India Through The Ages
A Popular And Picturesque History Of Hindustan

by

Flora Annie Steel

India Through The Ages
A Popular And Picturesque
History Of Hindustan
by Flora Annie Steel

ISBN: 978-93-59952-59-8

Published by

DOUBLE 9 BOOKS

2/13-B, Ansari Road
Daryaganj, New Delhi – 110002
info@double9books.com
www.double9books.com
Tel. 011-40042856

ABOUT THE AUTHOR

She was a writer who lived in British India for 22 years and was born on April 2, 1847, and died on April 12, 1929. She was known for writing books that took place in or had something to do with the Indian subcontinent. In her 1896 book On the Face of the Waters, she writes about events in the Indian Mutiny. Flora Annie Webster was born at Sudbury Priory in Sudbury, Middlesex. She was George Webster's sixth child. The woman who raised her, Isabella MacCallum, was a rich woman. Henry William Steel was in the Indian Civil Service when she married him in 1867. They lived in India until 1889, mostly in the Punjab, which is where most of her books are set. She became very interested in the lives of local Indians and started to ask the Indian government to make changes to the way schools work. As an adult, Mrs. Steel worked as an Inspector of Government and Aided Schools in the Punjab. She also helped promote Indian arts and crafts with Rudyard Kipling's father, John Lockwood Kipling. At times when her husband was sick, Flora Annie Steel took on some of his duties. She passed away in Minchinhampton, Gloucestershire, on April 12, 1929, at the home of her daughter. Biographers Violet Powell and Daya Patwardhan have written about her.

CONTENTS

PART III
THE MODERN AGE

PREFACE

A history, above all one which claims to hold no original research, but simply to be a compilation of the work of others, needs no introduction save the compiler's thanks to many who have been consulted.

One word, however, may be said regarding the only accent used--the circumflex.

This is put always on the tone of stress; that is to say, on the syllable to be accented. Thus Mâlwa, Ambêr, Jeysulmêr, Himâlya, Vizigapatâm. Where no accent appears the syllables are of equal value.

F. A. STEEL.

Talgarth, Machynlleth.

PART I

THE ANCIENT AGE

As the mind's eye travels backwards across the wide plains of Northern India, attempting to re-people it with the men of olden time, historical insight fails us at about the seventh century B.C. From that date to our own time the written Word steps in to pin protean legend down to inalterable form.

And yet before this seventh century there is no lack of evidence. The Word is still there, though, at the time, it lived only in the mouths of the people or of the priesthood. Even if we go so far back as B.C. 2000, the voices of men who have lived and died are still to be heard in the earlier hymns of the Rig-Veda.

And before that?

Who knows? The imaginative eye, looking out over the vast sea of young green wheat which in many parts of the Punjâb floods unbroken to the very foot of the hills, may gain from it an idea of the wide ocean whose tide undoubtedly once broke on the shores of the Himalayas.

The same eye may follow in fancy the gradual subsidence of that sea, the gradual deposit of sand, and loam brought by the great rivers from the high lands of Central Asia. It may rebuild the primeval huts of the first inhabitants of the new continent--those first invaders of the swampy haunts of crocodile and strange lizard-like beasts--but it has positively no data on which to work. The first record of a human word is to be found in the earliest hymn of the Aryan settlers when they streamed down into the Punjâb. When?

Even that is beyond proof. The consensus of opinion amongst learned men, however, gives the Vedic period--that is to say, the period during which the hymns of the Rig-Veda were composed--as approximately the years between B.C. 2000 and B.C. 1400.

But these same hymns tell us incidentally of a time before that. It is not only that these Aryan invaders were themselves in a state of civilisation which necessarily implies long centuries of culture, of separation from barbarian man; but besides this, they found a people in India civilised enough to have towns and disciplined troops, to have weapons and banners; women whose ornaments were of gold, poisoned arrows whose heads were of some metal that was probably iron.

All this, and much more, is to be gathered in the Rig-Veda concerning the Dâsyas or aboriginal inhabitants of India. Naturally enough, as inevitable foes, they are everywhere mentioned with abhorrence, and we are left with the impression of a "tawny race who utter fearful yells."

Who, then, were these people?

Are we to treat the monotonous singing voice which even now echoes out over the length and breadth of India, as in the sunsetting some Brahman recites the ancient hymns--are we to treat this as the *first* trace of Ancient India? Or, as we sit listening, are we to watch the distant horizon, so purple against the gold of the sky, and wonder if it is only our own unseeing eyes which prevent our tracing the low curve that may mark the site of a town, ancient when the Aryans swept it into nothingness?

"The fiction which resembles truth," said the Persian poet Nizâmi in the year 1250, "is better than the truth which is dissevered from the imagination"; so let us bring something of the latter quality into our answer.

Certain it is that for long centuries the reddish or tawny Dâsyas managed to resist the white-skinned Aryas, so that even as late as the period of that great epic, the Mâhâbhârata--that is, some thousand years later than the earliest voice which speaks in the Vedic hymns--the struggle was still going on. At least in those days the Aryan Pandâvas of whom we read in that poem appear to have dispossessed an aboriginal dynasty from the throne of Magadha. This dynasty belonged to the mysterious Nâga or Serpent race, which finally blocks the way in so many avenues of Indian research. They are not merely legendary; they cross the path of reality now and again, as when Alexander's invasion of India found some satrapies still held by Serpent-kings.

It is impossible, therefore, to avoid wondering whether the Aryans really found the rich plains of India a howling wilderness peopled by savages close in culture to the brutes, or whether, in parts of the vast continent at least, they found themselves pitted against another invading race, a Scythic race hailing from the north-east as the Aryan hails from north-west?

There is evidence even in the voice of the Rig-Veda for this. To begin with, there is the evidence of colour--colour which was hereafter to take form as caste. We have mention not of two, but of three divergent complexions. First, the "white-complexioned friends of Indra," who are palpably the Aryans; next, "the enemy who is flayed of his black skin"; and lastly, "those reddish in appearance, who utter fearful yells."

It seems, to say the least of it, unlikely that a single aboriginal race should be described in two such curiously different ways.

As for the fearful yells, that is palpably but another way of asserting that the utterers spoke a language which was not understood of the invaders. "Du'ye think th' Almighty would be understandin' siccan gibberish," said the old Scotch lady when, during the Napoleonic war, she was reminded that maybe many a French mother was praying as fervently for victory as she was herself. The same spirit breathes in many a Vedic hymn in which the Dâsyas are spoken of as barely human. "They are not men." "They do not perform sacrifices." "They do not believe in anything." These are the plaints which precede the ever-recurring prayer--"Oh! Destroyer of foes! Kill them!" And worse even than this comes the great cause of conflict--"*Their rites are different.*"

So the story is told. These Dâsyas, "born to be cut in twain," have yet the audacity to have different dogma, conflicting canons of the law. Even in those early days religion was the great unfailing cause of strife.

These same hymns of the Rig-Veda, however, give us but scant information of the foes who are called generally Dâsyas, or "robbers." But here again divergence creeps in. It is impossible to class "the wealthy barbarian," the "neglecters of sacrifices," who, "decorated with gold and jewels," were "spreading over the circuit of the earth," whose "iron cities" were to be destroyed, who were to be "slain whether weeping or laughing, whether hand to hand or on horseback, whether arrayed in hosts or aided by missile-hurling heroes"--it is impossible, surely, to class these enemies with the mere robber brutes of whom it is written that they "were slain, and the kine made manifest."

Were then these tawny-hued foes, with the mention of whom wealth is invariably associated, in reality the ancestors of the treasure-holding

Takshaks or Nâgas, that strange Snake race of which we read in the Mâhâbhârata, and of which we hear again during the invasion of Alexander?

At least there is nothing to prevent us dreaming that this is so; and while we listen to the voice of some Brahman chanting at sunset-time the oldest hymns in the world, there is nothing to hinder us from trying to imagine how strangely these must have fallen on the ears of the "neglecters of sacrifices, the dwellers in cities, rich in gold and beautiful women," of whom we catch a passing glimpse as the stately Sanskrit rhythm rolls on.

The sun sets, the voice ceases, and the far-away past is no nearer and no further from us than the present.

THE VEDIC TIMES

B.C. 2000 TO B.C. 1400

Before entering on its history it is necessary to grasp the size of the great continent with which we have to deal. Roughly speaking, India has fourteen and a half times the area of the British Isles. Of most of this country we have next to no history at all, and in the time which is now under consideration we have to deal only with the Punjâb, the "Land of the Five Rivers," the area of which about equals that of Great Britain. That such lack of information should exist is not wonderful, since, for all we know, this upper portion of India may then have been on the shores of a still-receding sea; indeed, colour is given to this suggestion by the remembrance that the five rivers of the Punjâb plain to this day act as huge drain-pipes which deprive the intervening country of surface moisture. Naturally, this fact, in the days when all India, save for its few isolated ranges of central mountains, must have been one vast swamp, was an immense boon to humanity.

The geographical area, therefore, with which we have to treat in the Vedic period is very limited. It is a mere patch on the present continent of India, bounded on the north by the snowy Himalayas, on the south by the Indus (and probably by the sea), on the west by the Suleimân Mountains, while on the east lay the unknown, and possibly marsh, land of the Ganges and Jumna Rivers.

Curiously enough, although we speak of this very tract nowadays as the "Land of the Five Rivers," in Vedic times the rivers were counted as seven. That is to say, the Indus was called the mother of the six--not five-- streams which, as now, joined its vast volume. In those days this juncture was most probably in comparatively close proximity to the sea. Of these six rivers only five remain: the Jhelum, the Chenâb, the Râvi, the Beâs, the Sutlej. The bed of the sixth river, the "most sacred, the most impetuous of streams," which was worshipped as a direct manifestation of Sarâswati, the Goddess of Learning,[1] is still to be traced near Thanêswar, where a pool of water remains to show where the displeased Goddess plunged into the earth and dispersed herself amongst the desert sands.

The stream never reappears; but its probable course is yet to be traced by the colonies of Sarâswata Brahmans, who still preserve, more rigidly than other Brahmans, the archaic rituals of the Vedas. The reason for this purity of rite being, it is affirmed, the grace-giving quality of Mother Sarâswati's water which, with curious quaint cries, is drawn in every village from the extraordinarily deep wells (many of which plunge over 400 feet into the desert sand), at whose bottom the lost river still flows.

Into this Land of the Seven Rivers, then, came--somewhere about two thousand years before Christ--wanderers who describe themselves as of a white complexion. That they had straight, well-bridged noses is also certain. To this day, as Mr Risley the great ethnologist puts it, "a man's social status in India varies in inverse ratio to the width of his nose"; that is to say, the nasal index, as it is called, is a safe guide to the amount of Aryan, as distinguished from aboriginal blood in his veins. One constant epithet given to the great cloud-god Indra--to whom, with the great fire-god Agni, the vast majority of the hymns in the Rig-Veda are addressed--is "handsome-chinned." But the Sanskrit word *sipra*, thus translated "chin," also means "nose"; and there can be no doubt that as the "handsome-nosed" one, Indra would be a more appropriate god for a people in whom, that feature was sufficiently marked to have impressed itself, as it has done, on countless generations.

Whence the Aryans came is a matter still under dispute. That they were a comparatively civilised people is certain. The hymns of the Rig-Veda, which were undoubtedly composed during the six hundred years following on the Aryans' first appearance in the Punjâb, prove this, as they prove many another point concerning these the first white invaders of India. How the idea ever passed current that they were a pastoral people is a mystery, since from the very first we read in these hymns of oxen, of the cultivation of corn, of ploughing, and sowing, and reaping.

"Oh! Lord of the Field!" reads one invocation. "We will cultivate this field with thee! May the plants be sweet to us; may the rains be full of sweetness; may the Lord of the Field be gracious to us! Let the oxen work merrily; let the man work merrily; let the plough move merrily! Fasten the traces merrily; ply the goad merrily.... Oh! Fortunate Furrow! speed on thy way, bestow on us an abundant crop--sow the seed on this field which has been prepared. Let the corn grow with our hymns, let the scythes fall on the ripe grain. Prepare troughs for the drinking of animals. Fasten the leathern string, and take out water from this deep and goodly well which never dries up. Refresh the horses, take up the corn stacked in the field, and make a cart to convey it easily."

Practically Indian agriculture has gone no further than this in close on four thousand years.

It is true that a hymn to the God of Shepherds finds occasional place in the Rig-Veda, but in these there is an archaic ring, which seems to point to the Aryan wanderings before India was reached. One of them begins thus: "Oh! Pushan, the Path-finder, help us to finish our journey!"

From purely religious hymns, naturally, one has no right to expect a full crop of information concerning the political and social life of the times in which they were composed, yet the light which the Rig-Veda throws upon these dark ages is luckily surprising; luckily, because we have absolutely no other source of knowledge.

From it we learn something of commerce, even to the extent of the laws regulating sale and usury. We learn also of ships and shipwrecks, of men who, "taking a boat, took her out to sea, and lived in the boat floating on the water, being happy in it rocking gracefully on the waves"; from which we may infer that our early Aryan brothers did not suffer from sea-sickness. There is also a phrase in fairly constant use, "the sea-born sun," which would lead us to suppose that these writers of hymns had often seen sunrise over an Eastern ocean.

Many kinds of grain were cultivated, but the chief ones seem to have been wheat and barley. Rice is not mentioned. Animals of all sorts were sacrificed, and their flesh eaten; and as we read of slaughter-houses set apart for the killing of cows, we may infer that the Aryan ancestors of India were not strict vegetarians.

But all mention of food, even sacrificial food, in the Rig-Veda fades into insignificance before its perfectly damnable iteration concerning a fermented drink called "Soma." Scarcely a hymn finds finish without some mention of it, and pages on pages are full of panegyrics of the "exhilarating juice," the "adorable libation," "the bright effused dew of the Soma, fit drink for gods." And apparently for men also, since we read that the "purifying Soma, like the sea rolling its waves, has poured out on men songs, and hymns, and thoughts." An apotheosis of intoxication, indeed!

It appears to have been the fermented juice of some asclepiad plant which was mixed with milk. The plant had to be gathered on moonshiny nights, and many ceremonials accompanied its tituration, and the expressing of its sap.

In later years, of course, the Soma ritual expanded into something very elaborate, and no less than sixteen priests were required for its proper fulfilment; but in the beginning, it is evident that each householder prepared the drink, and offered some of it, and of his food also, to Indra the cloud-god first, then to Agni the fire-god, and so by degrees (increasing with the years) to a host of smaller gods--the Winds, the Dawn, Day, Night, the Sun, the Earth.

For these ancient Aryans had not far to look for godhead. They found it simply, naturally, in themselves, and in all things about them, as the secret verse which to this day is held in sacred keeping by the twice-born amply shows. For there can be small doubt that the closest rendering to the original meaning runs thus:--

"Let us meditate on the Over-soul which is in all souls, which animates all, which illumines all understandings."

Mankind makes but small advance with the years in metaphysics, and it needed a Schopenhauer to reinvent the Over-soul--after how many generations? Who can say?

Only this we know, that a few centuries after Christ, a Chinese pilgrim to India committed himself to the assertion that "Soma is a very nasty drink!"

There is no trace in these Vedic hymns of the many deplorable beliefs, traditions and customs, which in later years have debased the religious and social life of India.

The Aryans worshipped "bright gods," and seem to have been themselves a bright and happy people. We hear nothing of temples or idols, of caste or enforced widowhood. Indeed, the fact that the language contains distinct, concrete, and not opprobrious terms for "the son of a woman who has taken a second husband," and for "a man who has married a widow," proves that such words were needed in the common tongues of the people. Neither is there any trace of, nor the faintest shred of authority for, either suttee or child-marriage.

So the ancient Aryan rises to the mind's eye as a big, stalwart, high-nosed, fair-skinned man, with a smile and a liking for exhilarating liquor, who, after long wanderings with his herds over the plains of Central Asia-- where, reading the stars at night, he sang as he watched his flocks to Pushan the Path-finder--looked down one day from the heights of the Himalayas over a fair expanse of new-born land by the ripples of a receding sea, and found that it was good.

So for many a long year he lived, fighting, ploughing, and praying--with copious libations--to Indra, the God of Battles, and to Agni, the humble, homely God of Fire, who yet was the invoker of all Gods mysteriously connected with the Sun, the Moon, the Stars, the very Lightning.

And one of the prayers to the god who "comprehended all things," who "traversed the vast ethereal space, measuring days and nights and contemplating all that have birth," ran thus:--

"Take me to the immortal and imperishable abode where light dwells eternal."

We have not gone much further. The cry which rises in the Rig-Veda is the cry of to-day:--

"From earth is the breath and the blood; but whence is the soul? What or Who is that One who is ever alone; who forms the six spheres; who holds the unborn in His Hand?"

Yet the religious feeling of these primitive Aryans was not all tinged by doubt, by sadness; some of their hymns to the Dawn breathe the spirit of deep joy which is in those who recognise, however dimly, that the One of whom they question is no other than the Questioner.

So let us conclude this chapter with a few verses collated from these hymns.

"Many-tinted Dawn! Th' immortal daughter of Heaven!
Young, white robed, come with thy purple steeds;
Follow the path of the dawnings the world has been given,
Follow the path of the dawn that the world still needs.

"Darkly shining Dusk, thy sister, has sought her abiding,
Fear not to trouble her dreams; daughters, ye twain of the Sun,
Dusk and dawn bringing birth! O Sisters! your path is unending;
Dead are the first who have watched; when shall our waking
be done?

"Bright, luminous Dawn; rose-red, radiant, rejoicing!
Shew the traveller his road; the cattle their pastures new;
Rouse the beasts of the Earth to their truthful myriad voicing,
Leader of rightful days! softening the soil with dew.

"Wide-expanded Dawn! Open the gates of the morning;
Waken the singing birds! Guide thou the truthful light
To uttermost shade of the shadow, for--see you! the dawning
Is born, white-shining, out of the gloom of the night."

Surely there is something in these phrases, taken truthfully from the original and strung together consecutively so as to give the spirit which animates the whole, that makes us of these later times feel closely akin to those who sang thus in the Dawn of Days.

THE DAYS OF THE EPICS

ABOUT B.C. 1400 TO ABOUT B.C. 1000

The area of India which has now to be considered is much larger. Oudh, Northern Behar, and the country about Benares are comprised in it; but Southern India remains as ever, unknown, even if existent.

The sources of information concerning this period of six hundred years are also much larger, though in a measure less trustworthy; for the two great epics of India, the Mâhâbhârata and the Râmâyana, are avowedly imaginative, and not--as are the hymns of the Rig-Veda--the outcome of the daily life of a people, which, like the accretions of a coral reef, remain to show what manner of creature once lived in them.

Even the remaining Vedas, the Yajur, the Sâma and the Athârva, partake of the same purely literary spirit, although the first and second of these were probably in existence towards the end of the Vedic period. The last named is--at least in its recognition as a Sacred Text--of far later date. All three consist largely of transcripts from the Rig-Veda, and around each of them, as indeed around the Rig-Veda-Sanhita itself, there grew up a subsidiary literature called Brahmânas, the object of which was to explain, consolidate, and elaborate both the ritual and teaching of the Vedic age, as it became archaic under the pressure of a greater complexity in life.

It is to the epics and to the Brahmânas, then, that we must look for what sparse information is to be gleaned concerning India during this six hundred years or so. It should be remembered that even these books were to remain truly the "spoken word" for at least two centuries longer, until the art of writing became known about B.C. 800. As against this, however, we may set the undoubted fact that such was the marvellous memory of those early days, that by the close of the Epic period every syllable of the Rig-Veda had been counted with accuracy, and the whole carefully compiled, arranged, analysed as it now stands.

To tell the honest truth, the Brahmânas are but a barren field. Full of elaborate hair-splitting, cumbered with elaborate regulations for the performance of every rite; prolix, prosy, they reflect only a religion which was fast breaking down into canonical pomposity. It is true that towards the end of the Epic period matters improved a little, and in the teachings of the Ûpanishads--last of the so-called "revealed Scriptures" of India--we find a very different note; but as these seem to belong, by right of birth, more to the Philosophical period which follows on the Epic, we will reserve them for subsequent consideration.

It is, then, to the Mâhâbhârata and to the Râmâyana that we must look.

Not, however, for history as history; for the personages, the incidents in these two great poems are purely mythical.

But that a strong tribe called Bhâratas or Kurus who had settled near Delhi did for long years struggle with another strong tribe called the Panchâlas, who had settled near Kanauj, is more than likely. With this background, then, of truth, the story of the Mâhâbhârata is a fine romance, and throws incidentally many a side-light on Hindu society in these remote ages. But it is prodigiously long. In the only full English translation which exists it runs to over 7,500 pages of small type. Anything more discursive cannot be imagined. The introduction of a single proper name is sufficient to start an entirely new story concerning every one who was ever connected with it in the most remote degree. But it is a treasure house of folk-lore and folk tales, interspersed, quaintly, by keen intellectual reasonings on philosophical subjects, and still more remarkable efforts to pierce the great Riddle of the World by mystical speculations. It is, emphatically, in every line of it, fresh to the uttermost. It is the outcome of minds--for it is evidently an accretion of many men's imaginations--that still felt the first stimulus of wonder concerning all things, to whom nothing was common, nothing impossible.

A redaction even in brief of the Great Epic is beyond the power of any writer. To begin with, many of the side-issues are to the full as worthy transcription as those of the main thread of the story; and then it is almost impossible to make out what the latter really was in the beginning, before the endless additions and interpolations came to obscure the original idea.

To most critics this main thread presents itself as a prolonged war between the Kaurâvas and their first cousins the Pandâvas--in other words, between the hundred sons of Dhritarâshta, the blind king, and the five sons of his brother Pându--but to the writer the *leit motif* is the story of Bhishma. It is a curious one; in many ways well worthy of a wider knowledge than it has at present in the West.

Bhishma, then, was the heir of Shantânu, the King of Hastinapûr. His birth belongs to fairy tale, for he was the son of Ganga, the river goddess, who consented to be the wife of the love-struck Shantânu on condition that, no matter what he might see, or she might do, no question should be asked, no remark made. There is therefore a distinct flavour of the world-wide Undine myth in the tale. In this case the lover-husband is of the most forbearing type. It is not until he sees his eighth infant son being relentlessly consigned to the river that he cries: "Hold! Enough! Who art thou, witch?" In consequence of this, in truth, somewhat belated curiosity, the goddess leaves him, after assuring him that her purpose is accomplished. Seven Holy Ones condemned to fresh life by a venial fault have been released by early death, and this last child is his to keep as being, indeed, the pledge of mutual love.

So far good. Bhishma is brought up as the heir until he is adolescent. Then his father falls in love with a fisherman's daughter who is obdurate. She refuses to marry, except on the condition that her son, if one is born, shall inherit the kingdom. Even a promise that this shall be so is not sufficient for her. She claims that Bhishma must not only swear to resign his own claim to the throne in favour of her son, but must also take a solemn vow of perpetual celibacy, so closing the door against future claims on the part of his children. Devoted to his father, the boy, just entering on manhood, accedes to the proposal; his father marries, and dies, leaving a young heir to whom Bhishma becomes regent. An excellent one, too, as the following extract concerning his regency will show:--

"In these days the Earth gave abundant harvest and the crops were of good flavour. The clouds poured rain in season and the trees were full of fruit and flowers. The draught cattle were all happy, and the birds and other animals rejoiced exceedingly, while the flowers were fragrant. The cities and towns were full of merchants and traders and artists of all descriptions. And the people were brave, learned, honest and happy. And there were no robbers, nor any one who was sinful; but devoted to virtuous acts, sacrifices, truth, and regarding each other with love and affection, the people grew up in prosperity, rejoicing cheerfully in sports that were perfectly innocent on rivers, lakes and tanks, in fine groves and charming woods.

"And the capital of the Kurus (Hastinapûr), full as the ocean and teeming with hundreds of palaces and mansions, and possessing gates and arches dark as the clouds, looked like a second Amaravati (celestial town). And over all the delightful country whose prosperity was thus increased were no misers, nor any woman a widow, but the wells and lakes were ever full, full were the groves of trees, the houses with wealth, and the whole kingdom with festivities.

"So, the wheel of virtue being thus set in motion by Bhishma, the subjects of other kingdoms, leaving their homes, came to dwell in the golden age."

A golden age indeed! A millenium dating a thousand years before the Christ. And for this, Bhishma the Brother Regent and Sâtyavâti the Queen-Mother were responsible. The Boy-King appears to have been but a poor creature. Even Bhishma's famous exploit of carrying off the three beautiful daughters of the King of Benares--Amva, Amvîka and Amvalîka--as brides for the lad, does not seem to have kept him from evil courses. True, the elder of these three "slender-waisted maidens, of tapering hips and curling hair," cried off the match by bashfully telling the softhearted Bhishma that she had set her affections on some one else; whereupon he, holding that "a woman, whatever her offence, always deserveth pardon," bid her follow her own inclinations. Still the two remaining brides did not avail to prevent the young bridegroom from succumbing to disease, leaving them childless.

Here, then, was a situation. Bhishma and the Queen-Mother, both of an age, left without an heir! After Eastern fashion she urges him to take his half-brother's place, and raise up offspring to his father and to herself. But Bhishma is firm to his oath. "Earth," he says, "may renounce its scent, water its moisture, light its attribute of showing form, yea! even the sun may renounce its glory, the comet its heat, the moon its cool rays, and very space renounce its capacity for generating sound; but I cannot renounce Truth." Pressed to the uttermost he can only reiterate: "I will renounce the three worlds, the empire of heaven, and anything which may be greater than this, but Truth I will not renounce."

Poor Bhishma! One feels that he is a veritable Sir Galahad, beset by loving women, for when another father for possible heirs is found, Amvîka, who had expected Bhishma, refuses to look at his successor, the result being that her son Dhritarâshta is born blind, and being thus unfitted for kingship, Amvalîka's son Pandu becomes heir to the throne.

Hinc illæ lachrymal! Bhishma's vow of celibacy produces the rivals, and his part in the epic henceforward shows but dimly on the bloody background of the long quarrel between the hundred God-given sons of Dhritarâshta, and the five God-begotten sons of Pandu.

Yet, overlaid as it is by diffuse divergencies, the story of self-sacrifice, of a man whom all women love and none can gain, goes on. Bhishma, on Pandu's death, installs the blind Dhritarâshta as Regent King, and continues, as ever, faithful to his trust. Once or twice a ring of human pathos, human regret, is heard in the harmony of his good counsels, his unswerving loyalty, his fast determination to "pay the debt arising out of the food which has been given me."

Once when Arjuna, third of the five Pandus, climbs up on his knees, all dust-laden from some boyish game, and, full of pride and glee, claims him as father--"I am not thy father, O Bhârata!" is the gentle reply.

Again, when Amva, the eldest princess of the three maidens whom Bhishma had carried off as brides for his brother, returns in tears from seeking the lover he had allowed her to rejoin, saying that the prince will have none of Bhishma's leavings, there is human regret in the latter's refusal to accept the assertion that the carrying off was equal to a betrothal, and that he is bound in honour to marry the maiden himself! Yet of this refusal comes much. The injured girl calls on High Heaven for requital, and though her champion Râma is unable to conquer the invincible Bhishma, Fate intervenes finally.

Amva's penances, prayers, austerities, find fruit in revenge. She is born again as Chikandîni, the daughter of a great king whose wife conceals the child's sex for twenty-one years, until, according to the promise of the Gods, Chikandîni becomes in reality Chikandîn, the most beautiful, the most valiant of princes, who is destined in time to cause the death of Bhishma. For amongst the many confessions of a soldier's faith which the latter here makes is this: "With one who hath thrown away his sword, with one fallen, with one flying, with one yielding, with woman or one bearing the name of woman, or with a low, vulgar fellow--with all these I do not battle." So Chikandîn is beyond Bhishma's retaliation, and when in the final fight he "struck the great Bhârata full on the breast," the latter "only looked at him with eyes blazing with wrath; remembering his womanhood, Bhishma struck him not."

This, however, was not yet to come. Bhishma had as yet to bring up the five Pandu princes and the hundred sons of Dhritarâshta to be good warriors and true, and in the process we come across many quaint interludes. The story of Princess Drâupadt's Self-choice is charming, and the description of the ceremony worth giving as a picture of the times.

"The amphitheatre," we read, "was erected on an auspicious and level plain to the north-east of the town, surrounded on all sides by beautiful mansions, enclosed with high walls and a moat with arched doorways here and there. And the vast amphitheatre was also shaded by a canopy of various colours, and resounded with the notes of a thousand trumpets, and was scented with black aloes, and sprinkled with sandal wood water and adorned with flowers. The high mansions surrounding it, perfectly white, resembled the cloud-kissing peaks of Himalaya. And the windows of these mansions were covered with lattice of gold, and the walls thereof set with diamonds and precious stones. The staircases were easy of ascent, while the floors were covered with costly carpets and rugs. Now all these mansions were adorned with wreaths of flowers and rendered fragrant with excellent aloes. They were white and spotless as the necks of swans. And they were each furnished with a hundred doors wide enough to admit a crowd of persons. And in these seven-storied houses of various sizes, adorned with costly beds and carpets, lived the monarchs who were invited to the Self-choice, their persons adorned with every ornament, and possessed with the hope of excelling each other. Thus the denizens of the city and the surrounding country, taking their seats on the platforms, beheld these things.

"And the concourse of princes, gay with the performances of actors and dancers, increased daily, until on the sixteenth morning the daughter of the King entered the arena, richly attired and bearing in her hand a golden dish on which lay offerings to the gods, and a garland of flowers.

"Then a priest of the Moon race ignited the sacrificial fires and poured libations, uttering benedictions; and all the musical instruments that were playing, stopped, and in the whole amphitheatre was perfect stillness. Then the Princess' brother, taking his sister by the hand, cried in a voice low and deep as the kettledrums of the clouds: 'Hear all ye assembled Princes, hear! This is the bow, these are the arrows, yonder is the mark! Given Beauty, Strength, Lineage, he who achieveth the feat hath Princess Drâupadi to wife.' Then, for the sake of her unrivalled Beauty, the young Princes vied with each other in jealousy, and rising in their royal seats each exclaiming: 'Princess Drâupadi shall be mine!' began to exhibit their prowess."

It would take too long to give in extensor how one after the other the Princes failed to string the mighty bow. How Karna, the Disinherited Knight of the Romance--in reality uterine brother to the five Pandu princes, but passing as their deadliest Kuru enemy--strung it easily, but "turned aside with a laugh of vexation and a glance at the Sun, his real father," when Princess Drâupadi cried: "Hold! I will have none of mixed blood to my lord!"

How the young Arjuna, second of the five Pandu princes, "first of car-warriors and wielders of the bow," came disguised as a Brahman youth and achieved the feat; rousing no remonstrance, it may be remarked, as to admixture of race from the fair Princess Drâupadi.

Then follows the incident of Drâupadi marrying the whole five Pandu brothers, in obedience to their mother's mistaken command. She, when her five sons appeared in the dusk, "bringing their alms," bid them share it as ever; so, despite much heart-questioning, the fivefold wedding took place. It is an incident which is glozed over by ardent admirers of the Mâhâbhârata, and spoken of deprecatingly, as a mere myth. Why, it would be difficult to say, since it is palpably held up to honour as an instance of almost superhuman virtue. It is a voluntary self-abnegation on the part of the Five Princes, who swear to set aside jealousy for ever; an attempt on their part to right the relations between the sexes, and to return to the purer teaching of old times when, as we are distinctly told, "men and women followed their own inclinations without shame or sin." Certainly the record of this union of the Five Brothers to the devoted, almost divine Drâupadi, holds no suspicion of either the one or the other; surely, therefore, it requires neither disguise nor apology.

Thereinafter, amid ever-recurring sweep of furious blasts and counterblasts, ever-changing chances of fortune and misfortune, comes the great gambling scene which, deprived of disagreeable details and properly staged, should make the fortune of any dramatist who could really touch it. A fine scene, truly! Yudishthira, eldest of the Pandu princes, their ruling spirit, the brain, so to speak, of Bhima's strength, Arjuna's skill, Nakula's devotion, Sahadeva's obedience, had been challenged to a gambling bout by his chief enemy, Dhritarâshta's eldest son Duryôdhana. To this, according to the soldier's code of honour, there could be no refusal. But Yudishthira, gambler at heart, would not acknowledge himself beaten. He stakes his riches, his kingdom, his brothers, himself--last of all, his wife.

Losing her, she is sent for to the gambling saloon. She refuses to come. Finally, dragged thither by force, she pleads that Yudishthira, having first gambled away himself, was a slave, and so had no right to stake a free woman. Then ensues a scene of conflicting passions and protest which, once read of, lingers in the mind, rising superior to the certain disagreeable details which undoubtedly disfigure it in the original.

So the story sweeps on and on, ending really with Bhishma's death on the field of battle after a final encounter in which Arjûna, realising that victory is unattainable so long as "the Grandsire" lives, uses Chikandîn, the man-woman, as his shield, and so brings about the defeat of the otherwise invincible Bhishma. The latter, "lying on his bed of arrows," surrounded by all the princes, then proceeds to discourse for long days ("until the sun, entering its northern declension, permitted him to resign his life-breath") on the whole duty of mankind, and especially on the duties of kingship.

These discourses, which in the English translation run to over 2000 pages, are marvellously illuminating. When we read in them doctrines of kingly science which long centuries later were to be re-enunciated by Machiavelli, when we find in them many a theory of modern science forestalled by some bold, theoretical plunge into the Infinite, that Infinite to which "it is impossible to set limits since it is limitless," we may well pause to ask ourselves how much nearer we are to discovering the Great Secret than those were who, nearly three thousand years ago, puzzled themselves over the problem of consciousness, and why, "when the mind is otherwise engaged, the life-agent in the body heareth not."

Have we, even in science, gone much further than the assertion that "Space, which even the Gods cannot measure, is full of blazing and self-luminous worlds?"

Perhaps we have; but of a certainty we cannot outclass the Mâhâbhârata in the imagination with which it treats the Insoluble.

"In the Beginning," we read, "was infinite Space motionless, immoveable. Without Sun, Moon, or Stars, it seemed to be asleep. Then a darkness grew within the darkness, and water sprang to life."

So, gaining force as it goes like some giant wave, the vast epic sweeps on, gathering worthless pebbles and hopeless wreckage, with its thousand facets of bright bold sea, to leave us, after it has crashed over us, bewildered, storm-shaken on the shore, our heads whirling with wild memories of flashing, jewel-set cuirasses, "beautiful like the firmament of night bespangled with stars," of floating veils "like wind-tossed clouds," of celestial voices, "deep as the kettledrums of the skies," of "sparkling showers of keen arrows like the rays of the sun," of "tender, small-waisted maidens," and "mighty, high-souled car-warriors."

It is a marvellous dream, and as one reads it the ceaseless fall of seas upon a shore seems to fill the ear with the eternal message of indestructible life.

The Râmâyana, great though the epic is, and, in a way, more poetical, has none of this storm and stress. As R. C. Dutt, in his "Ancient India," says:--

"On reading it one feels that the real heroic age of India had passed. We miss the rude and sturdy manners and incidents which mark the Mâhâbhârata. The heroes of the Râmâyana are somewhat tame and commonplace personages, very respectful to priests, very anxious to conform to all the rules of decorum and duty, doing a vast amount of fighting work mechanically, but without the determination, the persistence of real fighters. A change has come over the spirit of the nation. It is more polished, more law-abiding, less sturdy, less heroic. In brief, the two epics give us the change which Hindu life and society underwent from the commencement to the close of the Epic age."

Griffiths, in the introduction to his metrical version of the Râmâyana, remarks that one of its most salient features is the complete absence of any mention of "that mystical devotion which absorbs all the faculties," to which we have constant reference in the Mâhâbhârata. The remark is full of critical acumen, and at once differentiates the varying planes on which the two dramas move.

That of Râma and his long-suffering wife Sîta, is, doubtless, the more human of the two; but there is a grandeur about the story of Bhishma before which the former crumbles to commonplace. Still, as R. C. Dutt asserts:--

"There is not a Hindu woman in the length and breadth of India to whom the story of Sîta is not known, and to whom her character is not a model to strive after and to emulate. Râma, also, though scarcely equal to Sîta in the worth of character, has been a model to man for his truth, his obedience, his piety. Thus the epic has been for the millions of India a means of moral education, the value of which can hardly be over-estimated."

Historically, there is little to be gleaned from it beyond the conquest of Southern India and Ceylon. Socially, it shows the accretion of custom, the consolidation of dogma, and the passing of power from the soldier to the priestly caste. Yet even here it is but a very modified Brahmanism of which we catch glimpses, and even caste itself is not as yet crystallised into hard and fast form.

So, with the Râmâyana and some few Purânas which, however, will be better considered in the next chapter, the Epic period closes.

Some few points in it may lay claims to distinct historical basis. The existence of Janaka, King of Kosâla, the father of Sîta, the befriender of wisdom, is so far attested by later writings and by legend, that his personality gains reality; but it is in the crashing, confused welter of the Mâhâbhârata that we must look for a just estimate of what India was like a thousand years before Christ.

THE MARVELLOUS MILLENNIUM

B.C. 1000 to A.D. 1

A millennium indeed! A thousand years of Time which (despite many purely historical events in its latter half, to which return will be made in the next chapter) must be treated, as a whole, as perhaps the most wonderful period in the history of the world. For, just as in the fifteenth and sixteenth centuries humanity appears to have set its mind on art, and such names as Shakspeare, Dante, Rafael, Leonardo da Vinci, Palestrina, Cervantes, and a hundred others are to be found jostling each other in history, so, during these thousand years, the mind of man throughout the whole world appears to have been set on solving the great secret of Life and Death.

The answer was given in many ways by the Greek and Roman philosophers, by Confucius in China, by Christ in Judea, by Buddha and the great systems of Indian philosophy in Hindustan; and yet the question is still being asked with the old intensity, the old keen desire for answer!

Now, since these thousand years have, in India, left behind them a very remarkable literature which, even in these latter days, is the root of all life and thought in that vast peninsula, it is as well to attempt a slight sketch of the time, as a whole, before embarking on actual history; though to do the latter we shall, after treating of the religious age, have to hark back to the year 620 B.C.

At the commencement, then, of this thousand years, the Aryans were still pushing their way westwards and southwards from the alluvial plains of Northern India.

It seems likely that the tide of their conquest followed that of the retreating sea. However that may be, certain it is that they found before them dark, almost impenetrable, swampy forests, swarming with enemies of all kinds. Who or what these were we have at first small record. Doubtless the human foes belonged to the aboriginal tribes which are still to be found clinging to the far mountain uplands and inaccessible fastnesses which the Aryans did not care to annex. But in the literature of which mention has been made, all and sundry are disdainfully dismissed with the epithet "*Rakshas,*" or evil demons.

Behind this shrinking verge of devildom, however, we know that "the children of light" were settling down; towns were springing up, waste land was being cleared and cultivated, schools were being established, and many principalities rising into power. But of all this we have as yet no record at all, until about one-half of the millennium was over. On the other hand, we have exhaustive literary evidence of what the minds of men were busying themselves about, first in the Ûpanishads, and then in the myriad Sûtras or Aphorisms, on every subject, apparently, under the sun, which are still extant.

Regarding the former--of which the German philosopher, Schopenhauer, wrote: "They have been the solace of my life; they will be the solace of my death"--though some of these treatises or essays belong, undoubtedly, to the dying years of the Epic age, they fall far more naturally into place during the opening years of this, the succeeding one. Their bold hypotheses covering all things were the first reaction against the soul-stifling formalisms of the Brahmânas; these, again, being due to the development of the dignity of the priestly class, which followed naturally on the excessive militarism so noticeable in the Mâhâbhârata. Of a truth, its stalwart warriors, for ever engaged in deadly combat and stirring adventures, could as heads of households have had little time for the due performance of domestic ceremonials after the customs of their fathers. Hence the rapid growth of the professional priesthood.

The fatal facility, however, with which speculative thought, after throwing off the shackles of canon and dogma, finds fresh slavery for itself in scientific formalism, is shown by the succeeding Sûtra literature, in which every department of thought and action is crystallised and codified into cut-and-dried form.

A reaction from this, again, is to be found in the succeeding philosophy of Kapîla and his disciples, which must have been promulgated a century or so before the birth of Gâutama Buddha. Frankly agnostic, many of the conclusions of this Sankhya system are to be found in the works of the latest German philosophers. Like theirs it is cold, and appeals not to the masses, but to speculative scholars. Still, it is strange that the very first recorded system of philosophy in the world, the very first attempt to solve the Great Question by the light of reason alone, should differ scarcely at all from the last. The human brain fails now, as it failed then; for Kapîla's doctrine never really overset those of the Ûpanishads, though the system of philosophy founded upon these last (and therefore called the Vedanta) was not to come for many years. But what, indeed, can or could overset the doctrine laid down in these same Ûpanishads, of a Universal Soul, a Universal Self, which is--to use the very words of the text:--

"Myself within the heart smaller than a corn of rice, smaller than a mustard seed, smaller than the kernel of a canary seed: myself within the heart greater than the earth, greater than the sky, greater than heaven. Lo! He who beholds all beings in this Self, and Self in all beings, he never turns away from it. When to a man who understands, the Self has become all things, what sorrow, what trouble can there be to him who has once beheld that unity? He, the Self, encircles all, bright, incorporeal, scatheless, pure, untouched by evil; a seer, wise, omnipresent, self-existent, he disposed all things rightly for eternal years. He therefore who knows this, after having become quiet, subdued, satisfied, patient and collected, sees Self in Self, sees all in Self. Evil does not overcome him, he overcomes all evil. Free from evil, free from stain, free from doubt, he becomes True Brahman. The wise who, meditating on this Self, recognises the Ancient who dwells for ever in the abyss, as God--he indeed leaves joy and sorrow far behind; having reached the subtle Being, he rejoices because he has obtained the cause of rejoicing."

Such words as these live for ever, a veritable Light in the Darkness of many philosophies.

Yet even the Vedanta teaching failed to satisfy the masses; its atmosphere was too rarefied for them. So about the middle of the millennium a new Teacher arose. Gâutama Buddha was born about the year B.C. 560 at Kapilavâstu, and the followers of the religion of which he was the founder number at this present day nearly one-third of the whole human race.

A magnificent work truly, look at it how we may! Yet it becomes the more astounding when we enquire into the religion itself; for it holds out no bait to humanity. It neither gives the immediate and certain grip on a spiritual and therefore eternal life which the Vedanta promises, neither does it proclaim the personal individual immortality for which the Christian is taught to look.

Yet it holds its place firmly as first favourite with humanity. There are some five hundred million Buddhists, as against some three hundred million Christians; while about the tenth century of our era fully one-half the world's inhabitants followed the teaching of Gâutama.

Why is this? Wherein lies the charm? Possibly in its pessimism, in the declaration that all is, must be, suffering.

"Hear! O Bhikkhus! the Noble Truth of Suffering. Birth is suffering, decay is suffering, illness is suffering, Death is suffering.

"Hear! O Bhikkhus! the Noble Truth of the cause of suffering. Thirst for pleasure, thirst for life, thirst for prosperity, thirst that leads to new birth.

"Hear! O Bhikkhus! the Noble Truth of the cessation of Suffering. It is the destruction of desire, the extinction of thirst.

"Hear! O Bhikkhus! the Noble Truth of the Pathway which leads to the cessation of suffering. Right Belief, Right Aspirations, Right Speech, Right Conduct, Right Means of Livelihood, Right Exertion, Right-mindedness, Right Meditation."

In these few words lies the whole teaching of Buddhism. To king and beggar alike, the world is evil; there is but one road to freedom, and that must be trodden alike by all. In that road none is before or after others.

Now to the poor, to the oppressed, there is balm in this thought. Lazarus does not yearn for Abraham's bosom! Before all lies forgetfulness, peace, personal annihilation.

This, then, was the teaching which Gâutama Buddha, the son of a king, gave as a gift to his world; and his world, wearied yet once more with formalism, with the ever-growing terrorism of caste and creed, welcomed it with open arms. The progress of the Buddhistic faith was fairly astounding, and half India was converted in the twinkling of an eye. Of the life led by the founder himself much has been written. Many of the incidents bear a strange resemblance to those in the life of Christ. Perhaps none is more beautiful than the story of the woman who applied to Gâutama, begging him to restore her dead child to life. As given in Sir Edwin Arnold's *Light of Asia*, it runs so:--

"Whom, when they came unto the river side,
A woman--dove-eyed, young, with tearful face
And lifted hands saluted, bending low:
'Lord! thou art he,' she said, 'who yesterday
Had pity on me ...

* * * * *

when I came
Trembling to thee whose brow is like a god's.
And wept, and drew the face-cloth from my babe,
Praying thee tell what simples might be good.' ...
'Yea! little sister, there is that might heal
Thee first and him, if thou couldst fetch the thing.
Black mustard-seed a tola; only mark
Thou take it not from any hand or house
Where father, mother, child or slave hath died.'
'Thus didst thou speak, my Lord.
... I went, Lord, clasping to my breast

The babe grown colder, asking at each hut:
"I pray you, give me mustard, of your grace
A tola, black," and each who had it gave.
But when I asked: "In my friend's household here
Hath any, peradventure, ever died?
Husband or wife or child or slave?" they said:
"Oh, Sister! what is this you ask? The dead
Are very many, and the living few." ...
Ah sir! I could not find a single house
Where there was mustard seed, and none had died.'

* * * * *

"'My sister! thou hast found,' the Master said,
'Searching for what none finds that better balm
I had to give thee....
Lo! I would pour my blood if it could stay
Thy tears, and win the secret of that curse
Which makes sweet love our anguish ...
I seek that secret: bury thou thy child.'"

Buddha, it will be observed, answered no questions. He left the insoluble alone. He simply preached that holiness meant peace and love, that peace and love meant pure earthly happiness.

So, even while they accepted the morality of Buddhism, and acquiesced in its negation, the keener speculative minds were still busy trying to find some key to fit the Great Lock.

The Yoga system of philosophy followed on the Sankhya, the Nyaya and the Vaisasika on the Yoga; finally, the two Mimamsa or Vedanta philosophies. Of these the Yoga is merely a repetition, with some alteration, of the Sankhya; the Nyaya--which is to the Hindu what the Aristotelian system was to the Greek, and which is still the school of logic--finds its complement in the scientific and atomic theories of the Vaisasika. This last, which is the first effort made in India to enquire into the laws of physics, is curiously provocative of thought. A Rip-van-Winklish feeling creeps into the mind as the eyes read that all material substances are aggregates of atoms, that the ultimate atom must be simple, that the mote visible in the sunbeam, though the smallest perceptible object, must yet be a substance, therefore a thing composed of things smaller than itself.

Once again the question arises, "How much further have we gone towards solution?"

Of the Vedanta system enough has already been said. It is pure Monism, matter being but a manifestation of the Supreme Energy, the Supreme Soul, the Supreme Self which comprises all things, holds all things, is all things.

So much for the speculative thought of this remarkable age. But when we turn to other subjects, we find the same truly marvellous acumen displayed in almost every field of enquiry.

Panini, whom Max Muller called the greatest grammarian the world has ever seen, lived in the middle of this millennium, and by resolving Sanskrit to its simple roots, paved the way for the Science of Languages. It is strange, indeed, to think of him in the dawn of days discovering what was to be rediscovered more than two thousand years afterwards, and adopting half the philological formulas of the present century.

So with geometry, a science which certainly developed from the strict rules concerning the erection of altars, as the science of phonetics grew from the study necessary to ensure absolutely accurate intonations of the sacred text. Of the former science much is to be found in the Sulva Sûtras; amongst other things, the celebrated theorem that the square of the hypothenuse is equal to the square of the two other sides of a rectangular triangle. This proposition is ascribed by the Greeks to Pythagoras, but it was known in India long before his time, and it is supposed that he learnt it while on his travels, which included Hindustan.

Geometry, however, was not destined to take hold of the Indian mind. The cognate science of numbers speedily took its place, and the acute Asiatic intellect soon evolved Algebra out of the arithmetic which they had rendered of practical use by the adoption of the decimal system of notation.

For all these many discoveries the world is indebted to this marvellous millennium.

Regarding the social life of this time the Dharma Sûtras give us endless laws--which are the originals of later and codified laws--concerning almost every subject under the sun. As every Hindu student (and every Hindu had to be student for a definite number of years) had to learn these Sûtras by heart, it may safely be predicted that they faithfully reflect the general conduct of affairs. They are extraordinarily minute in particular, and from them it may be gathered that life had become much more artificial. Amongst the king's duties is that of "guarding household weights and measures from falsification." It may also be noticed that "the taxes payable by those who support themselves by personal labour differ materially from those paid by mere possessors of property." Any injury, also, to a cultivator's land or to an artisan's trade was punished with great severity, and violence in defence of them was held justifiable. A legal rate of interest was settled, and the laws of inheritance were laid down minutely, as also were those of marriage. Indeed, as Mr R. C. Dutt puts it:--

"Everything that was confused during the Epic period was brought to order--everything that was discursive was condemned; opinions were arranged and codified into bodies of laws, and the whole social system of the Hindus underwent a similar rigid treatment."

Briefly, it was at once an age of keen speculation and rapid crystallisation almost unequalled in the history of any nation. Nor have we to found this estimate of it solely by inference from the literature which it has left behind it. We have other evidence on which to draw. True, the earliest foreign notice of India is that of Hekataios of Miletus, who wrote about B.C. 520, but he seems only to have been aware of its existence. The next is that of some inscriptions of the Persian king, Darius, which may be dated about B.C. 486, while Ktesias of Knidos, who collected travellers' tales about the East, wrote a little later. But Alexander's Indian campaign, which began in the year B.C. 327, brought many Western eyes to wonder at what they saw, and from this time Greece practically gives us the chronology of Hindustan.

Of what these Western eyes saw we gain glimpses in the few fragments of the works of Megasthenes which have withstood the destruction of time. Living, as he did, in the fourth century B.C. as Ambassador at the court of Pâlipûtra, he gives us a picture of the times well worth reading, with a few extracts from which this chapter may well conclude.

"The inhabitants, having abundant means of subsistence, exceed, in consequence, the ordinary stature, and are distinguished by their proud bearing. They are also found to be well skilled in the arts, as might be expected of men who inhale a pure air and drink the very finest water ... they almost always gather in two harvests annually; and even should one of the sowings prove more or less abortive, they are always sure of the other crop. It is accordingly affirmed that famine has never visited India, and that there has never been any general scarcity in the supply of nourishing food.... But, further, there are usages observed by the Indians which contribute to prevent the occurrence of famine among them; for whereas amongst other nations it is usual, in the contests of war, to ravage the soil, and thus to reduce it to an uncultivated waste, among the Indians, on the contrary, by whom husbandmen are regarded as a class that is sacred and inviolable, the tillers of the soil, even when battle is raging in their neighbourhood, are undisturbed by any sense of danger, since the combatants allow them to remain quite unmolested. Neither do they ravage a land with fire nor cut down its trees.... The Indians do not raise monuments to the dead, but consider the virtues which men have displayed in life and the songs in which their praises are celebrated, sufficient to preserve their memory.... All the Indians are free, and not one of them is a slave. The Indians do not even use aliens as slaves, and much less one of their own countrymen.... They live frugally and observe very good order. Theft is of very rare occurrence. The simplicity of their laws and their contracts is proved by the fact that they seldom appeal to law. They have no suits about pledges or deposits, nor do they require either seals or witnesses, but make their deposits and confide in each other. They neither put out money at usury or know how to borrow.... Truth and virtue they hold alike in esteem.... In contrast to the general simplicity of their style, they love finery and ornaments. Their robes are worked in gold, adorned with precious stones, and they wear flowered garments of the finest muslin. Attendants walking behind hold umbrellas over them; for they have a high regard for beauty, and avail themselves of every device to improve their looks....

"Of the great officers of state, some have charge of the market, others of the city, others of the soldiers, while some superintend the canals and measure the land, some collect the taxes, and some construct roads and set up pillars to show the by-roads and the distances....

"Those who have charge of the city are divided into six bodies of five each. The first body looks after industrial art. The second attends to the entertainments of strangers, taking care of them, well or ill, and, in the event of their dying, burying them and forwarding their property to their relatives. The third enquires of births and deaths, so that these among both high and low may not escape the cognisance of Government. The fourth deals with trade and commerce, and has charge of weights and measures. The fifth supervises the sale of manufactured articles which are sold by public notice, and the sixth collects the tithe on such articles. There is, beside the city magistrates, a third body, which directs military affairs. One division of this has charge of the infantry, another of the cavalry, a third of the war chariots, a fourth of the elephants; while one division is appointed to co-operate with the admiral of the fleet and another with the superintendent of the bullock trains used for transporting the munitions of war."

So much for the East before it was gripped by the West. With a full-blown War Office, and a statistical registration of births and deaths, it appears to have gone far on the course of our civilisation.

Concerning the "Brahmanes," as the old writers term the Brahmans, Megasthenes says of them that they live in groves, and

"spend their time in listening to sermons, discourses, and in imparting knowledge to such as will listen to them. The hearer is not allowed to speak, or even to cough, and much less to spit, and if he offends in any of these ways, he is cast out from their society that very day, as being a man who is wanting in self-restraint. Death is with them a very frequent subject of discourse. They regard this life as, so to speak, the time when the child within the womb matures, and death as the birth into a new and happy life. They go about naked, saying that God has given the body as sufficient covering for the soul."

One may still hear this teaching given in the mango groves, or in the shade of a banyan tree, throughout this India of the twentieth century.

And it still satisfies the hearers.

THE SESU-NÂGA (and Other) KINGS

B.C. 620 TO B.C. 327

We stand now on the threshold of actual history. Before us lie two thousand five hundred years; and behind us? Who can say? From the far distance come the reverberating thunders of the Mâhâbhârata, still filling the ear with stories of myth and miracle. But the days of these are over. Henceforward, we are to listen to nothing save facts, to believe nothing to which our ordinary everyday experience cannot give its assent.

Who, then, were these Sesu-nâga kings of whom we read in the lists of dead dynasties given in the Purânas--those curious histories of the whole cosmogony of this world and the next, some of which can now be fairly proved to have existed in the very first centuries of our era, and with them an accredited claim to hoar antiquity?

How came these kings by their name Ses, or Shesh-nâga? A name which indubitably points to their connection with the sacred snake, or "nâg."

Were they of Scythic origin? Nothing more likely. Certain it is that Scythic hordes invaded India from the north-east, both during and after the age of the Epics. It is conjectured, also, that they met in conflict with the Aryan invaders from the north-west on the wide, Gangetic plains, possibly close to the junction of the Sone River with the Ganges.

Here, at any rate, lay the ancient kingdom of Magadha, the kingdom of these Ses-nâga kings.

There were ten of these kings, and of the first four, we, as yet, know nothing. But almost every year sees fresh inscriptions deciphered, new coins discovered, and therefore it is not unlikely that some day these mere dry-as-dust names, Sesu-nâga, Sakavârna, Kshema-dhârman, and Kshattru-jâs, may live again as personalities. At present we must be content with imagining them in their palace at Raja-griha, or "The kings abode surrounded by mountains."

It has a curiously distinguished, dignified sound, this description. One can imagine these Ses-nâga princes, their Scythian faces, flat, oblique-eyed, yet aquiline, showing keen under the golden-hooded snake standing uræus-like over their low foreheads, riding up the steep, wide steps leading to their high-perched palaces, on their milk-white steeds; these latter, no doubt, be-bowed with blue ribbons and bedyed with pink feet and tail, after the fashion of processional horses in India even nowadays. Riding up proudly, kings, indeed, of their world, holders of untold wealth in priceless gems and gold--gold, unminted, almost valueless, jewels recklessly strung, like pebbles on a string.

This legend, indeed, of countless uncounted gold, of fair women, and almost weird, rough luxury, lingers still around the very name of Snake-King, and holds its own in the folk-lore of India.

In these days the kingdom of Magadha--so far as we can judge, a Scythic principality--was just entering the lists against that still more ancient Aryan kingdom of Kosâla, of which we read in the Râmâyana. But there were other principalities in the settled country which lay between the extreme north-west of the Punjâb and Ujjain, or Mâlwa. Sixteen such states are enumerated in various literary--chiefly religious--works, which were probably compiled in the fifth century B.C.; but these, again, are mere dry-as-dust names.

The first breath of real life comes with Bimbi-sâra, the fifth Sesu-nâga king. He, we know, conquered and annexed the principality of Anga and built the city of New Rajagrîha, which lies at the base of the hill below the old fort. But something there is in his reign which grips attention more than conquests or buildings. During it, and under his rule, the founders of two great religions gave to the world their solutions of the problem of life. In all probability both Mâhâvîra and Gâutama Buddha were born in Bimbi-sâra's days; certain it is that he must have heard the first teachings of Jainism and Buddhism preached at his palace doors. He is supposed to have reigned for nearly five and twenty years, and then to have retired into private life, leaving his favourite son, Ajâta-sutru, as regent.

And here tragedy sets in; tragedy in which Buddhist tradition avers that Deva-datta, the Great Teacher's first cousin and bitterest enemy, was prime mover. For one of the many crimes imputed to this arch-schismatic by the orthodox, is that he instigated Ajâtasutru to put his father to death.

Whether this be true or not, certain it is that Bimbi-sâra was murdered, and by his son's orders; for in one of the earliest Buddhist manuscripts extant there is an account of the guilty son's confession to the Blessed One (*i.e.*, Buddha) in these words: "Sin overcame me, Lord, weak, and foolish, and wrong that I am, in that for the sake of sovranty I put to death my father, that righteous man, that righteous king."

If, as tradition has it, that death was compassed by slow starvation, the prompt absolution which Buddha is said to have given the royal sinner for this act of atrocity becomes all the more remarkable. His sole comment to the brethren after Ajâta-sutru had departed appears to have been: "This king was deeply affected, he was touched in heart. If he had not put his father to death, then, even as he sate here, the clear eye of truth would have been his."

Apart from this parricidal act, the motive for which he gives with such calm brutality, Ajâta-sutru seems to have been a strong, capable king. He had instantly to face war with Kosâla, the murdered man's wife--who, it is said, died of grief--being sister to the king of that country. Round this war, long and bloody, legend has woven many incidents. At one time Magadha, at another Kosâla, seems to have come uppermost. Ajâta-sutru himself was once carried a prisoner in chains to his opponent's capital; but in the end, when peace came, Kosâla had given one of its princesses in marriage to the King of Magadha, and had become absorbed in that empire.

But this was not enough for ambitious Ajâta-sutru. He now turned his attention to the rich lands north of the Ganges, and carried his victorious arms to the very foot of holy Himalaya.

In the course of this war he built a watch-fort at a village called Patali, on the banks of the Ganges, where in after years he founded a city which, under the name of Patâliputra (the Palibothra of Greek writers), became eventually the capital, not only of Magadha, but of India--India, that is, as it was known in these early days.

Patali is the Sanskrit for the bignonia, or trumpet-flower; we may add, therefore, to our mental picture of the remaining four Ses-nâga kings, that they lived in Trumpet-flower City.

For the rest, these two great monarchs, Bimbi-sâra and Ajâta-sutru, must have been near, if not actual contemporaries of Darius, King of Persia, who founded an Indian satrapy in the Indus valley. This he was able to do, in consequence of the information collected by Skylax of Karyanda, during his memorable voyage by river from the Upper Punjâb to the sea near Karâchi, thus demonstrating the practicability of a passage by water to Persia. All record of this voyage is, unfortunately, lost; but the result of it was the addition to the Persian Empire of so rich a province, that it paid in gold-dust tribute to the treasury, fully one-third of the total revenue from the whole twenty satrapies; that is to say, about one million sterling, which in those days was, of course, an absolutely enormous sum.

There is not much more to tell of Ajâta-sutru; and yet, reading between the lines of the few facts we actually know of him, the man's character shows distinct. Ambitious, not exactly unscrupulous, but uncontrolled. A man who, having murdered his father, could weep over his own act, and seek to obliterate the blood-stain on his hands by confessions and pious acts. When Buddha died, an eighth portion of his bones was claimed by Ajâta-sutru, who erected at Râjgrîha a magnificent tope or mound over the sacred relics.

But, if tradition is to be believed, he handed down the curse of his great crime to his son, his grandson, and his great grandson; for the Ceylon chronicle asserts, that each of these in turn were parricides. It is--to use a colloquialism--a tall order; but assertion or denial are alike unproven.

If it be true, there is some relief in finding that the last of these criminal kings--Mâhâ-nundin by name--was ousted from his throne and killed by his prime minister, one Mâhâ-padma-Nanda, who is said, also, to have been the murdered man's illegitimate son by a Sudra, or low-caste woman.

Whether this latter be true or not, certain it is that about the year B.C. 361, or thereabouts, the reign of the Ses-nâga kings ends abruptly. The dream-vision of the steps of old Râjgrîha with Scythian princelings--parricidal princelings--riding up to their palaces on processional horses, or living luxuriously in Trumpet-flower city, vanishes, and something quite as dream-like takes its place.

For in the oldest chronicles we are told that there were but two generations in the next, or Nanda dynasty--viz.: Mâhâ-padma and his eight sons--yet we are asked to believe that they reigned for one hundred and fifty-nine years!

In truth, these nine Nandas seem in many ways mythical, and yet the very confusion and contradictions which surround their history point to some underlying reason for the palpable distortion of plain fact. They are said to have reigned together, the father and his eight sons. The name of only one of these is known, Sumâ-lya; but when Alexander the Great paused on the banks of the Beâs, in the year B.C. 326, he heard that a king was then reigning at Patâliputra, by name Xandrames (so the Greek tongue reports it), who had an army of over two hundred thousand men, and who was very much disliked, because of his great wickedness and base birth. For he was said to be the son of a barber, and as such, "contemptible and utterly odious to his subjects."

This king must have belonged to the Nanda dynasty, and the story, if it does nothing else, proves that the family was really of low extraction. That it gained the throne by the assassination of a rightful king, is also certain. But revenge was at hand. The tragedy was to be recast, replayed, and in B.C. 321

Chandra-gûpta, the Sandracottus of the Greeks, himself an illegitimate son of the first Nanda, and half-brother, so the tale runs, of the eight younger ones, was, after the usual fashion of the East, to find foundation for his own throne on the dead bodies of his relations.

But some four years ere this came to pass, while young Chandra-gûpta, ambitious, discontented, was still wandering about Northern India almost nameless--for his mother was a Sudra woman--he came in personal contact with a new factor in Indian history. For in March, B.C. 326, Alexander the Great crossed the river Indus, and found himself the first Western who had ever stood on Indian soil. So, ere passing to the events which followed on Chandra-gûpta's rude seizure of the throne of Magadha, another picture claims attention. The picture of the great failure of a great conqueror.

THE ANABASIS

B.C. 326 TO B.C. 320

"Some talk of Alexander...."

Who does not know the context? Who also does not think that he knows who Alexander was, who could not, if necessary, reel off a succinct account of his character, his conquests?

And yet, though most know of his Anabasis, how few have really grasped the picturesque points of his grand sweep on India. Who, for instance, has properly appraised and inwardly digested, until it remains as a living picture in the mind's eye for ever, that quaint thirty days' halt of the Macedonian legions on the western bank of the Indus, while on the eastern lay, ripe for plucking, the rich harvest of the fertile plains of India?

It was not a halt of preparation. Hephaistion had already swung the barges across the tumultuous swirls of the great river, and a bridge, unstable, yet firm, lay ready for use. The cohorts were eager. Taxîles, the Indian king, had sent from the Takhsha, or Snake-City, over the water, half a million of tribute, and an advance guard of seven hundred horsemen and thirty caparisoned elephants. For he was wily, and the Western army would aid him against his hereditary enemy the great Porus, or Puar, a representative, doubtless, of the Râjput tribe of that name, who reigned beyond the next river--the Jhelum.

So there was no real need for this prolonged rest, for this fateful pause, ere the West reached out its hand and gripped the East. Still, Alexander deemed it necessary for the purpose, as Arrian puts it naïvely, of "offering sacrifice to the gods to whom he was in the habit of sacrificing."

Wherefore?

He had conquered many other lands. Whence came this hesitation, this desire for divine guidance? And wherefore did Taxîles, sacrificing to the gods to whom he was *not* in the habit of sacrificing, send over three thousand oxen and ten thousand sheep as victims?

Who can say? All we know is, that the sacrifices were favourable to the crossing, as they were bound to be since Alexander had made up his mind to it. Whereupon he "celebrated a gymnastic and horse contest near the river"; those who took part in it, doubtless, wearing crowns of the ivy leaves which the Macedonian legions, as Arrian writes, had found at Mount Merus to their great delight, "for they had not seen any for a long time. So they eagerly made garlands of it, singing hymns in honour of Dionysus."

It must have been a pleasant rest, a jolly time, those thirty days of February and March spent by the sliding river. Those of us who know Northern India have memories of many such a sojourn in the enchanted no-man's-land of a Punjâb river-bed, where the soil on which the tent is pitched one year may be deep stream the next, and the great solemn cranes stalk amongst the young green wheat, and the flocks of flamingoes show rosy-red in the sunrises. Bright, bracing memories these, full, as it were, of the wild wings of many quaint aquatic birds, full of the deep spoors of the heavy black buffaloes, and the motionless grey logs of bottle-nosed crocodiles.

Alexander's army, however, had no such *mise en scene*. At Attock-- about which place the bridge must have spanned the Indus--the river rushes between fixed rocky banks; the uneven country is broken by ravines, or, rather, deep clefts, which look as though they had been split open in the barren, undulating valley by the burning summer heat of the sun. And all around, upon a near horizon, rise, curiously opalescent at all times, whether red by day or white by moonlight, a circle of rocky hills. Elusive hills, distant at one moment, seeming to crush in the valley at another.

One can imagine them rose-red in the dawn, when the order came at last, and Alexander the Invincible closed in grips with his new antagonist.

Plain sailing at first, despite the false alarm of the last day's march to Taxîla, when a complete army in order of battle was seen on the horizon, and startled Alexander into instant dispositions for attack, until this display of force was proved to be an Indian form of honourable reception. The Serpent-City, yielded up to him by its willing ruler without a blow, gave occasion "for more sacrifices which were customary for him to offer."

Once again, however, *not* customary to "Taxîles the Indian," who must have watched this honouring of strange gods with furtive, wily eyes, thinking the while of Porus, with the whole of his mighty army waiting on the further side of the Jhelum River for this upstart Western conqueror as a spider waits a fly.

Here at Taxîla, also, "the king of the Mountaineer-Indians sent envoys, the embassy including the king's brother, as well as the other most notable men." This is one version of the story. Another is that Alexander fought a pitched battle with the mountaineers, defeating them, of course; but this is negatived by Arrian's distinct assertion that when the conqueror moved

Jhelum-wards in May, he left behind him only "soldiers who were invalided by sickness."

In those days Taxîla was a University city, one of the largest in the East-- rich, luxurious, populous--noted as the principal seat of learning in Northern India. All that is left of it now is some miles of ruins between Hasan-Abdâl and Rawalpindi, and a few copper and silver pieces, more ingots than coins, punched in quaint, rude devices. To Alexander it was a hospitable resting-place, where king vied with conqueror in lavish generosity of mutual gifting. Golden crowns for the Macedonian and all his friends; caparisoned chargers, Persian draperies, banqueting vessels for the king and courtiers.

Pleasant rain fell also, laying the Punjâb dust, and hastening the flower-buds to bursting.

But behind all the policy and the pleasure, like a low, distant thunder cloud, lay Porus, with an army fifty thousand strong, biding his time beyond the river.

He had to be faced; so, early in May, Alexander, his small force augmented by a contingent from Taxîla, arrived on the banks of the Hydaspes. Very different weather now from what it had been in March. The hot winds were blowing, the rocks and sand were all aglow, and in its widening bed, as the Jhelum debauched from the hills, the river, swollen by the melting of Himalayan snows, showed a turbulent flood, separating him from his enemy, who, with all his army and his huge troop of elephants, could be seen lining the opposite shore.

How to cross to him, how to give the invincible Macedonian cavalry time to recover and re-form after a forced passage, was the problem before Alexander.

He set his camp face to face with his enemy's, and sent back for the boats with which he had crossed the Indus. A veritable burning of the bridge behind him in a way; but Alexander never considered defeat.

The easiest plan would no doubt have been to wait comfortably encamped till October chill should have checked the melting of summer snow; but, once again, Alexander considered no delay.

So there ensued what Arrian terms "the stealing of a passage." Day and night long the sentinels of Porus were given no rest. Flotillas of boats went up and down the river, reconnaissance parties were here, there, everywhere, menacing a ford; and all the while it was being spread about that Alexander, baffled, disappointed, was fast making up his mind to wait till winter.

Yet 16 miles upwards, almost among the mountains, behind a wooded island which shut out the view southward, galleys, rafts, skins stuffed with hay, everything needful for a forced passage was secretly being prepared.

Night after night brought a feint of attack. As Arrian writes:--

"The cavalry was led along the bank in various directions, making a clamour and raising the battle cry ... as if they were making all preparations for crossing the river.... When this had occurred frequently ... Porus no longer continued to move about also; but, perceiving his fear had been groundless, he kept his position."

It was not, however, as Arrian calls it, by "marvellous audacity" only, that Alexander finally succeeded in his object. As one reads the minute precautions, the stringent orders, the foresight displayed for every possible complication, one is forced to acknowledge the master mind of the commander. Small wonder if the very heavens fought for him. It was now July, month of torrential rains, fierce storms; and one of these fell suddenly like a pall over Alexander's forced night march of 16 miles--"The noise of the thunder," Arrian writes, "drowned with its din the clatter of the weapons."

Thus, noisily yet secretly, the position was gained by the 11,000 picked troops led by Alexander in person. The storm passed; the dawn rose, calm and bright, to find the Western soldiers across the stream, crashing through the low undergrowth of what their general deemed was the mainland. For it was July now, and the rains had brought that marvellous luxuriance of sudden life which springs ever from the union of sun and water. So we can imagine the well-greaved Greeks brushing aside the low daphne bushes, and crushing under foot the trailing arches of the ground maidenhair fern. To find disappointment await them, as, standing on a further shore, they realised that they were on an island, that before them lay another formidable channel, swollen by the night's rain. For a while the cavalry could find no ford; when found, it was but a swimming one. Yet even so, dripping, half-drowned, the legions were over and deployed in the open, before any attempt at opposition could be made.

So with Alexander at the head, the West did battle for the first time with the East.

The result was foregone. Outnumbered as it was by nearly five to one, Alexander's force was still one of veterans, and Alexander himself the foremost military genius of his own or any age.

The story, then, of the great battle of the Hydaspes remains as a lesson in warfare, and soldiers of to-day may pore over the sketch map of it in admiration. Here, in this attempt to give Indian history in picturesque form, all minor things, the magnificent charges of the Macedonian cavalry, the desperate courage of the Indians, even the awful carnage wrought by the maddened elephants cooped up within narrow space, all these fade into insignificance before the tale--so seldom told as it should be told--of the meeting of Alexander and Porus after the battle was over in the eighth hour of the day. Let it be told in Arrian's own words.

"When Porus, who exhibited great talent in the battle, performing deeds not only of a general, but of a valiant soldier, observed the slaughter of his cavalry ... and that most of his infantry had perished, he did not depart, as Darius the Persian king did, setting an example of flight to his men.... At last, having received a wound ... he turned his elephant round and began to retire.

"Alexander, having seen him valiant in battle, was very desirous of saving his life. Accordingly, he sent to him first Taxîles the Indian, who, riding up ... as near as seemed safe, bade him ... listen to Alexander's message. But when he saw his old foe Taxîles, Porus wheeled and prepared to strike him with a javelin, and would probably have killed him, if he had not quickly driven his horse beyond reach. But not even on this account was Alexander angry ... but kept sending others in succession, and last of all Meroës the Indian ... an old friend of Porus.

"As soon as the latter heard the message of Meroës, and being overcome by thirst from his wound, he dismounted from his elephant. After he had drank water and felt refreshed, he ordered Meroës to lead him without delay to Alexander....

"And Alexander rode in front of the line with a few of the Companions to meet him, and stopping his horse, admired the handsome figure and the stature of Porus, which reached somewhat about 5 cubits (6 ft. 6 in.). He was also surprised that he did not seem to be cowed in spirit, but advanced to meet him as one brave man would meet another brave man.... Then, indeed, Alexander was the first to speak, bidding him say what treatment he would like to receive.

"'Treat me, O Alexander, in a kingly way!'

"Alexander, pleased, said: 'For my own sake, O Porus, I do that, but for thine, do thou demand what is pleasing unto thee.'

"But Porus said all things were included in that, whereupon Alexander, being still more pleased, not only granted him the rule over his own Indians, but also added another country of larger extent than the former to what he had before. Thus he treated the brave man in a kingly way, and from that time found him faithful in all things."

A fine picture this; one which does not readily desert the mind's eye when once it has found place there. And a fine beginning also to the dealings of the West with the East. Pity that in the years to come the same policy was not always adopted.

In commemoration of this victory a town was founded on the battle-field, and another near the present one of Jhelum, in memory of the horse "Bucephalus," who died there full of years and honour; not, as Arrian says,

"from having been wounded by any one, but from the effects of toil and old age; for he was about thirty years old, and quite worn out with toils. He had shared many hardships and incurred many dangers with Alexander, being ridden by none but the King, because he rejected all other riders."

The triumphal progress through the Doabs, which ensued on Alexander's passage of the Hydaspes, was only checked by the stout resistance of Sangâla, a fortified town as yet unidentified. But with the help of a fresh contingent brought by Porus, it was razed to the ground as a punishment for its stubborn and useless resistance.

And now before the conqueror lay the river Beâs; beyond it, a nation by repute brave, well equipped, more civilised than those through which he had passed like a flaming sword. His own courage rose high; to him "there seemed no end of the wars so long as anything hostile to him remained."

But the spirit of the soldiers had begun to flag. It was now September, the most trying month in Upper India. The lassitude born of long heat disposed the men to listen to the tales of gigantic heroes beyond the water, and so the exhortations of their leader fell on deaf ears. Yet, as given by Arrian, the words were stirring beyond compare.

"If they had come so far, why should they shrink from adding further lands to their Empire of Macedonia? To brave men there was no end to labours except the labours themselves, provided they led to glorious achievements. The distance to the Eastern ocean was not great, and that must be united to their own familiar sea, since the Great Waters encircled the earth. If they went back, the races they had conquered, not being as yet firm in allegiance, might revolt. Oh! Macedonian and Grecian Allies stand firm! Glorious are the deeds of those who undergo labours, who live a life of valour, and die, leaving behind them immortal glory."

But the words only provoked a long silence. And so the flaming sword turned back; but the great fighting heart of its holder seems to have been left behind in the old bed of the Beâs River, where, on its furthest bank, as a memorial of what would have happened but for dull humanity, he erected twelve huge altars--

"equal in height to the loftiest military towers, while exceeding them in breadth; to serve both as a thank-offering to the gods who had led him so far as a conqueror, and also to serve as monuments of his own labours. And after completing them, he offered sacrifices on them" (to the gods to whom he was in the habit of sacrificing, doubtless!), "and celebrated a gymnastic and equestrian contest."

A very different festivity this from that upon the banks of the Indus; and we can imagine the great leader coming back across the wide stream in his oared galley from the useless, unreal ceremonial, with bent head and arms crossed like Napoleon on his way to St Helena.

A picture that fittingly may end the story of Alexander in India; for the record of his retreat is a record of success without aim, beyond the discovery of the Great Sea which encircles the whole Earth.

There is something intensely pathetic in this story of his choice of the river Hydaspes as his means of retreat, of the infinite care for every unit in his force which he showed before that approach of the dawn in late October, when, without confusion, without disorder, he poured a libation out of a golden goblet from the prow of his vessel into the stream, in the name of his gods and the three great rivers, the Jhelum, the Chenâb, the Indus, to whom he trusted; then, doubtless, flinging the cup of gold far into the sliding water, ordered the signal for starting seawards to be given with the trumpet. So in slow, stately, orderly procession (the "noise of the rowing" mingling with "the cries of the captains, the shouts of the boatswains," and the choric "songs of farewell from the natives who ran along the banks, into a veritable battle cry"), he passed down to the Great Ocean. The voyage took a year, and he reached the sea coast not very far from where Kurrachee now stands. Practically, Alexander was in India proper but nineteen months, and the outward result of his flaming sword had passed almost before his premature death at Babylon, a year and a half after he left its shores. But, though India remained outwardly as ever "splendidly isolated," forgetful of the West, she had felt the Hellenic power; she feels it still. In every little village "Jullunder" (Alexander) is still a name wherewith to conjure, and the village doctor still claims, with pride, to follow the Yunâni (Ionian) system of medicine.

That the former should be the case is surely small wonder. India is ever the slave of vitality, and Alexander was vital to the finger-tips. What else could be said of the man who, finding himself checked in an assault on a stronghold, leapt from the bastion into the fort, and, supporting himself against the wall, kept the enemy at bay with his sword, till one by one his followers, maddened by the sight of their beloved leader's danger, followed him in time to rescue him, wounded, fainting?

But the deed which, of all others, Arrian extols as the most noble deed ever performed by Alexander, took place in this wise in the desert. His army, parched with thirst, were stumbling on blindly, led, as usual in times of distress, by Alexander on foot.

To him, weary and exhausted, returned scouts, bearing with them water collected in a helmet with great difficulty from some cleft in a distant rock.

He took it, thanking the bearers, but immediately poured it upon the ground in sight of all. "As a result of this," Arrian writes, "the entire army was reinvigorated to so great a degree that any one would have imagined that the water so lavished had furnished draught for every man."

Truly, though he left little of sovereignty behind him, Alexander left enough pictures imprinted on the soil of Hindustan to furnish forth many a gallery.

THE GREAT MAURYAS

B.C. 321 TO B.C. 184

We come here to one of the landmarks of Indian History. There were seven kings of the Maurya dynasty; of these, two gained for themselves an abiding place in the category of Great World Rulers. Their names are Chandra-gûpta and Asôka. Grandfather and grandson, they made their mark in such curiously divergent ways that they stand to this day as examples of War and Peace.

Concerning Chandra-gûpta's usurpation of the throne of the Nine Nandas, something has already been said. It has also been mentioned that while still almost a lad, he met with Alexander during the latter's brief summer among the Punjâb Doâbs or Two-waters, so called because they are the fertile plains which lie between the rivers.

The identification, indeed, of the Sandracottus mentioned by Greek writers with Chandra-gûpta has been of incalculable value in enabling historians to fix other dates. It has been, as it were, a secure foundation for a superstructure which has grown, and still grows, year by year, and in which every new stone discovered is found to fit accurately in its place.

At the time of this meeting, Chandra-gûpta was a nameless adventurer, a political exile from Magadha. Who he really was seems doubtful. The illegitimate son, it is said, of one of the Nine Nandas by a beautiful low-caste woman (from whose name, Mura, the titular designation of the dynasty Maurya is taken), it is hard to see whence came the young man's undoubted claim to be of the Shesh-nâg, or Serpent race; for the Nandas were as undoubtedly of low-caste origin themselves. It is possible, therefore, that some further history of wrong may have existed to make Chandra-gûpta claim kinship with the Serpent-Kings whom the Nandas had ousted, and hold himself, like any young pretender, a rightful heir.

Be that as it may, he was ambitious, capable, energetic, and seized the first opportunity given him of rising to power.

This came with the news of Alexander's death in B.C. 323. In the instant revolt of conquered India which followed, he took a prominent part, and found himself, in B.C. 321, with an army at his back which, having accomplished its purpose and given its leader paramount power in Punjâb, was eager to follow his fortune elsewhere.

He led it to Magadha, and taking advantage of the Nanda king's unpopularity, slew every male member of the family.

This was the Eastern etiquette on such occasions; the sparing of a brother or an uncle being considered a weakness sure to bring speedy repentance in its train.

Except in as far as the principals were concerned, this revolution appears to have been easy and bloodless. At least so we gather from the play called the "Signet of the Minister," which, though not written till nearly twelve hundred years after the event, seems fairly trustworthy in fact.

In itself it is so studiously realistic, so palpably free from all appeal to the imagination, as to form a marked contrast to all other dramas of the period. It is most likely the first purely political play that ever was written, for, excluding love passages and poetical diction, it deals entirely with the stir of plot and counterplot. Chânakya, the wily Brahman--whose advice had been Chandra-gûpta's best weapon in gaining the throne--realising the insecurity of that throne without the hearty support of the nobles and, above all, of the late King's Prime Minister, sets himself by sheer diplomacy to cut the ground from beneath the feet of his master's enemies, and, succeeding, yields up his signet of office to the appeased Rakahâsa, whose final aside when he accepts it--"Oh! vile Chânakya--say rather, Wise Chânakya, a mine of wisdom inexhaustible! Deep ocean stored with excellent rare gems"-- shows that he feels himself overmastered by sheer wit.

But the whole play is well worth reading; some of it--notably the parts in prose-reminding one of Shakspeare.

The remainder of Chandra-gûpta's career, however, was anything but bloodless. It was scarcely possible that it should be so, considering that he began life as a nobody and ended it as undisputed Emperor of India from the Bay of Bengal to the Arabian Sea. A man of iron nerve, born to conquer, born to rule, he went on his way undeviatingly, holding his own despite the constant threats of his enemies, despite the danger of constant plots; a danger which made perpetual precaution necessary. He never occupied the same bedroom two nights in succession; he never during the daytime slept at the same hour.

A story is told of Chânakya's wily vigilance for his master. He noticed one day a long caravan of ants on the wall of the king's room carrying crumbs. This was enough for Chânakya. Without an instant's hesitation, the royal pavilion was ordered to be set on fire and, as the plaint runs:--

"The brave men who were concealed
In the subterrene avenue that led
To Chandra-gûpta's sleeping chamber, so,
Were all destroyed."

So far as one can gather, Chandra-gûpta's character was not a lovable one; but there can be no question of his power to rule men wisely and well. Megasthenes' account of Pâlipûtra (which applies more to the reign of Chandra-gûpta, during whose lifetime the Grecian was ambassador to the court, than to that of any other monarch) gives us a marvellous picture of the grip which Government kept on the people; and kept for their good. Every department (especially the land revenue and irrigation, both of paramount importance in an Indian State) was legislated for with the utmost care, and though the whole system of government was based on the personal power of the king, it was far from being a mere arbitrary autocracy. His greatest contemporary was Seleukos Nikator, who in addition to ceding Kâbul, Herât, and Kandahâr to him, bestowed on him his daughter in marriage.

Chandra-gûpta died in B.C. 297, having reigned for twenty-four years. A short enough time in which to have accomplished so much; for at the day of his death, the only portion of the vast continent of India which did not acknowledge his rule was a strip of sea coast country about Cuttack, on the Bay of Bengal, and that part of the lessening peninsular which lay southward, beyond a line drawn through Mangalore and Madras.

His son Bindu-sâra reigned in his stead. Of him we know nothing; not even if he was born of the Grecian princess. Only this is on record, that he was extremely fond of figs, and, presumably, of learning; for a letter of his to Antiochus, the son of Seleukos Nikator, asks naïvely for the purchase and despatch of green figs and a professor! To which the dignified reply is still extant that the figs shall be procured and forwarded, but that by Grecian etiquette it was indecorous either to buy or sell a professor!

Bindu-sâra had this merit: he handed on the empire which he had received intact to his son, after a reign of five and twenty years.

So let us pass to Asôka, who, next to Akbar the Great Moghul, was the greatest of all Indian kings. Curiously enough, both these monarchs, Asôka and Akbar, ruled India through its imagination. Both claimed pre-eminence as apostles of a Faith in the Unknown; both appealed to the people on transcendental grounds.

At the time of his fathers death in B.C. 272, Asôka was Viceroy of the Western Province. He had previously ruled in a similar position in the Punjâb, where his headquarters had been Taxîla, the Serpent City. Chosen as Crown Prince from amongst numerous other sons on account of his ability, he had been given this semi-independent control, partly because of his ungovernable temper, which earned him the nickname of "The Furious." He thus seemed to take after his grandfather, Chandra-gûpta, who, with all his many virtues, was unquestionably cruel and arrogant. But Asôka was not to follow in his ancestor's footsteps. Forty years afterward, when his long and peaceful reign, marred by but one war, had come to an end, he had earned for himself the well-deserved title of "The Loving-minded One, Beloved of the Gods." A great change in any man's life; but nothing to the change which his life was to bring into his world.

In B.C. 260, when he came under the mingled influence of Buddhism and Jainism, those creeds were little more than sectarian beliefs confined to the India which had given them birth. When he died, Buddhism had spread through Asia, and had touched both Africa and Europe. Asôka has been called the Constantine of Buddhism, but he was more than that. The creed which brought him comfort was not, as Christianity was in Constantine's time, already a power to be reckoned with, it was simply the belief of a few enthusiasts, a few select souls who sought almost sorrowfully for some solution of the Great Secret.

What was the cause which led the Emperor of India, in his luxurious autocracy, to join himself to this Search? Undoubtedly it was remorse; remorse for the numberless lives needlessly sacrificed, the needless suffering entailed on humanity by the one war of his reign--the conquest of Kalînga, a maritime province on the sea-board of the Bay of Bengal. We have this remorse with us still (as we have so much of the innermost soul and thoughts and aspirations of Asôka) in the marvellous edicts engraven on rock and pillar, which, outlasting Time itself, tell to wild waste and deserted ruins their story of one man's struggle towards the light. One can almost hear the break, as of tears, in the voice that clamours still of "the regret which the Beloved-of-the-Gods felt at the murders and the deaths and the violence."

This regret, then, was the cosmic touch which drove Asôka to find comfort in preaching the doctrine of the sanctity of life. Was it Jainism (amongst the tenets of which this takes first place) which influenced Asôka most, or was it Buddhism? Doctors differ; only this we know, that it was through Asôka's exertions that the latter became the creed of one-third of the human race. For the energy of the man was incomparable. His missionaries were everywhere. "Let small and great exert themselves," is the cry still carven upon stone. "The teaching of religion is the most meritorious of acts.... There is no gift comparable to the gift of religion ... it is in the conquests of religion that the gods takes pleasure." So his yellow-robed monks went forth beyond the confines of his visible, tangible world, and found their way to Egypt, to Greece, to Syria. Their influence is still to be traced in other religions, though no record exists of their labours.

Thus for some thirty years of his life Asôka set himself to alter the faith of the world. Why? And how? Because he believed with a whole heart, not in ritual or dogma, but in something which--hard to be translated--is best rendered by the "Law of Piety." And this his edicts explain to be "mercy and charity, truth and purity, kindness and goodness."

A good creed even in these later days. Not to be improved upon by conformists or non-conformists!

As to how this gospel of good-will was to be preached we learn from these edicts also. It is by example, by tolerance, by "gentleness and moderation in speech."

"Government by religion, law by religion, progress by religion." This was Asôka's rule, and in it he stands alone as the only king who has subordinated all things to a faith which must only be preached in gentleness and moderation.

The first series of fourteen edicts were cut on rocks in various parts of his kingdom, from Attock on the Indus to Cuttack on the Eastern Sea, during the twelfth and thirteenth year of Asôka's reign. They are, therefore, the first-fruits of his conversion. They range over a vast number of subjects, but in each of them there is a personal note which justifies the belief that they are verily the words of the king, and not the mere drafts of some secretary.

On the other hand, the Minor Rock edicts were carven in the last year of Asôka's reign, and thus gain an additional interest from being the farewell of a king to the people whom he had striven so hard to lead into the Way of Peace. In one of them he says that the truest enjoyment for himself has been making men happy by leading them to follow the path of religion, that "with this object he has regulated his life"; yet, though he has "promulgated positive rules, it is solely by a change in the sentiments of the heart that religion makes true progress." The edict ends thus: "So spake Piyadâsi, Beloved-of-the-Gods. Wherever this edict exists on pillars of stone let it endure to remote ages."

It has endured. The Prakrit language in which it was engraven--the spoken language of those times--has passed; but Asôka's words are not of Time, they are of Eternity.

He was a great builder, but few of his buildings remain to this day. What their magnificence must have been we may judge by the topes at Sanchi, where the eye wearies in following the intricacy of ornament, the brain is bewildered in attempting to re-fashion in imagination the whole stupendous structure as it must have been. But here and there some monolithic sandstone pillar still remains, slender, perfect in proportion and execution, still bearing in close-carven character Asôka's message to his people, to the world.

Strange, indeed, that the West knows so little of him! Strangest of all that the twentieth century, with its Peace Party and its Anti-Vivesectionists, should not put Asôka's name as President in perpetuity of their organisations. Asôka, who more than a thousand years upheld the equal rights of animals with men to the King's care, and openly adjured his successors to follow in his steps, and not "to think that a conquest by the sword deserves the name of conquest."

What manner of man Asôka was outwardly, we have no means of knowing; but those who know of his life can picture him in his yellow monk's robe, wearied yet unwearied, pondering over his lifelong problem. "By what means can I lead my people into the path of peace?"

Unwearied because of the spirit which inspires the words, "Work I must for the public benefit"; wearied because, "Though I am ready at any hour and any place to receive petitions, I am never fully satisfied with my despatch of business."

He died in B.C. 231, leaving his empire intact, and was apparently succeeded by a grandson. After him came five kings, all mere names. The duration of the dynasty was 137 years, and as 89 of these belonged to the combined reigns of Chandra-gûpta, Bindu-sâra, and Asôka, the remaining six kings have but eight years apiece. Long enough, however, to disintegrate, to dissipate the vast empire of Asôka. So much so, that before continuing the story of what may be called the central kings of India, it is necessary to give a side-glance at the outlying provinces where, on the removal of Asôka's firm grip on Government, various minor dynasties began to rise into a power superior to that of Magâdha.

THE OUTLYING PROVINCES

B.C. 231 TO A.D. 45

A growing tide as it nears the springs claims more and more of the shore at each rise and fall. So it was with the tide which on Asôka's death set in around his throne.

On the north-western frontier, that battle-ground of India, there had been peace since Chandra-gûpta wrested half Ariana from the grip of Seleukos Nikator. But the country itself had remained more or less under Hellenist influence. Antiochus, Demetrios Eukratides, such are the names of the passing rulers of whose existence we know by the multitude of coins which form almost their only history.

Indeed, as in some museum we gaze with keen yet clouded interest at some case of coins labelled "Indo-Greek, Indo-Parthian *civ*: B.C. 250, A.D. 50," we are really gaining at a glance an impressionist picture of the strange welter of principalities and powers, of sudden diminutions and almost causeless exacerbations of influence, which marked the passage of these few centuries upon the borderland of India. Here a big gold plaque arrests our eye, just as the name of Arsakes or Menander heaves into sight out of the confused medley of their more insignificant surroundings; or some quaint half-Aryan, half-Parthian inscription leaves us wondering of the why and the wherefore, just as some trivial incident which has survived Time in the pages of obscure Greek writers makes us pause to wish for more. Strange, ghost-like personalities are those which live rudely hammered out on a rough ingot of bronze, or silver, or gold, telling their tale truly,--succinctly at times however, as when the name and portrait of one prince forms at first the obverse of another, then the name alone remains, and finally Hermaios disappears, and Kadphîses rules supreme.

Map: India to B.C. 231

Who are they all? Historians peer and ponder; they add date to date, and divide the total by their own desires--for in no branch of knowledge is the personal equation more powerful than in history--yet still that glance at the case of coins gives to the uninitiated the best impression of the period.

One thing which militates against a concise pigeon-holing of such information as we can gather into this brief review of Indian history, is the fact that much of it has really nothing to do with India at all. The Hindoo Kush range of mountains may be taken as the western boundary of Asôka's empire, and the powers which encroached on that empire matured their plans, conquered and governed such provinces as they gained from beyond that boundary. The Bactrians, for instance, who appeared on the banks of the Indus, came from the valleys and fertile plains about the Oxus. They were a semi-civilised, semi-Hellenised race, who boasted the possession of a thousand cities. The Parthians, on the other hand, hailed from the wide steppes about the Caspian Sea, and were barbarian utterly in the sense of not caring for either luxury or culture. Mounted shepherds, mere moss-troopers, they were a hardy race, and under the leadership of Arsakes, gripped at the crown of Central Asia, and so, inevitably, after a time reached out to the fat lands about the Indus; for the most part leaving the princelings who parcelled out the land in possession, as feudatories to the foreign power.

It will be remembered that Seleukos Nikator's attempt to recover India for Greece in Chandra-gûpta's time failed. Thenceforward for a hundred years no other attempt was made. In B.C. 206, however, Antiochus the Bactrian made a sweep on Kandahâr, and Demetrios, his son, in B.C. 190, following his example, captured both the Punjâb and Sinde. To his own cost, however; for, weakened by these distant wars, he had to yield his throne to one Eukratides, and be content for a time with the title of "King of the Indians." Not for long, however, for Eukratides, being bad to beat, eventually got a grip even on these eastern provinces.

Justin the historian gives a few personal details of this Eukratides. How he and three hundred held a fort for five months against Demetrios and sixty thousand; and how he was killed in cold blood by his son and colleague, who drove his chariot wheels over his father's dead body and refused it burial. A poor return for trust, and honour, and devoted love! It is satisfactory to know that the monstrous crime brought its own punishment The dead hero's hold once gone, the successes he had gained drifted from the murderer's hands, and thereinafter ensued one of those confused welters of conflicting names, powers, principalities, which send us back to our outlook on the case of coins. Menander's name rises out of the obscure in B.C. 155, when he attempted to follow Alexander's footsteps. With a large army he marched on India, and crossing the Beâs, which had defied his predecessor, actually threatened the capital of Pâlipûtra itself. At that time, however, the sovereignty of Magadha lay with a strong man; the man who, ousting the degenerate Mauryas, had shown himself to have the qualities of both a soldier and general. So the Greek king had to beat a hasty retreat, thus ending the last attempt of Europe upon India until Vasco de Gama's, in A.D. 1502.

About this time two nomad tribes from the wide Roof-of-the-World began a march southward, which, like a flood, was eventually to sweep everything before it. The first were the Sâkas, who, driven from behind by the following tribe, the Yuehchi, overwhelmed Bactria, forced their way into the Punjâb, and penetrated as far south as Mathura, while another section founded a Sika dynasty at Kathiawâr. They seem to have owned allegiance to the Arsakian or Parthian kings of Persia, and bore the Persian title of satrap.

Thus, from the pell-mell of petty princelings and wild, nomadic chieftains another name springs to notice. On the coins it runs: "*Maues basileus basileon.*"

This king of kings, as he proudly calls himself, was Maues, the first, or nearly the first, of an Indo-Parthian dynasty replacing the Indo-Greek and Indo-Bactrian ones. As our eye runs over the coins--the only relics of dead kings--it is arrested by the name of Gondophares.

Now who was Gondophares? The question clamours vainly for answer, until a faint recollection of the early fathers brings Origen and the Acts of St Thomas back to memory. Yes! Gondophares was the King of India in the days when

"the twelve Apostles, having divided the countries of the world amongst themselves by lot, India fell to the share of Judas, surnamed Thomas or the Twin, who showed unwillingness to start on his mission."

Poor St Thomas! It was a far cry, but Habbân, the Indian merchant, conveyed his saintly purchase (for the Lord sold the unwilling missioner to him in a vision for twenty pieces of silver) to King Gundephar in safety. And the king bade the apostle, who was an architect, build him a palace in six months.

"And St Thomas, commanded therefore by the Lord, promised to build him the palace within the six months, but spent all the monies in almsgiving. So when the time came, he explained that he was building the king a palace, not on earth, but in heaven, not made with hands--and multitudes of the people embraced the faith."

So runs the old Monkish story. Is it true? Who knows! Gondophares was a real man, he was a real Indian king, he is associated in legend with a Christian mission, and the claim that St Thomas was the missioner is not at variance with known facts or chronology. With that we must be content.

And now the coins tell another tale. In their turn the Indo-Parthian princes were being driven southward. Their names disappear before those of the horde of Turki nomads called the Yuehchi, who about the middle of the second century B.C. followed the path taken years before by the Sâkas, and with two hundred thousand bowmen and a million persons of all ages and sexes poured themselves into India in search of pastures new.

So much for the north-western frontier. In the south-west, while Greek prince after Greek prince in the north was minting coins that were to carry his name idly, ineffectively, through the centuries, an aboriginal Dravidian people, driven, no doubt, thousands of years before from the fertile fields of the Gangetic plain by the steady advance of the Aryan immigrants, were as steadily regaining their hold upon Central India. The Andhra race was not slow to seize opportunity. The death of Asôka gave them the chance of casting off their allegiance to the Maury a empire, and they took it. A few years later the King of the Andhras, self-styled the "Lord of the West," was able to send an army to the eastern sea-coast, and so help Kalînga to revolt also. The capital of the Andhra kingdom appears to have been an unidentified city called Sri-Kâkulum, on the banks of the Krishna River; and the area of Andhra rule gradually increasing, crept closer and closer to that of Magadha. The memory of Hâla, the seventeenth king, lives still by virtue of an anthology of love-songs called "The Seven Centuries," which he is said to have composed. That, a collection entitled "The Great Storybook," and a Sanskrit Grammar all belong by repute to the reign of this king. Finally, the inevitable collision occurred between the powerful Andhra dynasty and the degenerate, dissolute monarchy at Magadha, which resulted in the annihilation of the latter. But before turning to this, the course of the years since the Maurya kings disappeared from sheer inanition must be traced briefly. It was in B.C. 194 that Pusŷa-mitra, commander-in-chief to the last of the Mauryas, lost patience with his weak master, assassinated him, and founded the Sunga line. A strong, unscrupulous man evidently, he held his own, succeeded in stemming the steady tide of disintegration on both the south-east and the north-west, and drove back the Greek invasion of Menander.

Still unsatisfied, he revived, in order to strengthen his rule, the old traditional Horse-sacrifice, of which we read in the Vedas.

A quaint old ceremony without doubt. Imagine a grey horse, approved by lucky marks, sanctified by priests, turned loose to wander at its will. And behind it, following it from field to field as it ranges, a complete army ready to claim pasturage for it from all and sundry during the space of one whole year. Hey presto! by beat of drum the fiat goes forth, as it grazes, that proprietors, principalities, powers, must submit or fight. So, if an unconquered army returned when the trial was ended, he who sent it forth had right to claim suzerainty, to call himself Lord-Paramount of all the others.

This particular "Asva-medha," as it is called, has a peculiar significance, in that it proves a determined return from Buddhism to Brahmanism on the part of the holders of the Magadha throne. It is said, indeed, that Pushŷa-mitra, like so many bloody usurpers, was *dévote*, and that his piety included persecution of the new faith. One thing seems certain: his ten successors in the Sunga dynasty were all more or less in the hands of the Brahmans, who managed the state while the titular monarchs amused themselves in various discreditable ways, until in B.C. 75, one Vasu-deva, Brahman prime minister, lost patience with *his* hereditary master, killed him while engaged in a dishonourable intrigue, and started a new dynasty--the Kanva--by mounting the throne himself! an idle proceeding, since it was soon to pass from the hands of his ineffectual successors to those of an Andhra prince.

But by this time--B.C. 75--another advancing flood--the Yuehchi migration--had appeared in the north-west, and for the first two centuries or so of our era was to claim equal share with the Dravidian kings in the Government of India.

And what of Vikramadîtya? Vikramadîtya the hero, the demigod, the king *par excellence* of the Indian populace of to-day? The monarch whose victory over some Scythian invaders in B.C. 57 was celebrated by the introduction of the Samvat era, which dates from that year? Are all the stories of him that are told about the smoke-palled winter fires in the Punjâb fields, the hundred and one tales of his munificence, his courage and his goodness--are all these mere legends?

So far as this early date is concerned, historians tell us that they are. More than five hundred years later one of the Gupta kings bore the name, and answers in some way to the description.

But how came he to be connected with the Samvat era which undoubtedly dates from B.C. 57? Who can say! Vikramadîtya is a terrible loss to India. How can we bear to part with the king whose swans sang always:

"Glory be to Vikramajeet,
He gave us pearls to eat!"

The king whose puppets of stone that bore aloft his throne refused to bear the weight of his successor, and wandered out into the wide world, each telling a tale of departed glory!

No! Vikramadîtya, the beloved of every Indian school-boy for his valour, of every little Indian maiden for his gentleness, cannot be given up without a protest.

"The fiction which resembles truth is better than the truth which is dissevered from the imagination." Let us hark back to those words of wisdom, and search round for some faint foothold for blessed belief.

Let us turn to our case of coins in hope. Stay! What is this?

A nameless one. The date is close to the era we are seeking; the only inscription runs thus, "*Soter Megas.*"

The "Great Saviour!" Is not that enough for the imagination? So let us pass by the cogitations of the historian as to what nameless king minted the coin, and listen with renewed confidence to the tale told by a childish voice of how King Vikramadîtya slew the foul fiend.

What does it matter whether he was Vikramadîtya or another? Foul fiends must always be killed; as well by a nameless king, provided he be a "Great Saviour."

But one point more requires a few words ere we pass on--the extent to which Greek culture influenced India.

Curiously little. A glance at the Græco-Buddhist carvings which still, in some places on the frontier, are to be had for the mere picking up as they lie littered about among the rough-hewn stones which once were fort or palace, temple or shrine, shows that while India accepted Greek art, she did not oust her own, but grafted the new skill on the old stock.

And though it fires the imagination to think of Greek customs, Greek philosophy, Greek valour and intellect making its home for hundreds of years among the young green wheat-fields by the bed of the Indus, we must not blind our eyes to the fact that the broad yellow flood of the river seems to have been an impassable barrier to the whole theory of life which was the root-stuff of such custom, such philosophy, such valour, such intellect.

India went on her way, as she has gone always, almost untouched by outside influences. Despite the brilliancy of the Macedonian cavalry, her own retained its ancient traditions; despite the intellectual keenness of European theorists, India has dreamt--as she dreams still--her old dreams.

There is a little temple near the supposed site of Taxîla. Or perhaps it was not a temple at all: it may have been anything else. But two or three of the broken pillars have Ionic capitals.

That is about the extent of Greek influence in India.

THE BACTRIAN CAMEL AND THE INDIAN BULL

A.D. 45 TO A.D. 225

The device of a camel and a bull on the reverse and obverse of a coin minted by Kadphîses, the first Kushân king in India, is, Mr Vincent Smith remarks, a singularly appropriate symbol for the conquest of Hindustan by a horde of nomads from Central Asia.

These wanderers, ever pressed from behind, had come far; they had met and overwhelmed by sheer numbers many hostile tribes. But all this was prior to their passage into India proper. That took place about the year B.C. 40, when Hermaios, the last of the Indo-Greek rulers, gave way to the first Mongolian king.

It is curious to note this transference of power viewed in the light of our case of coins. First, we find the names of both princes preserved in the legend, the portrait of the Greek, with his title in Greek lettering, still adorning the obverse. After a while the legend changes, the Mongolian's name monopolises it, though the portrait remains. Again a while, and Hermaios' face disappears in favour of the features of the Roman Emperor, Augustus; a piece of flattery due to the growing fame of Rome at its zenith, even in the Far East. So, after again a little while, the coin shows nothing but that symbol of conquest, the Bactrian Camel dominating the Indian Bull!

A pause for consideration will show us that this was no ordinary conquest. The domination of a highly civilised people such as the Indians were undoubtedly, even in those far ages, by a horde of upland wanderers, veneered with a culture picked up hastily as they journeyed, cannot have come about without much disturbance. Yet of this we have no record. The feet of those million or more of men, women, children, seem to have overwhelmed even their own noise and clamour. Still, we know that the final overthrow of the old dynasties in the Punjâb and the Indus valley was deferred until Kadphîses I. had been gathered to his fathers after a reign of forty years, and his son, Kadphîses II., reigned in his stead. As energetic, as ambitious as his father, he was keen enough to see the advantages of propitiating that great Western emperor of Rome, whose gold was now pouring into India in exchange for the latter's silk, gems, dye-stuffs, and spices; so, after conquering the whole of the North-Western Provinces, he sent an embassy to Rome in order to acquaint the Emperor Trajan of the fact.

Probably we have here the first political connection between East and West.

For the rest, was this in truth, not the golden age, but the age of gold, for in addition to the Roman Aurei, of which numberless specimens are to be found in our Museums, we have examples of Oriental gold coins of the same purity and weight, which must have been struck by the Kushân kings, as these leaders of the wanderers are called.

On the death of the second Kadphîses, one Kanîshka came to the throne. This is a name which still has a voice in Indian tradition, and, beyond India, is still known in the legendary lore of Tibet, Mongolia, and China.

Yet as to who he was, whether he came to the throne by honest succession, or even as to the date of his reign, we have next to no accurate information.

Here and there, as we dig at the grave of this dead king, our spade and mattock turn up a coin, an inscription, perhaps an allusion in later literature; but the point remains unsettled as to whether Kanîshka reigned in B.C. 57 or A.D. 120. The evidence of coins points to the latter date. There is a certain quaint four-pronged symbol to be found in most of the coins struck by Kadphîses II., which is found also in the innumerable coinage of Kanîshka; for, whoever he was, he minted much. Sure sign of a long and prosperous reign.

But there is evidence also which brings home to the enquirer the mysterious attraction which lingers alike in the search for buried treasure, and the search for buried history. For, close beside our traces of Kanîshka, of Kadphîses, we come upon those of that nameless King, the Great Saviour, whose unknown personality dominates for the imaginative the two centuries of time which holds in their grip of years the birth of Christ. A hundred years before that event, a hundred years after, this vision of a Great King flits vaguely through the obscure, making us say: "It cannot be, and yet--suppose it were?"

Good old Vikramadîtya! Will the years, as they bring new discoveries, bring you back from the realms of myth?

Meanwhile, "Soter Megas Basileus Basileon" remains free of the fetters of fact, and Kanîshka, the king, evades them in a fashion that is purely tantalising.

"Strangely open to doubt," is the verdict of the historian on almost everything concerning him.

‛And yet we know much.

We know that, like Asôka, he was an ardent Buddhist, though of how or why he adopted this faith we are ignorant. We know that he ruled as far east as Benares, as far south as the mouths of the Indus, as far west and north as the Pamirs. His capital was Peshawur; but he had subdued the old Indian capital of Pâlipûtra. We know, also, that he was a man of artistic tastes, a student and an admirer of Nature; for his favourite holiday ground was the valley and hills of Kashmir, where he erected many great monuments. At Peshawur itself, besides a monastery whose ruins may still be traced outside the Lahore gate of the modern town, he raised a great tower to cover some Buddhist relics. The spire or pinnacle of this was in thirteen stories, made of beautifully carved wood, and, surmounted by an iron finial, rose 400 feet in height. It is thus described by a Chinese pilgrim who visited it in the sixth century.

But what best deserves remembrance in connection with Kanîshka's name are the wonderful sculptures which of late years have been discovered in such quantities in the Hashtnûgar district, and elsewhere. They are known, generically, as the Gandhâra sculptures, as they are supposed to be the output of a distinct school which flourished in the district of that name. But in conception, style, and execution, they assimulate closely to the Græco-Roman school, which at this period of the world's history was nearly cosmopolitan.

Kanîshka is also to be remembered for the Great Buddhist Council he convened, in imitation, apparently, of Asôka. The story goes that certain commentaries, being approved by this Council, were ordered to be engraved on copper, and placed, for security, in a st'hupa or tumulus.

The site of this has not yet been discovered, the copper plates remain unread!

A find this, perchance, for the coming years! It is something to look forward to, something which may clear up many points concerning Kanîshka now "strangely open to doubt."

The history of his successors is, likewise, doubtful. We stand, indeed, on the threshold of one of those curious intervals in Indian story, when the curtain comes down on the living picture of the stage, leaving us to wonder what the next act of the drama will be, and when it will recommence. Still more like, perhaps, is the position of the spectator to one who, on some mountain top, watches the rolling clouds sweep through the valleys below him. A stronger breath of wind, a little rift in the hurrying white vapour, and a glimpse of the life that goes on and on below the mists comes into view for a moment, and is gone the next.

So we look back towards the beginning of the third century after Christ. A glint of sunlight, a passing peep of something recognisable, obliterated in an instant by the rolling clouds growing more and more obscure as they deepen and darken.

"Then there were in this land three kings, Hûshka, Jûshka, and Kanîshka, who built three towns."

So runs the Kashmir chronicle.

It reads like the beginning of a fairy tale, but nothing follows save a gold coin with the beautifully executed portrait of a striking-looking man upon it, a man with deep-set eyes and determination marked upon every feature. Beneath it, the legend of King Huwûshka, or Hûshka.

Another glimpse comes to us of one Vâsu-deva. Does he in truth belong to the Mongolian princes, with their strange uncouth names? His is a purely Indian one, and the coins which bear his name no longer bear the Bactrian camel. The bull, too, is attendant on the Indian God Siva, complete with his noose and trident.

Had Buddhism, then, gone by the board? Who can tell. The curtain is finally rung down about the year A.D. 230 on the confused passing of the Andhra dynasty in the south, the Kushân dynasty in the north, and does not rise again, not even for a moment, until a hundred years have passed.

And yet, before this little book is published, the grave may have given up its dead, and out of a few dry bones, a chance coin, a half-obliterated inscription, some new personality may have arisen to live again through those long, empty years.

India is very wide, and she is very secretive. How can it be otherwise, when beyond reach of the clash and welter of kings, of courts and conquests, the great mass of the people live untouched by change, watching their crops, ploughing, sowing, reaping, "undisturbed" (as Megasthenes pointed out with wonder), "even when battle is raging in their neighbourhood, by any sense of danger, since the tillers of the soil are regarded by the Indians as a race sacred, inviolable." To the world beyond such lives are a secret; they hold the unknown.

So from behind the curtain the "Song of the Plough" rises in monotonous chant as, in the same dress, using the same implements as he uses to-day, the peasant drives his white oxen, and sings:--

"Bitter blue sky with no fleck of a cloud!
Ho! brother-ox drive the plough deep.
Sky-dappled grey like the partridge's breast!
Ho! brother-ox drive the plough straight.
Merry drops slanting from East to West!
Oh! brother-ox drive home the wain.
The gods give poor folk rain."

THE GREAT GÛPTA EMPIRE

A.D. 308 TO A.D. 450

The curtain rises again upon a wedding; the wedding of Princess Kumâri Devi. Eight hundred years before, King Bimbi-sâra of the Sesu-nâga dynasty had strengthened his hold on Magadha by marrying her ancestress, a princess of that Lichchâvi clan which for centuries has held strong grip on a vast tract of country spreading far into the Nepaul hills.

This kingdom of the Lichchâvis had given Bimbi-sâra much trouble. It was to check the inroads of the bold hill folk that he first built the watch fort of Patâliputra, the modern Patna. Of the history of the warlike clan during these long intervening years nothing is known; but they must have kept their independence, for Princess Kumâri Devi (which, by the way, is tautological, since Kumâri means princess, the whole name therefore standing as Princess-Goddess) appears from the obscure as a person of importance, apparently an heiress. Whether she was the reigning princess history sayeth not; but it appears not unlikely that this was the case, and that at the time the Lichchâvis, instead of being checked by, were in possession of, Patâliputra.

Be that as it may, the Goddess-Princess chose to marry one Chandra-gûpta, a mere local chief of whose father and grandfather only the names have been preserved. Possibly he was good-looking; let us hope so! From the character of his son, Samûdra-gupta, it is reasonable to suppose that he rose above the common herd of princelings in both intelligence and accomplishments; though, on the other hand, these might have been derived from the princess.

Scarcely, however; unless the fairy god-mother had worked hard, since the bride's race warrants us in presupposing beauty. Even now, says a contemporary witness, "the delicate features and brilliantly fair complexion of the Lichchâvi women are remarkable."

Anyhow, the immediate result of what must have been a love match was the appearance for the first and last time in Indian History of a veritable Prince Consort, who, though calling himself king, struck coins which bore the name of his queen as well as his own, and whose son claimed succession as the "son of the daughter of the Lichchâvis."

Indeed, save as husband and father, Chandra-gûpta, the first of the Gûpta race, has little claim on attention. After the fashion of Prince Consorts, he is more or less of a figure-head, though the prospects of his dynasty were considered sufficiently dignified and secure to permit of his coronation date being made the beginning of yet another of the many Indian eras; one which has, however, passed entirely out of use.

Chandra-gûpta seems to have died when still quite a young man, leaving his son, apparently quite a boy, to reign in his stead.

A precocious stripling this Samûdra-gupta, who was to fill the throne of India as it has seldom been filled for more than half a century. Possibly there may have been some interval of Regency with the Queen-Mother at its back, but one of the most curious features in this fifty-year-long reign, is that we know nothing of it from the words of any historian, that we gather no allusion to it from any contemporaneous literature. Our knowledge, which year by year increases, comes from coins, from inscriptions; notably from a pillar which now stands in the fort at Allahabad. Originally incised and set up by Asôka six centuries earlier, Samûdra-gupta's court panegyrist has used its waste space for a record of his master's great deeds. A quaint contrast; since these were chiefly bloody wars, and Asôka everywhere was a peace propagandist.

In truth, Samûdra-gupta appears to have been an Indian Alexander. What he saw he coveted, what he coveted he conquered. From this same pillar we learn that his empire included all India as far south as Malabar, as far north as Assam and Nepaul. It was thus larger than any since the days of Asôka, though the southward sweep of Samûdra-gupta's victorious armies cannot, in the nature of things, have been much more than a raid. A campaign, involving fully 3,000 miles of marching, which cannot have occupied less than three years, and the furthest limit of which lands one more than 1,200 miles from one's base, must be a mere march to victory and a retreat with spoils.

The record of this march is fairly complete. The courtly panegyrist's stilted verses tell us in detail of Tiger-Kings subdued, of homage and tribute; but, so far as this slight history is concerned, all we need picture to ourselves is an apparently invincible hero, laden with loot from all the treasures of the south.

With honour also, for he made many treaties with foreign powers.

One gives us a quaint picture of the time. The Buddhist king of Ceylon sent two monks, one the king's brother, to visit the monastery which pious King Asôka of olden days had built by the sacred Bo tree at Bodh-Gya.

Now, India being at this time Brahmanical, the worthy brothers met with scant courtesy, and on return complained that they had literally found no place at the holy shrine wherein to lay their heads. The Buddhist king, therefore, anxious to redress this anomaly, despatched an embassy to Samûdra-gupta, asking leave to found a rest-house for the use of pious pilgrims, and sent with it rich jewels and gifts galore. These were duly accepted by the Hindoo as tribute, and gracious permission given. Whereupon the decision to build a special monastery close to the sacred tree was duly engraved on a copper plate, and, in due time, carried out by the erection of what was described two centuries later by the Chinese pilgrim, Hiuen T'sang (to whose literary labours we of to-day owe nearly all our knowledge of India in these far ages), as having three stories, six halls, three towers, and accommodation for a thousand monks,

"on which the utmost skill of the artist has been employed; the ornamentation is in the richest colours, and the statue of Buddha is cast of gold and silver, decorated with gems and precious stones."

Natheless this was the golden age of the Hindoo, not of the Buddhist, and, imitating Pushŷa-mitra, who overset the Buddhist Maurya dynasty, Samûdra-gupta determined to proclaim his supremacy by the ancient Horse sacrifice. So once more the doomed charger, followed by an army, set out on its wanderings for a year. This we know by reason of a few rare coins bearing the effigy of the victim standing before the altar, encircled by an explanatory legend, which have survived time, to be discovered of late years. There is also a rudely-carven stone horse now standing at the door of the Museum in Lucknow, which some archæologists label as belonging to Samûdra-gupta's great sacrifice.

But the coins of this king are somewhat lavish of information. Several, which represent him playing on a lyre, remain a proof that the court panegyrist was not a wholesale flatterer in counting him musician. This, again, gives ground for belief that he was also, as is claimed for him, a poet. That he took delight in patronising art of all kinds is proved beyond doubt by the great number of eminent men whose works date from the reign of Samûdra-gupta, and his son Chandra-gûpta II., who, on his coronation, took the name of Vikramadîtya; the latter being, of course, the one associated in the mind of every Hindu of to-day with the splendid renaissance of national learning and art, on which they love to dwell. To them Vikramadîtya is synonymous with the zenith of Hindu glory; but it is open to doubt whether the hero's father may not lay claim to a lion's share of the record of great achievements. We know of a certainty that he was sufficiently notable as musician to warrant his coins being stamped with majesty in that *rôle*; his poet-laureate tells us of keen intellect, love of study, and skill in argument.

Is not this sufficient to make us at any rate date the beginning of the Renaissance from the days of Samûdra-gupta?

Be that as it may, it is abundantly clear that in him we are dealing with another of those rare kings, who are kings indeed by right of their personal supremacy.

India is curiously fruitful in them, and, so far as we have come in Indian history, their individualities stand forth all the stronger in contrast with the mists and shadows which surround them. Bhishma, Chandra-gûpta, Asôka, Kanîshka, Samûdra-gupta--we gauge our admiring interest by our desire to know what manner of men these were in feature and form. But Fate, for the most part, denies us even the scant suggestion of a rude coin. She does so here. Whether Samûdra inherited his mother's beauty is for the present an unanswerable question. We do not know even the year of his passing, still less the manner of it: the story goes on without a pause to Chandra-gûpta-Vikramadîtya, his son, whose fame, until lately, quite overwhelmed all memory of his father; that father who conquered India, who allied himself with foreign powers, who made the subsequent achievements of his son possible.

The question which besets us now is the extent to which Chandra-gûpta-Vikramadîtya's fame is really his own; how much of it is due to the fact that we possess of his reign and administration an almost unique record in the account given of his travels and sojourn in India by the Buddhist pilgrim from China, Fa-Hien? This gives us information which fails us in the reigns of other kings. How much, again, of this Vikramadîtya's fame belongs by right to that other mythical Vikramadîtya of before-Christ days? That nameless king who flits like a Will-o'-the-Wisp through the mists of early Indian history?

How much, again, is rightfully due to his father--that striking personality which historians have forgotten, but which now comes surging through the shadows, a veritable man indeed?

Who can say? All we know is that the Gûpta dynasty was a mighty one; that it still serves the modern Hindu as a model of good government, just as the Mahomedan still points with pride to Akbar's rule.

What, then, were the salient points of this beloved control? Judging by Fa-Hien's account they may be summed up in personal liberty. The subject was left largely to follow his own intentions, and the criminal law was singularly lenient. This was rendered possible by the wide acceptation amongst the masses of Buddha's gospel of good-will; for although Brahmanical Hinduism had ousted Buddhist dogma, it had scarcely touched its ethics. Capital punishment was unknown; there was no need for an eye for an eye, a tooth for a tooth. "Throughout the country," we read, "no one kills any living thing."

An easy kingdom in good sooth to rule! According to our traveller, the people seem to have vied with each other in virtue. All sorts of charitable institutions existed, and the description of a free hospital, endowed by benevolence, is worth quoting:--

"Hither come all poor or helpless patients suffering from every sort of infirmity. They are well taken care of, and a doctor attends to them, food and medicine being given according to their wants. Thus they are made quite comfortable, and when they are well they may go away."

Thus, once more, the East saw light sooner than the West; for the first hospital in Europe only struggled into existence more than five hundred years after this one at Magâdha.

But the chief glory of the Gûpta empire was its patronage of the arts and sciences. Every pundit in India knows the verse which names the "nine gems of Vikramadîtya's court"; those learned men amongst whom Kâlidâsa, the author of "Sakûntala" (so far as fame goes, the Shakspeare of India), stood foremost. Poets, astronomers, grammarians, physicians, helped to make up the *nawa-ratani*, as it is called, and the extraordinary literary activity of the century and a quarter (from A.D. 330 to 455), during which long period Samûdra, Chandra, and his son, Kumâra, reigned, is most remarkable. The revival of Sanskrit, the sacred language of the Brahmans, points to an upheaval of Hindu religious thought, and so does the almost endless sacred literature, which, still surviving, is referred to the golden age of the Gûptas. The Purânas in their present form, the metrical version of the Code of Manu, some of the Dharm-shâstras, and, in fact, most of the classical Sanskrit literature, belong to this period.

Architecture was also revolutionised. As Buddhism slipped from the grip of the people under pressure from the ever-growing power of the Brahmans, the very forms of its sacred buildings gave way to something which, more ornate, less self-evident, served to reflect the new and elaborate pretensions of the priesthood. Mr Cunningham gives us somewhere the seven characteristics of the Gûpta style of architecture; but it is more easily summed up for the average beholder in the words "cucumber and gourd." These names serve well to recall the tall, curved *vimanas*, or towers, exactly like two-thirds of a cucumber stuck in the ground, and surmounted by a flat, gourd-like "Amalika," so called because of its resemblance to the fruit of that name.

That such buildings are interesting may be conceded, but that any one can call the collection of pickle-bottles (for that is practically the effect of them) at-let us say-Bhuvan-eshwar beautiful, passes comprehension.

Exquisite they are in detail, perfect in the design and execution of their ornamentation, but the form of these temples leaves much to be desired. The flat blob at the top seems to crush down the vague aspirings of the cucumber, which, even if unstopped, must ere long have ended in an earthward curve again.

To return to history.

Chandra-gûpta-Vikramadîtya died in A.D. 413. His greatest military achievement was the overthrow of the Sâka dynasty in Kathiawâr, and the annexation of Mâlwa to the already enormous empire left him by his father. In other ways we have large choice of prowess. All the tales which linger to this day on the lips of India concerning Râjah Bikra- or Vikra-majît are at our disposal.

Of his son Kumâra we at present know little, save that he reigned successfully for not less than forty years, keeping his kingdom intact, remaining true to its traditions.

Perhaps some day his fame also will rise from its grave, and coin or inscription may prove him true unit of the Great Trio of Gûpta emperors. This much we may guess: he was his grandmother's darling, for he bears her name in masculine dress.

THE WHITE HUNS AND GOOD KING HARSHA

A.D. 450 TO A.D. 648

The name Huns has quite a familiar sound. We think of Attila; we remember the 350 pounds weight of gold which Theodosius of Byzantium paid as an annual tribute to the victorious horde which swept into Europe about the middle of the fifth century; finally, we hark back to Gibbon's description of this race of reckless reiving riders; for the Huns seem to have been born in the saddle and never to have lived out of it. This is what he says:--

"They were distinguished from the rest of the human species by their broad shoulders, flat noses and small black eyes, deeply buried in the head; and, as they were almost destitute of beards, they never enjoyed either the manly graces of youth or the venerable aspect of age." (*En passant*, we can but wonder what our poor Gibbon would have said to the shaven chin of to-day!) "A fabulous origin was assigned worthy of their form and manners-- that the witches of Scythia, who for their foul and deadly practices had been driven from society, had united in the desert with infernal spirits, and that the Huns were the offspring of this execrable conjunction."

Again, poor Huns! We do not need such legend to know that they were utterly barbarian; that they rode like the devil, fought with bone-tipped javelins, clothed themselves in skins, and ate herbs and half-raw meat which they had first made tender by using it as their saddle! It is a sufficiently black indictment, and, though it applies only to the rolling swarm of savages which, on leaving that hive of humanity, the wide Siberian Steppe, turned westward, we have no reason to suppose that the swarm which turned eastward differed much from the type. It is true they are called the White Huns, but that is most likely because among the dark races of Hindustan, the yellow Mongolian complexion showed fair.

India had been overrun many times before, but it needs small consideration to see that this invasion must have been the worst, must have brought with it a perfect horror of havoc. Far more so than the Hun invasion in Europe. There the ultimate savage met, for the most part, with Goths and Visigoths. In India they stood between a Brahman and his salvation, between culture and comfort. For India was in these days far more civilised than Europe; its people were refined, bound hand and foot by ritual, curiously conventional in custom.

The long ages which had passed since the Vedic times had made religion more complex, had multiplied ceremonial to such an extent that the performance of the simplest duty was hedged about by the danger of fateful commissions, and still more fateful omissions. The revival of Hinduism during the paling days of the Gûpta empire had vastly increased the power of the Brahman. In brief, Purânic Hinduism--that is, religion based on the Purânas, as distinct from the Vedas--with all its hair-splitting, its overlay of ritual by ritual, was at its zenith. From birth to death a man--even the meanest man--was in the grip of innumerable petty commandments.

The very gods he worshipped had changed. The elemental deities of the Rig-Veda--the Winds, the Fire, the Sun, the Dawn--behind which lay ever (half recognised, wholly mysterious) the Unconditioned, the Absolute, were lost; crowded out, as it were, by the three hundred and thirty millions of Purânic godlings, which rumour says had replaced the thirty-and-three of the Vedas. And beset by an Athanasian *furore* for faith, the Purânas had defined the undefinable. The doctrine of a Trinity seems about this era of the world's history to have been more than usually in the air, and we find it here, hard and fast, crystallised unchangeably.

Brahma the Creator, Siva the destroying Spirit, Vishn or Krishn the Saviour, the Man-God, kind to the weaknesses of humanity. The three hundred and thirty millions of little gods were contained in the Three; they were emanations, attributes, as such imaged and worshipped. A great change this from the singing of a hymn to Agni the Fire-God, as the victim's flesh shrivelled in the flame, and the cooling of the ashes with a libation of soma juice.

And the worshipping of images brought with it a veneration for temples, a reverence for a paid priesthood, with its inevitable corollary of cult and custom and ceremonial. This complexity of religion naturally showed itself in the character of the people. As Mr Dutt writes:--

"Pompous celebrations and gorgeous decorations arrested the imagination and fostered the superstitions of the populace; poetry, arts, architecture, sculpture, and music lent their aid, and within a few centuries the nation's wealth was lavished on these gorgeous edifices and ceremonials which were the outward manifestations of the people's unlimited devotion and faith. Pilgrimages, which were rare or unknown in very ancient times, were organised on a stupendous scale; gifts in land and money poured in for the support of temples, and religion gradually transformed itself to a blind veneration of images and their custodians. The great towns of India were crowded with temples, and new gods and new idols found sanctuaries in stone edifices and in the hearts of ignorant worshippers."

Add to this the testimony of the literature of the period. The dramas of Kâlidâsa, beautiful as they are, concern themselves entirely with Love. The very descriptions of nature have reference to it, as when we read:--

"The oleander bud

Shows like the painted fingers of the fair,
Red tinted on the tip and edged with ebony."

His very reflections also are tinged with the same soft note of underlying passion:--

"Not seldom in our hours of ease,
When thought is still, the sight of some fair form
Or mournful fall of music breathing low
Will stir strange fancies thrilling all the soul
With a mysterious sadness."

And, leaving poetry alone, such knowledge as we have of social life in these days points to a certain effeminacy. In fact, there is evidence that woman played a larger part in society than she does in the India of to-day. The perennial joke against learned ladies, indeed, appears in the drama of the "Toy Cart," where the comic man says he always laughs when he "hears a woman read Sanskrit, or a man sing a song!" Then the heroine of this drama is frankly a courtesan, an Indian Aspasia, who received her lovers in a public court furnished with books, pictures, gambling-tables, etc., and who was

"Of courteous manners and unrivalled beauty,
The pride of all Ujjain."

Such, then, were the people who "felt, dreaded, and magnified" (as Gibbon says of the Goths--a far less civilised nation--in like predicament) "the numbers, the strength, the rapid motions and implacable cruelty of the Huns; who beheld their fields and villages consumed with flames and deluged with indiscriminate slaughter."

Perhaps it is as well, therefore, that history is for the most part silent concerning the horror and the havoc of the century or so of time during which the Huns ravaged India. We hear only of the greater tragedies, of Toramâva the Tyrant, and his son Mihîragûla, who out-Heroded his father in implacable cruelty towards the cultured, caste-bound Hindus, to whom all things were sacred. Of him it is written that his favourite amusement in Kashmir was watching elephants goaded into impassable, precipitous hill-paths, so that he might laugh like a fiend if they slipped and fell; fell with a wild shriek of terror and anger, to be dashed to pieces thousands of feet below. An unpleasing picture this! One cannot wonder at the criticism passed on his death, when "the earth shook, thick darkness reigned, and a mighty tempest raged." It was succinct, bald, but forcible: "*He* has now fallen into the lowest hell, where he shall pass endless ages."

After his death, which must have occurred about the year A.D. 540, the clouds gather darkly, and we are permitted few peeps as to what was going on behind them. Certain it is that no trace of a paramount power is to be found in the scant records of the last half of the sixth century.

The beginning of the seventh, however, finds the historian in very different case. He has first and foremost the detailed account of Hiuen T'sang's travels with which to deal, and this is supplemented by the "*Harsha-charita*," or "Deeds of Harsha," written by a learned Brahman who lived at the court of the good king. That this latter book partakes more of the character of a historical romance than a steady, straightforward chronicle of events is true; but even so, the information at disposal is fuller and more precise than that which has been forthcoming hitherto, excepting, perhaps, in regard to the great Maurya kings.

Harsha, then, was younger son of a Râjah of Thanêswar, in the Punjâb.

His father dying in A.D. 606, his elder brother ascended the throne, but was almost immediately most treacherously assassinated in conference by the King of Bengal; the conference apparently being for the purpose of arbitrating between the young Râjah of Thanêswar and the King of Mâlwa, who had murdered the former's brother-in-law for the sake of possessing his wife, and was keeping the Thanêswar princess a prisoner, with "iron fetters kissing her feet."

The assassinated king being too young to have a son, his brother Harsha was invited to take the throne. For some unknown reason he hesitated, and his formal coronation did not take place until nearly six years after he had assumed the actual responsibilities of kingship.

The story of the recovery of his widowed sister from the hands of her abductor is full of incident and romance. The rescue was but just in time, for the Princess Râj-yasri--a most attractive and learned young lady, and well versed in the Buddhistic schools, apparently--was about to commit *suttee* amid the pathless forests, whither she had fled to escape her persecutor, when her brother, led to her retreat by the aboriginal chieftains, arrived upon the scene. The hurry was so great, that in it the assassin-lover appears to have escaped.

It will be observed by this that the family of Harsha was of the Buddhist faith. How, or why, we know not. The very name of his kingdom, Thanêswar (*S'thaneswara*, or, The Place of God), is purely Hindu; nevertheless, this, the last great King of Hindu India, professed the religion of Gâutama.

In fact, in many ways his reign is a poor imitation of that of Asôka. He did not, however, follow that king's example as a peace prophet, for he spent nearly thirty-six years out of his forty-two in bloody warfare. And in all his long career of aggression he met with but one check. He was unable to push his forces through the narrow defiles of the Deccan passes, and had to confine himself to being Lord Paramount of the North. So his empire, though extensive, never touched that of Asôka; in truth, he did not touch that monarch in any way. Nevertheless, his rule was excellent, and our Chinese pilgrim is loud in praise of it. Harsha did not trust to officialdom; personal supervision was his theory of government, and he was constantly on the move inspecting, punishing, rewarding. His camp must have been quaint, for in those days tents were unknown, and the "King's Palace" was built at each halting-place of boughs and reeds, and solemnly burnt after it had been used.

Like all these Eastern kings whose personalities have survived the years, he appears to have been somewhat of a genius. Besides being a most expert penman and draughtsmen, he wrote various learned books, and in his salad days produced several plays which still remain part of the literature of India. One, "The Necklace," is quite the liveliest of all Indian plays, and with appropriate songs and dances must have been rather like a Savoy comic opera. There is a legend that Harsha spent so much money on poets, actors, dancers and artists of all descriptions, that he had eventually to sell the gold and silver ornaments of the Hindu temples in order to pay for his pleasures; but this is pure legend. Following the example of Asôka, he established rest-houses for travellers, hospitals for the sick, magistrates for the regulation of morals; yet in all this, somehow, the sense of pose is never absent. Asôka's voice is still to-day a *cri du cœur*; Harsha's is--*fin de siècle*.

He could not help it. The curious religious eclecticism of the period favoured it. His family showed keenly the general tendency to self-consciousness, and it was written of his father:

"He offered daily to the Sun a bunch of red lotuses set in a pure vessel of ruby, and tinged, like his own heart, with the same hue."

Could Oscar Wilde have done more? Strange, indeed, how the cycles of culture come round and round.

It was in his later years that King Harsha became a pronounced Buddhist. This was largely owing to the preachings and teachings of Hiuen T'sang, in honour of whom a solemn assemblage was held at Kanaûj in the fresh spring-time of the year A.D. 644. The scene is admirably given in Hiuen T'sang's Record, and is well worth a reading. We can imagine the king carrying in person the canopy upheld over the golden statuette of Buddha; we can see him "moving along, scattering golden blossoms, pearls and other rare gems." We catch a glimpse of the flaming monastery accidentally catching fire, to be extinguished by the mere sight of the good Harsha. The rush of the mad Hindu fanatic to slay this "favourer of Buddhists" comes as a startling incident, to be followed by the immediate exile of five hundred Brahmans for high treason.

Then we learn of the journey to Prâg (Allahabad), where every five years Harsha, in accordance with ancient custom, had held a distribution of alms.[2]

The description of this is even more entrancing, and we can take part in all the ceremonials of the seventy-five days during which Buddha, the Sun, and Siva were apparently worshipped indiscriminately. The proceedings were opened by a magnificent procession of feudatory princes, and ended with a forty-days' distribution of alms to all and sundry.

After this, Hiuen T'sang writes

"the royal accumulation of five years was exhausted. Except the horses, elephants and military accoutrements ... nothing remained.... The king gave away his gems and goods, his clothing and neck-laces, ear-rings, bracelets, chaplets, neck jewels, and bright head jewel; all these he freely gave away without stint."

Was it a real gifting, we wonder, or, after duly worshipping in a borrowed second-hand suit, did Harsha return to his palace to find his wardrobe much the same as ever?

The hint of unreality in all things provokes the question.

King Harsha died in A.D. 648, shortly after his beloved Chinese pilgrim had departed for his native land. Once again it has to be written that the "withdrawal of the strong arm plunged the country into disorder."

Arjûna, his minister, seized the throne, but drew down on himself the wrath of China, and after a brief interval was carried thither as a prisoner.

Meanwhile, no one appeared to take the reins. In truth, degeneration had already set in. The people who had posed so long as a nation of culture, of refinement, who had spent their lives in applauding poetasters, who had laughed when the court wit said the commander-in-chief's nose was as long as the king's pedigree, who had been ready to worship any god if so be the ceremonial pleased their æsthetic sense, who had given free pass to their emotions in all ways, such people were not ready for action. And so once for all the clouds cover Hindu supremacy.

The next four hundred years are the Dark Ages of Indian history. Even the impressionist outlook of our case of coins is denied us. A thousand names jostle each other in commonplace confusion. In the chaos of conflicting claims, any attempt at classification is hopeless.

CHAOS

A.D. 700 TO A.D. 1001

These, as has been said, are the Dark Ages of Hindustan. She has ever been the prey of personality, the willing victim of vitality. From the year B.C. 620, when her real history begins, until now, that history has been that of individuals who have either risen from her ranks, or appeared on her horizon; who have dominated her imagination, and left her too often at their death confused, helpless, to fall back into the bewildering anarchy of petty princedoms.

The light shines clearly for a few years, reflected by one man's keen sword, or keener eyes; and then the strong arm falls, the vision fails, and India sinks back into the Great Apathy concerning things sublunary which is ever her most salient characteristic.

And these three hundred years give us no personality striking enough to be seen through the mist which settled down like a pall over India after the death of Harsha. This death, says Mr Vincent Smith, "loosened the bonds which restrained the disruptive forces always ready to operate in India, and allowed them to produce their normal result: a medley of petty states with ever-varying boundaries, and engaged in unceasing internecine war."

No new thing this in the past history of India; it will be no new thing in the future, for Hindustan will always need some strong, centralising, magnetic force to hold together its innumerable atoms.

It is true that in literature some few names hover doubtfully about the eighth century, and that round the outskirts of India, in Kashmir, Nepaul, Madras, Ceylon, we hear every now and again of events which arrest the attention for a moment. The reassertion of Chinese influence along the northern borderland, though brief, was noteworthy, and in Kashmir the names of several kings and one queen stand out from the general *posse*. Amongst them that of Lâlâditya, who built the famous Temple of the Sun at Martand, not far from Bâwun in Kashmir. A magnificent ruin this, standing out sharply against both the rising in the east and the setting in the west; set high on one of those lofty *karêwas*, or tablelands, which are so marked a characteristic of Kashmir. Fringing the mighty mountains, they stretch like promontories into the rice and saffron fields, still showing by their precipitous sides the force of the mighty flood which at some time must have swept through the valley, lowering its levels, and leaving these landmarks to tell of its passage.

Then we have two names--rather painfully reminiscent of comic opera--Avanti-vârman and Sankâra-vârman, good and bad boys of Kashmir history. The former remembered for his beneficent schemes, his kindly patronage; the latter for his ingenuity in squeezing the last drop of blood-tax from his oppressed subjects, and his aptitude in stealing temple treasures.

Finally, and alas! we have a queen called Didda. The less said of her the better. It is sufficient to record that she was the Messalina, the Lucrezia Borgia of Kashmîr for close on half a century.

A long time this! Could she by chance have had the secret of youth like Ninon d'Enclos?

Her death, however, brings us to A.D. 1003, and in A.D. 1001 Mahmûd, so-called of Ghuzni, was to begin his first raid into India, and so bring a new factor--Islâmism--to its welter of creeds and castes.

Here, therefore, ends the Hindu period of Indian history. There follows on it the Mahomedan age from A.D. 1001 to 1858, when the English formally took over the entire charge of Government.

Now as in this Mahomedan age the new faith of the conquerors had much to say to the general trend of events, it may be as well to occupy this empty chapter by a brief exposition of what that faith is, and how it inspired those constant invasions of India which make the next few hundred years the record of an almost continuous campaign. Before doing this, however, let us take still briefer stock of this past Hindu age.

It was an age of growth, of renaissance, of decadence.

The natural vigour of the Vedas grew to the more complex, more artificial energy of the Epics, and out of this arose strangely the quietism of the Buddhist. War and Peace, Glory and Dishonour, Riches and Poverty, all faded away to nothingness before the hope of Nirvana--of escape from Desire. Thus Asôka becomes the dominating figure, and even after his death the names of Kanîshka and Hûshka and Harsha faintly echo his fame.

But they failed to keep it alive. The Brahmans, rising to power, thrust out alike the simplicity of the Vedas and the nescience of Buddha. So came the Renaissance.

An epoch marked, as such epochs generally are, by a curious cult of the emotions in all things. The Indians of the Gûpta empire were emphatically *fin de siècle,* so they did not survive. King Harsha, Mithraist, Buddhist, Hindu, worshipping his several deities by giving in alms even "his bright head-jewel," pictures the time. A time when the court panegyrist Bana, writing of his dying master, can so juggle with words as to describe his agony thus:--

"Helplessness had taken him in hand; pain had made him its province, wasting its domain, lassitude its lair ... broken in utterance, unhinged in mind, tortured in body, waning in life, babbling in speech, ceaseless in sighs."

Of a truth, there is no wonder that the Indian world also had come to "the tip of death's tongue," to "the portal of the Long Sleep."

It was becoming neurotic, hyper-æstheticised. It needed a rest and a rude awakening.

Mahomedanism was to give it the latter, and the founder of this faith had been born at Mecca on the 10th November A.D. 570. By a curious coincidence, the date on which he began his teaching and that of King Harsha's coronation are very nearly synchronous.

Mahomed was an Arab, but was in every way unlike his race. A posthumous son, he had "inherited from his mother a delicate and extremely impressionable constitution, and an exaggerated sensibility." He was melancholy, silent, fond of desert places, solitude, and dreamy meditations.

Nature appealed to him. The sight of the setting sun inspired him with vague restlessness, and he would weep and sob like a child at slight provocation.

His religious excitability was of the most acute character, and passed at times into attacks of epilepsy.

A true revivalist this! Small wonder if, having in his mountain solitude seen, or thought he had seen, a vision of the Great Unity which men call God, he should have claimed inspiration, and claimed it militantly. The time was ripe for a revival. Religion was being discussed on all sides, and Mahomed having, it is said, gained nine converts by his first vision, set to work to gain more. Ere he died all Arabia frankly followed his teaching. This, however, was not the result of what Asôka advocated as the only legitimate method of a mission, for "example, tolerance, gentleness and moderation in speech" have never found much place in Mahomedan proselytising; the rather fire and sword, a sharp blade held to the throat that hastily gabbles the Kalma or Mahomedan creed.

And yet it is a faith which has held, which still holds, its own, and which was to be responsible for much in the future history of India. Like all faiths, however, it has gone far beyond its founder, and it is doubtful for how much of the Mahomedanism of to-day the seer-prophet of A.D. 610 is really responsible. Within six years of his death his successors had carried their version of the dreamer's thoughts to Syria and Egypt. Ere Harsha died the whole of Persia as far east as Herât was added to the Arab empire. Thence in the slow centuries it drifted towards India; for the lust of personal and temporal power amongst the leaders checked its progress much. The great dispute as to the rightful succession to the Prophet provoked almost instant schism; while the assassination of Ali, the fourth *kalifa*--he was son-in-law of the Prophet--and the subsequent murders of his two sons Hussan and Hussain, was productive of a strife which lasts to the present day between the rival sects of *Shîahs* and *Sunnis*.

So, while the Dark Age of India drifted on, the Awakener was creeping closer to the border, and in A.D. 976 one Sabaktagîn, a Turkish slave who had married the Governor of Khorassan's daughter, began the invasion by sweeping the western bank of the Indus, and retiring laden with loot.

PART II
THE MIDDLE AGE

CAMPAIGNS OF THE CRESCENT

A.D. 1001 TO A.D. 1200

Part I

For close on these two hundred years the northern plains of India were a battle-field. Winter after winter, as the sun's power declined, and the curious second spring began of cold-weather crops and fruits and flowers, which to this day make the Punjâb seasons hover between the tropics and the temperates, there debouched from the snow-clad hills, all along the western and north-western frontier of India, long files of wild-looking horsemen, followed by camels, by foot soldiers; and somewhere, in their midst always, was the green flag of the Prophet, with its over-riding, overbearing crescent, telling its tale of rising power; the crescent which is an apt symbol of a fighting faith.

What tempted these hardy northern folk into the wide plains of India? Was it, indeed, zeal for Souls? Hardly. By the way, as a sort of salve to conscience, such zeal was good to break an idol or two, or an idolater's head; but *au fond*, the money bags outweighed all other reasons for these recurring raids.

For during those three centuries of Chaos, during the dark ages of degeneracy, India had grown rich-inordinately rich. Overlaid, and yet again overlaid with finikin fanciful ornamentations, almost incoherent in their diffuse discursive details, the temples were perfect mines of wealth; in some cases of useless, buried treasure, since in the gradual downfall OF the Hindu nation at large, the privileged class of Brahmans had closed their grip even on the power of the princes. The only thing which remained comparatively untouched, as in India it has ever remained untouched, being the slow-moving mass of the peasantry, who, willing bondsmen to Mother Earth, took no heed of anything save famine.

The first swoop for plunder was made by one Mahmûd, King of Ghuzni, in November A.D. 1001. He must have entered India by the Khyber Pass, for on the 27th of that month, near Peshawar, he met and defeated King Jaipal of Lahôre. One can imagine the contest. The long-nosed, long-curled, long-bearded Ghuznivites, rough and ready in their skin-coats, their burly bosoms aflame with covetousness for creed and gold, their guttural throats resounding with the war-cry of Islam: "Kill! Kill! For the Faith!" And on the other side, the clean-shaven, oiled, scented Hindus lax with long centuries of ease, yet still full of pride, full of high courage.

It was a foregone conclusion, despite the mailed elephants and the elaborate old War Office dispositions and compositions of corps and *cadre* which had come down, we may be sure, from Chândra-gûpta's days. For once the East gets hold of a thing, it sticks to it.

It was new blood against old--a new faith against one so ancient that it had almost been forgotten. Almost, not quite, as the story shows of what Jaipal did, when the Mahomedan conqueror, driven back to the cool by the approach of a new summer, carelessly gave the royal prisoner--whom he had dragged about with him in his victorious raid--a contemptuous freedom. But ere this time came, Mahmûd of Ghuzni had to set one of his many marks--he invaded India no less than twelve times--as far south in the Punjâb as Bhattinda, a town in the Patiala State. A marvellous place this even nowadays, set as it is amid deserts of sand, patched with green grain-fields. The low, insignificant city seems lost in the old fort; a perfect mountain of a place, visible for miles and miles, a rose-red mass of sun-scorched bricks with white-edged, crenulated parapets so quaintly stern, so still more quaintly fragile-looking in its suggestion of some huge iced cake.

Here, doubtless, in the half-desert land, it was the sound of the *koël* knelling his sonorous note in the *kikar* trees, or the sudden transformation, mayhap, of the uncanny, witchlike, gnarled thickets of the low *dhâk* trees into coral-pink stretches, showing like sunset clouds on the gold of the sun-saturate sands, that warned Mahmûd he must be up and away from the oncoming of the heat.

As he passed up the Peshawar valley, laden to the last limit with loot, the peach gardens must have been a-blossom; and, being a man with the odd strain of imagination in him, which all have had who have left their mark on India, he must, despite his plunder, have regretted leaving so much beauty behind him.

But he left tragedy also; for Jaipal, the beaten king, went straight back to Lahôre, and having formally proclaimed himself unworthy to reign after having suffered defeat at the hands of the unclean, mounted a funeral pyre, and burnt himself in sight of his people, leaving his son Anang-pal to reign in his stead.

Truly Indian history is provocative of picture-making. We have one here which would tax most painters' power. Yet the look which must have been on the proud king's face, as, remembering his name, "The Guardian of Victory," he defied defeat, defied disgrace, by defying death, is worth recording, worth recalling in these later days when the primitive virtues are somewhat overclouded.

So there was peace for three years. Apparently the plunder was sufficient unto the day until 1004, when Mahmûd again appeared with the return of the wild birds from Lake Mansarawar, on the Siberian Steppes; but this was more a primitive campaign against a tributary chief on the western side of the Indus, than a real raid.

The following year, however, things were organised on a larger scale, and he was opposed by Anang-pal, who met no better fate than his father, and fled incontinently to Kashmir. But Mahmûd's progress southward was checked by the news of revolt in Ghuzni, and he had to return in order to count scores with his pet converted Hindu, one Sek Pal, who, left governor, had resumed his Brahmanical thread, and was in full swing of conspiracy with his fellows in India.

It took the burly Mahomedan short time to settle his shrift, and send him to cells for life, so that the next fall of the leaf found Mahmûd ready for his fourth invasion of India.

A real invasion, a real resistance this time. For the Rajas of Lahôre, Delhi, Gwalîor, Ujjain, Ajmir, Kanauj, had joined confederacy to rout the Unclean Stranger. It was a holy war: women sold their jewels, and men sent their hoards to furnish forth its munitions.

To no purpose. It is true that at the outset Mahmûd suffered a reverse. The Ghakkars, Scythic warrior race of the Salt Range, laughed at the invader's entrenched camp amongst their bare hills, bore down on it, overpowered his outposts, and accounted for some four thousand of his army.

But even that failed to stop these big, burly men, bent on plunder, bent on proselytising at the sword's point. The result of this raid was the destruction of Nagar-kôt, ancient town hard by the temple called Jawâla-Mukhi, or Flame's Mouth, where, since the beginning of Time, the jets of combustible gas issuing from the ground amongst the dark shadows of the sheltering spire have burnt bravely as emanations, manifestations, of the Goddess Dûrga, that Fury of Womanhood. According to native historians Mahmûd's returning army must have been a perfect caravan, for it carried with it about seven thousand pounds weight of gold coins, six thousand of gold and silver plate, fifteen hundred of golden ingots, a hundred and twenty-eight thousand of unwrought silver, and more than a hundred and fifty pounds weight of pearls, corals, diamonds and rubies.

But the combustible gas must have remained to be re-lit in honour of Mai Dûrga, and so have remained to help the memories of the iconoclasts! A fine trade this, that of smashing golden idols in the name of the Prophet, and carrying the bits and the diamond and sapphire eyes away in the name of Mammon!

It found its apotheosis in the twelfth and last expedition to India, when Mahmûd directed all his energy towards Som-nâth, a temple renowned throughout India, set proudly on a peninsula in Guzerât, surrounded on all sides save one by the sea.

The intervening seven excursions were all marked by noteworthy incidents, all full to the brim of reckless romance, and each left India the more helpless, the more ready to let the invader pass to fresh, more southern conquests. Indeed, a certain suzerainty was acknowledged by many Hindu rajahs, and on one occasion Mahmûd's march was ostensibly to the relief of a feudatory.

But it would take too long to follow in detail events which were in general so alike. Swift marching, utter unpreparedness, almost pitiful submission, and then "a halt at some sacred city, during which the town was plundered, the idols broken, the temples profaned, and the whole fired." Yet, as the ravaging raids touched Râjputana, resistance became more spirited. At one place the garrison rushed out through the breaches in true Kshatriya fashion to do or die, whilst the women and children burned themselves in silence in their houses. Not one, we are told, survived. This is the first mention in history of the *johâr*, or great war-sacrifice of the Râjputs. It is not the last.

So let us turn to Som- or Soma-nâth. Now "Soma" is the Moon-God, "Nâth" is Lord. We have, therefore, a simple Temple to the Moon by name; but in reality Som-nâth, or Som-eswara, is one of the forms of the God Siva- -his self-existing form.

The crescent moon on the forehead with which the God always is portrayed alludes to this, and to the intimate relation between the phases of the planet as a measure of time, and the upright stone or lingam, which as all know is worshipped as a symbol of material Life. It is customary to condemn this nature or phallic worship in India as unclean, almost obscene; it is not so, anyhow, in spirit.

Som-nâth, then, was a shrine of Life. The idol in its holy of holies bore no semblance of created beings. It was the symbol of Creation itself, a tall, rounded, black monolith of stone, set six feet in the ground, rising ten feet above it. One of the twelve lingams believed by the Hindus to have descended from Heaven, it was unexpressedly holy, marvellously mighty in miracle. Small wonder, then, with a priesthood of clutching hands, that Som-nâth stood renowned as the richest shrine in India.

It must have been fine to see this temple, with its fifty-six pillars set in rows, all carven and inlaid with gems, its gilded spires above the dark, unlit sanctuary, where the great bell swung on a solid gold chain which weighed some fifteen hundred pounds.

Steps led down from it to the sea--that sea which was a miracle in itself to the ignorant, up-country pilgrim, accustomed to parched deserts, unwitting of such natural phenomena as tides; for did it not bow, did it not rise and fall incessantly in constant adoration of the Great Lord of Life? So, at any rate, said the priests, and the pilgrim went back to his parched desert with empty pockets, to dream for the rest of his life of the solemn, ceaseless adoration of the sea. Aye! even when it raged black with monsoon winds, and spat white with fury at the temple walls, yet still in subservience, still as a slave.

This was not a place to be yielded up of the Brahmans without a struggle. So we read of a three days' battle, of scaling ladders, of heavy reinforcements of the "idolatrous garrison," of an "idolatrous"--surely there is no better word in the language with which to fight a foe!--array in the field which withdrew Mahmûd's personal attention. And then there is the crucial moment: Mahomedan troops beginning to waver, their leader leaping from his horse, prostrating himself on the ground before the Lord God of Battles, and imploring aid for the True Faith.

To speak trivially, it did the trick. One wild, cheering rush, and "the Moslems broke through the enemy's line and laid five thousand Hindus dead at their feet; so the rout became general." So general that the garrison of four thousand, abandoning the defence, escaped by the sea in boats.

Nothing left, then, but to enter the temple in pomp. A goodly procession of warriors! Mahmûd, his sons, his nobles; all, no doubt, spitting profusely, while keeping their weather eye open on the gems starring the heavy, carven pillars. Darker and darker! The pillars close in. No light now, save,--high up in the shadows--one pendent jewelled lamp, reflected in the glistening stones, showing dimly the huge, massive golden chain, the swinging bronze bell.

And what more? Only a roughly-polished, black marble, upright boulder, hung round, doubtless, as such lingams are to-day, with faded *champak* chaplets and marigold wreaths.

Was it disappointment which made Mahmûd strike at it with his mace? One could imagine it so, but that he had had experience of the idle objects of which men make idols. Perhaps the backward swing of the mace-head hit the bell and sent its last hollow boom of appeal--which so many worshippers had raised--straight to the ears of the Lord of Life.

It is a rare picture this, of one faith defying another. It does not need the amplification which legend brings to it, in order to grip attention.

That legend runs thus. When Mahmûd had ordered two fragments to be hewn off the idol, one for the threshold of the mosque at Ghuini, another for the threshold of his own palace, some of the two thousand priests of Baal in attendance offered untold gold to arrest further destruction; an offer viewed with favour by the king's sons, and the attendant nobles. Smashing one idol out of millions was but mildly meritorious, whereas the money thus gained might be given to the poor But the Judas argument failed.

"The King"--to quote the text--"acknowledged there might be reason in what they said, but replied that if he should consent to such a measure his name would be handed down to posterity as 'Mahmûd the idol-seller,' and he wished it to be 'Mahmûd the idol-breaker.' He therefore directed the troops to proceed in their work. The next blow broke open the belly of Som-nâth, which was hollow, and discovered a quantity of diamonds, rubies, and pearls of much greater value than the amount which the Brahmans had offered."<

Very dramatic, no doubt, but, unfortunately, none of these lingams are hollow. It is possible, however, that the story found base in the discovery of sacred vaults.

Be that as it may, Mahmûd, "having secured the wealth of Som-nâth," apparently fell in love with the country round about it; so much so that he proposed remaining there and sending his son Masûd back to reign at Ghuzni. It needed pressure on the part of his officers to induce him to stir; but after some difficulty in securing a Governor for Guzerât, he started to march direct towards Ghuzni by way of the desert.

This same difficulty gives us another picture.

Apparently there were two cousins Dabeshleems--fateful name, of what nationality or family absolutely uncertain--one a hermit, the other a rajah. The hermit was made governor, the prince became pretender.

Mahmûd, ere leaving, reduced the latter, and handed him over prisoner to the former. To this the hermit objected. But one course, he said, was open to him, since by the tenets of his religion no king could be put to death; he must build a vault under his throne and place the unfortunate gentleman therein for life. This would be inconvenient, therefore he prayed the conqueror to carry the rajah back with him to Ghuzni.

So Mahmûd, his army, and his vast loot, set out for the desert, set their faces for the last time away from the wealth and idolatry of India. Set them, as it turned out, very nearly away from all wealth, all faiths; for in the desert the whole army was misled for three days and three nights by a Hindu guide, "so that many of the troops died raving mad from the intolerable heat and thirst." A Hindu guide who, under torture, confessed exultantly that he was one of the priests of Som-nâth, and so died, satisfied with his measure of revenge.

Mahmûd, however, had only to prostrate himself once more, and lo! a guiding meteor, and after a long night-march, water! Water, even though it must have been the Great Salt Lake.

After this, time passed in comparative uneventfulness, until on the 23rd of April A.D. 1030, in the sixty-third year of his age, "this great conqueror gave up his body to death and his soul to immortality amid the tears of his people."

One of his last recorded remarks was his exclamation when, in answer to his enquiry, the Lord High Treasurer told him that before becoming extinct, the last dynasty had accumulated seven pounds weight of precious stones. "Thanks be to Thee, All-Powerful Being!" cried Mahmûd, prostrating himself yet once more. "Thou hast enabled me to collect more than a hundred pounds."

What did he do with all the vast wealth which in the course of his missionary work he managed to annex? We know that he built a magnificent mosque at Ghuzni called "The Celestial Bride"; but that could not have absorbed it all.

Indeed we know much of it was still in the treasury; for two days before his death he ordered all the gold and the caskets of precious stones to be brought before him, and "having seen them, he wept with regret, ordering them to be carried back, without exhibiting his generosity at that time to anybody."

Gold had evidently gripped at the heart and soul of this middle-aged, well-shaped, ugly man, who was strongly pitted with the smallpox. His was not a lovable personality in any way. Gifted with a touch of genius, gifted above all things with that marvellous vitality which is always as magic to the Indian, he was just, curiously callous, and absolutely sceptical.

He openly doubted if he was really the son of his father, and scoffed at the idea of a future state. Certainly annihilation would be a kinder fate than the one which the poet Sa'adi gives to him in the Gulistan, and which may be paraphrased thus:--

> "The King of Khurasan saw in a dream
> Mahmûd the son of Subaktigeen,
> Dead for this hundred years or more,
> His head and his heart, his arms and his thighs
> Dissolved to dust, and only his eyes
> Moved in their sockets and saw
> His gold, his empire, everything
> He loved in the hands of another King."

CAMPAIGNS OF THE CRESCENT

A.D. 1001 TO A.D. 1200

Part II

The Great Raider Mahmûd being now put past, the Campaigns of the Crescent continued in feebler fashion. In truth, for a few years Mahomed and Masûd, the dead king's twin sons, were occupied in settling the succession. Mahomed, the elder by some hours, mild, tractable, was his father's nominee and on the spot; Masûd, on the other hand, was a great warrior, bold, independent, and promptly claimed as his right those provinces which he had won by his sword. So they came to blows.

At the outset Mahomed's piety failed him; for having decorously halted his host during the whole of the Month of Fasting--Ramzân--Masûd thereinafter fell upon him, armed at all points, defeated him, and put out his eyes after he had reigned a short five months.

Masûd, the new king, appears to have been a man of considerable character and grim humour, for one of the first acts of his reign was in cold blood to hang an unfortunate gentleman who once, long years before, when the question of succession was the subject of conversation, had been heard to say crudely that if Masûd ever came to the throne he would suffer himself to be hanged.

So he suffered.

But in truth, as we read the story of this Ghuznevide dynasty, and of the Ghori dynasty which followed it, we rub our eyes and wonder how many centuries we have gone back. For these big, bold, burly men are fairly savages in comparison with the cultured Hindu whom they harried. And Masûd, though by repute an affable gentleman, generous even to prodigality, and of uncommon personal strength and courage, was as turbulent as a king as he had been as a prince.

His favourite maxim was, "Dominion follows the longest sword." His was not only long, but heavy. No other man of his court could wield it, and an arrow from his bow would pierce the hide of a mailed elephant. During the ten years of his reign he entered India with an army three times. But the first of these raids was followed, A.D. 1033, by a terrible famine, a still more terrible outbreak of plague, from which in one month, more than forty thousand people died in Isphahân alone.

This was in its turn followed by a severe defeat of the Ghuznevide arms by the Turkomâns on the north-east frontier; for it must not be forgotten that though these dynasties of which we are treating are counted as of India, they have in reality but little to do with it. They were but titular suzerains, and very often not that, of the more northerly provinces of Hindustan.

Apparently as a salve to resentment and shame at this defeat, Masûd began to build a fine palace at Ghuzni, over which he must have spent some of his father's treasures, for a golden chain and a golden crown of incredible weight appears as a canopy in the Hall of Audience.

It must have been this depletion of the royal treasures which led to his last and most successful campaign against the kingdom of Sivalak, where he is said to have found enormous wealth; and so on to Sônput, ancient Hindu shrine and city to the north of Delhi, whence he made a Mahmûd-like return laden with loot.

A quaint old city is Sônput, and a curious authenticity of its hoar antiquity turned up not long ago, when some cultivators were digging a well. This was a small clay image of the Sun-God, a deity to which there is now in India but one single shrine.

But here the star of Masûd's fortune touched its zenith. The Turkomâns, encouraged by success, renewed operations, finally forcing the king to abandon his border principalities and seek time in India to recover strength for renewed efforts.

Urged, perhaps, by kindness, perhaps by fear, he ordered his blinded and imprisoned brother to be brought to Lahôre, with the unforeseen result that his household troops suddenly revolted, and hoisting the blind prisoner on to their shoulders, incontinently proclaimed him once more King.

It was all over in a moment; and Masûd, whose life was spared by the mild Mahomed, found himself forced to beg a subsistence of his brother. His pride, however, would not stand the pitiful dole of £5 which was sent him, so he promptly borrowed £10 from his servants and bestowed them as *bakshish* on the messenger who had brought, and who took back, the shabby gift.

Not a very tactful way of beginning what was practically an imprisonment. But it was not to last long, for Prince Ahmed, Mahomed's son, in whose favour the blind king resigned the crown, would have no half-measures, and prevented further complications by burying Masûd alive.

The historian explains that the prince was suspected of a "strong taint of insanity."

In truth, homicidal mania appears to set in generally, for the remaining records of the Ghuznevide dynasty are as irrational, as murderous as transpontine melodrama.

Prince Ahmed was in due time murdered by the murdered Masûd's son, who reigned long enough to see his Indian empire almost reft from him; since with violent internal dissensions racking the body politic, there was naturally no time for foreign affairs. So in the year A.D. 1048 the Râjah of Delhi, taking counsel with his compeers of Ajmîr, Kanauj, Kalungar, Gwalîor, once more made themselves practically independent of the Crescent. Only Lahôre remained Mahomedan, repelling a siege of seven months, and after actual street fighting, succeeded in driving off the investing force.

Thus in a History of India there is small need to note that Masûd II., a child of four years, succeeding his father, reigned six days; or that Hussan Ali and Absal Raschîd between them numbered but four years.

In the general turmoil, wonder comes faintly how Ibrahîm--a worthy soul who, as the historian says, "begot 36 sons and 40 daughters by various women"--ever managed to rule for forty-two years. Apparently by a peaceful policy; but, as the same historian goes on to say that this monarch "was remarkable for morality and devotion, having in his youth succeeded in subduing his sensual appetites," one hesitates before accepting either the narrator's facts or his deductions.

Finally, after the Ghuznevide dynasty had touched a bakers' dozen, came one Byrâm, who was destined to lose the throne for his race by two useless and brutal murders. The first was the public execution of his son-in-law, an apparently harmless prince of Ghor--as the country of the Afghâns was then called. The reason of this act is obscure, though it seems probable he was suspected of high treason. Be that as it may, Kutb-din Ghori-Afghân was an ill man to assail, for he had two big brothers. The first of these, Saîf-ud-din, had no little success in his immediate campaign of revenge. Byrâm fled, Ghuzni was occupied; but finally, by a stratagem, the victor fell into his enemy's hands, whereupon the latter doubled and excelled his former crime, by blackening his captive's face, and sending him face tailwards round the town on a bullock as a preliminary to torturing him, beheading him, and impaling his grand *wazîr*.

Allah-ud-din, the last brother, then took up the gloves, after defying Byrâm in these words: "Your threats are as impotent as your arms! It is no new thing for kings to make war on their neighbours, but barbarity like yours is unknown to the brave, and such as none have heard of being exercised towards princes. You may therefore be assured that God has forsaken you, and has ordained that I, Allah-ud-din, should be the instrument of that just revenge denounced against you for putting to death the representative of the independent and very ancient family of Ghor."

A quaint touch! that of the "very ancient," showing the value set on blue blood in those days.

Allah-ud-din proved a true prophet. In the resulting battle the two "Khurmiels," gigantic brothers-in-arms, the Gog and Magog of those days, brought victory to his arms by the ripping up of elephants' bellies and other prodigies of strength and valour. Byrâm fled, to die miserably in India overwhelmed by misfortunes, while the conqueror earned for himself the title of "The Burner of Worlds," by the deadly revenge he took on Ghuzni and its inhabitants.

"The massacre," writes the historian, "continued for the space of seven days, in which time pity seems to have fled from the earth, and the fiery spirits of demons to actuate men. A number of the most venerable and learned persons were, to adorn the triumph, carried in chains to Feroz-Kuh, where the victor ordered their throats to be cut, and tempering earth with their blood, used it to plaster the walls of his native city."

Allah-ud-din thus ended the House of Ghuzni; for though two descendants of Byrâm's kept a feeble hold on power from Lahôre during the space of a few years, he was the last real king. His actions are strangely at variance with his character, for he is said to have "been blest with a noble and generous disposition!"

We hear also of an uncommon thirst for knowledge. But in truth these wild, revengeful Mahomedans of the borderland were then very much as they are to-day; that is to say, proud, lawless, quick to respond in kind to good or evil, above all, possessed by a perfect devil of revenge--the cruel revenge which is ever associated with sensuality.

So, naturally, Allah-ud-din, after plastering the city walls with blood, spent the gold he had taken from Ghuzni on pleasure, until he died four years later, in A.D. 1156.

His son only reigned for a year. A fine fellow this, apparently, both physically and mentally, if we are to believe what is said of him; but, as usual, passionate, revengeful. So, seeing a chief who had fought against and defeated his father wearing some of the family jewels which had been stripped from his own wife after that occasion, he out with his sword and slew the offender forthwith. Whereupon the dead man's brother, choosing a convenient moment in the middle of a subsequent battle, out with his lance and ran the young king through the body.

Scarcely any of them, however, died in their beds. The procession of murders and sudden deaths becomes indeed monotonous, but was now to be broken for a while by the advent of another of those strong men who every now and again make, as it were, a landmark in Indian history.

This was Shahâb-ud-din who, counting the time during which he was his elder brother's deputy, was to reign for close on fifty years, and once more weld the principalities of India proper into one solid empire.

A strange history is this of the devoted brothers, who appear from their babyhood to have gone through life hand in hand in fortune and misfortune; but the house of Ghori seems to have been remarkable alike for its family feuds and for its family affection. The latter it was, be it remembered, which led to the establishment of the dynasty. Another peculiarity was their sonlessness. Ghiâss-ud-din, the elder brother, succeeded to the throne by virtue of cousinship only, and as neither he nor Shahâb-ud-din had sons, it passed at their death to a nephew.

Before that, however, India had to be reconquered, and for this purpose the Campaigns of the Crescent had to recommence.

The first was in A.D. 1176, when Mahomed Shahâb-ud-din--for ere commencing his task he added the name of the Prophet to his own, which signifies the "Meteor of Faith"--swept through the low-lying lands about the junction of the Punjâb rivers with the Indus. He must have had in his mind's eye the exploits of Mahmûd nigh on two hundred years before. Perhaps it was this memory which made him choose what is practically the same name; on the other hand, he may only have been seeking an excuse for plunder, like the dead conqueror had done in the religious enthusiasm roused by the name of the prophet.

Be that as it may, in reading the account of his exploits, one is tempted to rub one's eyes and ask, "Is this Mahmûd of Ghuzni, or Mahomed of Ghori?" So curiously alike are they in every way.

He did not, however, lead quite so many raids: on the other hand, he was more permanently successful in them, despite far more organised resistance than that which had opposed his great predecessor.

In fact, it is in this resistance that the real interest of the period lies, so it may be as well to make a complete *volte face*, and having viewed the introduction of Islâm to India through Mahomedan eyes, look at these final Campaigns of the Crescent from the Râjput side.

Before passing on to this, let us picture the man who, for close on half a century, found his sole occupation in a soldier's life. Here we have no added reputation of the arts or sciences. We are told he was a great king and a just man, but he appears to have been quite unscrupulous towards every one excepting his brother. Many of his successes were due to treachery, and when he died--an old man, assassinated in his sleep by those same wild tribes of the Punjâb Salt Range who inflicted so much damage on Mahmûd of Ghuzni--he was the richest king in the world. "The treasure," says the chronicler, "which this prince left behind him is almost incredible. In diamonds alone of various sizes he had five hundreds *muns* (at the lowest computation about 1,000 lbs.), the result of his nine expeditions into Hindustan, from each of which, excepting two occasions, he returned laden with wealth."

Yet India was still rich!

THE RAJPUT RESISTANCE

A.D. 1176 TO A.D. 1206

More than a hundred years had passed since Mahmûd of Ghuzni's strong grip had relaxed on India. During that time she had reverted, as she always will revert, to those ideals of life which suit her dreamy yet fireful temperament.

The fierce on-sweep of the Moslem scimitar had mowed down the tangle of petty chiefships which had grown up in the Dark Ages, and so left room for the spreading of four great kingdoms, Delhi, Ajmîr, Kanauj, Guzerât, which were all held by the representatives of certain Râjput clans.

Now the Râjputs are born soldiers. They represent the second, or military (called the Kshatriya) caste of ancient Vedic time; they have provided India for long centuries with her warriors, her nobles, her monarchs. Râj-pûtra means, in fact, a king's son. Their history is a magnificent one. They have faced and fought every enemy which Fate has brought to their native land in the past; they are ready still to face and fight whatever may come to it in the future. They are the Samurai of India, each clan led by a hereditary leader, and forming a separate community, bound by the strongest ties of military devotion and pride of race.

They claim to have sprung from the sun, or from the moon, or from the fire; and between them lies ever the faint jealousy of a different origin. Thus the Tomâras or Tuars of Delhi claimed the kinship of flame with the Chauhans of Ajmîr, while the Râthors of Kanauj stood by their distant sun-cousins of Guzerât. For to this day the pride of ancestry is the Râjput's most cherished inheritance. Often he has little else; but he stills scorns to turn his lance into a plough-share.

For the rest there is no people in the world whose history yields more pure romance. The chivalry of Europe seems strained and artificial beside the stern, straight-forward code of honour by which the early Râjputs regulated their dealings alike with women and with other men; and no roundel of troubadour or challenge of knight-errant could have roused more enthusiasm than did the wild love and war songs of the Râjput bards.

These, then, were the people whose resistance Mahomed Shahâb-ud-din of Ghor had to overcome, when, after an ineffectual attempt to reach the heart of India through the sandy deserts of Multân and Guzerât, and a further swoop on the country about Lahôre (in which, by treacherous stratagem, he seized on the persons who still prolonged the dying Ghuznevide dynasty and sent them northwards to imprisonment and death), he finally marched on Hindustan proper in the year A.D. 1191.

And here once more the pink-and-white mass of the huge fort of Bhatînda heaves into view as our *mise en scene*. The flowers of the *dâkh* trees had long since been picked as dye-stuff by the village women, when once more the hosts of hardy horsemen swept over the horizon. For, as ever, the *Toovkhs*-- as the peasantry learned to call these wild raiders--came with the flights of winter birds. The fort gave in at once to the fierce attack of the Mahomedans. The filagree sugar-work on its battlements seems, indeed, to have infected the mass of stone beneath it with frailty, for despite its apparent strength, Bhatînda has been taken and retaken ofttimes. So, leaving a garrison there, Shahâb-ud-din commenced his return; for the hardy horsemen always seem to have been more afraid of melting in the heat of India than meeting the onslaught of her armies.

Ere he had gone far, however, news of recall came to him. The great Prithvi-Râj, conjoint King of Delhi and Ajmîr, with many other Indian princes, two hundred thousand horse, and three thousand elephants was behind him.

Here was challenge indeed! The heat was forgotten; he faced round to the relief of the garrison he had left, and boldly passing Bhatînda, paused to give battle on that wild plain between Karnâl and Delhi, where half the struggles for the possession of India have been fought to the bitter end.

He must have awaited his enemy with anxiety, for the fame of Prithvi-Râj had spread even amongst Mahomedans. To the Hindus he was a demi-god: the personification of every Râjput virtue, the pattern of all Râjput manhood. A bold lover, a recklessly brave knight-errant, the story of his exploits, as told by his bard, Chand, fills many books, and is still listened to of winter nights beside the smoke-palled fires by half the men and women in India. It will be sufficient to recount one here to show what manner of man he was, and how he comes still to hold the admiration, not only of the romantic Râjputs, but of all India.

Prithvi-Râj, then, was of the Chauhan, Fire-born race. Râjah of Ajmîr only, by father-to-son descent, the kingship of Delhi had come to him by the death of his maternal grandfather without male issue.

But the Râjah of Kanauj was also grandson, and elder grandson, of the dead king by another daughter. Hence arose envy and strife between the cousins; the more so, because the sixteen-year-old Prithvi carried all things before him with an *élan* not to be imitated. It was all very well to match the young hero's Great Horse sacrifice (the last one, it is believed, in India), with which he claimed empire, by instituting a Sai-nair, accompanied by a Self-choice (also the last), for one's only daughter, the Princess Sunjogâta of Kanauj. Now the ceremony of Sai-nair is a most august one. It is virtually a claim for universal supremacy, for divine honour. Every one concerned in it, even the scullion in the kitchen who helps to cook the feast, must be of royal blood. So all India's princes were bidden to take their part in it, excepting Prithvi-Râj, and in his place an image of clay was made and set to the lowest job--that of door-keeper.

Thus the Râjah of Kanauj strove to save his dignity, for the rites were equally old, equally honourable; but what man, even though he were king, could calculate on what a young girl, just blossoming into womanhood, would say or do?

As a matter of fact, the young Princess Fortunata (a literal translation of the name) did a very distressing thing. No doubt as she entered the splendid arena (decorated, possibly, in imitation of the celebrated one, described in the Mâhâbhârata as the scene of Drâupadi's Swayâmbara), where all the assembled princes of India--excepting, of course, her wicked cousin, Prince Prithvi--were eagerly awaiting her choice, she looked very sweet and innocent--quite entrancing, briefly, in her fresh young beauty, about which every one was raving; but who would have dreamed of the mischief which was lurking behind the eyes down-dropped as she stood hesitating, the marriage garland--which every prince longed to feel, even as a yoke, round his neck--in her dainty little hands.

And then? Hey presto! Her dainty little feet sped determinedly over the Court to the door, and there was the garland, not round any living man, but be-decorating the misshapen image of clay which Jai-Chand, her father, had caused to be put in absent Prithvi's place!

There must have been wigs on the green in the women's apartments that fateful day, with papa cursing and mamma upbraiding, while all the little culprit's female relations held up pious hands of horror. But the deed was done, and there in broad daylight, on the wings of fierce love and pride, awakened by the tale of that maiden garland on cold clay, was the twenty-one-year-old Prince Prithvi himself, the flower of Râjput chivalry, followed by youthful heroes, ready, like their chief, for soft kisses or hard blows. The last came first in that desperate five-days-running fight all the way back to

Delhi, with willing Princess Fortunata in their midst, her cheek paling but her eyes dry, as one by one the dear, brave lads fell out from her cortege dead or dying.

But the bravest, the dearest, the best, held her close, unharmed, and so the soft kisses came at last.

For Prince Prithvi, though he lost some friends--lost, as the historians put it, "the sinews of India"--kept his prize, and gained for himself immortal memory in the hearts of all Râjput maidens even to the present day.

This, then, was the paladin who took the field against the bearded, middle-aged Mahomed Shahâb-ud-din, and deftly outflanking his wings, drove them back and back until the whole Mahomedan army showed a circle surrounded by the enemy. In the centre the great general himself, mad with passion at the counsel sent to him by his subordinates to save himself as best he could. His reply was to cut down the messenger, and calling on all who would to follow him, rush out on the enemy, dealing reckless, almost futile death. To no purpose. Prithvi's younger brother, marking down his quarry, drove his elephant full against the burly-bearded leader of the desperate sally; but Mahomed Ghori lacked no courage, and the charge was met half-way, horse against leviathan, lance couched to lance.

And the honours lay with the Moslem, for Châwand Rao took the lance-head full in his mouth, to the destruction of many teeth. But Prithvi was in support of his brother, and a well-aimed arrow twanged and quivered in the northerner's scimitar arm; he reeled in his saddle and would have fallen, had not a faithful servant, taking advantage of the wild, swift closing in of rescue for the wounded monarch, leapt up behind him in the saddle, and turning the horse's head to the open, carried the almost fainting king from the field. He was followed by his whole army, harassed for full 40 miles by the victorious Hindus.

Princess Fortunata's kisses must have been sweet that night to her victorious hero. But Mahomed Shahâb-ud-din's calm had gone. Smileless, he waited for the healing of his wound at Lahôre, then, returning to Ghor, publicly disgraced every officer who had not followed his forlorn hope, by parading them round the city like horses or mules, their noses in "nose-bags filled with barley, which he forced them to eat like brutes," and afterwards flinging them into prison. So two years passed in moody anger and sullen disgrace, crushed into forgetfulness by reckless pleasure and festivity. Then, taking heart of grace, he got together a picked force of 120,000 Toorki and Afghân cavalry recruits, for the most part men of his own class and calibre, whose helmets were encrusted with jewels, their cuirasses inlaid with gold; and so off Peshawur ways.

"Since the day of defeat," he said to an old sage, "despite external appearances, I have never slumbered with ease, or waked but in sorrow. I go, therefore, to recover my lost honour from these idolaters, or die in the attempt."

"My king," replied the wise old man, kissing the ground, "wherefore should not those whom you have so justly disgraced likewise have opportunity of wiping away the stain of their defeat?"

The plea struck him by its justice. He issued orders for the disgraced officers' freedom, and gave leave for those desirous of redeeming their character to follow his example. A picked force this, indeed, with a vengeance!

And on the other side was haughty defiance, marked still by the chivalrous sense of honour which, to such as Prithvi-Râj, was dearer than life.

A proud acceptance of the issues met the curt declaration of war should the Indians refuse to embrace the true faith, which the Mahomedan general sent to Ajmîr by accredited ambassador. A 'cute move this; one to enhance the martial ardour of his men; perhaps to still further inflame his own determination to turn past defeat to present victory. Then ensued a pause for parley, in which the Princess Fortunata had her share--a worthy share, as the following extracts will show. Till then her kisses had lulled Prithvi-Râj to forgetfulness of sterner things; now they were to rouse him from his dream. For this was her reply when her husband, leaving his War-Council to deliberate, sought wisdom where he had so often found pleasure:--

"What fool asks woman for advice? The world
Holds her wit shallow.... Even when the truth
Comes from her lips men stop their ears and smile.
And yet without the woman where is man?
We hold the power of Form--for us the Fire
Of Shiv's creative force flames up and burns:
Lo! we are thieves of Life and sanctuaries
Of Souls. Vessels are we of virtue and of vice,
Of knowledge and of utmost ignorance.
Astrologers can calculate from books
The courses of the stars, but who is he
Can read the pages of a woman's heart?
Our book has not been mastered; so men say
'She hath no wisdom' but to hide their lack
Of understanding. Yet we share your lives,

Your failures, your successes, griefs and joys.
Hunger and thirst, if yours, are ours, and Death
Parts us not from you; for we follow fast
To serve you in the mansion of the Sun.
Love of my heart! Lo! you are as a swan
That rests upon my bosom as a lake.
There is no rest for thee but here, my lord!
And yet arise to Victory and Fame.
Sun of the Chauhans! Who has drunk so deep
Of glory and of pleasure as my lord?
And yet the destiny of all is death:
Yea even of the Gods--and to die well
Is life immortal---- Therefore draw your sword,
Smite down the foes of Hind; think not of self--
The garment of this life is frayed and worn,
Think not of me--we twain shall be as one
Hereafter and for ever.--Go, my king!"

So the fiery cross sped round Râjputana, and ere long Prithvi-Râj could confront the enemy with an army of 300,000 horse, 3,000 elephants, and a large body of infantry. They encamped opposite and within sight of each other on the old battle-field, with the river Saraswati, which was soon to lose itself in the desert sands beyond, running between the opposing armies. Despite the disparity in numbers the forces were not ill-matched, for the Indians were hampered by a thousand old traditions, old accoutrements, old scruples. The Mahomedans, on the other hand, were full up with desire for gold, for souls. But it was a holy war on both sides. The Hindus had sworn on Ganges water to conquer or die, the Moslem had sworn likewise on the Korân; so heads were bowed in humble prayer to the Lord of Hosts, and human hearts beat high with murderous hope. Quaint conjunction when all is said and done!

Thus far, well. Now comes Mahomed Shahâb-ud-din's diplomatic strategy, which some might call by another name, even though the account of what occurred comes to us through the pen of an ardent Mahomedan, and cannot, therefore, but put the best face on what happened. Prithvi-Râj, then, facing his foe, so much smaller in numbers, so altogether insignificant beside the splendid lavishness of the Râjput camp, wrote a letter to Mahomed Shahâb-ud-din. Whether dictated by mere pride or martial honour, by contemptuous pity, religious dislike to take life, or, as the Mahomedans aver, by mere brag, the terms of it are worth reading:--

"To the bravery of our soldiers we know you are no stranger: and to our great superiority in numbers, which daily increases, your eyes bear witness. If you are wearied of your own existence, yet have pity on your troops who may still think it a happiness to live. It were better, then, you should repent in time of the rash resolution you have taken, and we shall permit you to retreat in safety."

Not an undignified appeal, this first recorded attempt at peace with honour. Its reply was, as the historian puts it, "politic." It consisted in Mahomed Shahâb-ud-din's assertion that he was only the general of his brother's forces; that therefore he dare not retreat without orders, but he would be glad of a truce until such time as information could be sent to Ghuzni and an answer received.

A simple and admirable adjunct to the night-attack which followed, and which found the Râjputs unprepared, in fancied security.

About the false dawning, when even the noise of revelry in the opposite camp had quieted down to sleep, the Mahomedan army forded the river in silence, and drew up in order on the sands beyond. Some portion of it was actually within the Hindu lines ere the alarm was raised.

Even so, the Râjput cavalry was to the front immediately, and checked the advance.

For what followed, Mahomed Shahâb-ud-din deserves unstinted praise. It was good general-ship.

He formed his bowmen into four divisions, and placing them one behind the other, ordered the first to come into fighting line, discharge their arrows, and wheel to the rear, thus giving place to the second fighting line, the whole army to retreat slowly, giving ground whenever hard pressed.

All that day he fought, biding his time with such patience as he and his twelve thousand steel-armoured horsemen could muster. The sun was just setting when, judging the delusion of victory had done its work in the hot heads of the Râjputs, he gave the orders for one desperate charge.

It did its work!

"Din! Din! Fateh Mahomed!" once and for all overcame the Hindu war-cry of, "Victory, Victory!" In the years to come success and failure were to attend both; but only in detail. The great issue between Brahmanism and Mahomedism was fought out on the vast Karnâl battle-plain in A.D. 1193, when, as the chronicler of Islâm says,

"one desperate charge carried death and destruction throughout the Hindu ranks. The disorder increased everywhere, till at length the panic became general. The Moslems, as if they now only began to be in earnest, committed such havoc, that this prodigious army once shaken, like a great building tottered to its fall, and was lost in its own ruins."

How many thousand pagans "went below?" Who knows? But one is sure that Mahomed Shahâb-ud-din duly praised God from whom all blessings flow. His subsequent atrocities prove that he must have relied on something which he deemed Divine Guidance; mere humanity could never have been so cruel.

Half Râjput chivalry lay dead under the stars, but the flower of it was hiding in the sugar-cane brakes, stealing his way back to Delhi, to the Princess Sunjogâta his wife, who, as she had watched him go forth, lance in rest, his sword buckled on by her own steady hands, had said with foreboding courage to her maidens: "In Yoginâpur (Delhi) I shall see him no more: we will meet in Swarga." The tale of what happened is almost beyond telling.

Prithvi Râjah was murdered in cold blood, murdered ignominiously. The Princess Fortunata escaped a like, or a worse, fate by a funeral pyre, and Delhi was given over to such hideous devils work as even that long-suffering city has never seen before or since. The followers of the Prophet wiped out their own and their God's disgrace in torrents of blood, filled their pockets by the way, went on to Ajmîr, enacted a like tragedy, and so returned northwards when the pink clouds of the low-lying groves of *dâkh* trees began to blossom about the battle-field where the sun of the Hindus had set for ever.

But Mahomed Shahâb-ud-din left his pet Turki slave Kutb-din-Eîbuk behind him at Delhi, and he, assuming almost regal honours, "compelled all the districts around to acknowledge the faith of Islâm."

How many murders go to the making of a Moslem is a question which might fairly be asked. Converts, however, hardly came in fast enough for Shahâb-ud-din's zeal, so the next year saw him back again to help his slave in crushing the Râjah of Kanauj, who, doubtless, had not been of Prithvi-Râj's host. Thence he marched to Benares, in which hot-bed of idolatry he thoroughly enjoyed himself by smashing the idols in a thousand temples, which he subsequently purified by prayer and purgation, and thereinafter consecrated to the worship of the true God.

This was his last real outing, for Fate--can it have been that she dissociated herself from his doubtful use of the white flag--began to play him false. His slave-viceroy showed inclination to plunder on his own behalf, and though the master once more returned to India, it was but a flying visit, apparently to check independence. To no avail, for Kutb-din-Eîbuk, "ambitious of extending his conquests, led an army into Râjputana, where, having experienced severe defeat, he was compelled to seek protection in the fort at Ajmîr."

For the fighting spirit in the Râjput was not to be quenched by blood, or burned out by fire. It was to flame up fiercely for many a century to come, until the wisdom of Akbar won it over to his side.

Mahomed Shahâb-ud-din's hands were, however, too full to permit of his giving much attention to India. His brother, Ghiâss-ud-din, the mere figure-head of a king, died in A.D. 1202, and though Shahâb-ud-din was crowned in his stead without any opposition, bad luck seemed to attend him afterwards. His army was literally cut down to a mere body-guard of a hundred troopers in Khorassan, and though his fortunes were recovered in some measure, his time seems to have been taken up in quelling the rebellions of his favourite slaves whom he had promoted to honour.

In India, Kutb-din, it is true, remained faithful in name, though his power and prestige rose above his master's, and he was virtually king, not viceroy.

Finally, in A.D. 1206, the leader of the last real raid of the Crescent into India was assassinated by the Ghakkars of the Salt Range upon the banks of the Indus.

"The weather being sultry, the King had ordered the screens which surround the royal tents to be struck in order to give free admission to the air. This afforded the assassins an opportunity of seeing into the sleeping apartments. So at night time they found their way up to the tents and hid themselves, while one of their number advanced boldly to the tent door. Challenged by a sentry, he plunged his dagger in the man's breast, and this rousing the guard, who ran out to see what was the matter, the hidden assassin took that opportunity of cutting a way into the King's tent.

"He was asleep, with two slaves fanning him. They stood petrified with terror as the Ghakkars sheathed their daggers in the King's body, which was afterwards found to have been pierced by no fewer than twenty-two wounds."

THE SLAVE KINGS

A.D. 1206 TO A.D. 1288

"The Empire of Delhi was founded by a slave."

So runs the well-known jibe. And it is true; for although India, despite the combined resistance of the Râjputs, was overcome during the reign of Mahomed Shahâb-ud-din Ghori, the real glory of conquest belongs by rights to Eîbuk, the slave; Eîbuk of the "broken little finger," who took the name of Kutb-ud-din, or Pole-star of the Faith.

To those who know India the name conjures up one of the most marvellous sights in the world. A dark December morning in the Punjâb, when the Christmas rain-clouds gather black on the horizon, and on them, above the rolling, brick-strewn ridges of Old Delhi, rises a thin shaft of light--the Kutb Minâr, the finest pillar in the world.

It was built by the Turki slave Eîbuk, and one can forgive him much in that he left the world such a thing of beauty to be a joy for ever.

And yet as one stands beneath it, marking here and there the half-obliterated traces of previous cutting on the stones of the wonderful tapering pillar, all corbeilled with encircling balconies, and banded in dexterous art with interlaced lettering; as one looks round on the dismantled ruins of still more ancient temples, the mind suddenly ceases to give the glory to Kutb-ud-din, and turns almost with amaze to the thought of the Hindu architects who built it to order out of their dishonoured shrines.

Think of it! Art, true Art rising superior to Self! Surely as they chiselled at those interlaced attributes of the One Unknowable, Unthinkable, they must have been conscious that though all things in this life were--as their religion told them--but Illusion, behind that Illusion lay Reality.

And so their work comforted them.

How much of India is built into this watch tower of her gods? The best of her, anyhow, and English civilisation can scarcely add an additional story to this record of her past.

To Kutb-ud-din Eîbuk, however, belongs the glory of inception; therefore also some forgiveness, which, in truth, he sorely needs. For from the beginning his attitude towards strict morality is, to say the least of it, doubtful. He was a beautiful Turki slave, the avowed pet and plaything of his master Shahâb-ud-din, who gave him "his particular notice, and daily advanced him in confidence and favours."

He appears to have been diplomatic, for on one occasion, being questioned by the king as to why he had divided his share of a general distribution of presents amongst the other retainers, he kissed the ground of Majesty's feet, and replied, that being amply supplied already by that Majesty's favours, he desired no superfluities.

This brought him the Master of the Horse-ship, from which he went on to honour after honour, until in the year A.D. 1193 he was left as viceroy in India. Thenceforward he was practically king. It was he who took Delhi after a conflict in which the river Jumna ran red with blood. It was he who commanded the forces at Etawah, and it was his hand which shot the arrow that, piercing the eye of the Benares Râjah, cost him his life and the loss of everything he possessed.

A quaint picture that, by the way, of the search for Jai-Chund's body amidst the huge heaps of the slain, and its final recognition after weary days by "the artificial teeth fixed by golden wires." Had dentistry got as far in the West, I wonder?

Then it was Kutb-ud-din who presented to his master the three hundred elephants taken at Benares; amongst them the famous white one which refused to kneel like the others before the *M'lechcha*, king though he might be. The beast's independence serving him better than a man's would have done, since it brought no punishment, but the honour of being pad elephant to the viceroy thenceforth.

And it was he who marched his forces hither and thither, "engaged the enemy, put them to flight, and having ravaged the country at leisure, obtained much booty."

The eye wearies over the repetitions of this formula, as the hand turns the pages of Ferishta's history, while the heart grows sick at the thought of what such a war of conversion or extermination meant in those days.

The victorious procession of the Mahomedan troopers was only broken once in Guzerât. Here Kutb-ud-din, despite six wounds, fought stubbornly and with his wonted courage, until forced by his attendants from the field, and carried in a litter to the fort at Ajmîr, where he managed to hold out until reinforcements came to his aid from the King of Ghuzni.

Defeat seems ever to have been the mother of victory with these passionate, revengeful Afghâns, for on the very next occasion on which

Kutb-ud-din "engaged the enemy," he is said to have killed fifty thousand of them, and to have gathered into his treasury vast spoils.

Nothing seemed to stop him. Even the swift assassination by his own prime minister of a cowardly râjah who was coming to terms with the *M'lechcha* instead of resisting the Unclean to the death, did not avail to preserve almost impregnable Kalûnjur; for a spring incontinently dried up in the fort, and there once more was one last sally, and then death for the garrison.

It was in A.D. 1205, after Kutb-din had had twelve years of battles, murders, and sudden deaths, twelve years of absolute if not nominal kingship, that Mahomed Shahâb-ud-din's successor, feeling himself not strong enough to assume the reins of government in India, made a bid for peace for himself in Ghuzni by sending Eîbuk the slave, the drums, the standards, the insignia of royalty, and the title of King of India.

Eîbuk received them all with "becoming respect," and was duly crowned. This fact did not prevent his being crowned again in Ghuzni the following year!

He then, having attained to the height of his ambition, seeing no more worlds to conquer, having for the time being crushed even Râjput resistance, gave himself up "unaccountably to wine and pleasure."

This seems to have irritated the good citizens of Ghuzni. They invited another claimant to the throne to try his luck. He came, found Eîbuk unprepared, possibly drunk. Anyhow, there was no time to attempt a defence. He fled to Lahôre, thus finally severing the Kingship of Ghuzni from that of India.

There, we are told, he became "sensible of his folly," repented, and thereinafter "continued to exercise justice, temperance, morality."

He was killed while playing *chaugan* (the modern polo) in A.D. 1210. At that time he was supposed to be the richest man in the world; but, unlike Mahmûd, he was generous. "As liberal as Eîbuk" is still a phrase in the mouth of India.

His son Arâm (Leisure) appears to have deserved his name. He never gripped the kingdom, and lost it fatuously after less than a year. Apparently he was not deemed worth the killing, and Altâmish, a favourite slave of the slave Eîbuk, took his place by virtue of being son-in-law to the dead king.

Altâmish was also of Turki extraction. As a youth, the fame of his beauty and talents was noised abroad, and Shahâb-ud-din was in the bidding for him, but hung back at the price; whereupon Eîbuk the Lavish put down the fifty thousand pieces of silver, and carried off the prize.

Years after, he was married to the Princess-Royal, and so, adding Ṣhums-ud-din (Sword of the Faith) to his name, ascended the throne, and reigned for no less than twenty-six years.

So Delhi, indeed, was founded by slaves!

Atlâmish appears to have been of the regulation type. He was, so to speak, Kutb-ud-din and water. The largest number of Hindus he is recorded to have killed at one time is three hundred; a sad falling-off in *Ghâzi*-dom. [3] On the other hand, he was the barbarian who, taking Ujjain, destroyed the magnificent temple of Mâhâ-Kâli which it had taken three hundred years to build. The idols thereof, and also a "statue of Vikramadîtya, who had been formerly prince of this country, and so renowned that the Hindus have taken an era from his death," were conveyed solemnly to Delhi, and there broken at the door of the great mosque of which the magnificent ruins--spoils of many a Jain and Hindu temple--still lie about the foot of the Kutb Minâr, a monument to the slave Eîbuk who commenced it, the slave Altâmish who finished it.

This solemn smashing was doubtless a fine ceremony, yet as we of the present day contemplate it, regret goes forth, especially for the statue of Vikramadjît. How many a riddle might it not have solved concerning the Unknown King!

We are told that Altâmish was an "enterprising, able, and good prince"; he has, however, another, and in the history of the world, quite unique claim to regard. The father of seven children, six of them in turn mounted the throne with more or less success.

Considerably less as regards the first occupant, Ruku-ud-din (Prop of the Faith), who spent his six months and twenty-eight days tenancy in lavishing his inherited treasures on dancing girls, pimps and prostitutes.

This might have been borne for longer, but the hideous cruelties of his mother, a Turki slave to whom he entrusted the reins of government, were such as to rouse even the dull humanity of a thirteenth-century Mahomedan. She had murdered horribly every one of the dead king's women, and had begun on his son's, when the patience of the various viceroys gave way. They entered into a conspiracy, deposed the king, and threw his mother into prison--a lenient punishment for such a monster of cruelty.

And then? Then they did a thing unheard of in Indian history--they raised a woman to the throne.

But Sultana Râzia Begum was no ordinary mortal! Indeed, there is something so quaint about the recapitulation of her virtues, as given in the pages of Ferishta, that, perforce, one cannot but quote it.

"Râzia Begum (my Lady Content) was possessed of every good quality which usually adorns the ablest princes; and those who scrutinise her actions most severely, will find in her no fault but that she was a woman."

Alas! Poor Lady Content! Of what avail that you changed (as it is solemnly set down) your apparel; that you abandoned the petticoat in favour of the trews; that your father, when he appointed you regent during one of his long absences, defended his action by saying that though a woman, you had a man's head and heart, and were worth more than twenty such sons as he had? All this was of no avail against womanhood. Let this be thy comfort, poor shade of a dead queen, that the argument still holds good against thy sisters in this year of grace 1907!

Setting this aside, the career of Queen-Content matches in tragedy that of Mary Queen of Scots. A clever girl, evidently, her father made her his companion, and while her brothers were dicing and wenching, drinking and twanging the *sutara*, she was frowning with him over endless pacifications, endless violences, becoming, apparently, an adept at both. For it would have needed great qualifications to ensure the almost unanimous vote of the nobles which placed a woman on the throne.

At first even these contemptuous Mahomedans were satisfied. Then came discontent. Did Râzia Begum really favour the Abyssinian slave whom she allowed--*horribile dictum!*--to "lift her on her horse by raising her up under the arms"? Or had she really forgotten the petticoat in the trews? Who can say? All we know is that Malik-Altûnia, the Turki governor of Bhattînda--curious how that name crops up in all the really exciting tales of Indian history!--revolted on the plea of the queen's partiality to the Abyssinian; that she marched against the rebel, leading her troops; that a tumultuous conflict occurred in the old place of battles, in which the Abyssinian favourite was killed, the queen taken prisoner, and sent to Altûnia's care in the fort.

So far good. But here affairs take a turn which is fairly breathless, and which gives pause for doubting Altûnia's disinterested care for morality and *les convenances*.

He promptly married the empress, and with scarce a comma, we find him raising an army to espouse her cause, and fighting her battles, the Bothwell of his time. He failed, and he and his wife were put to death together on the 14th of November A.D. 1239.

A tragic tale indeed! Best finished by another excerpt from the historian.

"The reign of Sultana Râzia Begum lasted three years, six months, and six days. Those who reflect on the fate of this unfortunate princess will readily discover from whence arose the foul blast that blighted all her prospects.--What connection exists between the high office of Amîr-ul Omra and an Abyssinian slave? Or how are we to reconcile the inconsistency of the queen of so vast a territory fixing her affections on so unworthy an object?"

And no one, apparently, remembered that she herself was the daughter of a Turki slave who achieved empire.

Byrâm was the next brother to ascend the throne. The two years, one month, and fifteen days before he also "sipped the cup of fate" is a welter of crimes. Enemies were trodden under foot of elephants, slaves suborned to feign drunkenness and assassinate friends; in short, "these proceedings, without trial or public accusation, justly alarmed every one," so Masûd, the next brother, had his innings. A poor one, though it lasted twice as long as Byrâm's. He found time in it, however, to repel the first Moghul invasion by way of Tibet into Bengal. This was in A.D. 1244, and it was followed by a similar incursion the next year, by way of Kandahâr and Sinde. Masûd seems to have become imbecile over wine and women, and when deposed, was contemptuously allowed to live by his brother, Nâsir-ud-din, the only one of Altâmish's sons who appears to have been worth anything; possibly because he had passed the whole of the last four reigns in prison!

Adversity may be a hard, but she is a good taskmistress, and in Nâsir-ud-din she had evidently good mettle on which to work. He was a man, distinctly, of original parts, for while in prison he had always preferred supporting himself by his writings to accepting any public allowance; a "whimsical habit" which he continued after he came to the throne. He was also almost scandalously moral according to the orthodoxy of the day in refusing to have more than one wife, and in cutting down all outward show and magnificence on the ground that, being only God's trustee for the State, he was bound not to burden it with useless extravagance.

As he reigned for no less than twenty years, he had time to gather together the *disjecta membra*, of the Indian empire which Eîbuk had built up, and which was fast coming to be a series of semi-independent provinces, and even once more to annex Ghuzni to the kingdom of Delhi. He followed his predecessors' example also in rousing yet again the Râjput resistance. During the previous reigns the clans had recovered themselves, and, from the Mahomedan point of view, needed a lesson. So some few thousands were killed in battle, some few hundred chiefs put to death, and innumerable smaller fry condemned to perpetual slavery. And yet a story is told of Nâsir-ud-din which shows him not devoid of heart.

A worthy old scholar, criticising the king's penmanship, pointed out a fault. He, smiling, erased the word, but when the critic was gone, began to restore it, remarking that it was right, but it was better to spoil paper than the self-confidence of an old man.

He died, after a long illness, in A.D. 1266, and thereinafter Ghiâss-ud-din the *wazîr*, who had married a sister of Sultana Râzia's, ascended the throne, possibly in the absence of more direct heirs. He must have been nearly sixty at the time, for he died twenty-one years after in his eightieth year.

He also was a Turki slave, first employed as falcon-master by Altâmish, who promoted him again and again; wherefore, Heaven knows, for history gives us but a poor character of him. He appears to have been a pious, narrow-minded, intolerant, selfish tyrant, with a hypocritical dash of virtue about him which took in his world completely. Circumstances also aided him in posing as perfection; for about this time the Moghul invasion had reached the western borderlands, and hundreds of illustrious and literary fugitives crowded thence, to find in Delhi the only stable Mahomedan government.

These, flattering and fawning, helped to noise his fame abroad as a paragon. Then the son of his old age, Prince Mahomed, was a potent factor in his popularity. The apple of his father's eye, he seems to have been an Admirable Crichton, and his death, in the moment of victory, not only "drew tears from the meanest soldier to the General," but came as a final blow to the old king, "who was so much distressed that life became irksome to him."

This great affection between father and son--for "Prince Mahomed always behaved to him with the utmost filial affection and duty"--is, indeed, the one human interest of a life devoted to pious pretences, to pomp and pose.

His grandson Kêik-obâd came to the throne at his death, and promptly gave the reins to pleasure and the guidance of public affairs to his *wazîr*. He succeeded in painting Old Delhi very red indeed during his short reign of three years. "Every shady grove was filled with women and parties of pleasure, every street rang with riot and tumult; even the magistrates were seen drunk in public, and music was heard in every house."

His minister kept him at this task also; for, perceiving a faint check in the pursuit of pleasure, he "collected graceful dancers, beautiful women, and good singers from all parts of the kingdom, whom he occasionally introduced as if by accident."

So, finally, the three-year-old Prince Keî-omurs--the only child of a miserable father who was now paralytic--was smuggled out of the harem to be King-designate, while the wretched, debauched, half-dying man had his brains beaten out with bludgeons while he was lying on his bed helpless; and so, battered out of all recognition, his body was hastily rolled up in the bed-clothes, and flung through the window into the sliding river.

A horrid tale, with which the history of the Slave Kings fitly comes to an end.

They were not a good breed. Even Ferishta the historian, who has a weakness for kings, feels this, for he ends his account of them with the sphinx-like remark: "Eternity belongs only to God, the great Sovereign of the Earth!"

THE TARTAR DYNASTIES

A.D. 1288 TO A.D. 1398

As can easily be imagined, India at the end of those ten Slave reigns (which between them lasted but eighty-two years) was a very different place to what India had been when Eîbuk's iron hand first closed on it. Half the Punjâb, almost all Râjputana, and the better part of the United Provinces, had run red with Hindu blood in those days; but as the stream subsided, the terrible legacy of the flood had remained as a lesson welding the whole land into apathetic acquiescence, until absorption set in with the years, and as time went on, the crushed, half-dead organism began once more to feel life in its veins. For Hinduism is India--India is Hinduism. When the last trace of the metaphysical Monism which underlies every aspiration, every action, has disappeared, India and Hinduism will have disappeared also, but not till then.

So as time crept on, and under slack rule Mahomedan began to fight Mahomedan, each petty governor playing for his own hand, his own independence, the Râjputs raised their dejected heads, and, seizing every opportunity, strove to recover part at least of their own. Gwalîor with its rock,--that almost impregnable fort--for instance, changed hands many times, and, save during the reign of Nâsir-ud-din, no attempt was made on the part of the Mahomedans after the time of Altâmish, either to increase their conquests, or do more than temporarily bolster up their rule.

Nor when the Slave dynasty ended, and one Jelâl-ud-din, of the House of Khilji, established himself on the throne of Delhi by the murder of the three-year-old Keî-omurs, was there any change of policy. He was seventy years old; old for kingship in any country, extraordinarily so for India. And he was weak, hesitating. For a while distracted by feeble remorse he refused royal honours, and after a very short time delegated his authority to his nephew, Allah-ud-din, who succeeded him, and who for many years prior to his uncle's death arrogated to himself almost absolute independence.

The seven years of Jelâl-ud-din's reign, then, are but a prelude to Allah-ud-din's twenty.

A vigorous man this, and an unscrupulous. One of his first emprises was the conquest of the Dekkan which, as yet, had been untouched by Mahomedan adventure.

He got no further, however, than Deogîri, the capital of the Mâhârâjah of the Mahrattas. Far enough, however, for pillage *à la* Kutb-din-Eîbuk. He found the Râjputs unprepared--they had strict scruples of honour regarding the necessity for a formal declaration of war, by which their adversaries were not bound--and the usual slaughter took place. For the first time, also, mention is made of merchants being tortured to make them disclose their treasures. *"L'appetit vient en mangeant,"* and a rich Hindu *banya* was to the Mahomedan what the Jew was to a Crusader.

The result was prodigious. Allah-ud-din left Deogîri--surely misnamed thus the "Shelter of the Gods"--with "2,400 pounds weight of pearls, 12 pounds of diamonds, rubies, emeralds, and sapphires, 6,000 pounds of silver, 4,000 pieces of silk, besides a long list of other precious commodities to which reason forbids us to give credit." In truth, reason appears as it is somewhat over-taxed!

It was on Allah-ud-din's return from this campaign that he perpetrated the foulest murder of Indian history; and that means much.

His expedition had been absolutely unauthorised by his uncle, the king, who, almost dotingly affectionate though inwardly relieved at his favourite's success, was persuaded to ask on Allah-ud-din's return for explanations, and express displeasure. The latter feigned remorse, went so far as to hint that the excess of his regret might put an end to his melancholy life; so lured the old man to meet him on the banks of the river Ganges, where the villain halted, fearful, he protested, of just punishment. The king, deceived, crossed the river in the Royal Barge almost unattended, bidding those who did accompany him unbuckle swords lest the beloved prodigal might take affright. He reached the landing-stage, and found Allah-ud-din backed by trusty friends. The old man advanced, the prodigal fell at his feet, to be raised with almost playful tenderness. "Lo!" said the tremulous old voice, as the tremulous old hand patted the villain's cheek, "how couldst thou fear me, Allah-hu? Did I not cherish thee from childhood? Have I not held thee dearer than mine own sons?"

The words had hardly left his lips, the first step hand-in-hand towards the Royal Barge had hardly been taken, when Allah-ud-din gave the signal. The feeble old man was thrown down. One cry, "Oh, Allah-ud-din, Allah-ud-din!" and all was over. His head, transfixed on a spear-point, was paraded about the city, and his murderer, making a pompous and triumphant entry into Delhi, ascended the throne in the Ruby Palace, and thereinafter utilised part of his loot by spending it on magnificent shows, grand festivals, and splendid entertainments, "by which the unthinking rabble were made to forget in gaiety all memory of their former king, or of the horrid crime which had placed the present one on the throne."

So much for Allah-ud-din's accession. His reign is literally crammed full of picturesque incidents, and would almost require a volume to itself. Before attempting a few details, there is one tale of Jelâl-ud-din's which deserves record--that of the Mysterious Stranger. He was called Sidi--Dervish Sidi. He appeared in Delhi suddenly, opened a large house, and commenced to distribute charity on a scale of magnificence which led instantly to the belief that he must possess the philosopher's stone. He thought nothing of giving three thousand pieces of gold in casual relief to some noble but distressed family. Every day he expended about 8,000 pounds of flour, 400 pounds of meat, with sugar, spices, and butter in proportion to feed the poor, while he lived on rice alone, and foreswore both wine and women. So, after a time, his influence almost exceeding that of Majesty itself, he was accused of high treason, and by the king's orders condemned to the ordeal by fire.

It was to be carried out *coram populo*. On the plain between the town and the river all preparations were made: a circle round the blazing pile to give fair view to the populace; Sidi Dervish, and his companions in suspicion, saying their prayers; then, at the last moment, objection raised and upheld by learned doctors that such ordeals were both contrary to the law of God and against Reason. So Sidi Dervish and his friends are being hauled off to prison once more, until the foiled king gives a hint to some shaven monks hard by: "I leave him to you to be judged according to his deserts."

Cut down by the shaven ones' razors, Sidi offers no resistance, begs them to be expeditious in sending him to God, lays his curse heavily on the king and his posterity, and dies; whereupon a black whirlwind rises and envelopes all for the space of half an hour. A terrifying end to one whose piety was unquestioned, but whose dogma was disturbing; for Sidi Dervish held, we are told, "very peculiar opinions, and never attended public worship."

A quaint, incomprehensible tale, surely, that reads true, and brings wonder as to who the poor man could possibly have been.

To return to Allah-ud-din. One of the most picturesque stories of Râjput history is associated with his name: the story of the Princess Padmani and the first sack of Chitore--that terrible happening which still haunts the memory of the race, and provides its ultimate inviolable oath, "By the sin of the sack of Chitore."

Padmani, then, was peerless. Her very name survives to the present day as synonymous with perfect womanhood. And Allah-ud-din--who seems to have been eclectic in his pleasures--hearing of her beauty while still only commander-in-chief to his uncle, forced his way to the sacred stronghold of the Râjputs, and threatened instant attack if he were not allowed to see her, if it were only her reflection in a mirror. Now such hardy, yet in a way honourable, requests were not foreign to the Râjput spirit, and Râjah Bhim-si, her husband, granted it. With due pomp and ceremonial he escorted Allah-ud-din to his palace, with due pomp and ceremony showed him the reflection of the most beautiful woman in India, with due pomp and ceremony escorted the Mahomedan general back to his tents, trusting to his honour. But Allah-ud-din's honour was a mutable quantity: he seized the husband as ransom for the wife, and swore instant death if the princess were not delivered to him without delay. So forth from the frowning rock came seven hundred litters, Padmani and her women offering themselves up in exchange for a life that was the dearest thing on earth to every Râjput man and woman. Into the camp they came; and then? Then each litter belched out reckless manhood armed to the teeth; each disguised litter-bearer threw off his swathing shawl and proclaimed himself warrior.

So the husband was brought back to the wife, and in the ensuing battle the Râjputs died hard. There is a story of how one widow of the slain, standing with foot ready to mount the funeral pyre of her dead hero, called in a loud voice to the page who had followed him in the fight:

"Boy! Tell me once more ere I go how bore himself my lord?"

"As reaper of the harvest of battle! On the bed of honour, he spread a carpet of the slain, whereon, a barbarian his pillow, he sleeps ringed about by his foes."

"Yet once again, oh boy, tell me how my lord bore himself?"

"Oh mother! Who can tell his deeds! He left none to fear or to praise!"

The memory of Padmani's trick rankled. After ascending the throne Allah-ud-din returned to Chitore. Up till then, A.D. 1303, the fort was maiden, had been held unassailable, impregnable. But Allah-ud-din was rich beyond belief. He gave gold for every basket of earth brought to raise the pile, whence, overtopping the rock, he could pour his missiles into the doomed city.

Night and day, day and night through the long hot weather the baskets worked, the gold was paid, until the end drew near.

The tale which is still told round many a watch-fire runs that one night Râjah Bhim-si, to whom twelve sons had been born by the beautiful

Padmani, woke in fear. Before him, in a lurid light, stood Vyan-Mâta, the tutelary goddess of his race. "I am hungry," she wailed. "Lo! I drink Râjput blood, but I am hungry for the blood of kings. Let me drink the blood of twelve who have worn the diadem, and my city may yet be inviolate."

So one by one eleven of the young princes were raised to the throne. Then, after three days' reign, they went forth to meet the foe, to meet fate.

But the youngest, Prince Ajey-si, was the darling; so when his turn came, his father's heart failed him, and he called his chiefs together. "The child shall go free to recover what is lost. I will be the twelfth king to die for Chitore."

"Yea-we will die for Chitore," was the reply.

So each Râjput man put on the bridal coronet and the saffron robe, and every Râjput woman her wedding garment. And when the dawn came, the city gates were set wide, and through them poured desperate manhood surrounding a little knot of picked heroes who had sworn to see the child safe; while from behind rose up on the still morning air a column of smoke from the vast funeral pyre on which desperate women had sought the embrace of death in the dark vaults and caves which honeycomb the rock, and which, since that fatal day, have never been entered but once by mortal man. Their very entrance is now forgotten.

So runs the story. This, at least, is fact: the great Sacrifice of Honourable Death--the Johâr--was performed at Chitore, and Allah-ud-din, entering victorious, found a silent city.

Given an unscrupulous man, possessed of boundless wealth, and all things are possible in a country distracted by jealousies as India was at this time. And all things were achieved. The frequent incursions, growing year by year on larger scale, of the Moghuls who had already gained foothold to the west and north, were repelled. The Dekkan was finally conquered and annexed by the king's worthless slave and favourite, the eunuch Kafûr, a man whose life was one long tale of infamy. Originally the seat of the great Andhra dynasty, the Dekkan, divided into many principalities, had passed into many hands. In the seventh century King Hârsha had attempted to gather it into his empire, but had been foiled by the skill of Pulikêsin the king, during whose reign the wonderful caves in the Ajanta valley were excavated and adorned.

Another dynasty, another king in the eighth century gave to the Dekkan the marvellous rock-cut temple at Ellora. At first a stronghold of the Jain religion, it oscillated between that and Brahmanism, until in the twelfth century the latter finally came uppermost with the Haysâla line of kings.

It was in A.D. 1310 that Kafûr swept through the kingdom, despoiled the capital, laid waste the country, and carried off the reigning Râjah, though its final absorption in the Mahomedan empire was not until A.D. 1327. Kafûr, however, set his mark so far south as Adam's Bridge, opposite Ceylon, the furthest point yet reached by any northern invasion.

This was the zenith of Allah-ud-din's power. His health had yielded to intemperance of all kinds; he became more and more despotic, more and more cruel, more and more under the baleful influence of his creature Kafûr.

Rebellion grew rife. Little Prince Ajey-si's heir, Hâmir, recovered Chitore, Guzerât revolted, and almost ere it was annexed, the Dekkan rose and expelled half the Mahomedan garrison.

These tidings coming to the already suffering king brought on paroxysms of rage, and he died, his end accelerated by poison administered by that slave of his worst passions, Kafûr. Thereupon followed the usual murders and sudden deaths of an Indian succession, followed by the death of Kafûr, and the final enthroning of Allah-ud-din's third son, Mobârik. He was a weak sensualist, who, nevertheless, was human. So he removed some of his father's more oppressive taxes, and did away with his restrictions on trade and property. After which he and his creature Khûshru, a converted Hindu slave, outraged all decency, and gave way to sheer dissolute devilry, which ended in the master's murder by his favourite, who thereinafter snatched at the crown.

But this man even the Mahomedan India of the time could not stand. Mobârik, "whose name and reign would be too infamous to have a place in the records of literature, did not our duty as historian oblige us to the disagreeable task," was bad enough. Khûshru was worse. So he was killed, and a worthy warrior, by name Ghâzi-Beg Toghluk, who had repelled many invasions of Moghuls, was invited to the throne.

Ferishta's description of this is rather nice, and bears quotation:

"So they presented him with the keys of the city, and he mounted his horse and entered Delhi in triumph. When he came in sight of the Palace of a Thousand Minarets" (this must have been somewhere close to the Kutb) "he wept, and cried aloud:

"'Oh, subjects of a great empire! I am no more than one of you who unsheathed my sword to deliver you from oppression, and rid the world of a monster. If, therefore, any member of the royal family remain, let him be brought, that we his servants should prostrate ourselves before his throne. But if none of the race of kings have escaped the bloody hands of usurpation, let the most worthy be selected, and I swear to abide by the choice.'"

Not a bad speech. Small wonder that there followed on it the first historical notice of "chairing"--"the populace, laying hold of him, raised him up, carried him to the throne, and hailed him as Shâhjahân, Master of the World; but he chose the more modest title of Ghiâss-ud-din...."

For the curse of Sidi Dervish had been effectual, and the House of Khilji was extinct.

Warned by the past, one of the first acts of Ghiâss-ud-din was formally to nominate his successor from amongst his four sons. He made an unfortunate choice, for there is little doubt but that Prince Jonah was accessory to his father's death four years afterwards, when he invited him into a wooden palace which promptly fell upon, and crushed the king and five of his attendants.

Neither was Prince Aluf-Khân--under which title Jonah became heir-apparent--a lucky choice in other ways. He lost a large army in attempting to regain Deogîri, and was not particularly successful against the Râjpûts. The king, meanwhile, spent most of his energy in building a new citadel at Delhi, the ruins of which still survive under the name of Tôghlukabâd. A fine, massive piece of work it must have been, with its huge blocks of dressed stone and curiously sloping walls, reminding one of a modern dam.

So with the death of honest Ghiâss appears the typical Eastern potentate, complete as to arrogance, cruelty, power, and pride, who for seven-and-twenty years was to cry, "Off with his head!" to any one he pleased.

He seems to have been clever. We are told that he was the "most eloquent and accomplished prince of his time, and that he was not less famous for his gallantry in the field than for those accomplishments which render a man the ornament of private society."

It sounds well, but, judged by his acts, it appears doubtful if pride and arrogance had not made Mahomed Toghluk partially insane. No other supposition explains the extraordinary contradictions of his rule. He "established hospitals and almshouses for widows and orphans on the most liberal scale," but "his punishments were not only rigid and cruel, but frequently unjust. So little did he hesitate to spill the blood of God's creatures, that one might have supposed his object was to exterminate the human species." On more than one occasion, going out for a royal hunt, he suddenly announced his intention of hunting men, and not beasts; so the unoffending peasantry were driven in by the beaters and slain as if they were blackbuck. He imagined and started vast schemes for conquering China and Persia, in order to enrich his coffers, yet bribed a Moghul invasion to return whence it came by a huge subsidy which completely crippled him. He attempted to face famine--one of the worst India has ever known--by projects for agricultural improvements, and then added to the horrors and distress by ordering Delhi to be evacuated, and its inhabitants on pain of death to migrate with his court to Deogîri, which he rechristened Dowlutabâd, or the "Abode of Wealth." He founded an admirably regulated postal system throughout the country, but the roads themselves were bad, and absolutely unsafe for travellers. He tried to escape insolvency by coining copper at silver values--the first instance of token money in India--then fell upon his people tooth and nail because the public credit was not stable enough to stand the strain. Consequently, vast tracts of land were left uncultured, whole families fled to the woods to subsist on rapine and murder, while famine desolated wide provinces.

But the potentate remained a potentate. So strong was his grip on the people, that when, after having once been allowed to return to Delhi he again ordered them to Dowlutabâd, they obeyed, leaving "the noblest metropolis, the Envy-of-the-World, a resort for owls, and a dwelling-place for the beasts of the desert."

Thus it was not the hand of an assassin, but a surfeit of fish which eventually carried him off. This much may be said in his favour--he was no sensualist.

He was succeeded by his cousin Ferôze in A.D. 1351, who until his death, at the great age of ninety, in A.D. 1388, bent his whole mind towards restoring peace and prosperity to his distracted empire; which, while the largest, nominally, that India had ever seen, was in reality at the breaking-up point from sheer disorder. His great panacea appears to have been irrigation, and many an old canal in India dates from the time of Ferôze Toghluk. Despite his efforts, however, the empire began to disintegrate. The Dekkan and Bengal gained independence by the reception of ambassadors at court, and various smaller states seceded into autonomy. India was, in fact, at this time semi-fluid, half-gelatinous. Its form was for ever changing. Each principality at one moment, amœba-like, reached out an invertebrate arm and clutched at something, the next it had shrunken to a mere piece of jelly, quiescent, almost lifeless. And Ferôze Toghluk's hand was not strong enough for the task set it. Yet he was a good and kindly soul, as is evidenced by the resolutions which he caused to be engraven on the mosque he built at Ferôzebad (another portion of Old Delhi). In one he abolished judicial mutilation, claiming that God in His goodness having conferred on him the power, had also inspired him with the disposition to end these cruelties. Another orders the repeal of many vexatious taxes and licences. Yet another reduced the share of war plunder due to the sovereign from four-fifths to one-fifth, while it increased that of the troops to four-fifths from one. A fourth recorded his determination to pension for life all soldiers invalided by wounds or by age. A fifth declared his intention of severely punishing "all public servants convicted of corruption, as well as persons who offer bribes." The latter being a nicety in legal morality which one would hardly expect of the fourteenth century.

Ferôze was followed in about six years by no less than five kings whose only record of interest is that they stood by and watched the great empire which Kutb-ud-din Eîbuk had wrested from the Râjputs, and which Allah-ud-din had consolidated by sheer tyranny, fall to bits. Anarchy reigned supreme, civil war raged everywhere, and in Delhi itself two nominal kings were in arms the one against the other when, in A.D. 1398, news came that for an instant checked quarrel, and made all India hold its breath.

The Moghuls, under Timur, on their way to Delhi, had crossed the Indus, The long-dreaded, ofttimes-delayed invasion had come at last.

THE INVASION OF TIMUR

A.D. 1388 TO A.D. 1389

There is one cry of terror which from time immemorial has echoed out over the wide wheatfields of Northern India. Sometimes it has come when the first sword-points of the new-sprouted seed give a green shading to the sandy soil, and the flooding water from the wells which cease not night or day follows obedient to the naked brown figure with a wooden spud which directs it first to one patch of corn, then to another. Sometimes, again, it has come when the village has emptied itself upon the harvest field, when men are cutting and threshing, and women winnowing, while the children lie asleep in the great heaps of chaff, or make quaint images out of the straw.

At times, again, but not often, it has come, as it did in the Mutiny days, when the bare burnt fields lie idle, resting against next crop-season, and the peasant women sit outside the breathless village, picking and carding and spinning. But the cause is always the same: a knot of hurried horsemen showing on the level horizon, messengers, as it were, from the outside world beyond village ken.

"The Toork! The Toork!" rises the cry, and in an instant jewels are torn off and hidden, everything that can be concealed concealed, and with a wild prayer to some god for protection, the ultimate atom of India awaits destruction or dishonour or death in apathetic despair.

It must have needed a bitter biting indeed to have engraven this fear so indelibly on the Hindu heart.

Yet looking back on the four hundred years of Mahomedan inroads which we have just followed, small wonder can be felt at the persistence of this terror. How many times had not this knot of horsemen appeared, done their worst, and disappeared, leaving behind them miserable, dishonoured women, maddened by the sight of their murdered husbands, and the very dead boy-babies at their breasts.

A horrible legacy of fear, in truth!

And of late, in addition to the endless incursions of the Mahomedans proper, there had been persistent appearances and reappearances of the yellow-skinned Moghuls. From north, from east, from west, this rising race had ridden, had ravaged, and had returned whence they came.

In truth they were more of a rising race than these poor peasants knew; more so than the effete monarchies and nobilities of Mahomedan India realised. Close on a hundred and fifty years before, Chengiz Khân, a Moghul chief, had barbarously swept through the plains of North-Western Asia, and now his descendant Timur--though born in comparatively civilised times, and by profession a Mahomedan--was to carry on the destruction which his ancestor had begun. History hardly presents a more terrible personality than that of this man, as judged by the autobiography he left behind him. It is one of the most remarkable records ever written. Here is no mere rude barbarian, but a wily man of the world, ready to practise on every weakness of his fellows, ready with cant, with real devotion, full of courage as well as full of address, and with and through it all the most unscrupulous selfishness, the utmost admiration for his own perfidies.

But he was a great man; in his way, a genius. There is nothing in its way finer than the record he gives in this autobiography of his--which he entitles, "Political and Military Institutions of Tamârleng," or the Lame Timur--of his reasons for advancing on India, and his experiences there.

"I ordered 1,000 swift-footed camels, 1,000 swift-footed horses, and 1,000 swift-footed infantry to bring me word respecting the princes of India. I learnt that they were at variance one with the other.... The conquest appeared to me easy, though my soldiers thought it dangerous.

"Resolved to undertake it, and make myself master of the Indian Empire.

"Did so."

Brief to the point almost of bathos; but surely a brevity which brings with it a shiver as at something inhuman in its strength.

So in September 1398 the "admirably regulated horse and foot post" which Mahomed Toghluk had given to India, brought news that a huge host of Turks and Tartars and Moghuls, led by Timur in person, had crossed the river Indus by a bridge of rafts and reeds.

The tidings seem to have brought about no concerted action in India. It was too much given over to anarchy for cohesion. And so the celebrated march of the "Lame Firebrand of the World" began in earnest.

It is a horrid record of brutal butchery. As if fascinated by some unholy spell, the inhabitants of India seem to have yielded their necks to the smiter, without, as Ferishta puts it, "making one brave effort to save their country, their lives, or their property."

His first halt was at Talûmba, a strong fort and city at the junction of the Chenâb and the Râvi rivers. He plundered the town, but as the fort was strong, left it comtemptuously alone and went forward on his path of desolation and destruction. Not a village was left unburnt, not a male left alive, not a female unravished. The next pause was at a town famous for the shrine of a Mahomedan saint, for whose sake he spared the inhabitants, and after (doubtless) saying his prayers, dutifully pressed on to Bhatnîr, the headquarters of the Great Lunar Race of Râjputs. This he reached in two days by forced marches, the last being one of close on 100 miles. Here his ferocity broke beyond bounds. He slew by thousands the helpless country folk who had fled for protection to their Râjah, and who, overcrowding the city, were huddled together like sheep beyond its walls. The garrison gave battle, but, hard-pressed, sought refuge in the citadel, and Timur, gaining the gates of the town ere they could be shut, drove the unfortunates from street to street. Overmastered by numbers, by sheer terror, the place capitulated on terms. To no purpose. For, even while the Tartar was receiving the delegates and accepting their presents, orders were given to sack and slay. Whereupon, struck with horror, with despair, the cry, "Johâr! Johâr!" arose from the men, wives and children were slain, and the Râjputs sought nothing but revenge and death. "The scene," says Ferishta, "was awful. The inhabitants in the end were cut off to a man, though not before some thousands of the Moghuls had fallen."

This so exasperated Timur that every living soul in the city was massacred, and the place itself reduced to ashes.

To Sarâswati, to Fatehâbad, to Râjpur, he carried his flaming sword; then at Kâitul he rejoined the main body of his army--for he had only commanded a flying column hitherto--and settled his face fairly towards his goal--Delhi.

But now abject fear was beforehand with him, and he marched through desolate fields, deserted houses, empty cities.

A strange march of Death indeed! The young green wheat showing green as ever, the hearth fires still burning bravely, the litter and leavings of human life lying about in the sunlight; but life itself?--nowhere! Everything, gold, gems, home, country left, but that had gone. It must have angered the horde of butchers to find no blood with which to wet their swords, to hear no piteous cries for mercy as they rode. The very hands must have grown listless as they gathered in the unresisting spoils.

Perhaps that was the reason why Timur, arriving within touch of Delhi, sought to revive his soldiery by an order for the wholesale slaughter of all prisoners.

And all this time at Delhi the puppet-king Mahmûd, the last degenerate scion of the House of Toghluk, had sate in the massive palace of his forefathers, waiting.

"Delhi dûr ust."

["It is a far cry to Delhi."]

This had been his hope as he waited. But early in January an old man-- for Timur was now past sixty years of age, and his life had been a strenuous one--crossed the river with a small body of seven hundred horse, and calmly reconnoitered Tôghlukabad.

Seven hundred horse only! Mahmûd took courage, sallied out with five thousand, was contemptuously driven within the walls again, until Timur, "having made the observations he wished, repassed the river, and rejoined his army."

A good general this, trusting to no Intelligence Department, but to his own eyes.

That night the one thousand prisoners (the figure is that given by Mahomedan historians) were slain in cold blood. Next day, 13th January, he and his army forded the river without opposition and entrenched themselves close to the gates of Tôghlukabad. Despising the astrologers, who pronounced the 15th of January to be an unlucky day, Timur chose it for his attack, and drew up his army in order of battle. His foes were barely worthy of such trouble. They certainly returned the challenge by marching out, elephants covered in mail, warriors in armour, pennants flying, drums sounding; but at the first charge of Moghul horsemen, the elephants' drivers were unseated, and leviathan in terror fled to the rear, communicating confusion to the ranks.

So almost without a blow the Tartar found himself by nightfall at the very gates of the city.

A fateful night! The king fled in it, the chief men in the city resolved during it on submission, and were promised protection on payment of a heavy indemnity.

Next morning, Timur was proclaimed Emperor in every mosque, guards were placed at Treasury and gates, and troops sent to enforce immediate payment.

What followed may have been due to insubordination on the part of the pillaging soldiery; on the other hand, it occurred far too often in Timur's career to make us quite unsuspicious of perfidy. Anyhow, whether by collision between the populace and the troops, or by mere wanton violence, resistance was aroused even amid the panic-stricken inhabitants, and the greatest tragedy Delhi has ever seen began. Once more the cry, "Johâr! Johâr!" echoed out helplessly, the gates were overpowered by mob-force and closed, the houses were set on fire, and while women and children perished in the flames, the men fought desperately to death in the streets, hand to hand with their butchers. The lanes were barricaded by the bodies of the dead, lives were sold dear, and a scene of carnage beyond description ensued; until the gates being once more forced, the whole Moghul army was let loose, to deal inevitable death on the almost unarmed crowd.

Five days afterwards Timur offered up to God "his sincere and humble tribute of grateful praise for his victory" in the splendid mosque of marble which Ferôze Toghluk had built on the banks of the Jumna.

Once more we are reminded of that idle rhyme--

"Three thousand Frenchmen sent below,
Praise God from whom all blessings flow."

The primitive passions change very little.

After that he departed, his work accomplished, his task done. He took with him plunder inconceivable, and with a few minor excursions to "put every inhabitant to the sword," made his way back to Samarkhûnd by the Kâbul route. To the last exposing himself to every fatigue, every privation which he imposed upon his army.

So he quitted India, taking no trouble to make provision for holding the empire he had won. He left anarchy, famine, pestilence, behind him. For two months Delhi was a city of the dead, and for thirty-six years India owned no government either in name or in reality. Dazed, depopulated, despairing, she dreamt evil dreams--dreams almost worse than the nightmare of the past.

No greater proof of the totality of Timur's destruction is needed than this--a whole generation had to pass away ere men could be found with hope enough wherewith to face the future.

DEVASTATED INDIA

A.D. 1389 TO A.D. 1514

For over a hundred and twenty years India remained free from a master hand. It is true that the puppet-king Mahmûd, who had fled from Delhi on that fateful night of the 15th of January 1389, returned to it, first as a mere pensioner, afterwards as nominal ruler; but the whole continent had split up into petty principalities governed by Mahomedan rulers. Guzerât, Mâlwa, Kanauj, Oude, Kârra, Jaûnpur, Lahôre, Dipalpûr, Multân, Byâna, Kalpi, Mahôba, these were but a few of the countless kings who rose up and warred with one another.

Beyond these, again, to the southward, lay the great kingdom of the Dekkan, which one Allah-ud-din Hassan had reft bloodlessly from Mahomed Toghluk. This Hassan had a curious history. The servant of a Brahman astrologer, he appears to have lived a life absolutely without colour, until one day, when ploughing, the share caught in a chain attached to an old copper vessel full of antique gold coins. This treasure trove introduced him to the king's notice; he was made captain of a hundred horse, so rose gradually to power. And wherever he went he took with him his former master, the Brahman Ganga, who long years before had predicted for him great distinction. When Hassan reached royalty, the Brahman became finance-minister, and from this fact the whole dynasty was called Bâhmani, or Brâhmani. It lasted for close on two hundred years; a most unusual stability for India. But ere the period now before us had closed, the Dekkan also had split up into five separate states--Bîjapur, Golcônda, Berâr, Ahmudnâgar, Hyderabâd.

About the time of Timur's invasion, the Brâhmani dynasty was in the zenith of its fortunes. We have in the description of it, then, a picture of Eastern despotism that fits in with the preconceived ideas of most Westerns on this subject. Absolute power, untold wealth, munificence, cruelty, passion, pride, prejudice; all the concomitants of an Eastern potentate are there. The celebrated Turquoise Throne itself fills the imagination with its "enamel of a sky-blue colour, cased in gold which was in time totally concealed by the number of precious ornaments"; but when we add to this the golden ball over the throne "all inlaid with jewels, on which sate a bird of paradise composed entirely of precious stones, in whose head was a ruby of inestimable price," we desire no more. The Eastern glamour is complete.

So the kings of the Dekkan went on ruling, every now and again letting themselves loose on some minor râjah, and killing a few thousand Hindus for the sake of the Faith; every now and again ruling wisely and well, but as often as not badly and brutally. Sometimes they combined the epithets, as in the case of Mahomed Shâh Bâhmini, A.D. 1358-1375, during whose reign it is said "all ranks of the people reposed in security and peace," and that "nearly five hundred thousand unbelievers fell by the swords of the warriors of Islâm, by which the population of the Carnatic was so reduced that it did not recover for several ages"!!!

Some of these precious potentates died in their beds, a larger proportion of them were assassinated. This much, at any rate, may be said of Indian public opinion in these times, that it sided with morality, for the most condign punishments on record are invariably meted out to the biggest villains. Perhaps the most picturesque of these records is that concerning King Ghiâss-ud-din Bâhmini and Lâlchi, one of the principal Turki slaves of the household. This man possessed a daughter of exquisite beauty, whom the seventeen-year-old young monarch happened to see and instantly desired. The father refused, the king persisted. So Lâlchi laid his plans. He invited the passion-struck lad to an entertainment at his house, plied him with wine, and then induced him to order his attendants to withdraw, in order that the exquisite beauty might appear. The half-intoxicated prince attempted flight when Lâlchi returned from the harem not with a girl, but a naked dagger, rolled down some steps, and the next instant both his eyes were blinded; whereupon Lâlchi coolly sent for the royal attendants one by one, as if by the king's order, and put them to death severally as they appeared. As these were mostly nobles and officials of high rank, he found no difficulty in deposing Ghiâss-ud-din, who had only reigned for six weeks!

The history of the Dekkan finds echo in the kingdoms of Kandeish, Mâlwa, Guzerât, all of which came into existence about the same period. But in addition to these Mahomedan principalities a great and powerful Râjput confederacy--for the semifeudal system of the race was antagonistic to empire--was springing up among the hills in Mêwar, the "middle mountain" country now called Oudipur, and in the deserts of Mârwar or the "Region of Death," now called Jodhpur and Jeysulmeer. The two former kingdoms were ruled by princes of the Sun, but Jeysulmeer claimed, as it does now, descent from the Moon.

Such slight differences, however, were as naught before a common enemy, and ever since Mahmûd of Ghuzni had defeated Anangpal, Lunar king of Delhi--representative of a dynasty which, legend has it, had lasted since the days of Yudishthira of Mâhâbhârata fame--down through the time when Mahomed Ghori had annihilated Prithvi-Râj, grandson of the last Anangpal, and Kutb-uddin Eîbuk, his Slave-general, had carried on his butchery, until the present day, the common enemy of every Râjput had been the Mahomedan.

So, naturally, the conflict of the conquerors was the opportunity of the vanquished.

It is true that the young Ajey-si, saved from the sack of Chitore by so much bloodshed, did not fulfil his father's hope that the child should recover what the man had lost, but his appointed heir, Hamîr, more than redeemed the promise; for, during the two centuries following on the recapture of his kingdom, it rose to a pitch of power and solidarity never before touched, and received the homage of all surrounding principalities. The story of Hamîr's success is a strange one, and is reminiscent of the legend of Sir Gawaine, or the Knight of Courtesy, since the success came as a consequence of chivalry to womanhood.

Hamîr's perseverance had brought him to the very walls of Chitore, but the real struggle for possession was before him. At this juncture the city gates opened, and a peaceful procession passed out, bearing the recognised symbol of a marriage proposal, a cocoa-nut. It came from the mercenary but highborn Hindu Governor of Chitore, offering his daughter as a preliminary to peace. The young prince's advisers voted for a return of the offer. Hamîr bid its retention, boldly saying that, come what might, his feet would thus tread the rocky steps which his ancestors had trodden.

Forth, therefore, with but the stipulated five hundred horse, went the Bridegroom-Prince. He was met at the gate by the bride's five brothers, gloomy of face, solemn of mien. But on the city portal was no mystical triangle of marriage, no wedding garlands decorated the streets. Yet ceremony was not absent. The ancient hall of his ancestors was filled with chiefs awaiting him with folded hands; the bride's father welcomed him gravely. One can imagine the young man, ready to take what the gods chose to give for the sake of a hold on Chitore, waiting while the bride was led forth.

No cripple this! The young heart must have breathed more freely as the slim, veiled figure stood silent by his side. A promise of beauty here, surely! The young blood shivered through his veins, as the strong sword-hand met the soft, slender fingers; then seemed to flow almost tumultuously towards the new, the unknown, as the attendant priest knotted the marriage garments together. Yet still no smile, no word of congratulation. What did it mean? What matter! it was for the sake of Chitore.

So to the marriage chamber, where the family priest lingered hesitatingly to preach patience.

Patience! with a bride before one, every fold of whose veiled figure told of beauty!

Beauty indeed! but--one glance was enough--she was a widow!

He had been tricked indeed! A virgin widow, no doubt, and beautiful, exceedingly; yet still a widow, and accursed, almost unclean.

What did she say to him? History does not tell us. All we know is that "her kindness and vows of fidelity overcame his sadness."

Doubtless, the pity which is akin to love swayed him, but it was her cleverness, and not her kindness that gained the victory. For that strange marriage night was spent in a woman teaching a man how to win back his ancestral kingdom. Not by war, that was too crude. The people must be won over. Let her husband ask next morning as the marriage gift which no Râjput bridegroom is refused, for one Jâl, a humble scribe of the city.

So Hamîr went home burdened by a widow-wife and a scribe.

A year passed, and a prince was born; another year spent in what wiles and guiles only the widow mother and her scribe adviser knew, and the little prince, sick, had to be taken back to Chitore in order to be placed for healing before the shrine of Vyan-Mâta. Taken, oddly enough, while his grandfather, the mercenary governor, was away with most of the troops on an expedition.

A beautiful injured queen, a lovely baby prince, a hero husband ready to regain the throne of his ancestors, a devoted adherent prepared for every emergency; these were the factors in the sudden acclaim by which Hamîr, in consequence of his courtesy, was able once more to raise the standard of the Sun on the walls of Chitore. Where it remained for long years gloriously, comparatively peacefully; for while in Mahomedan Delhi no less than twenty-five monarchs were needed--such was the perpetual procession of assassinations, rebellions, dethronement--to bridge the period between Kutb-ud-din's seizure of Delhi and Timur's invasion of India, in Chitore--that is to say, Mêwar, or as it is now called, Oudipur--eleven princes had sufficed to fill the throne.

But in addition to Mêwar we have to reckon with Mârwar, or Jodhpur and Jeysulmeer. The former, however, was at this time a comparatively modern principality. After the defeat of Jâichand, the Râjah of Kanauj--who had so unavailingly performed the Sai-nair rite at which Prithvi-Râj had carried off the Princess Sunjogâta--his grandsons Shiv-ji and Sâyat-Râm, set out towards the great Indian Desert, hoping to carve fresh fortune from its barren stretches. They succeeded; but it was not until A.D. 1511 that Prince Jodha laid the foundation of a new capital, and brought Mârwar into line with the other great Râjput powers.

Jeysulmeer had a longer record. Headquarters of the Bhatti clan, its legendary history goes back to the eighth century; but from A.D. 1156 the chronicle is fairly continuous, and is full of romance and interest. Proud, passionate, clean-lived princes, these descendants of the Moon--for they were of the Yâdu race--seem to have been. One of them, still quite a lad, giving way to Berserk rage, struck his foster-brother. The blow was returned; whereupon, stung with shame, both at the insult and the lack of self-control which brought it about, the offender stabbed himself with his dagger. Another still more typical story is told of the passing of Râwul (an honorific title equalling Râjah) Chachîk, who, finding disease his master, sent an embassy to the Mahomedan ruler of Multân, begging from him the last favour of *jûd-dan*, or the gift of battle, "that his soul might escape by the steel of his foeman, and not fall sacrifice to slow disease."

The challenge was accepted, after the Mahomedan had been assured that honourable death was the sole end and aim.

So on the appointed day Râwul Chachîk, followed by seven hundred nobles, who, having shared all his victories, were prepared to follow him to death, marched out "to part with life."

"His soul was rejoiced, he performed his ablutions, worshipped the sword, bestowed charity, and withdrew his thoughts from this world. The battle lasted four hours, and the Yâdu prince fell with all his kin, after performing prodigees of valour. Two thousand Mahomedans fell beneath their swords, and rivers of blood flowed in the field; but the Bhatti gained the abode of Indra, who shared His throne with the hero."

Such, then, were the people who were gradually recovering some of the possessions and the prestige which they had lost when Prithvi-Râj fell victim to Mahomed Shahâb-ud-din Ghori.

Meanwhile, at Delhi the thirty-six years of kinglessness passed into seventy-three, during which the government was in the hands of three comparatively strong men, Belôl Lodi, Secûnder Lodi, Ibrahîm Lodi.

The first was a warrior, the second a bigot, the third a tyrant. Of the three, Belôl did most for his country, since at his death his empire extended eastwards as far as Benares.

Secûnder seems to have subordinated policy to religion. He destroyed every image and temple which he could see, or of which he could hear, and promptly put to death a Brahman who preached that "all religions, if sincerely practised, were equally acceptable to God."

Tolerance was not a virtue in those days.

It was during the reign of Ibrahîm Lodi that Babar, the first of the great Moghuls, entered India in A.D. 1514; but this was an event of such vast importance that it will be necessary to hark back some thirty years to the little kingdom of Ferghâna, where Babar was born on the 14th of February, A.D. 1483.

THE GREAT MOGHULS

BABAR THE ADVENTURER

A.D. 1483 TO A.D. 1514

Born on St Valentine's Day, A.D. 1483, the boy-baby, who was hereafter to be called Zâhir-ud-din Mahomed, and nicknamed Babar, must have been plentifully supplied with fairy godmothers, for he was gifted with almost every possible gift.

To begin with, he had good looks, even judging by the curious portraits of those days. Then, there can be no question of his ability as a soldier, while intellectually he would have been remarkable in any age. Besides this, he was possessed of the true artistic temperament to a quite unusual degree; he was painter, poet, author, and in the smallest thing that he wrote showed unerring literary skill and taste.

Beyond, and above all, however, he had that nameless charm which makes him, surely, the most delightful personality known to history.

Given such a man, it would be sheer perversity to treat of him solely in reference to the part he played in India, as this would be to deprive ourselves of no less than thirty-six years of the very best of company.

So let us begin at the very beginning. It is possible to do this with an accuracy unobtainable with any other Indian king--or, indeed, with any king of any clime--because Babar left to the ages an autobiography of himself, his thoughts, his acts, his failures, his successes, which is, truly, a quite extraordinary record. Between the covers lies a whole, real, live, human being.

It opens, however, with these words, "In the year 1494, and in the twelfth year of my age, I became King of Ferghâna." We have therefore to go back eleven years for the birth of Babar. Before doing this, a glance round the world will give us the *milieu* in which our hero was to play his part.

Briefly, then, Vasco da Gama had but just discovered India, Henry VII. was King of England. Michelangelo was revolutionising the world of art, Copernicus creating that of science. For the rest, a hundred years had passed since Timur the "Earth Trembler" had shaken literally the whole world; for his grip on it had reached West to Moscow and East to China. Yet a hundred years further back again Chengiz Khân had swept over the same ground like a devastating flame.

Babar had both these unamiable ruffians as ancestors, but, apparently, was by no means proud of his Mongal or Moghul descent. He called himself a Turk, and wrote hardly of the race whose name, by the irony of fate, was to be attached to the dynasty he founded.

> "If the Moghul race had an angel's birth,
> It still would be made of the basest earth;
> Were the Moghul name writ in thrice-fired gold,
> It would ring as false as it did of old;
> From a Moghul's harvest sow never a seed
> For the seed of a Moghul is false indeed!"

Babar was the son of Omâr-Shaîkh, King of Ferghâna, or as it is now called, Khôkand. At his birth a courier was sent post-haste to inform his maternal grandfather, the Khân of the Mongols, who, despite his seventy years, came back post-haste to join in the festivities, and--his uncouth, Mongolian tongue trippling over the polished Persian name Zâhir-ud-din (the Evidence of Faith)--to dub the child Babar, or "the tiger," a nickname which stuck to him for life. A fine old man this grandfather of Babar's, and a fine old woman his grandmother must have been. A woman not to be trifled with, to judge by her action when one Jâimul-Khân, having for a time defeated her husband, seized her and made her over to one of his officers.

Isa-Begum raised no puerile objections. She received her new master quite affably, but once he was within her chamber door she locked it, bade her maids stab him to death, fling the body to the street, and send this message to Shâikh-Jâimul: "I am the wife of Yunâs. Contrary to law, you gave me to another man, so I slew him. Come and slay me if you choose."

The erring Jâimul must have had good in him, for, struck by her courage, he restored her honourably to her husband.

At the age of five Babar was betrothed to his cousin Ayêsha, and the next six years must have been spent at the millstone of education, since this was all the schooling Fate granted him, and he emerged from it with two languages at his fingers' end, and an amount of literary skill and general knowledge which was fairly surprising. His father, still in the prime of life, was killed by an accident while away from his capital, and the incident is thus described by the boy-king, who, 36 miles away, "immediately mounted in the greatest haste, and, taking such followers as were at hand, set out to secure my throne."

"The river flows under the walls of the castle, which is situated on the very edge of a high precipice, so that it serves as a moat. And some of the ravines down to it being scarped to support the castle, in all Ferghâna stands no stronger fortress. Thus one of the walls giving way, my father, feeding his pigeons, was, with the pigeons and the pigeon-house, precipitated from the top of the steep, and so himself took flight to another world."

A quaint description, giving a picture which lingers in the mind's eye. The fortress hanging over the abyss, the king, in Eastern fashion, making his pigeons tumble for their corn. Then the sudden slip, and a startled soul among the startled white wings on its way to another world. Even the body which the soul had left remains alive for ever in Babar's words:--

"My father was of lowish stature, had a short, bushy beard, and was fat. He used to wear his tunic very tight, and as he drew himself in when he put it on, when he let himself out the strings often burst. He plaited his turban without folds, and let the end hang down. He was but a middling shot with the bow, but had such uncommon force with his fists that he never hit a man but he knocked him down. His generosity was large, and so was his whole nature. He was a humane king, and played a great deal at backgammon."

Peace be to thine ashes, oh, Omâr-Shâikh! Even after all the centuries we seem to know the man himself, as we read the words in which his son has pictured him.

So, let us hark back to Ferghâna, the little kingdom watered by the river Jaxârtes, and give one more extract from Babar's journal to show what manner of place it seemed to the eleven-year-old king.

"Ferghâna is situate on the extreme boundary of the habitable world. It is a valley clipped by snowy mountains on all sides but the west, whither the river flows, and on which side alone it can be entered by foreign enemies. It is of small extent, but abounds in grain and fruits. Its melons are excellent and plentiful. There are no better pears in the world. Its pheasants are so fat that four persons may dine on the stew of one and not finish it. Its violets are particularly elegant, and it abounds in streams of running water. In the spring its tulips and roses blow in great profusion, and there are mines of turquoise in the mountains, while in the valley the people make velvet of a crimson colour."

Surely this description is sufficient, not only to show us Ferghâna, but also to give us a clear idea of the boy who saw it thus. Truly the temptation to quote from this delightful record is well nigh irresistible, but space forbids, for there is much to say of Babar as poet, painter, musician, astronomer, knight-errant, soldier-lover, king, and *bon vivant*. He was all of these in turn; and in addition, kindly, valorous, courteous. A real paladin if ever there was one.

From the very first he gripped the reins of kingship with a firm hand. And it was no easy task to guide the little kingdom through the dangers which beset it; but he succeeded "through the distinguished valour of my young soldiers" (he himself being but twelve!) in besting his uncles the Kings of Samarkhûnd and Tashkûnd, so holding his own. Shortly after this the young king nearly fell a victim to conspiracy, owing to his confidence in one Hassan-Yukûb, "the best player of leap-frog I have known." From this infatuation he was rescued by his shrewd old grandmother, of whom Babar speaks with sneaking awe: "She was uncommonly far-sighted; few of her sex equalled her in sagacity." This incident evidently sobered him, for he "began to abstain from forbidden meats, and seldom omitted midnight prayers."

For there is always something absolutely translucent in Babar's accounts of himself, and of everything which he heard and saw. It is impossible even for a moment to doubt their accuracy. His self-revelation is frankness itself, and his views of men and manners bring conviction with them.

Ambition seems to have seized on him early, for ere he was fifteen, his uncle the king having died, he marched on Samarkhûnd to make a bid for the throne. And he succeeded. He was Emperor of Samarkhûnd, as his ancestor Timur had been, for exactly one hundred days, during which he appears to have enjoyed himself hugely. One is apt to think of these Eastern cities beyond the verge, as they are now--half-ruined, dreary, dead-alive. But in those days they were centres of commerce, learning, and art. To Samarkhûnd Timur had brought the untold riches of India, her clever craftsmen, her skilled artisans. It was a beautiful, a cultured city, and Babar came to the conclusion "that in the whole habitable world there are few places so pleasantly situated."

His dream of success lasted but those hundred days; then evil news of rebellion at Ferghâna and an appeal for help came from his mother. "I was ill," he writes, "but had not the heart to delay an instant, so being unable to nurse myself, I had a relapse."

He came so near death, indeed, that some of his followers, despairing of life, shifted for themselves, and brought the news of his demise to Ferghâna. Thus when the young king came back to consciousness, it was to find himself without a kingdom; for his friends, believing him dead, had surrendered.

"Thus for the sake of Ferghâna I had given up Samarkhûnd, and now found I had lost the one without securing the other."

Such is his philosophical comment. But Babar's remarks are always inimitable. When they hanged his envoy over the gate of the citadel, he sets down his instant belief that "without doubt Khwaja Kazi was a saint: he was a wonderfully brave man--which is no mean proof of saintship. Other men, brave as they may be, have some nervousness or trepidation in them. The Kazi hadn't a particle of either."

This reverse necessitated two years of wandering in the hills. He took his mother with him and his old grandmother, giving them the best shelter he could find. And wherever he wandered, he himself was always cheerful, always kindly, always ready to enjoy the beauties and the gifts of Nature; especially "a wonderful delicate and toothsome melon, with a mottled skin like shagreen."

Until one day, just as the sun was setting, a solitary horseman bearing a message sped up the valley towards his mountain fastness, and in less than half an hour Babar was up and away through the deepening night in response to those who loved him; and there were many of them. Indeed his capacity for winning over most men to his side is one of his most salient characteristics. He was *bon camarade* with half his world.

An eventful ride this over hill and dale, through darkness and through light. "We had passed three days and three nights without rest, neither man nor horse had strength left," when, hanging on the edge of a hill, the city of his hope showed rose-red in the dawn. Then for the first time fear came. Had he been over-hasty? What if this were a trick to decoy him and his handful of followers to their death?

But "there was no possibility of retreat, no refuge even to which we could retreat. So, having come so far, on we must go. (Nothing happens but by God's will.)"

The trite little sentence of consolation was justified. Babar found himself once more King of Ferghâna; but he promptly lost his kingdom again by attempting to make his ill-disciplined Mongolian troops make restitution to the peasantry of the loot they had taken from them.

He admits his error frankly.

"It was a senseless thing to exasperate so many men with arms in their hands. In war and in statecraft a thing may seem reasonable at first sight, but it needs to be weighed and considered in a hundred lights before it is finally decided upon. This ill-judged order of mine was, in fact, the ultimate cause of my second expulsion."

This was in A.D. 1500, when he was seventeen years old. Still his buoyancy remained, despite his evil fortune, and for the next few months his itinerary is full of the joys of "a capital hunting-ground, with good covers for game," in which he coursed, and shot, and hawked, to his heart's content.

Not for long, however. Samarkhûnd tempted him again in the summer; but he had to retire and seek shelter in the hills once more,

"by dangerous tracks among the rocks. In the steep and narrow ways and gorges which we had to climb, many a horse and camel dropped and fell out. After four or five days we came to the col of Sir-i-Tuk. This *is* a pass! Never did I see one so narrow and steep, or follow paths more toilsome and strait. We pressed on, nevertheless, with incredible labour, through fearful gorges and by tremendous precipices, until, after a hundred agonies and losses, at last we topped those murderous steep defiles and came down on the borders of Kân, with its lovely expanse of lake."

When eighteen he finally managed to conquer Samarkhûnd, and in the same year his first child, a daughter, was born; for he had wedded his cousin Ayêsha while in hiding in the hills. He called the baby "The Glory of Womanhood," and chronicles regretfully that "in a month or forty days she went to partake of the Mercy of God."

Marriage, however, appears to have roused him to no emotion, for he admits first that he had "never conceived a passion for any woman, and indeed had never been so placed as even to hear or witness words of love or amorous discourse"; secondly, that in the beginning of his wedded life, shyness almost overcame affection; "and afterwards," he adds quaintly, "as my affection decreased my shyness increased."

A curious record of clean-living this for an Eastern king in the very hey-day of youth.

Babar's success did not last for long. Two years after he was once more a fugitive, and this time he did not succeed in saving all his womenkind. His favourite sister, older than he was by some years, remained behind, part of the price paid for bare freedom, and entered his victorious enemy's harem. This was a bitter pill to swallow, and Babar never forgot it. This sister figures in the Memoirs of Babar's daughter, Gulbadan, as "Dearest Lady." She seems to have kept her brother's deep devotion to the last.

So for three long years Babar wandered once more. This is perhaps the most exciting portion of his Autobiography. It is absolutely packed full with hair's-breadth escapes, crowded in each word with human interest. We see the young king, now in the very prime of his manhood, standing stripped for his bathe in "a stream that was frozen at the banks, but not in the middle, by reason of its swift current." We watch him "plunge in and dive sixteen times, but the biting chill of the water cut through me." We follow breathlessly the vain endeavour made by him and three trusted friends to induce his frightened troops to rally: "I was constantly turning with my three companions to keep the enemy in check, and bring them up short with our arrows; but we could not make the men stand anyhow." We mourn with him on another occasion his ignorance that "the horsemen who followed were not above twenty or twenty-five, while we were eight." We agree with him that had he "but known their number at first, he would 'have given them warm work.'" We share his faith in his own nimbleness in climbing a hill as the only escape from the arrows of bowmen, and we positively hold our breath in the amazing story of the Garden at Tambal, where he waited for Death, and found Life, and friends, and new hope.

This was the capture of Kâbul. The kingly blood in him craved a kingdom. He felt he must have one if he died for it.

Surely never was claimant for royalty worse fitted out for the quest than was Babar! Even Prince Charlie, with his head in Flora Macdonald's lap, does not come up in forlornness with Zâhir-ud-din Mahomed Babar, who gave his only tent to his mother, and whose followers, "great and small, were more than two hundred and less than three. Most on foot with brogues to their feet, clubs in their hands, and tattered cloaks over their shoulders." Yet a short time afterwards he finds himself, "to my own great surprise," at the head of quite a respectable army.

A short time, again, and he is King of Kâbul; such are the amazing ups and downs of this most unfortunate, most fortunate of princes.

By this time his wife, Ayêsha, had left him, giving as her reason the perfectly true plaint that he did not love her. He had, however, fallen in love with some one else; the woman who was to be the mother of his son Humâyon, and of his three daughters, who were named by Babar's express wish, "Rose-face, Rose-blush, Rose-body." It was at Kâbul that Humâyon was born. At Kâbul, also, Babar lost his mother, whom he helped to carry shoulder high to her grave in the Garden of the New Year, outside the city, "the sweetest spot in all the neighbourhood."

He remained King of Kâbul until he made his first expedition to India in 1514. He gives us detailed accounts of his new kingdom. He seems to know everything that is to be known about it. The names and habits of every animal, bird, and beast, even to the fact that in stormy weather the migratory birds are stopped by the everlasting snows of the Hindu-Kush hills, and so are taken in hundreds by the bird-fowlers. He knows the place where the rarest tulips are to be found, and is unceasing in his praise of three-and-thirty different kinds, one "yellow, double, scented like a rose." Doubtless, the parents of that favourite in modern gardens, "Yellow Rose."

He knows also of the different clans and people of Kâbul, their past history, their present languages. In fact, he knows all things that are possible to vivid vitality, all things that are given to friendly hand and seeing eye.

It was from Kâbul that he went on a visit to his cousins, the Princes of Herât. Here, for the first time, he learnt what luxury meant, for Herât was the home of culture and of ease. At first he is somewhat shocked. There are so many things "contrary to the institutions of Chengiz Khân"--that sacred rule from which his family never deviated.

Then he began to meditate that after all "Chengiz had no divine authority," and that if a "father has done wrong, the son should change it for what is right."

From this to doing at Rome what Rome did is but a step; and yet it seems as if he had kept his vow of drinking no wine sacred while at Herât. Pity he did not keep it so always.

It was in returning to Kâbul by the mountains from his twenty days' visit to the most charming "city in the whole habitable world," that Babar met with the following adventure which shows him at his best. He and his army were lost in the snow, and "met with such suffering and hardship, as I have scarcely endured at any other time of my life."

The poem about it which he sat down to write has not survived, but Babar's prose is sufficient for most things.

"For about a week we went on trampling down the snow. I helped with Kâsim Beg, and his sons, and a few servants. Each step we sank to the waist, or the breast; but still we went on. After a few paces a man became exhausted, and another took his place. Then we dragged forward a horse without a rider. The horse sank to the stirrups and girths, and after advancing ten or fifteen paces, was worn out and replaced by another. It was no time for using authority. Every one who has spirit does his best at such times, and those who have none are not worth thinking about.

"In three or four days we reached a cave at the foot of the Yerrin pass. That day the storm was terrible, and the snow fell so heavily, we all expected to die together. When we reached the cave the storm was at its worst. We halted at the mouth. It seemed small, so I took a hoe and, clearing away the snow, made a resting-place for myself about as big as a prayer-carpet, and found a shelter from the wind in it. Some were for my going into the cave, but I would not. I felt that for me to be within in comparative comfort while my soldiers were in snow and drift would be inconsistent with that fellowship and suffering which was their due. So, remembering the proverb, 'Death in the company of friends is a feast,' I continued to sit in the drift. By bedtime prayers 4 inches of snow had settled on my head and lips and ears."

The description is excellent, and gives a delightful background to the quaint comment with which it finishes: "*N.B.*--That night I caught a cold in my ear."

Then once again the haunting dream of Samarkhûnd, the desire to possess the throne of his ancestor Timur, came to obsess him, and bring disaster. He gained the throne once more, only yet once more to lose it. Whether by his own fault, or because Fortune's wheel had turned for the time, we know not. The Autobiography is silent.

All we know is that in A.D. 1519--that is, when he was thirty-six years of age--he finally gave up the thought of Samarkhûnd, and turned his eyes to India.

Timur had conquered it; why should not he?

THE GREAT MOGHULS

BABAR, EMPEROR OF INDIA

A.D. 1519 TO A.D. 1530

These eleven years are all that India really can claim of Babar's life; yet ever since the day when, after a fatal battle in 1503, he had taken refuge in a shepherd's hut on the Kuh-i-Sulimân hills, and (as he sate eating burnt bread like another Alfred, and looking out to where in the dim distance the wide plain of Hindustan rose up like a sea ending the vast vista of mountains) an old woman, ragged, decrepid, had told him tales of her youth when the earth trembled under Timur--ever since then the idea of India had been part and parcel of his adventurous mind.

To do as his great ancestor had done; that became his ambition. At thirty-six he tried to make that ambition a reality.

How the last twelve years from A.D. 1507 had passed, we have no record. The Memoirs are silent, the Diary has ceased to be written. Why, it is impossible to say. Perhaps Babar felt his life too tame and commonplace for record, especially after his melodramatic youth.

We left, therefore, a young man of four-and-twenty, inclined to be shocked at a wine party, we find him again a man of thirty-six and an inveterate toper. Anything and everything is an excuse for the wine-cup. "Looking down from my tent on the valley below, the watch-fires were marvellously beautiful; that must be the reason, I think, why I drank too much wine at dinner that evening." For Babar is still translucently frank. "I was miserably drunk," is an oft confession, and he does not hesitate to record the fact that he and his companions "sate drinking wine on the hill behind the water-run till evening prayers; when we went to Târdi-Beg's house and drank till midnight--it was a wonderfully amusing and guileless party."

It was the vice of his age. He had resisted it apparently until he was six-and-twenty, and he had every intention of giving it up at a stated time, for he writes in 1521: "As I intended to abstain from wine at the age of forty, and as I now wanted somewhat less than a year of that age, I therefore drank copiously."

One thing may be said in his favour: he never let wine interfere with his activities, either of body or of mind. He was ready, as ever, to detail the flowers he saw in his marches, to expatiate on a beautiful view, to turn a *ghazel* or quatrain, to rise ere dawn, to spend arduous days in the saddle or on foot.

The portraits of him belong to this period, and they show us a man tall, strong, sinewy, with the long straight nose of his race, a broad brow, arched eyes, and a curiously small, sensitive mouth.

Such was the man who conquered India, and in the beginning of his conquests set Timur before himself as an example to such purpose that it is hard to believe that the ardent and bloodthirsty Mahomedan of his first campaign is our sunny, genial Babar.

In fact the taking of Bajâur is sad reading. "The people," writes Babar, "had never seen matchlocks, and at first were not in the least afraid of them, but, hearing the reports of the shots, stood opposite the guns, mocking and playing unseemly antics."

By nightfall, however, they had learnt fear, and "not a man ventured to show his head."

This was, nevertheless, not the first time that we hear of guns and matchlocks in Indian warfare, although it is the first absolutely authentic mention of them. But a hundred and fifty years before this, Mahomed-Shâh Bhâmani, King of Guzerât, is said to have employed them. As a digression, it may be observed that Babar's Memoirs give us an interesting account of the casting of a big gun by one Ustâd-Ali, "who was like to cast himself into the molten metal" when the flow of it ceased ere the mould was full! Babar, however, "cheered him up, gave him a robe of honour," and "succeeded in softening his humiliation." Which, by the way, was unnecessary, since when the mould was opened the mischief was found to be reparable, and the gun, when finished, threw over 1,600 yards.

To return to Bajâur. The influence of Timur was strong upon Babar, and though women and children were spared, the less said about the fate of the town the better. Once or twice in his life the Tartar which lay beneath his culture showed in Babar's actions; but only once or twice. Ere he arrived at the next town he had found an excuse for clemency. He claimed the Punjâb as his by right of inheritance. "I reckoned," he writes, "of the countries which had belonged to the Turk as my own territory, and I permitted no plundering or pillage." An admirable compromise, which allowed him to read his great ancestor's account of his campaign with a clear conscience.

After a short expedition he returned to Kâbul, having set a faint finger-mark on the extreme north of India. In the next five years he is said to have made three more expeditions into the Punjâb, but the Memoirs are again silent as to these, and they appear to have been insignificant. But the idea of Indian conquest was not dead, and in A.D. 1524 it burst forth again into sudden life. The cosmic touch which roused it being the appeal of the rightful heir to the Kingdom of Delhi for help against his nephew Ibrahîm Lodi, who, he said, had usurped the throne. At the same time Babar's governor in the Punjâb begged the emperor to come to his aid.

It was the psychic moment, and Babar was prepared for it. He marched instantly on Lahôre, and finding affairs unsatisfactory, paused ere going further to return to Kâbul, and beat up reinforcements with which to secure his line of retreat. Coming back, he found it necessary to settle the governor, an old Afghân, who had broken into rebellion, and who, girding on two swords, swore to win or die. He did neither, for Babar, catching him red-handed in rebellion with the two swords still hanging round his neck, forgave him--as he was inclined to forgive all men.

So, free at last, he set his face towards Delhi. What the state of India was at this time we know. It was one of countless jealousies, seething rebellions, open disunion--on all sides conquest seemed possible; but Delhi had been the goal of Timur, so it must be the goal of his descendant.

Curiously enough, this last, and in all ways most decisive attack from the North-West on India did not come as those of Mahomed of Ghuzni, of Mahomed Shahâb-ud-din Ghori, and of Timur had come, with the returning flight of migratory birds from the summer coolth of the high Siberian steppes. The birds were winging westward in this April A.D. 1526, when Babar, choosing with the eye of a general the old battle-field on the plain near Panipût, set to work entrenching himself in a favourable position. This was a new method of battle to the Indians. So was the laager which he made out of his seven hundred gun-carriages linked together by raw cow-hide to break a possible cavalry charge, and strengthened by shield shelters for the matchlock men. For a whole week, though the army of Delhi--consisting of a hundred thousand troops and a thousand elephants--lay before him, Babar, whose total force numbered twelve thousand, was neither let nor hindered in his work. But then Sultân-Ibrahîm, who commanded the enemy himself, is briefly dismissed by the man whose whole life had been one long fight, as being "inexperienced, careless in his movements, one who marched without order, halted or retired without method, and engaged without foresight."

It was on the 21st that Babar accepted the challenge which followed on a repulsed night-attack which he attempted in order to draw the enemy.

It is interesting to note the formation Babar adopted. The laagered guns in front; behind them--the line broken at bowshot distances by gaps through which a hundred horsemen could charge abreast--the right and left centre, right and left wing. Behind that again the reserve, and the cavalry left over from the flanking parties at the extreme right and left.

On came the Indians at quick march, aiming at Babar's right; finding the enemy entrenched, they hesitated, and pressure from behind threw them into disorder. In an instant the Mongol cavalry charged through the gaps, took them in rear, discharged their arrows, and galloped back to safety. This is their national manœuvre, and proved once more of deadly effect, as it had done in the days of Timur.

But the battle waged fiercely, uncertainly. At one time Babar's left, over-rash, might have been overwhelmed, but for his watchful eyes, his instant support.

So as the sun rose high, the wavering victory chose the side of the Northerners. The Southerners, driven into their centre, were unable to use what strength they possessed, and by noon Sultân-Ibrahîm himself lay dead, with fifteen thousand of his finest troops. The rest were in full flight. It had been "made easy to me, and that mighty army in the space of half a day was laid in the dust."

So wrote the victor modestly, though there can be no question that the battle was won by superior generalship.

The way was now clear before him. He seized on Delhi and Agra without, apparently, much bloodshed, and immediately distributed the treasures gained amongst his followers, only reserving sufficient for the State to send a silver coin to every living soul in Kâbul, bond or free, and to pay the army and the Government.

He kept nothing for himself; he was not of those to whom gold brings pleasure. Yet in Hindustan he found few things for which he cared. There can be no question that it was a disappointment to him.

"It is a country," he writes, "that has few pleasures to recommend it. It is extremely ugly. All its towers and its lands have a uniform look. Its gardens have no walls; the greater part of it is level plain. And the people are not handsome. They have no idea of the charms of friendly society. They have no good horses, no good flesh, no good grapes, or musk-melons, no ice or cold water, no good food or bread in their bazaars, no baths or colleges, no candles or torches--*never even a candlestick!*"

Poor Babar! It was now the hottest of the hot weather, and the heat in the summer of 1526 "chanced to be unusually oppressive." Hitherto these northern invaders had sought relief from discomfort in return to their cooler climes; but Babar had other aims. He wished to establish himself Emperor of India, and all around him in Mêwar, in Mârwar, in Gwalîor, everywhere save in the line of his victorious march, lay enemies.

He determined to remain, but had to meet as determined an opposition on the part of his troops.

It irritated even his placid good-temper.

"Where is the sense of decency," he writes, "of eternally dinning the same tale into the ears of one who had seen the facts with his own eyes, and formed a calm and fixed resolve in regard to the business in hand? What use was there in the whole army, down to the very dregs, giving me their stupid, uninformed opinions?"

What indeed!

He gave them his in return at a full review.

"Are we to turn back from all we have accomplished and fly to Kâbul like men who have been discomfited! Let no man who calls himself my friend ever again moot such a thing, but if there be any of you who cannot bring himself to stay, let him go!"

Needless to say, this appeal to personal friendship was effectual, though apparently pleasantry passed between the comrades-in-arms.

One wrote on the walls of the fort:--

"Could I but cross the river Sind,
Damned if I would return to Hind."

To which Babar sent the following reply:--

"Babar thanks God who gave him Sind and Ind,
Heat of the plains, chill of the mountain cold.
Does not the scorch of Delhi bring to his mind
Bitter bite of frost in Ghuzni of old?"

He was always writing verses; always, as he puts it, "wandering into these follies. For God's sake, do not think amiss of me for them."

His determination to stick by what he had won proved a great factor for peace. Many of the Mahomedan governors and petty kings acknowledged him as suzerain; he forced others to submission, and, ere the rains fell, bringing a welcome cessation to the fiery heat, he found himself with only Hindus to conquer. He attempted this at first by generosity and kindness.

The son of Hassan-Khân, Râjah of Mêwat (who from his name must have been a converted Hindu), was a prisoner of war. Babar returned him to his father with a friendly message; but the overture failed. No sooner at ease about his son than the chief overtly joined the enemy, and with Râjah Sanga of Mêwar (sixth in succession from Hamîr, whose widow-wife won back Chitore), marched to attack Babar. They met at the ridge of Sîkri, about 20 miles from Agra, where in after years Babar's grandson, the great Akbar, was to found his city of victory.

We can imagine the meeting, for Râjah Sanga, though an old man, was, in his way, Babar's double in chivalry and vitality. Both knew it was war to the death. And the old "Lion of the Râjputs," minus an eye and an arm, lame of leg and with eighty scars of battle on his body, must have taken stock of his foeman with inward admiration.

Here was no weakling, unnerved by luxury, but a man after a Râjput's heart. A man who swam every river he crossed for sheer joy in breasting a strong stream, who lived in the saddle, who, if challenged, would snatch up a comrade in either arm, and run round the battlements of a fort, leaping the embrasures in laughing derision; a man, too, well versed in warfare, better armed, if with a far smaller force at his disposal.

But if Babar had advantages he had also disadvantages. The hot weather had told on his troops, a preliminary reverse at Byâna had unsteadied their nerves, which broke down absolutely when an astrologer, arriving unseasonably from Kâbul, talked about the aspect of Mars and loudly presaged disaster. It needed all Babar's marvellous vitality, all that self-confidence which is the very essence of genius, to keep his followers in hand. For he recognised the virtues of his enemies. He saw that they were animated by one all-vivifying spirit of devotion, of national pride.

To match this, if he could, in his own rough-and-ready hordes of horsemen, he proclaimed a "Jehâd," or Holy War. Yet something more was needed to "stiffen their sinews, and summon up the blood." His own mind reverted, despite his courage, to many a sin of omission and commission. It was a time for repentance, for vows, for anything which would, as it were, bring the fourth dimension into life. So one evening he assembled his troops; before them he broke his jewelled wine-cups and beakers, he emptied the wine of Shirâz, the wine of Tabrêz upon the dust, and solemnly made his confession of sin, his vow of total abstinence. His manifesto began well--"Gentlemen and soldiers! Whoso sits down to the feast of life must end by drinking the cup of death."

It was an inspiration! Wine-cups poured on to the pile, oaths were sworn, from that moment the army plucked up courage. There was no good in further delay. Babar had staked his all on this chance, he was eager to try conclusions. On 12th March he marched his army in battle array for 2 miles, he himself galloping along the line encouraging, giving special orders how each division was to act, how each separate man was to proceed and engage. But it was not until Saturday, the 16th March 1527, that the second great fight between the west and the east, between Mongol and Aryan, Islâmism and Hinduism began, this time on the plains of Kanwâha. What the force of the imperial troops was is unknown; most likely less than one-half of the two hundred thousand said to have been ranged on the Râjput side. In truth, there were almost too many there, and their interests were too divided.

So suspicion of some treachery is not lacking. Be that as it may, both sides fought bravely; but Babar's unusual disposition of his troops, by which fully one-half of his force was held in reserve, seems to have turned the tide of fortune in his direction, and by evening (the battle began at half-past nine in the morning) the last lingering remnant of concerted Râjput resistance was swept away, and Babar was unquestioned Emperor of India. Had he then pressed his victory home, the Râjput power would have been shattered absolutely. But he preferred to take the task in detail. It is a thousand pities that Babar's desire to do justice to this great battle induced him to give it in the grandiloquent and elaborate despatch of his Secretary, instead of in one of his own inimitable descriptions, but we have at least the satisfaction of reading the torrent of abuse with which he greeted the astrologer who--"*most unwisely*"--came to congratulate him on his victory. "Insufferable evil-speaker" is one of the mildest of his epithets; but he gave him a liberal present, and bid him quit the presence and the dominions for ever.

He spent the next few months in attempting to restore order to the Government, and when winter brought the fighting season once more, he marched on the town of Chandêri, which had become a stronghold of the remaining Râjputs. Here he saw, almost contemptuously, the final sacrifice of the *Johâr*. It did not impress him, possibly because he held the previous defence of the fortress to have been poor, half-hearted.

About this time prolonged attacks of fever warned him that he could not in India trifle with his health as he had trifled with it in the north.

He thought once that he had hit on a marvellous febrifuge--the translation of religious tracts into verse!--and he records with interest how one bout ended before he had finished his task; but the effect was not lasting. Still, nothing crippled his extraordinary energy, and so late as March 1529 he writes in his diary:

"I swam across the Ganges for amusement. I counted my strokes, and found that I swam over in thirty-three; then I took my breath and swam back. I had crossed by swimming every river I met, except (till then) the Ganges."<

He was very happy, apparently, in these days. India was at peace under stern military control. At Agra, where he had settled, beautiful gardens were growing up, in which flourished many a flower he had loved in the wild adventurous days of his youth. Nor did he confine himself to old favourites. We read of a wonderful red oleander, unlike all other oleanders, which he found in an ancient garden at Gwalîor. His old love of Nature, too, finds expression in a detailed account of the fauna and flora of his new possessions.

Finally, he was happy in his domestic relations. In the Memoirs of his daughter, Gulbadan, we read of the joyful evening when news came to him that the long-expected caravan from Kâbul was within six miles of the city, when, without waiting for a horse, bareheaded, in slipper-shoon, he had run out to meet his "Dearest-dear," had met her, and walked the weary miles along the dusty road beside her palanquin.

In Babar's Memoirs this stands in a single sentence, pregnant with meaning:--

"On Sunday at midnight I met Mahum again"--

Mahum being the pet name for the wife who had borne him the three daughters whom he loved so well, the son Humâyon of whom he was so proud.

Concerning the latter he writes:--

"I was just talking to his mother about him when in he came" (from Badakhshân). "His presence opened our hearts like rosebuds, and made our eyes shine like torches. The truth is, that his conversation has an inexpressible charm, he realises absolutely the ideal of perfect manhood."

Brave words these; but Babar was ready to stand by them to the death.

The story is a strange one, but it is well authenticated. In October A.D. 1530 Humâyon was brought back to Agra, sick. The physicians despaired of his life, the learned doctors declared that nothing could save him save the Mercy of God, and suggested some supreme sacrifice.

Babar caught at the idea. "I can give my life," he said, "it is the dearest thing I have, and it is the dearest thing on earth to my son."

And in spite of remonstrance--the learned doctors having apparently intended a present to God (through them!) of money or jewels--he adhered to his decision. He entered his son's room, he stood at the head of the bed in prayer, then walked round it three times, solemnly saying the while: "On me be thy suffering."

Was it the extreme nervous, tension acting on a constitution weakened by fever, by hardships of every kind, which made his prayer effectual? Who can say? Certain it is that he died in his forty-ninth year, and Humâyon lived on to die at the same age.

Babar, by his own request, was buried beside his mother in the Garden of the New Year at Kâbul. He rests there within hearing of the running streams, within sight of the tulips and roses which he so dearly loved, for which he had so often longed with a "deep home-sickness and sense of exile."

So the most romantic figure of Indian history vanishes from our ken.

THE GREAT MOGHULS

HUMÂYON

A.D. 1530 TO A.D. 1556

Humâyon was practically the only son of his father. There can be no doubt that Babar regarded Mahum, the mother of the four children of whom he was so passionately fond, Humâyon, Rose-blush, Rose-face, Rose-body, from a different standpoint from his other wives, of whom he seems to have had four. This, however, did not prevent there being three other princes, Kamrân, Hindal, and Âskari, in the direct line of succession. Apparently they must have been somewhat troublesome before Babar's death, since one of his last words to his beloved heir was the hope that kindness and forgiveness should ever be shown to them. And right well did Humâyon keep his promise. Had he been less affectionate, less tender-hearted, he had been a better and a more successful king. His patience was early tried. Almost before the deep and sincere mourning for the kindly dead, which Lady Rose-body describes in her Memoirs, was over, he had to decide between fraternal war and Kamrân's claim to supremacy in the Punjâb. He chose the latter, an initial mistake which cost him dear. There must, indeed, have been some impression abroad that the new king had less fibre than his father, for from the very first Humâyon found himself enmeshed in a perfect network of revolt and conspiracy. He was now a young man of three-and-twenty, tall, extremely handsome, witty, and of the most charming manners. Unfortunately, he had already contracted the opium habit, which, though as yet it had not set its mark on his vitality, undoubtedly disposed him to be more easy-going than even Nature had intended him to be; and that is saying much, for his sweetness of temper is surprising. His whole life appears to have been spent in forgiving injuries which, by all the rules of justice and expediency, he should not have forgiven. Succeeding to his father in A.D. 1530, he was instantly engaged in war--fruitless war. Brave to a fault, not without intelligence, something always seemed to stand between him and success. The story of his failure to relieve Chitore is typical of him. Its widowed Râni, in sore straits to save it for her infant son from the hands of Bahâdur-Shâh, King of Guzerât (one of the many kings who snatched at every opportunity of enlarging their borders), sent a Râm-Rukhi, or Bracelet-of-the-Brother, to Humâyon. Now this Brother-Bracelet is in Râjasthân what a lady's glove was to chivalry. Only in greater degree, for the recipient becomes a brother--a bracelet-bound brother. There is no value in the pledge. It is generally a thin silk cord, to which are attached seven differently-coloured tassels; but once given and accepted by the return of a tiny silken bodice, called a *kachli*, it is an inviolable tie. In her extremity Kurnâtavi sent hers to Humâyon, whose fame as a puissant knight had reached her ears. He was enchanted with the romance of the idea, and instantly left the campaign on which he was engaged to go to her rescue. And then? Then he dallied. Then he became involved in a wordy, witty, pedantic war in verse with Bahâdur-Shâh, in which much point was laid on the resemblance of the name Chitore to some other word; in the midst of which the city fell, and suffered yet one more sack.

But the most memorable event of the early years of his reign was, however, the siege of Chunar, where he found himself first matched against the man who was eventually for a time to wrest his kingdom from him, and send him out a wanderer on the face of the earth for twelve long years.

This siege, which Humâyon felt compelled to carry through before marching on Bengal, was in reality a deep-laid plan of the rebel Sher-Khân. It was a method--often adopted in modern warfare, but until then unheard of in the East--of holding up his enemy's forces until such time as he had consolidated his own powers. It answered admirably. The rock of Chunar, detached outpost of the Vindhya mountains which frowns over the Ganges, engaged all Humâyon's attention for months, and when, after reducing it, he pushed on, Sher-Khân once more met brute-force by guile, and leading Humâyon on, left him to stew for the rainy season in the delta of the Ganges, a prey to flood and fever, while he himself looked down on him from the low hills of Northern Berars. It was a bitter beating! A prey to mosquitoes, to malaria, it was with difficulty that Humâyon's troops managed to preserve their communications with their base. Every tank was a lake, every brook a river. Their spirits sank, and no sooner were the roads opened than they deserted in hundreds; Prince Hindal--who, despite the virtue of being nearly always faithful to his brother, appears to have been of little good to him--setting the example by leaving ere the rains had stopped.

So when the dry season brought the possibility of campaign, Humâyon had no choice but to retreat from the now daily increasing boldness of his enemy, and try to force his way back to Agra. In this he was stopped by the river Ganges, which it was necessary to cross in order to avoid an entrenched camp which he could neither pass nor hope to reduce.

The bridge of boats took close on two months to complete, and then, a night or two before retreat became possible, the imperial camp was surprised about daybreak by the watchful enemy. It must have been a very complete surprise, for the emperor himself had only time to mount his horse, and after a vain appeal to his officers for one effort at least to repel the attack, accept their advice and ride for his life to the river-side. The bridge was not finished, there was no time for hesitation, so Humâyon urged his horse into the stream. It sank ere it could reach the shore, and the emperor would undoubtedly have done so likewise, but for the intervention of a water-carrier who was crossing with his skin bag, inflated with air, doing duty as a float.

It proved enough to support two; Humâyon's life was saved, but his queen was left in Sher-Shâh's hands. The whole story has a smack of opium about it, and it seems more than probable that the young king, roused out of a drugged sleep, had not his wits about him. Nothing else can explain the fact of Babar's son running like a hare, and leaving his womenkind behind him. His wife appears, however, not to have suffered thereby in any way, not even in her affection for her handsome, thriftless king, for it was she, a childless widow, who after his death erected the splendid mausoleum at Delhi which bears his name.

There is also something of opium in the promise which Humâyon made to the water-carrier, that *if* he came to Agra, and *if* he found Humâyon alive, he might, as a reward, claim to be king for a day.

He did come, so we are told, and for a day sate on the throne of the Emperor of India. Humâyon, always fond of a joke, made merry over this one, and had prime fun in cutting up the water-carrier's skin bag into wads (which were duly stamped as coin in the mint), and in other merry antics, for he was light-hearted like his father. Nevertheless, the jest cost him dear, for it drew down on him the wrath of his sour brother Kamrân, who always nourished the secret belief--not an unfounded one--that he would have made a better king than his brother.

This, however, was after Humâyon's generous condonation of both his brothers' grievous faults, and should have closed their lips from criticism. For both Kamrân and Hindal, seizing the opportunity of this disaster, claimed the throne, and marching on Agra from different sides, fell out over the question, until recalled to a sense of their common danger from the Bengal enemy.

Then the three royal brothers made friends, Humâyon, as ever, eager to clasp hands with those of whom he used to say: "How can I quarrel with them? Are they not monuments of my dear, dead father?"

Practically this defeat on the banks of the Ganges was Humâyon's Waterloo. He held his head above water for a while, attempted another campaign next year, lost once more on the banks of the Ganges near Kanauj, and was, with his army, absolutely driven into the river. Thence he escaped with difficulty, and but for the timely aid of two turbans knotted and thrown out to him, would undoubtedly have been drowned under the high bank which was too steep for his elephant to climb. Joined by his brothers Hindal and Âskari, he fled to Agra, thence with his women and part of his treasures to Delhi, and so, gathering what he could at the latter place, to Lahôre. But he was no welcome guest to Kamrân, who, fearing to be embroiled in the quarrel with Sher-Shâh, withdrew to Kâbul, leaving Humâyon helpless. He turned then to Sinde as a refuge, and after two and a half years of many adventures, found himself a mere wanderer in the desert.

It was, then, at the lowest ebb of fortune, that Fate interfered to make him--which is, indeed, his only real claim to remembrance--the father of the greatest king India has ever known.

The story is romantic in the extreme. His brother Hindal was over the Indus-water, in the rich province of Sehwân, and Humâyon, who from bitter experience had reason to doubt the former's loyalty, was keeping an eye on his proceedings. He therefore crossed the river for an interview at the town of Patâr. He found Hindal in the midst of festivities; for what purpose history sayeth not, but from what followed it seems likely that it was preparatory to a marriage. His mother, at any rate, gave an entertainment to all the ladies of the court, and at this Humâyon saw, and instantly fell in love with, a girl of sixteen, called Hamida-Begum. Hearing she was not as yet betrothed, he instantly said he would marry her. Then ensued a violent quarrel between the brothers, from which it seems likely that Humâyon's fancy had chosen the bride-elect. The girl wept at both brothers. They stormed; but finally Hindal's mother counselled her son to yield, and the thirty-eight-year-old Humâyon carried off the prize. Their honeymoon cannot have been cloudless, for they spent it in danger of their lives; but Humâyon must from his temperament have been a most beguiling bridegroom, and the little bride's tears soon dried. She followed him bravely, early in the next year, through the Great Desert of India, where horse and man nearly died of thirst.

That ceaseless marching from fresh enemies by day and night must have been a terrible experience for the young wife, soon to become a mother; but she had at least the consolation of her husband's deep, absorbing devotion. Once when her palfrey fell never to rise again, the king put her on his charger, and walked beside her bridle rein all through the long, weary night-march.

The stars must have looked down kindly on them as they toiled along, hand fast in hand.

It is a pretty picture, anyhow. So, after unheard-of miseries, they gained the quaint, stern old fort of Amarkôt, which rises bare and square out of the desert sand. One can imagine that August day, with the parching wind beating the fine, sharp sand of the desert against the purple-stained bricks, and grinding them to grey frostiness.

Here the Pathân chatelain, taking pity on the outwearied princess, offered her asylum. Humâyon, however, must go on; there was no rest, no shelter for such as he. It was four days after the sorrowful parting that a courier rode post-haste after the wanderer, telling him that a son was born to him-his first, his only son. There was no gold in the camp to give the messenger. All of regal pomp that could be found was a bag of musk, and this the proud father broke upon an earthenware platter, and distributed to his followers as a royal present in honour of "an event which diffused its fragrance over the whole habitable world."

One historian gives a somewhat different version of the birth of Akbar. In it he was born under a tree in the desert, and the little sixteen-year-old mother wept with fear at the hard-featured village midwife summoned hastily to her aid, then flung her arms round her and cried for joy when the boy-baby was put into her young arms. Within a month she and the child were back sharing her lover-husband's danger. It increased day by day, hour by hour. When the young Akbar was but a year old, it reached its climax. Compelled to quit Sinde, Humâyon, his wife and child with him, and some half a dozen followers, was on his way to Kandahâr, when news came that his brother Âskari was marching against him in force. There was nothing for it but swift, immediate flight. But the weather was boisterous, the only safe road almost impassable.

How about the child? Rapidly calculating chances, they decided on leaving the infant prince behind them. What tears, what forebodings must not have been miserable Hamida's--what vain kisses and strainings to her heart!

But when Âskari entered the little camp, the deed was done. The baby Akbar was there regal in his nurse's arms, with all his equipage, all his poor mockery of state and service about him, but the two fugitives were riding hard for the Persian frontier.

Humâyon had lost all things, even his fatherhood.

THE HOUSE OF SÛR

A.D. 1542 TO A.D. 1554

Sher-khân, the man who, worsting Humâyon, seized on the throne, had no atom of royal blood in his veins. He was a plain soldier, though of good birth; but, his father neglecting him, he had run away from home and entered the ranks. A rough-and-ready soldier, too, who, even in Babar's time, had not scrupled to tell a friend that in his opinion it would be no hard task to "drive these foreign Moghuls from Hindustan; for though the king himself was a man of parts, he trusted too much to his ministers, who were corrupt."

The friend laughed; but Sher-Khân was right even in his estimate of the king who, curiously enough, singled him out unerringly a few days afterwards, when, at a military banquet, he called for a knife to carve a chicken withal, and, the servant taking no notice of his rough order, immediately drew his dagger and coolly used it with contemptuous disregard for the diversion of his neighbours. Babar's quick eye caught the incident, and he remarked: "He may be a great man yet; trifles do not disconcert him."

He does not, however, appear to have been either an amiable or an estimable person, though he was not vicious, and even his successes as a soldier are somewhat too crafty for admiration. He knew well when to attack, when to retreat, and, if imperialist and Râjput accounts are to be trusted, was not over-scrupulous in his use of the white flag.

Then there is no doubt but that a secret understanding existed between him and Humâyon's brother Kamrân; for on the withdrawal of the latter from Lahôre, Sher-Shâh instantly pounced down on it, and would have captured the fugitive king but for his hasty flight.

He does not in truth appeal to one's sympathies, this Afghân of the House of Sûr, though he was by no means without good points. It is, however, impossible to get up much interest in a man who picks a quarrel with an innocent Râjput râjah on the ground that he has Mahomedan women in his harem, and who, after a lengthy siege, induces capitulation by promise of the garrison being allowed to march out with their arms and their property: thereinafter, on the advice of a learned doctor of law (who declared it was a sin to keep faith with infidels), proceeding to surround the brave band and cut them off!

It is satisfactory to learn that they sold their lives dearly. But Sher-Shâh continued to be diplomatic. He gained his success against the Râjah of Mârwar by a stratagem. Finding himself in a tight place, he forged treasonable correspondence between himself and certain of the Râjput generals, which was then so disposed of as to fall into the generalissimo's hands. The distrust thus sown of his levees' loyalty caused the râjah to give way; and with disastrous results.

The death of this Machiavel in armour was a Nemesis, for it arose in consequence of the Râjah of Kalinjasr's refusal to capitulate, on the ground of Sher-Shâh's many treacheries.

In the subsequent mining which became necessary to reduce the fort, Sher-Shâh was blown to bits in an explosion of a powder magazine that had not been properly secured.

Despite his treachery, he did much for India in the way of public works. The caravanserais, the wells which still stud the course of the high road from Bengal to the Indus, are of his building; and the very trees which shade the weary traveller in the long marching, if not of his planting, stand in the places of those which he watered with care.

He reigned five years, and left two sons. The elder and rightful heir preferred obscurity to prolonged battle for the crown, and after a while disappeared and was no more heard of, leaving Islâm-Shâh, or, as he is called by a mispronunciation, Salîm-Shâh, to follow in his father's treacherous footsteps. The most noteworthy event in his reign was the insurrection of the Mâhdi sect, led by one Ilâhi. The tenets of their faith seem to have been curiously destructive of each other. Neither their profession of predestination nor their pure socialism prevented them from going about armed, meting out lynch-law to all and sundry whom they deemed to be disobeying any divine law.

They must have been uncomfortable people to deal with, but the faith spread to such alarming proportions, that Salîm-Shâh finally called a Court of Arches to decide whether "Ilâhi's pertinaciously disrespectful manner to the king was consistent with his situation as a subject, or was enjoined by any precept of the Koran?"

He was subsequently tried on the accusation of presuming to personate the Great Mâhdi--for whose advent all pious Mahomedans look--condemned, and refusing to abjure his faith, was brought up for punishment, though at the time suffering from the plague which was then raging. He died under the third lash.

Almost immediately after this, Salîm-Shâh himself died, when his cousin Mobârik succeeded by a singularly brutal murder. Prince Ferôze, Salîm-Shâh's son, was then twelve years old. His mother, Bibi Bhâi, was Mobârik's sister, and devoted to her dissolute, pleasure-loving brother, whose life she had begged of the king. Notwithstanding this, immediately on the latter's death Mobârik entered the harem, tore the wretched boy from his mother's very arms, and killed him with his own hand.

Fraternal affection with a vengeance. His subsequent career was in keeping with this initial act. Sensual to a degree and absolutely illiterate, he set a Hindu usurer called Hemu at the head of affairs, and contented himself with remaining in the harem, and parading the city with pomp, surrounded by a body of archers, whose duty it was to discharge gold-headed arrows worth ten or twelve rupees each amongst the crowd; the scramble for them amusing the jaded satiety of this truly Eastern potentate.

He succeeded in A.D. 1552, and for two years the throne was the centre of a perfect anarchy of revolt.

Hemu, who seems to have had wits, held his own until faced by the returning Humâyon, backed by that splendid old Turkomân soldier, Byrâm Khân. Backed also by the son, whom eleven years before he had left alone with his nurses in the royal camp on the road to Kandahâr, and who now--an extremely youthful warrior--won back empire for his father by precipitating an action before the walls of Lahôre, in which the Moghuls, "animated by the conduct of that young hero," seemed to forget that they were mortal.

So ended the usurping dynasty of Sûr.

THE WANDERINGS OF A KING

A.D. 1542 TO A.D. 1556

When Humâyon and his Queen Hamida-Bânu-Begum left the infant Akbar to face fortune by himself, their own hopes for the future were low indeed. Look where they would, there seemed small chance of success.

India itself had practically become independent of Delhi, where the dreamful, opium-drugged king had thought to consolidate his empire by building a new capital. It is curious to mark in that fourteen-mile-long expanse of faintly-broken ground strewn with purple-stained bricks, which stretches between the massive ruins about the Kutb Minâr to modern Delhi at the foot of the red ridge, how each succeeding dynasty had shifted its ground nearer and nearer the river, until at last it flowed beneath the very walls of the palace which Shâh-jahân built, and where his descendant Bahâdur-Shâh carried on, in 1857, the conspiracy which led at last to the extinction of the Moghul dynasty.

The long fight for Râjputana which had gone on for centuries so that the taking and retaking of its principal forts forms the standing dish of every reign, had for the time ended in temporary independence.

Even at Chitore, Humâyon's delay in coming to the rescue of his bracelet-bound sister had been unproductive of result; for the Princess Kurnâvati's young son Udâi-Singh had escaped, and was now back in his own.

The story of his escape is still a favourite one in India, and women, cuddling their babies, tell breathlessly how one Râjputni once gave her child to death to save a king.

Little Udâi-Singh, smuggled to safety with his foster-mother, found asylum in his half-brother's palace. But one night screams rose from the women's apartments, followed by the sudden ominous death-wail. Punnia, the foster-mother, knew what had happened. The half-brother must have been assassinated as a preliminary to the murder of her charge. She caught him up, thrust opium into his mouth with a last drop of her milk, hid him, still sleeping, in a fruit-basket, and sent him out by the hands of a faithful servant, to await her among the rushes of the river-bed.

Then, throwing the little king's rich coverlet over her own child, she sat down to wait--for what?

For a question which she must answer.

And yet, when it did come, human nature was almost too strong for her. She could only point to the little sleeper in reply to that clamour for "The King! The King!"

And still she had to wait. To weep reservedly over her own darling, to do him reverence, and so, the last ceremony over, steal away hastily to where her king waited her in the rushes. Then, dry-eyed, stern, she carried him, drawing life from her bereaved breast, over wild hill and dale, till, reaching the mountain fortress of Komulmêr, she could set her nurseling on the governor's knee, and say: "Guard him--he is the King!"

Udâi-Singh, unfortunately, grew up unworthy of his foster-mother's sacrifice. Still, he held Chitore, and many another Râjput prince held other portions of the central tableland of India, whose rocky mountains form an ideal country for independence and revolt. For the rest, as we have seen, the Dekkan, Guzerât, and Mâlwa were held by Mahomedan dynasties, as were the smaller principalities of Khandêsh, Bengal, Joûnpur, Multân, Sinde. Towards the south-east the vast kingdom, mostly forest, of Orissa remained unexplored, and in the west, the whole narrow strip which includes the Western Ghâts figures not at all in history. Yet it was on this narrow strip that the first grip of Europe on Hindustan was to be laid.

Columbus was sailing the High Seas. The maritime nations, Italy, England, Spain, were on the *qui vive* for new worlds, and in 1484--just a year after Babar was born on Valentine's day--one Pedro de Covilham set out for India, overland, by the orders of King John of Portugal, with instructions to return with a report as to the practicability of reaching Hindustan' by sea. He reached India, being, apparently, the first European to touch its soil, but was detained on the return journey by the Arabs.

Ere he reached home in A.D. 1525 (after close on six and-thirty years of imprisonment), Portugal had acted on the advice which he had managed to send, God knows how. Vasco da Gama, leaving the Tagus in 1497, "coasted Guinea southwards, until he rounded into the Indian Ocean"; so reached Calicut in A.D. 1498. It was the beginning. Almost each year that followed saw a fresh, and ever a larger armament sent out chiefly by the Portuguese Order of Christ, with the ostensible object of converting the heathen. We read of nine, of seventeen, finally, in 1507, of twenty-two ships carrying one thousand five hundred fighting-men, and the very first Viceroy of India, Dom Francesco Almeda. Goa was taken and made the seat of Government by Dom Alfonso Albuquerque--after a tussle for the Viceroyalty--in 1510, and in 1542 St Francis Xavier, joint founder of the Jesuits with Ignatius Loyola, went out on a mission and had an enormous success of marvellous stability, since to this day a large proportion of the population on the south-west coast is professedly Roman Catholic.

Thus all India is practically accounted for in this, the first half of the sixteenth century. At a casual glance it seems as if here we have the vast continent tabulated, scheduled, within our reach. But a closer look shows us that these dynasties, these wars, these annexations and depredations, are but scratches on the surface of life. The India of reality was, as ever, in the fields, heedless of politics, heedless of all things beyond the village cosmogony save that recurring cry of, "The Toorkh! the Toorkh!"

That brought ruin, perchance death; but after death comes life, after ruin prosperity. And the new masters, no matter who they were, were not on the whole bad masters. When the revenues of the state depend upon the peasantry and the peasantry only, it is not politic to press the revenue-giver too hardly. There can be small doubt, therefore, that the general state of the country was distinctly flourishing. The land-rent or land-tax, call it what you will, was high, but the land itself was abundant, the people who had to live on it not too numerous. And luxury did not come, as it came in Europe, to the lives of the poor to make them poorer still. The standard of living did not rise, women were content with the fashions of their mothers; men asked no more than to be let live and die; humanity was its own amusement.

Practically, there was little difference in the system of Government under Hindu and Mahomedan rule. In both, the supreme power was easy of access. Petitions could be brought to the final authority without any difficulty, and a certain rough justice undoubtedly prevailed.

The king hired and paid for a portion of the army which he mounted on his own horses, but a large number of men came in independent parties under leaders of their own.

Such was the India which Humâyon left behind him for twelve long years. His adventures during this time are less entertaining than the wanderings of that prince of Bohemians, his father, but they are still interesting.

When he crossed the Persian border, he found himself received with a certain contemptuous pity. Still, female servants were sent to attend on the queen, and demonstrations were made in his favour. Arrived at the court of King Tahmâsp, however, the exiled monarch of India found himself by no means on a bed of roses. Even the gift of the greatest treasure he possessed, a huge diamond, did not ameliorate his situation; for Shâh Tahmâsp affected to despise the jewel, and is said to have sent it away disdainfully in a gift to the King of the Dekkan. But the whole history of this diamond, which has now disappeared, is a fine romance. It is said to have been the eye of Shiv-ji in some shrine, and to have passed into the possession of many conquerors, until it was given to Babar in recognition of chivalrous kindness and courtesy shown to them by the family of the Râjah of Chitore. Babar, who kept nothing for himself, gave the stone, "worth half the daily expenditure of the world," to his son. It is said to have weighed about 280 carats, and to have been of the purest water; it is also conjectured that it reappeared as the Great Moghul diamond which Tavernier describes as belonging to Shâh-jahân, and that possibly it is this very stone which, cleft and badly cut, still shines as the Koh-i-nur.

It did not, anyhow, avail Humâyon much. More effective was his servile consent to wear the red cap of the Persian, and by this becoming a *khizil bash*, renounce his Sunni faith, and proclaim himself a Shiah. He did not do this without much pressure, and at the very last nearly broke bondage; but the promise of ten thousand horse wherewith to recover his kingdom was too tempting. With this force he attacked Kandahâr, where his brother Âskari still held little Akbar as a hostage; or, rather, had so held him until the attacking army loomed over the horizon, when, after some hesitation as to whether it would not be wiser to send the boy under honourable escort to his father, Âskari decided on obeying his brother Kamrân's orders, and despatched the little prisoner to Kâbul. The story of that inclement winter march across the hills, with its attempts at rescue and numberless adventures, would make a charming book for English children.

After five months siege, Kandahâr surrendered, "Dearest Lady" having succeeded in obtaining a promise of pardon for Âskari from his brother. It was revoked, however, in an altogether indefensible manner, and Âskari was kept in chains for the next three years. This is so unlike Humâyon's usual conduct towards his brothers, that it gives colour to the assertion made by some authorities that Âskari's punishment was due to the discovery of a further offence.

After Kandahâr had capitulated, Humâyon marched on Kamrân and Kâbul. This is the march rendered famous by Sir Donald Stewart in the Afghân War, and by Lord Roberts' subsequent and rapid repetition. It was now winter, which had set in with extraordinary severity, and much of the country was under snow. Half-way to Kâbul Humâyon was joined by his brother Hindal, who, with brief intervals of hesitation, appears to have been fairly faithful. Their amalgamated armies proved too formidable for Kamrân to face, though at first he had prepared for extremities by removing little Akbar from his grand-aunt "Dearest Lady's" care, and giving the lad to a trusted creature of his own; so flight to Ghuzni followed. The child, however, remained, and Humâyon's delight at recovering his little son was great. Taking the boy in his arms, he exclaimed: "Joseph was cast by envious brethren into the pit; but in the end he was exalted to great glory, as thou shalt be, my son."

Only remaining in Kâbul long enough to restore the young prince to safer keeping, Humâyon set off in pursuit of his brother, who, finding the gates of Ghuzni closed against him, had fled to the Indus; but while on this campaign Humâyon fell so sick that his life was despaired of. After two months' confinement to bed he recovered, only to find himself deserted by his troops, and to hear that Kamrân, returning to Kâbul one dawn, had managed to slip in with a chosen band of followers as the city gates were being opened, had murdered the governor in his bath, had put out the eyes of Fazl and Muttro, the young prince's foster-brothers and playfellows, and had given the young prince himself into the charge of unkindly eunuchs. It was an anxious moment, and the almost despairing father, still weak from illness, set himself to beat up recruits and march to recover his capital, recover his son. Kamrân's troops, meeting with a reverse in the suburbs of the city, where--this being April--the peach-blossom must have been all ablow, Humstyon was enabled to establish himself on an eminence which commands the town, and to commence shelling it. Whereupon Kamrân sent a message to say that if the cannonade continued, he would expose the young heir to all his father's high hopes on the wall where the fire was hottest. A brutal threat, upon the carrying out of which history stands divided, some authorities saying that Akbar was so exposed, others declaring that Humâyon ordered the artillery to cease firing.

Be that as it may, on the 28th of April he entered the city in triumph, Kamrân having fled the previous night.

So little Akbar was once more in his father's arms. In his mother's also, ere long, for Hamida-Bânu-Begum rejoined her husband in the spring. Regarding this, a pretty story is told by Aunt Rosebody in her Memoirs. Humâyon, ever a lover of pleasure, devised a sumptuous entertainment to welcome his wife, and amongst the many devices for amusement was this. All the ladies of the family, unveiled, resplendent in jewels, were to range themselves in a circle round a hall; and to this dazzling company the baby-prince--he was but four--was to be introduced to choose for himself a mother! One can imagine the scene. Those laughing faces-all but one-- around the child who had not seen her he sought for two long years. The pause for hesitation, the sickening suffocation of one heart, the sudden sense of shyness, of loneliness, making one little mouth droop.

And then?

Then a quick cry, "*Amna! Amna-jân!*" and Hamida's arms closed convulsively over the sobbing child. What laughter! What tears! As Auntie Rosebody loves to say of all things that bring the sudden vivifying touch of emotion, "It was like the Day of Resurrection." But the young Akbar's trials were not yet over, neither were his father's dangers. In the summer of 1548 Humâyon once more pursued Kamrân, taking with him at first both Akbar and Akbar's mother--for whom the king (or, as he was now called, the emperor) had an affection that never wavered. Finding the way rough, he sent them back to Kâbul; and when he marched out from that city the next time on the same bootless errand, he left the boy, who was now eight years old, behind him as Governor of Kâbul, under tutorship. Whereupon Kamrân, who appears to have had the faculty of doubling like a hare, taking advantage of a serious wound which delayed his brother in the Sertun Pass, slipped to his rear, and for the third time captured Kâbul and that apple of Humâyon's eyes, Prince Akbar.

This was the last of Kamrân's exploits, however, for Humâyon, after suffering agonies of fear lest evil should happen to his heir, gained a complete and final victory over his brother, who fled once more; not, however, to the emperor's great relief, taking Akbar with him. He was soon after captured by the King of the Ghakkur tribe, that warlike race of the Indian Salt Range who broke the ranks of the Ghuzni Mahmûd, and assassinated his successor in campaign, Ghori-Mahomed. Being immediately betrayed to Humâyon, he met his fate at last. Yet even now, after treasons seventy-and-seven, he was nearly forgiven; would have been forgiven but for the fact that Humâyon's favourite brother, Hindal, had been killed in the pursuit of him. He deserved death, but the blindness which was meted out to him leaves us with a revulsion of feeling against the man who was driven by his adherents into giving the order. A revulsion which Humâyon hardly deserved, since, opium-soddened, flighty in a way, unreliable as he was, cruelty was not one of his faults.

And the adherents were right. With Kamrân scotched, Humâyon's fortunes began at once to improve, and in 1535 he was able to invade the Punjâb with fifteen thousand horse. Within a year he was once more Emperor in Delhi; but not for long. Six months after he re-ascended the throne, before he had time even to take breath and look around him, he fell from the roof of his library, and died from the result of the accident four days afterwards. Visitors to Delhi are still shown the broken stairs from which he fell, and are told the story of how, descending the steps, he heard the call to prayer, and stopped to repeat the creed and sit down till the long sonorous sound of the *muâzzim* had ended. And how, in attempting to rise again, his staff slipped on the polished marble of the step.

The parapet is certainly but a foot high; but as one looks over it, and remembers that Humâyon was a man in the prime of life, the wonder comes if the opium which claimed so large a share in the emperor's life had not an equal share in his death.

AKBAR THE GREAT

A.D. 1556 TO A.D. 1605

Here is a subject indeed!

Considering the time--a time when Elizabeth of England found that England ready to support her in beheading her woman-cousin, when Charles IX. of France idly gave the order on St Bartholomew's Eve, and Pope Urban VIII., representing the highest majesty of the Christian religion, forced the tortured, seventy-year-old Galileo to his knees, there to abjure by oath what he knew to be God's truth: considering the country--a country to this day counted uncivilised by Europe--there is small wonder that the record of Akbar seems incredible even to the owner of the hand which here attempts to epitomise that record.

And yet it is a true one. Discounting to the full the open flattery of Abul-fazl's Akbarnâmâh, the source from which most information is derived, giving good measure to Budâoni's grudging criticisms, the unbiassed readers of Akbar's life cannot avoid the conviction that in dealing with him, they are dealing with a man of imagination, of genius.

Between the lines, as it were, of bare fact, the unconventional, the unexpected crops up perpetually, making the mind start and wonder. As an instance, let us take the account of the great hunt at Bhera, near the river Jhelum, and let us take it in the very words of the historians.

"The Emperor gave orders for a *gamargha* hunt, and that the nobles and officers should according to excellent methods enclose the wild beasts.... But, when it had almost come about that the two sides were come together, suddenly, all at once a strange state and strong frenzy came upon the Emperor ... to such an extent as cannot be accounted for. And every one attributed it to some cause or other ... some thought that the beasts of the forest had with a tongueless tongue unfurled divine secrets to him. At this time he ordered the hunting to be abandoned. Active men made every endeavour that no one should even touch the feather of a finch."

Now whether the legend which lingers in India be true or not, that it was the sight of a *chinkara* fawn which brought about the Emperor's swift change of front, we have here baldly set down certain events which apparently were incomprehensible and but vaguely praiseworthy, even to Abul-fazl's keen eye for virtue in his master. Viewed, however, by the wider sympathies of to-day, the fact stands forth indubitably that the "extraordinary access of rage such as none had ever seen the like in him before" with which Akbar was seized, was no mere fit of epilepsy, such as the rival historian Budâoni counts it to have been, but a sudden overmastering perception of the relations between God's creatures, the swift realisation of the Unity which binds the whole world together; for it seems certain that he never again countenanced a *battue*.

Now Akbar's life was full of such sudden insights. We see the effect of them in his swift actions; actions so swift, so unerring, that they startle the dull world around him. He was that rare thing--a dreamer who was also a man of action.

That he was full of faults none can deny, but, judging him by the highest canon, one feels bound to place him amongst those few names, such as Shakspeare, Michelangelo, Beethoven and Cæsar, who seem to have had equal control over their physical and their subliminal consciousness; and so, inevitably, head the lists of leaders amongst men.

Of Akbar's early years enough has been said. From his birth in the sand-swept desert, to the day on which, a lad-ling of eight, he finally escaped the clutches of his uncle Kamrân, and rode into his father's camp before Kâbul at the head of a faithful contingent, he had suffered such constant vicissitudes of fortune that there can be no surprise at the belief, which grew up later, that he bore a charmed life.

Of the next three years until, at the age of twelve, he marched with his father on India, and brought success by, with youthful energy, precipitating a decisive battle, nothing is known, save that he was married with much pomp to his cousin Râzia-Khânum, daughter of his dead uncle Hindal, a woman many years his senior.

Akbar, then, was thirteen years and four months old when at Hariâna, a town in the Jullunder district, he received the news of his father's accident, and almost at the same time those of his death. He, together with his governor, tutor, or, as it is called in Persian, *atalik*, Byrâm-Khân, was engaged in pursuing Sikûndah-Shâh, the last scion of the House of Sûr, and it seemed to them best, ere returning to Delhi, to secure the Punjâb by securing Sikûndah. But their decision proved of doubtful wisdom; for Kâbul instantly revolted, and Hemu, the shopkeeper-prime-minister of the third Sûri king, with an army of fifty thousand men and five hundred elephants, marched on Delhi, flushed by his victories, to restore the late dynasty, and took the city.

In this predicament, Akbar's counsellors advised retreat to Kâbul. Its recovery seemed certain, and he could there await future developments. But Akbar's instincts were for empire, and Byrâm-Khân, the old Turkomân soldier, was with him.

Delhi must be won back at all hazards; so, not without trepidation, the old man and the boy crossed the river Sutlej, and were joined at Sirhînd by Târdi-Beg, and the forces which had fled from Delhi. Now Târdi-Beg was a nobleman of the House of Chagatâi (which also claimed the young king as its most distinguished scion), and between him and Byräm-Khân there had ever been enmity. The latter, therefore, taking as his excuse the over-haste of Târdi-Beg's retirement from Delhi, called him to his tent, and without referring to their youthful master, had him assassinated. The event, common enough in Indian history, is noteworthy, because it caused the first rift in the confidence between Byrâm and Akbar, who, boy as he was, showed his displeasure, and refused to accept the rough soldier's excuse that violence was necessary to assert power.

The next breach was of the same kind. Passing by our old friend, the fort of Bhattînda, Akbar gave battle to Hemu on the old field at Pâniput, where, thirty years before, his grandfather, Babar, had decided his fate.

No doubt the thought of this had something to do with the renewed victory which left Hemu, sorely wounded, a prisoner in Byrâm's hands. Not satisfied with this, the savage old Tartar general brought him into Akbar's tent, and, presenting the boy with a sword, said: "This is your first war, my king. Prove your sword upon this infidel." But Akbar drew back indignantly. "How can I strike one who is no better than a dead man?" he replied hotly. "It is on strength and sense that a king's sword is tried." Whereupon Byrâm, incensed, no doubt, by the proud refusal, instantly cut down Hemu himself.

They say the boy-king wept; certain it is that he never forgot, never quite forgave, the incident. Next day, marching 53 miles without a halt, Akbar entered Delhi, the acknowledged Emperor of India.

What that India was, we know. On all sides was despotism; good or bad government being the result of the personal equation of the despot.

Akbar was to change much of this by wise, unalterable, and beneficent laws during the nine-and-forty years of his reign; for the present, however, he was under tutelage, and the first four years after his accession passed without the young king's showing any of the markedly-original tendencies which characterised him in after life.

But during those four years he was learning to recognise what he liked, what he disliked. Amongst the latter was the arbitrary exercise of Byrâm's power. This became more and more galling as the years sped by, and the boy, now growing to manhood, began to realise *himself*, began to dream dreams, began to see realities with a clearness and insight far beyond those of his tutor. But he had a generous, an affectionate heart. He hestitated long to throw off the yoke of tutelage and proclaim his determination to rule in his own way; and despite the efforts of Byrâm's enemies--and he had many--added to the persuasions of Mahâm-Anagâh (Akbar's foster-mother, who all his life, from the day when, a yearling babe, he was left in her charge while his father and mother fled for their lives across the Persian frontier, had been his chief adviser), it was not till A.D. 1560 that Akbar made up his mind to action. Then, leaving Byrâm engaged in a hunting expedition, he returned, on pretext of his mother's sudden illness, to Delhi and issued a proclamation announcing to his people that he had taken the sole management of affairs into his own hands, and that no orders, except those given under his own seal, should in future be obeyed. At the same time he sent a dignified message to Byrâm-Khân to this effect:--

"Till now our mind has been taken up with our education and by the amusements of youth, and it was our royal will that you should regulate the affairs of our empire. But, it being our intention henceforward to govern our people by our own judgment, let our well-wisher withdraw from all worldly concerns, and taking the pilgrimage to Mecca on which he has for so long been intent, spend the rest of his days in prayer far removed from the toils of public life."

The very dignity of this was, however, irritating, and Byrâm, after a brief feint of obedience, broke out into open revolt.

It needed Akbar himself to reduce his disloyalty by a display of clemency which must have convinced the old Tartar that he had here to do with some one, with something, the like of which he had never seen before. For when, driven to bay, in utmost distress he sent in an almost hopeless appeal for pardon, Akbar's reply was the despatching of a guard of honour equal to his own to bring the unfortunate man to his presence with every mark of distinction. It was too much for the old soldier. His pride broke down, he flung himself at his young master's feet in a passion of tears. Akbar's reply was to raise him by the hand, order a robe of honour to be flung round him, and to place him in his old seat by the king's side above all the other nobles.

So in "the very loud voice," and with "the very elegant and pleasant manner of speech" for which the young king was famous, he addressed him thus:--

"If Byrâm-Khân loves a military life, the governorship of Kâlpe offers field for his ambition. If he prefers to remain at court, our favour will never be wanting to the benefactor of our family. But if he choose devotion, he shall be escorted to Mecca with all the honour due to his rank, and receive a pension of 50,000 rupees annually."

Byrâm chose the last, and from that time Akbar reigned alone; and, to his credit be it said, except in his disastrous leniency towards his sons, there is scarcely a mistake to be laid to his charge. Before, however, embarking on what must necessarily be a very inadequate sketch of this remarkable man, a few words as to his personality and his looks may not be amiss. He was "inclined to be tall, sinewy, strong, with an open forehead and chest and long arms. He had most captivating manners and an agreeable expression." According to his son, "his manners and habits were quite different from those of other persons, and his visage was full of a godly dignity." For the rest, he was a great athlete, the best polo-player and shot at court, and ready for any exploit that required strength and skill.

His mind followed suit with his body, though he was absolutely unlike his grandfather Babar in versatility. Yet he had had, apparently, much the same opportunity of education. In both, the four years from eight to twelve were all that Fate gave them for schooling; but Babar emerged from his, a writer, a poet, a painter, a musician. Akbar, strange to say, could neither read nor write, but he was counted the first musician of his day.

Such was the man who at eighteen started to rule India on new lines, whose head held a new idea concerning kingship. The king according to this, should be the connecting link between his subjects. He should rule not for one but for all. Just as Asôka, nigh on two thousand years before, had protested that conquest by the sword was not worth calling conquest, so Akbar, whose soul in many ways followed close in thought to that of the old Buddhist king, felt, vaguely at first, afterwards more clearly, more concisely, that the king should be, as it were, the solvent in which caste and creed, even race, should disappear, leaving behind them nothing but equal rights, equal justice, equal law. To secure this, it was necessary to make all men forget conquest.

It was a big idea, and to carry it through in the face of a society which deemed kingship a personal pleasure to be gained by a long purse or a stout arm, needed a strong will.

But Akbar was young, and vital to his finger-tips. The first thing to be accomplished was to annex all India--as bloodlessly as he could. That is the first thing to be noticed in Akbar's rule. War, even from the beginning, was never to him anything but the lesser of two evils; the other being disunion, decentralisation, consequent misgovernment.

His first annexation was Mâlwa, where the governor, hard-pressed, "sought a refuge from the frowns of fortune" in Akbar's clemency. As a result of which he lived, and fought, and died, long years afterwards, in the service of the king, feeling his honour in no way impaired by his defeat.

Immediately after this, Akbar had to choose between personal affection and abstract justice. His foster-brother, Adham-Khân, son to that Mahâm-Anagâh whose kindly, capable breast had been the young king's refuge for so many years, began to give trouble. Lawless, dissolute, he presumed on the king's love for his former playfellow in a thousand ways. It was he who was chief actor in the tragedy of Rûp-mati, the beautiful dancing-girl with whom Bâz-Bahâdur of Mâlwa lived for "seven long happy years, while she sang to him of love," and who killed herself sooner than submit to Adham-Khân's desires. This brought down on him the king's anger, but he defied it still more by assassinating the prime minister as he sate at prayers in Akbar's antechamber on the roof. Some say, and this is probably true, that the king, hearing the old man's cry, came out sword in hand to avenge him, but, restraining his wrath, ordered the murderer to be instantly thrown over the battlements. The story, however, is also told that the young Akbar, coming out from his sleeping-chamber, himself gripped the offender in his strong arms, and forcing him backward to the edge, paused for a last kiss of farewell ere he sent the sin-stained soul to its account. It is, at least, more dramatic.

But either tale ends with the greatest of tragedies for the young king. Mahâm-Anagâh, his more than mother, died of grief within forty days--died unforgiving.

The task of consolidating his empire occupied Akbar for the next two years. It would be idle to attempt to follow him from the Nerbûdda to the Indus, from Allahabâd to Guzerât. One incident will give an idea of his swiftness, his extraordinary dash and courage.

Returned from a long campaign on the north-western hills against his young brother, Mahomed Hakîm, Akbar heard of renewed trouble with the Usbeks in Oude. Though it was then the height of the rainy season, he made a forced march over a flooded country, and arriving at the Ganges at nightfall, swam its swollen stream with his advanced guard, and after lying concealed till daybreak, sounded the attack.

"The enemy, who had passed the night in festivity, little supposing the king would attempt to cross the river without his army, could hardly believe their senses when they heard the royal kettledrums." Needless to say, the rebels, surprised, were defeated, and, as usual, pardoned. This was Akbar's policy. To punish swiftly, then to forgive. Thus he bound men to him by ties of fear and love. Already he had conceived and carried out the almost inconceivable project of allying himself in honourable and peaceful marriage with the Râjputs. Behâri Mull, Râjah of Ambêr (or Jeypore), had given the king his daughter, while his son Bhagwan-dâs, and his nephew Mân-Singh, were amongst Akbar's most trusted friends, and held high posts in the imperial army. Toleration was beginning to bear fruit; but Chitore, the Sacred City, held out alike against annexation or cajolery. So it could not be allowed to remain a centre of independence, of revolt. It was in A.D. 1568 that Akbar began its siege. Udâi-Singh, the Fat King, had fled to the mountains, being but a bastard Râjput in courage, leaving one Jâimul in charge of the sanctuary of Râjput chivalry.

It was a long business. Once an accident in the mines which Akbar was pushing with the utmost care, brought about disaster, and the siege had practically to be begun again. In the end, it was a chance shot which brought success. Alone, unattended, in darkness, Akbar was in the habit of wandering round his guards at night, marking the work done in the trenches, dreaming over the next day's plans. So occupied in a close-pushed bastion, he saw by the flare of a torch on the rampart of the city some Râjput generals also going their rounds. To snatch a matchlock from the sentry and fire was Akbar's quick impulse.

It won him Chitore; for the man who fell, shot through the head, was Jâimul himself. Next morning, Akbar went through scenes which he never forgot. He saw, as his grandfather had done, the great war-sacrifice of the Râjputs; but, unlike Babar, he did not view it contemptuously. It made an indelible mark upon his soul. The story goes, that two thousand of the Râjput warriors escaped the general slaughter by the "stratagem of binding the hands of their women and children, and marching with them through the imperial troops as if they were a detachment of the besiegers in charge of prisoners."

If this extraordinary tale be true, the explanation of it surely lies in Akbar's admiration; an admiration which led him on his return to Delhi to order two huge stone elephants, formed of immense blocks of red sandstone, to be built at the gateway of his palace. And on the necks of these elephants he placed two gigantic stone figures representing Jâimul and Pûnnu, the two Râjput generals who had so bravely defended Chitore.

It was during this siege that Akbar's friendship with the poet Faizi commenced. Five years younger than the young king, who was then but six-and-twenty years of age, Faizi, or Abul-faiz, as he is rightly named, was by profession a physician, by temperament an artist in the highest sense. Charmed by his varied talents, fascinated by his goodness, Akbar kept him by his side until he died nineteen years afterwards, when it is recorded that the king wept inconsolably. One thing they had in common--an unusual thing in those days--they were both extraordinarily fond of animals, especially of dogs.

This friendship, bringing about as it did the introduction to Akbar of Abul-faiz's younger brother, Abul-fazl, marks an important change in the king's mental development.

Hitherto he had been strictly orthodox. In a way, he had set aside the problems of life in favour of his self-imposed task; henceforward his mind was to be as keen, as swift to gain spiritual mastery, as his body was to gain the physical mastery of his world. Possibly he may have been led to thought by the death in this year of his twin sons; apparently these were the only children which had as yet been born to him, and at twenty-seven it is time that an Eastern potentate had sons. With him, too, the very idea of empire must have been bound up with that of an heir to empire. So it is no wonder that we find him overwhelmed with joy at the birth, in 1569, of Prince Salîm. Yet his sons (he had three of them in Fate's good time) were to be the great tragedy of Akbar's life. Long years afterwards, when the baby Salîm, whom he had welcomed verily as a gift from God, had grown to be a man, a cruel man, who ordered an offender to be flayed alive, Akbar, with a shiver of disgust, asked bitterly "how the son of a man who could not see a dead beast flayed without pain, could be guilty of such barbarity to a human being?"

How indeed? Were they really his sons, these hard-drinking, hard-living young princes, who had no thought beyond the princelings of their age?

This resentment, this disgust, however, was not to be for many years. Meanwhile, Akbar, having built the fort at Agra, that splendid building whose every foundation finds water, whose every stone is fitted to the next and chained to it by iron rings, began on his City of Victory, Fatehpur Sikri.

And wherefore not, since sons had been born to his empire? It was wide by this time, but Guzerât was still independent and had to be brought within the net.

It was in this campaign that Akbar nearly met his end in the narrow cactus lane at Sarsa, when he and the two Râjput chieftains, Bhagwan-dâs and Mân-Singh, fought their way through their enemies, each guarding the other's head.

Akbar's life is full of such reckless bravery, such wonderful escapes; in this, at least, he was true grandson to Babar-of-the-Thousand-Adventures.

It was in the following year that the famous ride from Agra to Ahmedabâd in nine days was made; and, after all, somewhat uselessly made, since the emperor was too chivalrous to take his enemy unawares, and, finding him asleep, ordered the royal trumpeters to sound a *reveillée* before, after giving him plenty of time, the imperial party "charged like a fierce tiger." It is good reading all this, overburdened though the pages of the Akbarnâmâh-Abul-fazl's great History of his Master--may be with flatteries and digressions.

But it is not in all this that Akbar's glory lies. It is in the far-reaching justice of his legal and administrative reforms, above all, in the reasons he gives for these reforms, that he stands unique amongst all Indian kings. We have, however, still to record his conquest of Bengal (where, it may be noted, he swam his rivers on horseback at the head of every detachment for pursuit, every advance guard), still to tell the tale of the Fat King Udâi-Singh's son, Râjah Pertâp, before at Fatehpur Sikri, in the twentieth year of his reign, and the thirty-third of his life, we can find pause to consider Akbar's principles and practice. Bengal, then, was added to empire with the usual rapidity. Then arose trouble in Mêwar. Udâi-Singh was dead, still defying from a distance Akbar's power, still scorning the alliance by marriage which had brought his neighbours revenue and renown; but his son Pertâp lived--Pertâp, who was to the sixteenth century what Prithvi-Râj had been to the fourteenth; that is to say, the flower of Râjput chivalry, the idol of the men, the darling of the women. He had taken to the hills, he had outraged Akbar's sense of justice, and he must be crushed. The battle of Huldighât decided his fate. Wounded, wearied, he fled on his grey horse "Chytuc" up a narrowing stony ravine, behind him the clatter of another horse swifter than his own; for "Chytuc," his friend, his companion, was wounded, too, and more wearied even than wounded.

"Ho! *nîla-ghôra-ki-aswâr!*"

["Oh! Rider of the grey horse!"]

The cry rang out amid the echoing rocks. What! Was his enemy within call already? "Chytuc" stumbled on, urged by the spur.

"Ho! *nîla-ghôra-ki-aswâr!*"

Nearer and nearer! A cry that must be answered at last. One final stumble, "Chytuc" was down, and Pertâp turned to sell life dearly. Turned to find his brother.

"Thy horse is at its end--take mine," said Sukta, who long years before had gone over to Akbar's side, driven thither by Pertâp's pride.

"And thou?"

"I go back whence I came."

Those who had watched the chase from the plains below asked for explanations. They were given.

"Tell the truth," came the calm reply.

Then Sukta told it. Drawing himself up, he said briefly:

"The burden of a kingdom over-weighted my brother. I helped him to carry it."

Needless to say, the excuse was accepted. And to this day the cry, "*Ho! nîla-ghôra-ki-aswâr*," is one of the war-cries of the Râjput.

To return to Akbar, in the twentieth year of his reign. It was just ten years since Faizi had come into his life--Faizi, the first Mahomedan to trouble his head about Hindu literature, Hindu science. It had opened up a new world to Akbar, and when six years afterwards Abul-fazl entered into the emperor's life also, with his broad, clear, tolerant, critical outlook, and his intense personal belief in the genius of the man he served, it seemed possible to achieve what till then Akbar had almost despaired of achieving. The dream had always been there. In some ways he had gone far towards realising it. He had, early in his reign, abolished the capitation tax on infidels, and the tax on pilgrimages, his reason for the latter being, "that although the tax was undoubtedly on a vain superstition, yet, as all modes of worship were designed for the One Great Being, it was wrong to throw any obstacle in the way of the devout, and so cut them off from their own mode of intercourse with their Maker."

Then he had absolutely forbidden the slavery of prisoners of war; and having observed, both during his many campaigns and his still more numerous hunting expeditions, that the greater portion of the land he traversed remained uncultivated, he had set himself, alone, unaided--for his courtiers were content with conventionalities--to find out the cause. The land was rich, the cultivators were industrious; the reason must lie in something which made cultivation unprofitable. What was it? An excessive land-tax? He instantly started experimental farms, which convinced him that this, and nothing else, was the cause of the land lying idle. But on all sides he met with opposition. Convinced himself that the old methods were obsolete, he had almost given up the task of reform in despair, when he met Abul-fazl. In religious matters, too, he had gone far beyond his age. The intolerance the bigotry of those around him shocked his innate sense of justice. Here again Abul-fazl was a tower of strength, and, inch by inch, yard by yard, his support enabled the king to fight for his final position, until in 1577, after endless discussions in the House-of-Argument (which he had had built for the purpose, and where, night after night, he sate listening while doctors of the law, Brahmans, Jews, Jesuits, Sufis--God only knows what sects and creeds--discussed truth from their varying standpoints), he took the law into his own hands and practically forced the learned Ulemas to put their signatures to a document which proclaimed him Head-of-the-Church, the spiritual as well as the temporal guide of his subjects. The reason he gave for desiring this decision was, that as kings were answerable to God for their subjects, any division of authority in dealing with them was inexpedient.

So in 1579 he mounted the pulpit in his Great Mosque at Fatehpur Sikri, and read the Kutbah prayer in his own name in these words, written for the occasion by the poet Faizi:--

"Lo! from Almighty God I take my kingship,

Before His throne I bow and take my judgeship,

Take Strength from Strength, and Wisdom from His Wiseness,

Right from the Right, and Justice from His Justice.

Praising the King, I praise God near and far--

Great is His Power! Allâh-hû-Akbâr!"

They were not unworthy words; and they were, as Sir William Hunter well calls them, the Magna Charter of Akbar's reign. He was now free to realise all his long-cherished dreams of universal tolerance and absolute unity. In future, no distinctions of race and creed were held cogent. The judicial system was reorganised and the magistracy made to understand that the question of religion was no longer to enter into their work.

The whole revenue administration was altered, and it remains to this day practically as Akbar left it. In this, as in finance and currency, he was ably aided by Tôdar-Mull, a Hindu of exceptional ability and tried integrity.

But Akbar was fortunate in his friends. In addition to Faizi, who appears to have satisfied his philosophic instincts, and Abul-fazl, to whose clear eyes he always turned when in doubt, he had a third intimate companion who, in many ways, stood closest to him of the three.

This was Râjah Birbal, who began life as a minstrel. His pure intellectuality, his quaint humour and cynical outlook on life, seem to have given Akbar the nerve tonic, which, dreamer as he was at times, he seems to have needed; for like all really great men, the emperor was almost feminine in sensitiveness.

It is difficult to decide what his own personal creed was. That which he promulgated as the Divine Faith is a somewhat nebulous Deism. That which is credited to him in the following words is poetically mystical:--

"In every Temple they seek Thee, in every Language they praise Thee. Each Religion says that it holds Thee, the One. But it is Thou whom I seek from temple to temple; for Heresy and Orthodoxy stand not behind the Screen of thy Truth. Heresy to the Heretic, Orthodoxy to the Orthodox; but only the dust of the Rose Petal remains to the seller of perfume."

Behind all this there lies the conviction so strongly expressed that "not one step can be made without the torch of truth," that "to be beneficial to the soul, belief must be the outcome of clear judgment."

But the chronicle of the remainder of his reign claims us.

In 1584 he outraged the orthodox by choosing a Râjputni Jôdh-Bai, the daughter of Râjah Bhagwân-das, as the first wife of his son and heir, Prince Salîm.

He himself had left such things as marriage behind him, and, though still in the prime of years, led the life of an ascetic. Five hours sleep sufficed for him; he ate but sparingly once a day; wine and women he appears to have forgotten. There is a saying attributed to him of his regret that he had not earlier recognised all women as sisters. Certainly for the last five-and-twenty years of his life he had nothing in this respect wherewith to reproach himself. Wider interests absorbed him. Child-marriages had to be discountenanced, abolished by a sweep of the pen; education placed on a firmer, better basis. It seemed to him, as it seems to many of us to-day, that an unconscionable time was spent in teaching very little, and, hey presto! another sweep of the pen, and school-time was diminished by one-half. There is nothing so dynamic as a good despotism!

All this was crowded, literally crammed into a few peaceful years at Fatehpur Sikri, and then suddenly he left his City of Victory, the city that was bound up with his hope of personal empire, the city he had built to commemorate the birth of his heir and removed his capital, not to Delhi, but to the far north--to Lahôre.

Why was this?

It is said that a lack of water at Fatehpur was the cause. And yet with the river Jumna close at hand, and Akbar's wealth and boundless energies, what was a lack of water had he really been set on remaining there?

It seems as if we must seek for a cause behind this patent and pitiful one. Such cause, deep-seated, scarcely acknowledged, is surely to be found in the bitter disappointment caused to the emperor by his sons. From his earliest years Salîm had given trouble. At eighteen he was dissolute, cruel, arrogant beyond belief. His younger brothers, Murâd and Danyâl, were little better. Of the three, Murâd was the best; it was possible to think of him as his father's son. Yet the iron must have eaten into that father's soul as he saw them uncomprehending even of his idea, his dream. In leaving Fatehpur Sikri, as he did in 1585, therefore, it seems likely that he left behind also much of his personal interest in empire.

The ostensible cause of his northward journey was the death of his brother, and a consequent revolt in Kâbul; but he did not return for fourteen long years--years that while they brought him success, while they justified his wisdom, brought him also much sorrow and disappointment. Though both earlier historians and Western commentators fail, as a rule, to notice it, there can be no doubt to those who, taking Akbar's whole character as their guide, attempt to read between the lines, that the emperor's policy changed greatly after he left Fatehpur Sikri behind him. A certain personal note is wanting in it. Take, for instance, the war which he carried out in the province of Swât, and which ended in a disaster that cost him his dearest friend, Râjah Birbal. Now that disaster was due entirely to this new note in Akbar's policy. He did not desire conquest; not, at least, conquest on the old blood-and-thunder lines. He wished, and he ordered, what we should nowadays call a "peaceful demonstration to the tribes." The army was to march through the Swât territory, using as little violence as possible, and return. The idea was outrageous to the regulation general, so Abul-fazl and Birbal drew lots as to which of them should go and keep Zein-Khân's martial ardours in check. It fell on Birbal; much, it is believed, to Akbar's regret. Of the exact cause of disagreement between Birbal and Zein-Khân little is known; but they did disagree, and with disastrous results. The whole Moghul army was practically overwhelmed, and it is supposed that Birbal, in attempting escape by the hills, was slain. His body was never found. Elphinstone, in his History, accuses Abul-fazl of giving a confused and contradictory account of this event, "though he must have been minutely informed of its history"; but a little imagination supplies a cause for this: Abul-fazl knew that Birbal was undoubtedly acting on the king's orders.

The emperor for a long time refused even to see Zein-Khân, and he was inconsolable for the loss of his friend--his greatest friend--who had known his every thought. It is said, indeed, that these two men, both keenly interested in the answer to the Great Riddle of Life, the one Agnostic, the other hopeless Optimist by virtue of his genius, had agreed that they would come back the one to the other after death if possible, and that therein lay Akbar's strange eagerness to credit the many reports which gained currency, that Birbal had been seen again alive.

There can be no doubt but that the loss of his friend saddened the remainder of Akbar's life. Indeed, it may be said that from the year in which he quitted Fatehpur Sikri, thus abandoning his Town of Conquest to the flitting bats, the prowling hyenas, the year also of Birbal's loss, a cloud seems to fall over the gorgeous pageant of Akbar's royalty.

Just before this, however, on the very eve of departure, an event occurred at Fatehpur Sikri which in itself, had the Dreamer-King but possessed second sight, would have been sufficient to dim the lustre of his personal life.

For in 1585 three travellers from England arrived with a letter from Elizabeth their queen, to one "Yellabdin Echebar, King of Cambaya, Invincible Emperor."

The letter is worth giving:--

"The great affection which our subjects have to visit the most distant places of the world, not without good intention to introduce the trades of all nations whatsoever they can, by which meanes the mutual and friendly traffique of merchandise on both sides may come, is the cause that the bearer of this letter, John Newberie, joyntly with those that be in his company, with a courteous and honest boldnesse, doe repaire to the borders and countreys of your Empire; we doubt not but that your Imperiall Maiestie, through your royal grace, will favourably and friendly accept him. And that you wold doe it the rather for our sake, to make us greatly beholden to your Maiestie, wee should more earnestly, and with more words, require it, if wee did think it needful.

"But, by the cingular report that is of your Imperiall Maiestie's humanitie in these uttermost parts of the world, we are greatly eased of that burden, and therefore we use the fewer and lesse words; only we request, that because they are our subjects, they may be honestly entreated and received. And that in respect of the hard journey which they have taken to places so far distant, it would please your Maiestie with some libertie and securitie of voiage to gratify it with such privileges as to you shall seem good: which curtesie of your Imperiall Maiestie shall to our subjects at our request perform, wee, according to our royal honour, will recompense the same with as many deserts as we can. And herewith wee bid your Imperiall Maiestie to farewell."

Akbar's answer was to give the travellers safe conduct. So John Newbery, of Aleppo, after seeing all that was to be seen, journeyed Punjâb-ways, to be never again heard of. Ralph Fitch, merchant of London, went south-eastward to find the Great Delta of the Ganges, and so return to England, and by his report, help to start the first British venture to the East; and William Leedes, jeweller, who had learnt his trade in Ghent, remained to cut gems for Akbar.

A notable event, indeed, this first touch of England on India. And it happened when the Moghul dynasty was at the height of its power, when Akbar Emperor, indeed, had but one failure in his life--his sons.

Surely it must have been some prescience of what was to come, which made him, so soon after giving that safe conduct, leave the outward and visible sign of his personal hold on Empire--the City of his Heirs--a prey to the owl and the bat?

Akbar's fourteen-year stay in the Punjâb, spent partly at the Fort of Attock, which he built, and which still frowns over the rushing Indus, and at Lahôre, was marked by the annexation of Kashmir, which was effected with very little bloodshed. Owing to the difficulty of the passes, the first expedition made terms with the ruling power, by which, while the sovereignty of the Moghul was ceded, his interference was barred. This did not suit Akbar's dream of united, consolidated government. So he refused to ratify the treaty, and when the winter snows had melted, sent another expedition to enforce his claim to rule.

Dissensions due to bad government were rife in Kashmir. The troops detailed to defend the Pir-Punjâi pass were disloyal. Half, deserted to the invading force, the remainder retired on the capital. Whereupon, the whole valley lying at the mercy of the Moghul, terms were dictated.

Akbar himself went twice into Kashmir. Those who have been fortunate enough to see the indescribable beauties of its lakes, its trees, its mountains, can imagine how it must have appealed to a man of his nature.

Sinde and Kandahâr followed Kashmir swiftly into the wide net of Moghul influence, and took their places quietly in the emperor's Dream of Empire. Kâbul followed in its turn. While there, Akbar suffered a severe blow in the news of the death in one day--though at different places and causes--of two of his most trusted friends and adherents, Râjah Todâr-Mull, the great Finance-Minister, and Râjah Bhagwân-dâs, his first Râjput ally.

The Dekkan was in process of being netted also, when another and still heavier blow fell on the emperor in the death of his second--and, in many ways, most promising--son, Murâd. He died, briefly, of drink.

But the worst blow was the conduct of his son and heir, Salîm, which in 1598 made it necessary for his father to leave Lahôre for Agra, in order to check the prince's open rebellion. He was now thirty--arrogant, dissolute, passionate in every way; and, finding himself as his father's viceroy at the head of a large army, made a bid for the crown, while his father's forces were engaged in the Dekkan.

But Akbar's love made him patient. He wrote an almost pitiful letter of dignified tolerance. His affection, he said, was still undiminished. Let his son return to duty, and all would be forgotten.

Salîm chose the wiser part of submission, but even as he did so, prepared to wound his forgiving father to the uttermost.

Abul-fazl was on his way back from the Dekkan, and Prince Salîm instigated the Râjah of Orchcha to lay an ambuscade for this old, this most beloved companion of the king.

History says that he and his small force defended themselves with the greatest gallantry, but were eventually cut to pieces. Abul-fazl's head was sent to Prince Salîm, who, however, had craft; for his father, mercifully, never knew whose was the hand that really dealt the death-blow. Had he done so, his grief would have been even greater than it is reported to have been. He touched no food for days; neither did he sleep.

Akbar, indeed, was fast becoming almost unnerved by his tenderness of heart. Salîm, professedly repentant, abandoned himself to still further debaucheries at Allahabâd.

As a last resource, a last effort, Akbar resolved, in a personal interview, to appeal to his son's better feelings.

He had hardly started from Agra, however, when he was recalled to his mother's death-bed. It was yet another shock to Akbar, who, ever since that day of choice, when, surrounded by smiling, expectant faces, he had stood frightened, almost tearful, then with a cry found--he knew not how--Hamida-Begum's loving arms, had held his mother as he held no other woman in the world.

Something of the pity of it must have struck even Salîm's passion-torn heart, for he followed his father and gave in his submission. Not for long, however. Akbar could not be hard on those he loved. The restraint was soon slackened; the physicians who were to break the drug-habit sent to the right-about, and the patient restored to freedom and favour.

And still Fate had arrows in store for poor Akbar's wounded heart. Prince Danyâl, his youngest son, drank himself to death in the thirtieth year of his age, having accomplished his object by liquor smuggled to him in the barrel of his fowling piece.

A pretty prince, indeed, to be the son of the greatest king India has ever known.

This rapid succession of sorrow left the emperor enfeebled. He had always been a hard worker, had spared himself not at all; now Nature was revenging herself on him for his defiance of fatigue.

As he lay dying in the fort at Agra, the emperor, bereft of his friends, worse than bereft of his sons, had but one comfort--his grandson, Prince Khurram, who afterwards succeeded his father under the title of Shâh-jahân. A word from Akbar might have set him on the throne; but the father was loyal to his disloyal son. He summoned his nobles around him, and his personal influence was still so great that not a voice of dissent was raised against his declaration of Prince Salîm--little Shaikie, as he still called him at times--as his heir.

Akbar died at sixty-three, almost his last words being to ask forgiveness of those who stood about his bed, should he ever in any way have wronged any one of them.

The Mahomedan historians assert loudly that he also repeated the Orthodox creed; but this is not likely. He had wandered too far from the fold of Islâm to find shelter from death in it.

So died a man who dreamt a dream, who turned that dream into a reality for his lifetime; but for his lifetime only. Fate gave him no future.

Even his enemies admit with a sneer, saying he had it a gift from a Hindu *jogi*, his almost marvellous power of seeing through men and their motives at a glance. Did he ever, we wonder, look at his own face in the glass, and see written there his failure?

Most of his administrative reforms exist to the present day. Some, such as the abolition of *suttee* and the legislation for widow remarriage which he enforced easily, nearly cost us India to establish.

But Akbar had the advantage of being a king indeed.

"There is but one God, and Akbar is his Viceroy."

Such was his first motto. If it made him a despot, his second one made him tolerant.

"There is good in all things. Let us adopt what *is* good, and discard the remainder." And this admixture of despotism and tolerance is the secret of Indian statesmanship.

Akbar was the most magnificent of monarchs; but all his magnificences held a hint of imagination. Whether in the scattering amongst the crowd by the king's own hand, as he passed to and fro, of dainty enamelled rose-leaves, silvern jasmine-buds, or gilded almonds, or in the daily Procession of the Hours, all Akbar's ceremonials have reference to something beyond the weary, workaday world. In the midst of it all he was simplicity itself.

No better conclusion to this ineffectual record of his reign can be given than this description of him by a European eyewitness:--

"He is affable and majestical, merciful and sincere. Skilful in mechanical arts, as making guns, etc.; of sparing diet, sleeping but three hours a day, curiously industrious, affable to the vulgar, seeming to grace them and their presents with more respective ceremonies than those of the grandees; loved and feared of his own; terrible to his enemies."

One word more. He invariably administered justice sitting or standing below the throne; thus declaring himself to be the mere instrument of a Supreme Power to which he also owned obedience.

So not without cause did this record begin by calling Akbar a Dreamer.

JAHÂNGIR AND NURJAHÂN

A.D. 1605 TO A.D. 1627

These names, "Conqueror of the World" and "Light of the World," are inseparable.

It is as well they should be so, for they supply us with the only excuse which Prince Salîm could put forward for the curious animosity that for many years went hand in hand with his undoubted affection and respect for his great father, Akbar; the excuse being that he had been crossed in love, real, genuine love, by that father's absurd sense of justice.

The story will bear telling.

There was a poor Persian called Mirza or "Prince" Ghiâss, of good family but abjectly poverty-stricken, who, finding it impossible to live in his own country, determined to emigrate to India with his family. On the way thither, his wife, Bibi Azizan, somewhat of a feckless fashionable, was delivered of another daughter. Already in dire distress, the parents felt unable to cope with this fresh misfortune. So they left the child by the wayside. The chief merchant of the caravan by which they were travelling, happening to come along the same road a few hours afterwards, found the baby, and being struck by its beauty, determined to rear it as his own.

Now in a travelling caravan wet-nurses are rare. Small wonder, then, that the infant, whom the merchant had instantly called the "Queen of Women" (*Mihr-un-nissa*), should find its way back to its mother. This led to explanations. The merchant, discovering the father to be much above his present position, employed him in various ways, and became interested in his future.

This led to his being brought to Akbar's notice, who, finding him straightforward and capable, advanced him until he rose to be Lord High Treasurer of the Empire. A fine position, truly, especially for Bibi Azizan, who, amongst the ladies of the court, was noted for the *dernier cri* of fashion both in dress and perfume. It was she, briefly, who invented the attar of rose, which at first sold for its weight in gold.

Now Bibi Azizan was a matchmaking mamma, and in little Mihr-un-nissa she had a pretty piece of goods to bring to market. A thousand pities, indeed, that husband Ghiâss, honest man, had already allowed talk of betrothal with young Sher-Afkân of the King's Light Horse. All the more pity because there was Prince Salîm giving his father trouble despite the Râjput wife they had given him.

That Bibi Azizan cast nets is fairly certain; but it was Fate which sent the bird into them.

It was after one of Akbar's favourite diversions, a Paradise Bazaar, when the lords and ladies of the court had been playing pranks, that Salîm first saw the girl who was, long years afterwards, to be his good genius. The tale may be fully told in verse of how--

"Long ago, so runs the story, in the days of King Akbar,
'Mid the pearly-tinted splendours of the Paradise Bazaar,
Young Jahângir, boyish-hearted, playing idly with his dove,
Lost his boyhood, lost his favourite, lost his heart, and found his love.
By a fretted marble fountain, set in 'broidery of flowers,
Sat a girl, half-child, half-maiden, dreaming o'er her coming hours.
Wondering vaguely, yet half guessing, what the harem women mean
When they call her fair, and whisper, 'You are born to be a queen'.
Curving her small palms, like petals, for their store of glistening spray,
Gazing in the sunny water where in rippling shadow lay
Lips that ripen fast for kisses, slender form of budding grace,
Hair that frames with ebon softness a clear, oval, ivory face.
Arched and fringed with velvet blackness from their shady depths
her eyes
Shine as summer lightning flashes in the dusky evening skies.
Mihr-un-nissa, Queen of Women, so they call the little maid
Dreaming by the marble fountain where but yesterday she played.
Heavy sweet the creamy blossoms gem the burnished orange groves,
Through their shade comes Prince Jehângir, on his wrist two
fluttering doves.
'Hold my birds, child!' cries the stripling, 'I am tired of their play',
Thrusts them in her hands, unwilling, careless saunters on his way.
Culling posies as he wanders from the flowers rich and rare,
Heedless that the fairest blossom 'mid the blaze of blossom there
Is the little dreaming maiden by the fountain-side at rest
With the orange-eyed, bright-plumaged birds of love upon her breast.
Flowers fade and perfume passes; nothing pleases long to-day;
Back toward his feathered fav'rites soon the Prince's footsteps stray.

Dreaming still sits Mihr-un-nissa, but within her listless hold
Only one vain-struggling captive does the lad, surprised, behold.
'Only one?' he queries sharply. 'Sire', she falters, 'one has flown!'
'Stupid! How?' The maiden flushes at his quick imperious tone.
'So! my lord!' she says defiant, with a curving lip, and straight
From her unclasped hands the other circling flies to join its mate.
Heavy sweet the creamy blossom gems the burnished orange tree,
Where the happy doves are cooing o'er their new-found liberty.
Startled by her quick reprisal, wrath is lost in blank surprise,
Silent stands the heir of Akbar, gazing with awakening eyes
At the small rebellious figure, with its slender arms outspread,
Face half frowns, half laughter, royal right of maidenhead.
Slowly dies the flush of anger as the flush of evening dies,
Slowly grow his eyes to brightness as the stars in evening skies.
'So, my lord!' So Love had flitted from the listless hand of Fate,
And the heart of young Jahângir, like the dove, had found its mate!"

Such is the tale which, even nowadays, the women of India love to tell, bewailing the unkind destiny which separated the lovers for nearly twenty years. But, as a matter of fact, there is no evidence to prove that the little Queen-of-Women fell in love with the prince at all. On the contrary, it seems probable that, being a girl of great sense as well as great beauty, she preferred her father's young soldier to her mother's somewhat debauched heir to a throne. Certain it is, however, that the orthodox Mahomedan faction would have viewed with favour the introduction of a Mahomedan bride. Akbar, however, possibly from political motives, ostensibly because of the previous promise, vetoed the match, and giving the young soldier-bridegroom an estate in Bengal, sent him thither with his disturbing wife. Here they seem to have been very happy. But Jahângir did not forget, and the fact that fourteen years afterwards, at least, one of the very first acts of his reign was to send to Bengal, pick a quarrel with Sher-Aikân (who appears to have acted as an honest and upright gentleman by point-blank refusing to be bribed), and treacherously killing him, carry off his wife, makes one pause to wonder whether Jahângir's life might not have been a better one had his inclinations towards this most masterful woman not been thwarted.

It is a curious story altogether, one which needs reading between the lines. Not the least curious part of it being the fact that Jahângir, passionately lustful as he must have been by the time when, as a man of nigh forty, he gained actual possession of Nurjahân, used no force towards her. He accepted her scornful rejection of her husband's murderer, and after months spent in the endeavour to soothe and conciliate her, accepted his defeat.

For six long years Nurjahân lived at the court as one of the attendants of Jahângir's Râjput mother, refusing any pension from the hand of the man who had killed Sher-Afkân, and supporting herself entirely by her exquisite skill in embroidery and painting.

And then?

It is customary to say that ambition overcame her scruples; but the seeing eye, reading between the lines, may find a womanly pity for the man who in the prime of life had lost all control over himself, and who sorely needed help. She was a clever, a fascinating woman; and no woman could quite keep her head before such long constancy as his.

It needed little to bring him back. The story runs, that a single visit to her rooms, where, dressed in the simple white which she always wore after her widowhood, she received him gravely, kindly, was sufficient.

They were married almost immediately, and from that time the woman whom he had first seen as a little maiden beside the fountain was the one over-mastering influence in his life.

Thus before we begin even on Jahângir's career we must concede to him the grace of being a constant lover.

The six years which had passed since he had succeeded to his father had been fairly peaceful ones.

He had found the whole of his vast empire tranquil. The Râna of Oudipur, it is true, was still unvanquished; but the thorn of Chitore had almost ceased to rankle from its sheer persistence. The Dekkan was also disloyal; but there was no pressure of battle, no stress of struggle anywhere, for Jahângir's eldest son, Khushrou (Fair Face), had, after years of open enmity, subsided for the time into sullenness and dejection.

But almost the very first act of Jahângir's administration was one which, as it were, swept away the whole foundation of the empire which Akbar had built up.

He restored the Mahomedan confession of faith to the coins of the realm, thus giving the casting vote to a creed.

It was the first nail in the coffin of Unity.

For the rest, Jahângir evidently did his best for a while. He issued a few edicts, notably one against drug-takers and dram-drinkers, he all the while continuing his notorious habits.

Just before his marriage with Nurjahân, the Dekkan gave him serious trouble. An Abyssinian slave called Malik-Ambêr rose to power and swept all before him, compelling the Imperial troops to retire. But in Bengal peace was restored, and after many successes Oudipur succumbed to a final attack from Prince Khurram, Jahângir's second son, who afterwards reigned as Shâh-jahân. The emperor's delight on this occasion was childlike. In a rather inefficient and unreal diary, which he kept in imitation of his great-grandfather Babar, he records how the very day after the arrival of some captured elephants from Chitore, he sent for the largest of these and "went abroad mounted on Âlam-gomân, to my great satisfaction, and distributed gold in great quantity."

But in all ways he appears to have been blatant, even in his good humours. And these came to the front after his marriage. For Nurjahân was skilful. She held him hard in leash; her ascendency was absolute. It is usual, once more, to discount her influence by asserting its root to have been ambition; but there is absolutely nothing to warrant this assertion. It is true that she raised her own minions to office, that her father held the post of prime minister; but he was wise and just. Nor can there be any doubt that whole administration improved after Jahângir's marriage. As for his private character, he became, for a time, quite a decent and respectable monarch. If he drank, he drank at night in secret; his day duties were done with decorum.

Meanwhile, the report which a certain Mr Ralph Fitch had brought home to a certain "island set in steely seas" was beginning to bear fruit, and something more than hope of mere commerce filled the sails of the innumerable fleets which, not from England alone, but from Holland also, set forth to break through the monopoly of the shores of Ind which Portugal was endeavouring to maintain. The Dutch succeeded first, and their East India Company was formed in 1602. The first Royal Charter given to an English Trading Company was in 1601, but it was not until 1613 that a fleet of four joint-stock vessels, with Sir Thomas Roe aboard, as accredited ambassador from James I to Jahângir's court at Ajmîr, sailed for India.

The journal of this voyage, written by Sir Thomas Roe himself, is excellent reading, and gives us a quaint picture of life at the court of the Great Moghul. Jahângir himself, dead-drunk as often as not, with the figures of Christ and the Virgin Mary hanging to his Mahomedan rosary. A spurious Christianity (deep-dyed by the monkish legends which the Jesuit translators had coolly interpolated into the version of the gospels which Akbar had ordered and paid for!), hustling Hinduism and Islâmism combined. Nurjahân, with trembling lips, no doubt, at times, driving her despot gingerly what way he should go, proud of her power, but weary, a-weary of heart. A beautiful queen, beautifully dressed, clever beyond compare, contriving and scheming, plotting, planning, shielding, and saving, doing all things for the man hidden in the pampered, drink-sodden carcase of the king; the man who, for her, at any rate, always had a heart.

The inconceivable magnificence of it all, the courtesy, the hospitality, the devil-may-care indifference to such trivialities as English merchants or solid English presents! As Sir Thomas Roe writes sadly to his Company:--

"But raretyes please as well, and if you were furnished yearly from Francford, where are all knacks and new devices, £100 would go farther than £500 layd out in England, and *here better acceptable.*"

Thus the rivalry of "made in Germany" is no new thing to India. Sir Thomas himself seems to have been a most excellent, God-fearing man, who was both perplexed and distressed at the attitude of the heathen towards his own faith.

"I found it impossible," he writes, "to convince them that the Christian faith was designed for the whole world, and that theirs was mere fable and gross superstition. There answer was amusing" (?) "enough. 'We pretend not,' they replied, 'that our law is of universal application. God intended it only for us. We do not even say that yours is a false religion; it may be adapted to your wants and circumstances, God having, no doubt, appointed many different ways of going to Heaven.'"

Whether amusing or not, the argument was singularly unanswerable!

One of Sir Thomas Roe's most striking sketches is that of Prince Khurram, who moved through the court, a young man of five-and-twenty, cold, disdainful, showing no respect or distinction of persons; "flattered by some, envied by others, loved by none." "I never saw," writes the ambassador, "so settled a countenance, or any man keep so constant a gravity."

Sir Thomas Roe was not by any means the only Englishman at court. Captain Hawkins had come thither nearly six years before, and had-- Heaven knows why!--been beguiled by the capricious king into remaining, on the promise of a high salary. More than once he had attempted to escape in various ways; but even his plea that he lived in fear of poison was met by Jahângir with almost ludicrous firmness, and the presentation of a "white mayden out of his palace, so that by these means my meats and drinks should be looked into."

Poor Hawkins! His protest that he would take none but a Christian girl was of no avail. An orphan Armenian was promptly found, and the discomfited Captain could only write home:--

"I little thought a Christian's daughter could be found; but seeing she was of so honest a descent, and having passed my word to the king, could not withstand my fortunes. Wherefore I tooke her, and, for want of a minister, before Christian witnesses I married her; the priest being my man Nicolas; which I thought had been lawful, till I met with a preacher that came with Sir Harry Middleton, and he, showing mee the error, I was newly married againe."

An honest soul, apparently, this Captain Hawkins. Sir Harry Middleton was hardly so virtuous, for, disappointed in his desire to establish a factory at Surat, he started with his little fleet for piracy on the High Seas, waylaying other people's golden galleons! But all round the coast, nibbling, as it were, at India's coral strand, were strange ships out of strange nations, seeking for a foothold, seeking for merchandise, for money.

But of this the emperor took no notice; neither did his far more able son, Prince Shâhjahân. Backed by all Nurjahân's influence, he was fast superseding his father in a dual administration, leaving the latter free to amuse himself in Kashmir. But the death of Ghiâss, Nurjahân's father, about the year 1620, brought about complications. His sound good sense, his justice, had so far kept the impulsive womanhood of the empress inline with policy. Now she suddenly betrothed her daughter by her first husband to Prince Shariyâr, the youngest of Jahângir's sons, and naturally threw over the Knight-of-the-Rueful-Countenance, in whose inflexibility she saw danger to her own power. For Jahângir was ill of asthma, and like to die.

Aided by her brother, she set to work instantly to sow dissension between father and son, to such purpose that Shâhjahân, till then the undoubted heir-apparent, his father's fighting right hand, was forced to take refuge in the Dekkan, which once more was in the act of throwing off allegiance to the Moghul.

Having thus disposed, for the time being, of the inconvenient heir, Nurjahân took her emperor to Kashmîr, where, no doubt, he enjoyed himself, for he returned thither the next year. He was, however, living in a fool's paradise, while Nurjahân, bereft of her father's shrewd eyes and Shâhjahân's haughty insight, was but poor protection for a debauched and drunken monarch.

So one dawning the crisis came. Mohabat Khân, whilom Governor of Bengal, a worthy and excellent man, fell into disgrace with the empress. His son-in-law, sent to beg forgiveness, was bastinadoed and returned to him, face towards tail, on an ass.

So it came to pass that while the imperial camp, conveying the emperor to a summer in Kâbul, was marching northward, there followed behind it a half-defiant, half-repentant chieftain, commanding some five thousand stalwart Râjputs.

A word might have brought him to obedience once more; but the imperial camp was large, and proud, and self-confident. So Mohabat bided his time. There was a bridge of boats over the Jhelum River, nigh where the bridge stands now, and after the usual custom, the imperial troops, marching at nightfall, spent the dark hours in crossing and preparing the new camp on the opposite bank.

Thus by dawn little was left but the scarlet-and-gold imperial tents, wherein Majesty lay sleeping; a drunken sleep, it is to be feared.

This was Mohabat's opportunity. He swooped down, overpowered the guards at the bridge, burnt some of the boats, cut others adrift, and then awoke the confused monarch.

One can picture the scene. A protesting prince in pyjamas begging to be allowed to dress in the women's tents, and so gain a few words with his ever-ready counsellor. Mohabat wilily refusing; and so out into the dawn, down by the river-bed, with the red flush paling to primrose in the sky, and the wild geese calling from every patch of green pulse, a disconsolate despot bereft of his guide.

The empress, however, discovering her loss, was nothing daunted. She put on disguise; somehow--Heaven knows how!--managed to cross the Jhelum, and finding her generals somewhat doubtful, somewhat chill, upbraided them for allowing their rightful king to be stolen before their very eyes. That night an attempt was made to rescue him by a nobleman called Fedai-Khân, who swam the river at the head of a small body of horse; but it failed, and half the party was drowned.

Next morning, Nurjahân, having succeeded in rousing the army to a sense of its duty, herself headed a general attack. There was no bridge; the only ford was a bad one, full of dangerous deep pools. But the rashness of impulse was leader, and the woman was amongst the first to land of a whole army, drenched, disordered, dispirited, with powder damp, weighed down with wet clothes and accoutrements.

The result was a foregone conclusion. Nurjahân herself was as a fury. Her elephant circled in by enemies, her guards cut down, balls and arrows falling thick around her howdah, one of them actually hitting her infant grand-daughter, Prince Shahriyar's child, who was seated in her lap. A strange place, in truth, for a baby, unless it were put there as a loyalist *oriflamme*. Then, her driver being killed, and leviathan cut across the proboscis, the beast dashed into the river, sank in deep water, plunged madly, sank again, and so, carried down-stream, finally found shore; and the empress's women, looking to find her half-drowned, half-dead with fear, discovered her busy in binding up baby's wound.

Bravo, Nurjahân! One can forgive much for this one touch of grand-motherhood.

Of course she was beaten; whereupon she gave up force and instantly went to join her husband in the guise of a dutiful wife. It was her only chance of regaining him, and her empire over his enfeebled brain.

Already she was almost too late. Mohabat had been before with her, had treated him with deference, with profound respect, had made him see that she was the cause of all his troubles--which was hardly the case. Anyhow, she was met point-blank with an order for her execution.

Even this did not daunt her courage. She only asked for permission to kiss her lord's hand before death.

Grudgingly assent was given; it could not well be withheld. And one sight of her was enough. Jahângir's heart had really been hers ever since, as a boy, she had defied him in that matter of the doves.

Perhaps--who knows?--she may have stood before him--guilefully--in the very attitude in which she had stood while Love flitted from the listless hand of Fate; and all that Mohabat could do was to bow low and say: "It is not for the Emperor of the Moghuls to ask in vain."

So Nurjahân was once more in her old place beside the drunkard, free to begin again with her fine, feminine wiles. It did not take her long to undermine Mohabat's influence. Within six months her intricate intrigues bore fruit. Jahângir, whose person was so watched and guarded that he was practically a prisoner, was spirited away by a muster of Nurjahân's contingent in the middle of a review, and Mohabat having thus lost his hostage was compelled to come to terms.

One of these being an extremely guileful one, namely, that the ex-Governor of Bengal should turn his military capacity to the crushing of Shâhjahân, who was beginning to give trouble in the Dekkan.

This policy of the Kilkenny cats seemed to promise peace, and, relieved of all anxiety, the emperor and empress set off for their annual visit to Kashmîr. But this time death lurked amid the purple iris fields which they loved so well. The asthma from which Jahângir had suffered for many years became alarming. What were the floating gardens of the Dhal Lake, the Grove of Sweet Breezes, or the Festival of Roses to a monarch who could not draw his breath? They tried to get him back to the warmer climate of the plains, but he died almost ere he left the valley, being carried dead into the tent on one of the high uplands of the Himalaya.

So ended the reign, and with it, Nurjahân's. She made no effort to enter public life again; she put on the white robes of widowhood, and spent her days in prayer and charity, a sufficient answer to those who charge her with personal ambition. As far as India is concerned, Jahângir's was a neutral influence, except for that one first act of his, that rehabilitation of the Mahomedan formula. Under this, the whole of Akbar's dream of unity was dissolving into thin air. Yet the danger which perhaps he had foreseen, against which he had, perhaps, attempted to guard India, was becoming every day more dangerous.

The vultures--or, let us say, the eagles--were gathering over the carcase. From Holland, from Portugal, from England, even from France, came galleons, like birds of prey eager to carry off the riches of the East.

So for picturesque purposes we can think of this reign as of the picture of a man, pampered, bloated, half-drunken, looking in the lazy sunlight at the figure of a woman round whose head doves flutter amongst the hawks.

Jahângir's famous drinking-cup, cut from a single ruby about 3 inches long, after passing from hand to hand for many years down to the last century, has finally and mysteriously disappeared.

In some ways it would be worth while once to drain the good wine of Shiraz from the glowing red heart of that fatal cup which bears on it, in fine gold characters, a single name.

They say it is "Jahângir"--Or is it "Nurjahân"?

SHÂHJAHÂN

A.D. 1627 TO A.D. 1657

The Knight-of-the-Rueful-Countenance in his youth, remarkable for his lack of amiability, Shâhjahân's character appears to have changed to cheerfulness from the moment when, at the age of thirty-seven, he ascended the throne.

It was immediately evident also that not without purpose had he sate at the feet of that Gamaliel of administrative ability, Akbar. Without his grandfather's genius, a man, in brief, of infinitely lower calibre all round, he is yet palpably a lineal descendant of the Great Moghul. In reading of him we are continually reminded of that grandfather to whom he was so much attached, that when in the hour of Akbar's death he was urged by his father to follow his example and flee the court for fear of assassination by those who were pushing Prince Khûshru's claim, he replied proudly "that his father might do as he chose, but that he would watch by Akbar till the last."

It may be that this devotion had not been disinterested, and that disappointment at not being chosen to succeed may have had something to do with the moroseness of the young prince; but, on the other hand, it may have been the hidden impatience of knowing that filial affection, honour, everything his grandfather (who had been his boyhood's hero) held most dear compelled him to bide Nature's time for kingship, that made the long years seem wasted. For Jahângir's government was not good; after a very few years the whole administration of the country had visibly declined. It rose again under Shâhjahân, and some historians go as far as to say that, although "Akbar excelled all as a law-maker, yet for order and arrangement, good finance and government in every department of State, no prince ever reigned in India that could be compared to Shâhjahân." One thing is certain. India during his time was peaceful, easeful, and prosperous.

One reason for this is not hard to trace. Europe for the first time had really entered the Indian markets, and the superfluities it found there were being paid for in gold. There had been a time of truce, as it were, between the Dutch and the English after the massacre at Amboyna--a needless and brutal massacre which still stands to the discredit of the Dutch. England had threatened war, Holland had promised redress, and so the long years passed by, giving opportunities of commerce to both sides. But it was not until the seventh year of Shâhjahân's reign that the *firmân* granted by Jahângir to Thomas Roe, authorising the English to trade in Bengal, was acted upon, and a factory (as such trading centres were called) opened at Pepli, close to the estuary of the river Hugli.

That the commerce was growing by leaps and bounds may be judged from the fact that the original East India Company had to petition Parliament first; to restrain their own servants from taking undue advantage of a regulation which permitted a certain fixed limit of private trade; and secondly, against the formation of another trading company to the East India's. The chief cause of complaint made about the original one being its failure to fortify its factories, and so "provide safety or settledness for the establishment of traffic in the said Indies, for the good of posterity." Whence it may be observed that the policy of "pike and carronade" was beginning to find favour. For Charles I. granted a charter to this new company; whereupon time was lost, as well as tempers, in the consequent conflict of interests. The record written by the French physician, Francois Bernier, of his "Travels and Sojourn in the Moghul Empire," gives us clear insight as to what was happening in this first organised attempt of the West on the East. Scarcely a page passes without reference to new efforts of the Portuguese to outwit England, England to outwit Portugal, and of both to double-dam the Dutch. And behind all were the refuse leavings of all three nations, mixed up with Malays, Jews, Turks, Infidels, and Hereticks, in the redoubtable persons of the Pirates of Arracan; those foremost of buccaneers, who swept the Indian seas and harried its coral strands. Bernier's description of them is worth recording, as it shows graphically how the cancer of commerce and so-called civilisation was eating into the dreamful, slothful, ease-loving body-politic of the whole peninsula.

"The Kingdom of Arracan has contained during many years several Portuguese settlers, a great number of Christian slaves, or half-cast Portuguese and other Europeans collected from various parts of the world. That kingdom was a place of refuge for fugitives from Goa, Ceylon, Cochin, Malacca, and other settlements ... and no persons were better received than those who had deserted their monasteries, married two or three wives, or committed other great crimes.... As they were unawed and unrestrained by the Government, it was not surprising that these renegades pursued no other trade than that of rapine and piracy. They scoured the neighbouring seas in light galleys, entered the numerous arms of the Ganges, ravished the islands of Lower Bengal; and, often penetrating forty or fifty leagues up the country, surprised and carried away the entire population of villages on market days, and at times when the inhabitants were assembled for the celebration of a marriage, or some other festival.... The treatment of the slaves thus made was most cruel.... By a mutual understanding, the pirates would await the arrival of the Portuguese ships, who bought whole cargoes at a cheap rate; and it is lamentable to reflect that other Europeans have pursued the same flagitious commerce with the Pirates of Arracan, who boast that they convert more Hindus to Christianity in a twelve-month than all the missionaries in India do in twelve years."

Not a pleasing picture, though it whets the curiosity to know more, for instance, of the career of Fra Joan, the Augustine monk who, having by means unknown possessed himself of the island of Sundiva, reigned there King-of-the-Pirates for many years.

It was the encouragement given to these scourges of the seas which brought down on the Portuguese the vengeance of Shâhjahân, whose laconic reply to the complaint of his governor in Bengal against their new factory at Hugli is delightful in its peremptoriness, pathetic in its pride: "Expel those idolaters from my dominions!"

Easier said than done, even though the image-decorated church at Agra, which had been built in the reign of Akbar, and the newer one with chimes in its steeple, which had been erected at Lahôre in Jahângir's time, could easily be demolished. Still Hugli could be besieged and captured, and no doubt the success made a subject for general rejoicing. For above all things Shâhjahân delighted in fireworks; that is to say, he had a perfect passion for expensive entertainments, for gorgeous processions, for magnificent buildings. Half the architectural sights of to-day in Northern India are due to Shâhjahân's lavish love of beauty. Some of his *fêtes*, again, are estimated to have cost over a million and a half sterling. The famous peacock throne, of which Tavernier, a French jeweller by profession, asserts--with apparent credence--that it was commonly supposed to have been worth nearly six and a half millions, was constructed by this king's orders.

The question rises insistently: "How came the Emperor of India by such enormous wealth?" The answer is curiously simple: "L'etat c'est moi."

The State was the Emperor, or rather the Emperor was the visible State. Every atom of imperial revenue passed through his hands for distribution. Not in precise pay to clerks and collectors, to magistrates and ministers, departments and divisions, but in lavish gifts and prodigal scatterings abroad over the land. Whence the gold, gaining circulation, filtered down in smaller payments, smaller giftings. It was a quaint, but not a bad method of making the king the Fount-of-all-Goodness, the veritable Father-of-his-people. Indeed, Shâhjahân was counted, despite the fact that he spent the three-and-twenty millions sterling of revenue in right imperial fashion, to have been an economical king, getting his full money's worth in all ways. Nor was he privately an inordinately rich man, for Bernier states that when he died his whole personal estate was worth about six millions. Thus, while we read of peacock thrones, of marvellous mosques, of three millions spent without regret on a mausoleum, of half that sum squandered in what we have called fireworks, it is necessary to readjust our Western vision, and see public utility behind the personal extravagance. In fact the spectacle of Shâhjahân, the most magnificent of monarchs, raises the problem as to how far a millionaire's reckless squandering of a sovereign injures that coin of the realm for its final purpose of bringing bread to a hungry mouth.

Regarding the actual events of Shâhjahân's reign, there is very little to say. The Dekkan--in which we can now include the whole southward country down to Cape Cormorin, the hitherto unsurveyed, unrecorded triangle forming the apex of India having, chiefly by the nibbling of foreigners along the entire seaboard, by this time come into the equation--was as ever unsettled. It had, even in Akbar's time, been nothing more than a fief of the Crown, and though under his system it would doubtless have become in time an integral part of the empire, it was gradually making once more for independence. So, naturally, there was trouble in the Dekkan. The Râjputs, however, seem to have been fairly quiescent, and the chief disturbances of Shâhjahân's time were the constant quarrels of his four sons, Dâra, Shujah, Aurungzebe, and Morâd. These, with four daughters, Pâdshâh or Jahanâra Begum, Roshanrâi Begum, and two others, were undoubtedly the children of one wife; nor is there mention of others, so if it be true that Mumtâz Mahal, to whose memory the Tâj was built, died in giving birth to a thirteenth child, many of her family must have died, or been done away with in infancy; legend says the latter, Shâhjahân being three parts Râjput. It was, curiously enough, Shâhjahân's absolute adoration for his eldest daughter, Pâdshâh or Jahanâra Begum, which was the cause of England's first hold on Bengal. She was badly burnt in attempting to save a favourite companion, and an English doctor, Gabriel Boughton, hastily summoned from Surat, asked and received as his fee, the right for Great Britain to trade in Bengal.

To return to the sons. Dâra, the eldest, is drawn by Bernier in fairly pleasing colours. Frank and impetuous, liberal in his opinions, he made enemies with one hand while he made friends with the other, while his open profession of the tenets held by his grandfather Akbar, and the writing of a book to reconcile Hindu and Mahomedan doctrines, alienated the orthodox from his cause. Shujah, by his father's estimate, was a mere drunkard; Morâd, the youngest, a sensualist. There remains Aurungzebe. He was an absolute contrast to Dâra. A small man, with a big brain and absolutely no heart. A man of creeds and caution, of faith and faithlessness. He had what historians call an "early turn for devotion." In a thousand ways--and those the least estimable--he reminds one of Cromwell; Cromwell without his magnificent sincerity of purpose.

The history of the mutual misunderstandings and divisions and coalitions of these princes is indeed a weary one. Only Dâra comes out of it with comparatively clean hands. Indeed, in the last act of the drama of Shâhjahân's actual reign of thirty years our sympathies go entirely with Dâra, as he struggles to maintain his own future position, and still uphold that of the sick king.

As this final incident is an excellent example of what in lesser degree had been going on for years, it may be given with advantage. Shâhjahân was in his sixty-seventh year. His sons, therefore, all but the youngest, Morâd, touched and overpassed forty. His eldest, Dâra, had for some time had a large share in the Government, both as heir-apparent, and also because his father in his old age had turned to wine and women. Pâdshâh Begum, the elder daughter, to whom the aged emperor had devoted attachment, unbounded affection, was ever on her brother's side. Shujah, the second son, was Viceroy in Bengal; Prince Morâd, the youngest, Viceroy in Guzerât. Aurungzebe was occupied in Golconda carrying the Moghul arms into the diamond country.

Thus Dâra, on his father's sudden and dangerous sickness--of the cause of it the less said the better--found himself able for a time, with his sister's help, to keep all knowledge of the king's danger from spreading throughout the country. But as Pâdshâh Begum was Dâra's ally, so Roshanrâi, the younger sister, was fast friend to Aurungzebe. Through her he learnt the truth, and instantly took his part cautiously, diplomatically. He did not instantly proclaim himself king, as Shujah and Morâd did in their several viceroyalties when the news also reached their ears. He stood aside and waited, while Shujah marched with his army to engage Dâra, and then wrote to his younger brother Morâd one of the most fulsome letters of flattery ever penned, declaring that he, and he alone, was fit for the crown, and offering him the service of one who, weary of the world, was on the eve of renouncing it, and indulging the devotion of his nature by retirement to Mekka! Morâd must have been a fool to have swallowed the bait, but swallow it he did; and with this cat's-paw puppet in front of him, Aurungzebe, with their conjoined armies, moved to Agra, whence Shujah had been driven back by Dâra into Bengal. The old king was by this time convalescent, and, finding Dâra, instead of taking advantage of his illness, was, on the contrary, ready to yield up his brief regency with cheerfulness, was inclined to trust his eldest son more than ever. He therefore consented, somewhat against his own will, to the latter trying conclusions at once with the Morâd-Aurungzebe confederacy. Fortune went against him. During the battle Aurungzebe, who asserted that he warred alone against the irreligious, the heretical, the scandalous Dâra, was loud in prayerful protestations that God was on their side; after it he fell on his knees and thanked Divine Providence for the victory and the round thousand or so of souls sent below. Dâra fled, and three days afterwards Aurungzebe marched into Agra, coolly imprisoned the aged king in the fort, and having now no further use for Morâd, invited him to supper, plied him with drink (waiving his own pious scruples for the time), so, when hopelessly intoxicated, disarmed him in favour of chains, and packing him on an elephant, despatched him as a State prisoner to Selimgarh, the mid-river fort at Delhi! So ended poor, foolish Morâd's dream of kingship; nor was his life much more prolonged, for shortly afterwards he was executed in prison on a trumped-up charge. Shujah escaped a like fate by disappearance, and poor Dâra, after unheard-of dangers, difficulties, trials and terrors, met with a worse one.

But this record belongs to the reign of Aurungzebe, the man without a heart.

Shâhjahân, meanwhile, remained for seven years a captive in the fort, old, decrepid, tearful, counting his jewels, and comforted by his daughter, Pâdshâh Begum.

A sad ending this, for a man who had been the most magnificent monarch who ever sate upon the throne of India. But all his energies, all his capabilities seem to have deserted him. He made no effort to reassert his kingship, and what is still more strange, no friend or companion, no minister, no adherent, attempted it for him. Utterly deserted by all save his daughter, he died seven years afterwards, in 1665, and was buried at his own request beside his wife in the Tâj Mahal, that most marvellous monument of marriage which the world has ever seen.

And out of this there springs to light for the seeing eye a pitiful story which brings back a pulse of human sympathy for the man whose old age was so sordid, so degenerate.

How many years was it since with bitter grief he had buried the wife to whom he was so devotedly attached that history declares he kept faithfully to her, and to her only, till death did them part?

It was four-and-thirty years since the daughter she was bearing to him cried--so the story runs--ere it was born, and within a few hours, Ârjamund the Beloved lay dead with her still-born babe.

A tragedy indeed! Think what it means! Long years of hardship, exile, wandering, and then four only--four short years of content, of kingship, in which to heap comforts, luxuries, on the woman whom you love--who has borne with you the heat and burden of the day.

That was Shâhjahân's fate. But the history of these Moghul kings, these Great Moghuls whose name still lingers in conjunction with that of the Grand Turk and Bluebeard as something slightly shocking and decidedly despotic so far as women are concerned, is curiously disconcerting to one's preconceived ideas on this counter.

Babar, whose Mahum met him after long years "at midnight," as with bare head and slipper-shoon he ran to catch the earliest glimpse of her along the dusty road. Humâyon, whose sixteen-year-old bride, Hamida, wedded in hot love-haste, brought him his first son at the age of thirty-eight. Akbar, who, after a brief youth of normal passion, settled down into the life of an anchorite. Shâhjahân, who built the Tâj, who spent twenty-two years of his life in gathering together every conceivable beauty to lay at the dead feet of a woman who bore him thirteen children.

These are not the records which we should have expected from a line of Eastern kings.

Regarding this same monument of marriage, the Tâj. So much has been said about it, that little remains to say. Perhaps the most bewildering thing about its beauty is the impossibility of saying wherein that beauty lies. Colour of stone, purity of outline, faultlessness of form, delicacy of decoration--all these are here; but they are also in many a building from which the eye turns--and turns to forget.

But once seen, the Tâj--whether seen with approval or disapproval-- is never forgotten. It remains ever a thing apart. Something which the world cannot touch with either praise or blame--something elusive, beyond criticism in three dimensional terms.

It was Shâhjahân who first thought of it; but who designed, who built it?

The very question brings a certain revulsion. It is impossible to dislocate one stone of the Tâj from another, to think of it in fragments, as anything than as a perfect whole.

No! it was never built. It is a bit of the New Jerusalem which some yellow Eastern dawn coming after a velvet-dark Eastern night, found standing, as it stands now, amid the cypresses of the garden.

AURUNGZEBE

A.D. 1657 TO A.D. 1707

With Aurungzebe, the Middle Age of Indian History ends. From the date of his death, interest finally ceases to centre round the dying dynasties of India, and, changing sides, concerns itself absolutely with the coming sovereignty of the West.

Even during his long reign of fifty years, the attention is often distracted by the welter of conflicting commerces which, leaving the sea-boards, spread further and further up-country. It requires, therefore, some concentration to deal with Aurungzebe, the last of the Great Moghuls; the last, and, without doubt, the least estimable of them all.

In truth, the steps to his throne were littered with black crime. Shâhjahân, his father, had, it is true, made his seat more secure by the deaths by poison, bow-string, or sword, of the three next heirs to the throne--one of them his half-uncle; but Aurungzebe trod on the bodies of three brothers in reaching kingship, and for seven years of that kingship carried about with him the prison key of a deposed and dishonoured father. Of minor sins, such as the poisonings of nephews, cousins, even aunts, there were scores. Well might he exclaim upon his death-bed: "I have committed numerous crimes--I know not with what punishment I may be seized."

And yet he was, in his way, a good king. Had he been less of a bigot, he would have been a better one; but this bigotry was necessary to his peace of mind. He could not have borne the sting of conscience without some anodyne of hard-and-fast religious rectitude. It was after the murder of his brother Dâra, who, caught on the confines of Sinde, almost unattended (for he had sent his most trusted adherents back to Lahôre with the dead body of his wife, who had died of fatigue), was given a mock trial for heresy and done to death, that Aurungzebe built the celebrated Blood-money Mosque at Lahôre, in which no Mahomedan prayed for long years, feeling it to be defiled indeed.

But Aurungzebe was for ever hedging between this world and the next, so we must take him as we find him--an absolutely contemptible creature, who yet did good work. Needless to say, however, "Akbar's Dream" vanished into thin air from the moment he set his foot upon the throne.

The first five years of his reign were practically spent in ridding himself of relations. The whole family of Shujah suffered death, and even his own son was immured as a state prisoner in consequence of a trivial act of independence.

Then--and small wonder!--he was seized with a mysterious illness, which left him speechless. Nothing but his marvellous determination could have averted the chaos which must have followed in a state but half broken in to his murderous methods. But he sent for his great seal and his sister Roshanâra, and keeping them both by his sick-bed, held order by sheer insistency until he recovered.

So, after a brief holiday in Kashmir--that happy hunting-ground of all the Moghul kings, who seem to have inherited the love of beautiful scenery from their great ancestor, Babar--he came back to face the greatest foe to the Moghul power which had arisen since the combined Râjput resistance was finally broken by Mahomed-Shahâb-ud-din-Ghori.

This foe was the Mahratta race, which had been gradually growing to power in the Western Ghâts, that natural stronghold of mountains which rises in many places like a wall between the Western Sea and the high table-land of Central India. No more fitting birthplace for warlike tribes could be imagined. Towards the sea, breaks of rich rice-fields, tongued by spurred rocks and outlying strips of almost impenetrable forest. Then the bare, broken ridges, 3,000 or 4,000 feet high, ending often in a scarp of sheer precipice, and giving on wide, thicket-set woods, through which, after a while, ravines break into valleys to the eastward. A land of rain--clouds from the south-west monsoon, of roaring torrents and drifting mists; full of wild beasts fleeing fearfully from the small, sturdy huntsmen of the hills. These were the Mahrattas. Not a very interesting race when all was said and done. Brave, dogged, determined, but, by reason, doubtless, of their Sudra extraction, lacking the nobility of the Râjput and the Râjput nicety in honour.

It was in the time of Malik-Ambêr, the Abyssinian slave who in the reign of Jahângir gave new life to the dying dynasty in the Dekkan, that the Mahrattas first made their mark. Before this, history does not even recognise them.

Amongst the Mahratta officers of Malik-Ambêr was one Mâlo-ji, who had a five-year-old son called Shâh-ji. To a Hindu festival at the house of a Râjput this boy was taken, and by chance was lifted to one knee of the host, whose little daughter of three occupied the other.

"They are a fine couple," laughed the host and father. "They should be man and wife!"

This was enough for Mâlo-ji's ambition. He started up, and called the company to witness that the girl was affianced to his son.

Naturally enough, the claim roused indignation; but in the end, Mâlo-ji's fortunes improving, Shâh-ji gained his high-caste bride, and from the marriage sprang Siva-ji, the national hero of the Mahrattas, who was destined to wreck the power of the Moghuls in the south.

Siva-ji, by the time he was sixteen, was already notorious. His love of adventure, his knowledge of the popular ballads of the people, his complicity in the great gang-robberies which formed an ever-recurring excitement to life in the Ghâts, his intimate acquaintance with every footpath and defile in that wild country, his horsemanship, his sportsmanship, were on the tongues of all; and when, still in his teens, he fortified one of the neglected hill-citadels and set up a chieftainship of his own, there were not wanting those who laughed at the impertinence as a high-spirited, boyish freak.

But within a few years the boyish freak was found to be open rebellion, and Siva-ji was practically king of the wild western country. What is more, he had become an ardent Hindu, and laid claims to Divine dreams.

The court at Bîjapur attempted remonstrance, imprisoned poor Shâh-ji, his father, and threatened to wall him up unless Siva-ji repented of his errors: whereupon, with the cunning which distinguished him in all things, the latter made overtures to, and was taken into the service of, Shâhjahân, then engaged in the Dekkan. So for a few years affairs remained at a deadlock; Siva-ji, apprehensive for his father, Bîjapur of the Moghuls.

Then Shâh-ji being released, his son began his career of annexation afresh, being checked, however, in his depredations by fear of Prince Aurungzebe, who was then fighting the King of Golconda.

Both of the same kidney, artful, designing, specious, the diplomacies which passed between the Mahratta robber-chieftain and Aurungzebe, intent on stealing the throne of India, cannot have been edifying. The former took the opportunity of the latter's hasty retreat on the news of his father's illness, to increase his power by an act of double-dyed treachery. He induced the commander of the King of Bîjapur's forces to come unattended to the hill fort of Partabghar in order to receive his submission.

The scene is dramatic.

The generalissimo, in white muslin, carrying for ornament only a stiff, straight sword of state, awaiting on a rocky plateau with one single attendant the advance of Siva-ji, who, also in white muslin, was seen slowly descending the steps of his eyrie, apparently unarmed, and also with but one attendant. A slim little bit of a fellow this Siva-ji, timid, hesitating. But appearances are deceitful: underneath his muslin robing was chain armour, within his closed left hand were the "tiger's claws" (sharp hooks of steel fastened on to the fingers with which to grapple with the foe), and close to his outstretched, salaaming right hand was a poniard. It was all over in a second. The tiger's claws gripped and held, the dagger did its work. And then Siva-ji's wild robber hordes, conveniently disposed beforehand by secret paths round the royal troops, fell upon them and spared not until victory was secure. For in truth Siva-ji appears to have been of the noble highwayman type--that is to say, not set on murder if he can gain gold without it.

Siva-ji's next exploit was less blameworthy. Shayista-Khân, who commanded Aurungzebe's forces in the Dekkan, marched to annihilate the little robber, and, succeeding in worsting him in the open, took up quarters at Poona; curiously enough, occupying the very house in which Siva-ji had spent his youth.

Possibly the intimate knowledge of back-door passages, which he must thus have possessed, suggested what was more a boyish escapade than a serious attack. Siva-ji, with some twenty followers, entered Poona at night by joining a marriage procession, made his way straight to the house, entered by a side door, and was in Shayista-Khân's bedroom but half a minute too late, yet just in time to cut off with his sword the two fingers that clung to the window-sill as the Mahomedan general let himself down into the courtyard below. Whereupon, seeing that same courtyard full of ramping soldiery, Siva-ji retired as he came, until, once outside the city gates, he lit up torches and flambeaux; so making his way back to his hill eyrie, some 12 miles off, in a blaze of triumph that was visible to every Moghul in the place. This tale is still told by the Mahratta bards with immense enthusiasm, though the story of his march against Aurungzebe at Delhi is really more exciting.

They were birds of a feather these two: both small, slippery, absolutely untrustworthy; both playing consistently for their own hands. At one time, however, Siva-ji seems to have been inclined to yield to Aurungzebe, and honest, liberal treatment might have turned the rebel freebooter into a staunch adherent; but it was not in Aurungzebe to trust any one. So, mistaking his man utterly, he received the little Mahratta cavalierly, and when he stormed and raged and positively swooned with vexation, made him virtually a prisoner.

Almost alone in Delhi with his five-year-old son Samba-ji, Siva-ji was too wily to precipitate matters by any display of annoyance; but he laid his plans. His first move was to beg leave for his small escort to leave Delhi, the climate of which he said was insalubrious. To this Aurungzebe gave glad consent; it seemed to leave Siva-ji still more at his mercy. The latter next took to his bed on plea of sickness. This afforded him an opportunity of, first, being able to use the Hindu physicians, who were allowed to attend him, as spies and go-betweens; second, of sending sweetmeats and other offerings to various *fakirs*, Hindu and Mahomedan, with a request for their prayers. And as he grew more and more sick, the hampers and baskets containing the offerings grew larger and larger, until one day--hey presto!--little Siva-ji and his little son occupied the place of the sweetmeats. It was hours before the guards discovered that the sick-bed was occupied by a dummy, and by that time Siva-ji was in Muttra amongst his disguised followers. He himself adopted that of a wandering *jogi*, and, smeared all over with ashes, arrived in due time quite jauntily in his old haunts.

Aurungzebe took his defeat in good part. For the time he was occupied with Shâhjahân's death, and with embassies from Arabia and Abyssinia. Then Little Tibet had just been brought under his sway, and in Bengal the kingdom of Arrakan, which held the rich rice-fields of Chittagong, had been added to the crown.

It was some years, therefore, before Aurungzebe pitted himself once more against the Mahratta.

Then once again he found the impracticability of subduing an enemy which, at the first attack, reduced itself to a horde of units, each one animated by individual love of fight, love of plunder. It was guerilla war with a vengeance, so after a time the emperor was not sorry to have his attention drawn from it to the northwest frontier. On his return from this unsuccessful expedition, he settled down for a time to govern his kingdom, which he did in a way that irritated and exasperated both Hindus and Mahomedans. The former almost rose in revolt at the reimposition of the poll tax on infidels; the latter, especially in the court, objected to the prohibition of all amusements. Amongst other prohibitions was the curious one of forbidding history to be written, or court annals to be kept; the result being that no real record of the last forty years of this reign is extant.

As time went on, he bore more and more hardly on the Hindus, until discontent spread on all sides, and in the Dekkan every one was at heart a partisan of Siva-ji.

Finally, an attempt on Aurungzebe's part to get into his power the infant children of Râjah Jâi-Singh of Ambêr, whom he had caused to be poisoned in his distant viceroyalty of Kâbul, joined to the iniquity of the *jizya,* or infidel tax, set the whole of Râjputana in a flame. In this connection the letter sent to the Emperor by Rana Râj-Singh of Chittore may be quoted in part, as an example of the dignified remonstrances which preceded the appeal to the sword.

"How can the dignity of the sovereign be preserved who employs his power in exacting heavy tribute from a people thus miserably reduced?... If your Majesty places any faith in those books, by distinction called divine, you will there be instructed that God is the god of all mankind, not the god of Mahomedans alone. The pagan and the Mussulman are equally in His presence ... to vilify the religion or customs of other men is to set at naught the pleasure of the Almighty ... In fine, the tribute you demand from Hindus is repugnant to justice; it is equally foreign to good policy, as it must impoverish the country."

The appeal, needless to say, was fruitless; but after a long and mutually disastrous war a sort of peace was patched up between the Râjputs and the Moghuls, leaving Aurungzebe free to attempt yet once again to repress the irrepressible Siva-ji, who by this time had been crowned King of the Mahrattas, and had become a still more ardent Hindu, minutely scrupulous to ceremonial and caste.

Thus the two great rival powers in India were bigoted Hinduism, bigoted Islâmism. A far cry, indeed, from dead Akbar's Dream of tolerant Unity.

So the struggle recommenced. But Siva-ji was more elusive than ever. He fought by sea as well as by land, and the first record of a naval war in India is that which he waged along the shores of Western India. Only the English settlement at Surat defied him. They put their factory into what state of defence was possible, garrisoned it with their crews, and met the marauding Mahrattas with a sally which effectually drove them off. For which valiant defence of their own, Aurungzebe exempted the English for ever from a portion of the customs duty paid by other nations, and remitted the transit charges.

Siva-ji thus indirectly did a good turn to English commerce.

Years passed, bringing advantage to the Mahratta side, when, in 1680, death suddenly intervened and carried off the clever, astute little Siva-ji in the fifty-third year of his age.

A bit of a genius was Siva-ji, quick to seize on the mistakes of his adversary, and far-seeing enough to appeal to natural spirit and religious enthusiasm in his adherents. Thus, though his death was a great blow, it did not crush the rising fortunes of the Mahrattas, despite the fact that Samba-ji, his heir, had shown no capability for kingship during his youth, and on his accession gave himself up to cruelty and passion. Still the war dragged on; defeat was indeed impossible to an army which had no cohesion, and which now, in consequence of the failure of regular pay under Samba-ji's career of idle luxury, degenerated into plundering hordes of mere freebooters.

It was at this juncture that Aurungzebe himself, possibly suspicious of his generals, always distrustful of everything that did not actually come under his eyes, and pass through his hands, marched southwards. In a way, it was a fatal mistake; for he brought with him all his intolerant authority, his infatuation for his faith. Hitherto his officers, seeing the evil effects of levying the infidel tax strictly in this land of infidels, had let it slide; now affairs took a very different turn. But at first the imperial troops were fairly successful, though by the time they had marched through the Ghât country they were crippled by sickness, outwearied by the difficulty of the roads, harassed by the continual depredations of Samba-ji's guerillas both by sea and land. To add to difficulty, the latter concluded a sort of a defensive alliance with the King of Golconda; whereupon the emperor, tired of hunting a Will-o'-the-Wisp through mists and swamps, seized on a stationary enemy. Golconda reduced to terms, Bijapur next came under displeasure. A very small state, its capital was an extremely large town, the circumference of the walls being more than 6 miles. Garrisoned by a very small force it soon fell, and Aurungzebe was carried in a portable throne through the breach into the deserted city. It remains now much as it was then--a city, not of ruins, but of desertion. The walls, still entire, are surmounted by the cupolas and minarets of the public buildings within, so that from outside Bijapur shows bravely; but within all is desolation. The wide Mosque, the splendid palace, the great domed tomb of the kings, are alike deserted, the home only of bats and hyenas. Yet still, centering the desertion, stands the old brass cannon, weighing 41 tons, which "Rumi the European" cast in 1585.

While this was going on, be-drugged, dissolute Samba-ji watched the proceedings inertly, ineptly. The Mahratta historians accuse Kalusha the Brahman, his favourite, the pandar to all his vices, of having enchanted the young man; but the enchantment was mere sensuality, self-indulgence.

His time for enjoyment, nevertheless, ran short. Golconda and Bijapur taken, Aurungzebe, triumphant--after, as usual, alienating the people by his religious intolerance--added to religious hatred by capturing the person of Samba-ji while drunk and incapable in his favourite palace of pleasure, and thereinafter, having paraded him through the camp in disgrace, ordering him to prison. Whereupon Samba-ji, roused at last to sense, openly reviled the emperor, his prophet, his faith, in language so strong that it was considered necessary to cut his tongue out as a punishment for blasphemy, before beheading him and his favourite, the vile Kalusha.

Anything more injudicious could not well be conceived. Despised as Samba-ji had been whilst alive by the better class of Mahrattas, he was now a martyr. From this time, the fortunes of Aurungzebe, and with them the Empire of the Moghuls, began to fall; and for the few remaining years of his life, the emperor, now growing old, must have felt himself and his power on the downward grade. His indefatigable perseverance, his laborious energy, are almost pitiful. Over eighty years of age, he rested not at all, and despite our reprobation, the heart softens towards the tired old man as we see him, seemingly careless of the greater enemy along his sea-board, leading his armies through trackless forests and flooded valleys, enduring hardships that would have tried youth, in pursuit of the irrepressible, irresponsible Mahrattas. An old man, small, slender, stooping, with a long nose, a frosted beard, and a perpetual smile.

That smile was worn outside; but within? Within was weariness and fear even for this life. The remembrance of his father's fate at his hands seems never to have left him; every action of his during the later years of his reign showing his fear lest a like fate should be his. So he held every tiny thread of the great warp and woof of Government in his own hands. Only thus could he feel secure.

In such a system abuse is inevitable. No single eye can supervise a wide empire, and so corruption grew apace, and with corruption, inefficiency. The noblemen, waxing effeminate, wore wadded coats under their chain armour; their horses, laden with ornamentations, housed with velvet, were purely processional, and utterly unfit for war. The common soldiers, aping their superiors, followed suit, and became so slothful that they could neither keep watch nor picket, and discipline disappeared utterly.

Yet all the time, while Aurungzebe, old, enfeebled in health, outwearied himself in precautions, in providence, the greatest enemy to the Moghul dynasty was advancing, apparently unnoticed, in rapid strides. For the West had finally set its face towards the East. Commerce had already joined hands over the empire. In 1667 Britain, France, Holland, and Denmark, signed a treaty of common cause at Breda that was practically a league against the Pagan and the Portuguese. A few years previously the island and town of Bombay had been ceded to England as part of the dower of Catherine of Braganza, and had become thereby so much an integral part of Great Britain that every native in it, every child born there, had the right to claim every privilege of a British subject.

Fort St George, the nucleus of Madras, was finally established, and the group of factories around it formed into a presidency. Job Charnock had founded Calcutta, and Hugli was soon to be merged in it.

Then a new note had come into the dealings of the English with the accession of James II. A large shareholder, he promised the East India Company military support, and henceforward the "native powers were to be given to understand that the Company would treat with them as an independent power, and, if necessary, compell redress by force of arms." In consequence of this the President, Sir John Child, was appointed "Captain-General and Admiral of all forces by sea and land."

Poor Sir John Child! He was the first instance of a cat's-paw in the East (there have been many since!), and when the tortuous policy of the Company towards the Great Moghul failed, and they found it impossible to hunt with the hounds and run with the hare, by making war in Bengal, and wearing a mask of friendship in Bombay, he went to the wall promptly in obedience to Aurungzebe's "irreversible order" that "Mr Child, who did the disgrace, should be turned out and expelled."

But there was more disgrace than the making of a scapegoat out of one man in store for the old original East India Company. How much of the dirt flung at it in the next ten years or so deserves to stick? Who can tell? Or who can say how much of the moil and turmoil which arose around it was due to honest John Bull's honest love of clean hands, and how much to the itching of his palm? When gold is in dispute, motives are hard to dissever, impossible to pigeonhole. And in those days the Pagoda Tree was in full bearing, the gold lay on Tom Tiddler's ground ready to be picked up. So, at least, it must have seemed to England.

A terrible temptation to all sorts of sins. And so we have allegations of bribery, Parliamentary enquiries, scandalous disclosures, petitions, answers at length, impeachment of the Duke of Leeds, convenient disappearance of the Duke's servant, final hint by the disturbed king--William of Orange--that disclosures and exposures were out of season, as he was under the necessity of "putting an end to this session in a few days."

So at last we get at Act 9, William III., c. 44, for "raising a sum not exceeding 2,000,000 upon a fund for payment of annuities after the rate of £8 per annum, and *for settling the trade to the East Indies.*"

Thus the new company, started by solemn act of legislature, was left eyeing the old one. At first there seemed likelihood of their fighting it out like the Kilkenny cats. But in the pursuit of gold the main chance is a potent factor for peace. And so, while Aurungzebe, near his life's limit, was still, in his ninth decade of years, wearily pursuing the Mahratta, Earl Godolphin,

Lord High Treasurer of Great Britain, as referee, succeeded in reconciling the conflicting claims of commerce, and--to make his award binding on both parties--inserted a special clause in an Act of Parliament, by which the old London East India Company and the new English East India Company were for ever amalgamated under the title of the "United Company of Merchants of England trading to the East Indies."

By this arrangement there passed to one control in India alone, the ports and islands of Bombay, the factories of Surat, Sivalli, Broach, of Amadâd, Agra, Lucknow, and on the Malabar Coast, the forts of Kârwar, Tellicherri, Anjengo, besides the factory at Calicut. Rounding Cape Cormorin, the coast of Coromandel held Orissa, Chingi, Fort St George, the city of Madras and its dependencies; Fort St David, the factories of Cuddalore, Porto-Novo, Pettîpoli, Masulipatâm, Madapollâm, Vizagapatâm. Going northward to Bengal there was Fort William or Calcutta, with its large territory, Balasore, Cossimbazaar, Dacca, Hugli, Mâlda, Râjmahal, and Patna.

From which long list may be seen how steady had been the nibbling at India's coral strand during the last fifty years. The grant of Calcutta, with leave thereupon to erect fortifications, was practically the beginning of the end. This was almost the last act of Aurungzebe's reign. Shortly after, he lay dying, a man of eighty-nine, still in full possession of his faculties.

There is something very terrible about the death-bed of this man, who for fifty long years had held, without aid of any sort, the reins of Government. He had no friends; he could not trust any one sufficient for friendship. His one lukewarm affection seems to have been for his intriguing sister Roshanrâi, the woman who had sate beside his sick-bed guarding the Great Seal. For others he had literally no heart.

So in his death he was quite alone. Except for his remorse.

"Old age has arrived.... I came a stranger into this world, and a stranger I depart. I know nothing of myself; what I am, and for what I am destined. The instant which has passed in power, hath left only sorrow behind it. I have not been the guardian and protector of the Empire. My valuable time has been passed vainly. I had a guide given me in my own dwelling" (conscience), "but his glorious light was unseen by my dim sight. I brought nothing into this world, and, except the infirmities of man, take nothing out. I have a dread for my salvation and with what torments I may be punished.... Regarding my actions fear will not quit me; but when I am gone, reflection will not remain. Come, then, what come may, I have launched my vessel to the waves. Farewell, Farewell--Farewell!"

So he wrote from his death-bed to his second son, and to his youngest thus:--

"Son nearest to my heart! The agonies of death come upon me fast. Wherever I look I see nothing but the Divinity. I am going! Whatever good or evil I have done it was done for *you*."

He was a great letter-writer. Three huge volumes of his epistles are still extant; but even in these last solemn ones the absolute truth was not in them; for under his pillow when he died a paper was found--a sort of will, in which he appoints his eldest son Emperor, bids his second be content with Agra and Bengal, while to the one "nearest his heart," the doubtful kingship of Bijapur and Golconda was gifted. Aurungzebe was diplomatic to the last.

PART III
THE MODERN AGE

INDIA IN THE BEGINNING OF THE EIGHTEENTH CENTURY

A.D. 1707

Before making our *volte face*, and in future chronicling the history of India from the Western standpoint, it will be well to see what this India was which England set herself deliberately to annex.

So far as the East India Company was concerned, the vast peninsula was at this time what a huge slice of iced plum-cake upon a plate must be to a hungry mouse. That is to say, nice enough for outside nibblings, but with unexplored possibilities of plums within. Every now and again a bolder merchant would dive into the comparatively unknown centre, and come back laden possibly with idol-eyes, rich brocades, jewels in the rough.

It must--to repeat ourselves--have been a tremendous temptation having to live, as these early writers or clerks to John Company had, on the very verge of Tom Tiddler's ground--to have only to reach out their hands and touch a totally different world. A world which by virtue of immutable changelessness had not commuted the gold which the years had brought it into luxuries, but had stored it up uselessly in lavish ornamentation and idle, almost unappropriated treasure. Except as a gaud for a woman, a toy for a babe, or a flourish of trumpets for some man who called himself noble, gold in India had practically no value, for the rich man lived in all ways much as the poor man lived. The standard of personal comfort had not risen at all either for the wealthy or the poverty-stricken during the four thousand years and odd since the splendours of Princess Drâupadi's Swayâmvara had been chronicled in the Mâhâbhârata. An instant's thought will show us the effect which this hoarding of every diamond found in Golconda, of every bale of rich stuff made by some leisurely artificer, must have had upon the country. It became full to overflowing with scarcely recognised riches. To

English traders, keen on commerce, India must indeed have been the land of Upside-down; a land into which their gold was sucked down at the same time that astounding, almost undreamt-of treasures were literally vomited forth from every petty bazaar. Francois Bernier's views on this matter, and the conclusions which he draws from the indubitable facts which he observed, are so distinctly what may be called conventionally insular, that they serve well to show the attitude of mind in which the West, strong in conviction of its own worth, faced the East, all unfamiliar and startling.

"Before I conclude," he says, in a letter addressed to M. Colbert, the French Minister of State, "I wish to explain how it happens that though the gold and silver introduced into the Empire centre finally in Hindustan, they still are not in greater plenty than elsewhere, and the inhabitants have less the appearance of a monied people than those of many other parts of the globe.

"In the first place, a larger quantity is melted, re-melted, and wasted in fabricating women's bracelets, both for the hands and feet, chains, ear-rings, nose and finger rings, and a still larger quantity is consumed in manufacturing embroideries; *alachas* or striped silken stuffs, *touras* or tufts of golden nets worn on turbans; gold and silver cloths and scarves, turbans, and brocades. The quantity of these articles made in India is incredible."

He then goes on to paint, in vivid, horror-stricken phrases, the evils of a paternal despotism, pointing out that it is "slavery," that it "obstructs the progress of trade," since there is no encouragement to commercial pursuits when the "success with which they may be attended, instead of adding to the enjoyments of life, only provokes the cupidity of a neighbouring tyrant." This we are assured is the sole cause why the "possessor, so far from living with increased comfort, studies the means by which he may appear indigent: his dress, lodging, and furniture continue to be mean, and he is careful, above all things, never to indulge in the pleasures of the table."

Poor Bernier! And after more than a hundred years of comparative freedom under British rule there was still not a face-towel or a bit of soap in an Indian household; not a chair, not a table, and the simple food, cooked over a hole dug in the ground, was served on leaf-plates set upon the floor. For luxury has hitherto passed India by. Will it do so in the future? Who can say?

The state of the arts in India evidently puzzled Bernier's Western brain, and he sets to work to find out some occult cause for the undoubted skill of the artisan. He asserts that

"no artist can be expected to give his mind to his calling" without the stimulus of personal advantage, "and that the arts would long ago have lost their beauty and delicacy if the monarch and the principal nobles did not keep the artists in their pay to work in their houses."

Then:--

"The protection afforded by powerful patrons, rich merchants and traders, who give the workmen rather more than the usual wages, tends to preserve the arts; rather more wages, for it should not be inferred from the goodness of the manufactures that the workman is held in esteem, or arrives at a state of independence. Nothing but sheer necessity or blows from a cudgel keeps him employed."

And this in a country where, to this day, the pride of hereditary dexterity in hand and eye is handed down from father to son, and to say of a coppersmith or a carpenter or a weaver in brocades: "His grandfather, see you, was a real *ustad* (teacher)," is to raise that man above his fellows. Once more, poor Bernier! He might have learnt something from the eager-faced, lissome-fingured Indian smith, who, handling a gun made by Manton, laid it down reverently and salaamed to it as if it had been a god, with these simple words: "He who made that was a Great Artificer."

Here we have epitomised the true artistic temperament.

But it needs art to apply the solvent of sympathy; and the dealings of the West with the East were at this time purely commercial; so we meet with absolute, almost pathetic lack of comprehension. Indeed, as we read with painstaking care every record that exists of these Western dealings with the East at this period, we know not whether to laugh or to cry at the spectacle presented to us of mutual misunderstanding. India is a problem even now. What must it have been then, to these worthy Lombard Street merchants who knew nothing of ancient faiths and past civilisations, who looked on the native of India as a barbarian utterly. What a shock it must have been to them, when a native accountant, given some abstruse problem in arithmetic, solved it lightly, easily, by algebra! Small wonder that, finding the Hindu circle divided into 360 equal parts and the ratio of diameter to circumference expressed correctly at 1 to 3.14160 they credited Alexander's Greek phalanxes with being mathematical teachers as well as conquerors. Small wonder that every discovery of scientific knowledge amongst these "barbarians" should have been referred to some contact with the West.

It required long years before due credit could be given to the East; it is doubtful indeed whether sufficient credit is given to it even now. Who, for instance, knows of the accurate trigonometrical tables of India, in which *sines* are used instead of the Greek *chords?*--or of their framer, of whom Professor Wallace writes:--

"He who first formed the idea of exhibiting in arithmetical tables the ratios of the sides and angles of all possible triangles must have been a man of profound thought and extensive knowledge. However ancient, therefore, any book may be in which we meet with a system of trigonometry, we may be assured that it was not written in the infancy of the science. Hence, we may conclude that geometry must have been known in India long before the writing of the 'Surya Siddhanta.'"

Now this book on Astronomy was written at the latest computation about the year A.D. 400. Centuries before this, therefore, India was aware of certain of those inviolable laws of our Universe, in the apprehension of which lies humanity's best hope of immortality. And there is one curious fact about these vestiges of ancient knowledge which Professor Playfair has noted in a pregnant remark concerning these same trigonometrical tables. "They have the appearance, like many other things in the science of these Eastern nations, of being drawn by one *who was more deeply versed in the subject than may at first be imagined, and who knew much more than he thought it necessary to communicate.*"

It is a remark which stimulates the imagination.

But as a matter of fact the Western imagination of those days appears not to have been stimulated at all by anything save the prospect of plunder. And in truth the hoarded wisdom of the East was not nearly so much in evidence as its hoarded wealth. In Akbar's time some effort had been made to give such wisdom fair hearing. There is small doubt, for instance, but that his study of the kingcraft chapters of the Mâhâbhârata had done much towards making Akbar what he was--the best ruler India has ever seen, or is likely to see; but, taking it as a whole, the tide of Mahomedan conquest had simply submerged Hindu learning, and the rising flood of Mahratta power was not one whit less prejudicial to philosophy. But below the troubled surface of wars and rumours of wars the heart of India dreamt on undisturbed. All things, as ever, were illusion. The Wheel-of-Life revolved between the pivots of Birth and Death, so what mattered it whether the painted zoetrope showed the yellow face of a Toorkh from the North, or the white one of a trader from the West? Both sought gold; and even gold was illusion.

It is quaint to think, say, of those pirates of Arracan bursting in upon a crowd of pilgrims round some ancient shrine, and carrying off the whole concern, as it were--priests, worshippers, offerings, even the idol-eyes, leaving the empty sockets staring out helplessly at the deserted village.

But there are many such quaint items to be added to our picture gallery of India in the beginning of the eighteenth century, not the least of these being the spectacle of Job Charnock, the founder of Calcutta, carrying off from amongst the very flames of her husband's funeral pyre the Hindu widow who afterwards became his wife.

For on the confines of the various factories in the contiguous lands which had been won from Moghul rule by purchase, or bribe, or treaty, English laws had already begun to oust native customs. Indeed, quite an elaborate legal procedure, duly decked with Courts of Appeal, had been set up in the three presidencies. So far, it is to be feared, without much benefit to the people, for those who held the power seem ever to have been more occupied by the rules of commerce than those of justice.

Already, also, each presidency had its own regular army. This was composed first of recruits from England, sent out by the Company in their ships; secondly, of adventurers who had deserted from other European armies and had come out to the East to seek their fortunes; thirdly, of half-caste Indo-Europeans, the offspring of mixed marriages. In the beginning of the eighteenth century a few pure natives were enlisted, and from this time the Sepoy army of John Company grew by leaps and bounds.

As yet, however, there was no attempt at the policy of pike and carronade. That had been disastrous in the days of Sir John Child; so the small armies--the garrison of Calcutta in 1707 was *raised* to three hundred men--were kept simply for defence.

The insecure state of the country, also, which followed on Aurungzebe's death led to greater caution on the part of the Company. Hitherto, its clerks and merchants and agents had themselves carried their English goods to the various markets in the interior of the country; but now orders were issued directing everything to be sold by auction at the port of import, thus minimising the risk of loss.

A simple order which, nevertheless, must have had far-reaching results, since it introduced the middleman between the English merchants and the people of India; an unscrupulous middleman also.

Then the method employed, and necessarily employed, in the collection of the calicoes and other woven cotton-stuffs which at this time formed the staple of Indian trade was one which made fair dealing almost impossible. For there were no large merchants with whom the Company could deal. It had therefore to elaborate an agency of its own, by which it could come in contact with the weaver, who--ever one of the most poverty-stricken of Indian artisans--required raw material and sustenance given him before he could keep his rude loom going.

A fateful affair this! One European functionary issuing orders to a native secretary, he employing a native agent, who in his turn calls together the local brokers, who send out to village and towns by their paid messengers and advance cotton and money to the actual workmen. Here indeed were sufficient loopholes for fraud. Each one of these men had, in addition to his poor pay, to find secret gratification for himself and for those who were supposed to keep an eye upon him. The wretched weaver, of course, coming off worst in the scramble, being made, first, to work as he had never worked before, and secondly, as a set-off to the sustenance given, to take a price often 40 per cent. less than the work would have fetched in open market.

But the rate of pay which at this time the Company offered to its servants tells in unmistakable brevity the whole tale of its administration.

The salary of a president was but £300 a year, that of a factor but £20. Even when Bengal was practically ceded to it, and all power, judicial and executive, vested in its servants, the pay of a man who had almost unlimited power, and who had doomed himself to a life of exile, was but £130. Yet the actual profit of the East India Company at this time was nothing prodigious; it barely touched 8 per cent. on the capital employed. Still, the monopoly must have been valuable, for the efforts made to retain it would fill volumes; and one Act of Parliament followed another, prohibiting foreign adventure to India under penalty of forfeiture of triple the sum embarked, and declaring all British subjects found in India who were not in the Company's service liable to seizure and punishment, and generally crying "hands off" to all and sundry.

The Portuguese power in India had by this time dwined away; none too soon for its reputation. It had suffered reverses at many hands, not least of these being one dealt by itself; for the story of Bahâdur-Shâh, the king of Guzerât, is not one to bring credit with it.

He had entered into negotiations with the Portuguese, had granted them many favours, amongst others the right to build a factory. This, however, they surrounded with a wall which converted the whole into a fortification. Bahâdur-Shâh remonstrated, and was met with fair words from Nuno de Cunha, the Portuguese viceroy, who, however, came to the conference with a suspiciously martial fleet containing over four thousand fighting-men. Now, whether the Portuguese historians are right in attributing meditated treachery to the Mahomedans, or the historians of the latter are right in attributing it to the Portuguese, matters little in face of what actually happened. The viceroy, feigning sickness as an excuse for not paying his respects on land, the king, with but a few unarmed attendants, went to meet him on the admiral's ship. Once there, he became alarmed at whisperings and signs that were passing between the viceroy and his officers, and took a hasty leave. Hardly had he reached his boat, however, when he was attacked. Being a good swimmer he flung himself into the sea, was pursued, struck over the head with an oar, and when he clung to it, was finally despatched with a halbert.

The facts are brutal. Nothing can extenuate them, and though the affray may have originated in mutual distrust and alarm, there can be no doubt that such evidence of premeditated treachery as there is points to the Portuguese as the real criminals.

By the beginning of the eighteenth century, however, they had retired to Further India, there to repeat their brilliant but evanescent career of conquest, and in 1739 they finally ceded their few remaining possessions in the Konkan to the Mahratta power.

But their influence lives still all along the western coast, where to this day a large proportion of the people are professedly Roman Catholic, the descendants of the converts who, it is said, flocked in thousands to be baptized by St Francis Xavier. This, however, is extremely doubtful. Yet even the Portuguese power was but a sea-board influence, the nibblings, as it were, of the Western mouse upon the rich cake of India.

Inside this frayed and fraying fringe of contact with the outside world India was very much what it had been always, what in a way it will be always. So far as princes and principalities went it was a very distracted country; so far as the peasantry went it was a very peaceful one. But neither prince nor peasant seemed to realise that a great change was imminent.

One of the most curious points about this coming change was that though the greed of gold was undoubtedly the chief factor in bringing it about, the first two solid holds which the English got on India were due to the skill, not of British diplomacy or British commerce, but of British medicine. It was in consequence of the services rendered by Ship's surgeon Gabriel Boughton to the Emperor Shâhjahân's beloved daughter Jahanâra, when she was as a child badly burnt, that the Old East India Company gained the right to trade in Bengal free of all duty; this being the only fee asked--surely a public-spirited and disinterested one. And equally so was the only fee demanded by Staff Surgeon William Hamilton in 1715 for curing the decadent Emperor Farokhshir of a tumour in the back which had resisted the efforts of all the court physicians. He asked for the first sizable grant of land on the Indian peninsula which had ever been given to any foreign power: that is to say, for thirty-seven villages contiguous to the factory at Calcutta, which gave the English command of the river for 10 miles south of the port, for some villages near Madras, which consolidated that *pied à terre*; and for the island of Din on the western coast.

These two fees, given by gratitude for services rendered, were practically the fee simple of all India.

Some vague recognition of this fact doubtless prompted the epitaph on William Hamilton's neglected tombstone in Calcutta, which runs thus:--

His memory ought to be dear to his Nation

For the credit he gained the English

in curing Ferrukseer

the present King of Hindustan

of a malignant distemper

By which he made his own name famous

At the Court of that Great Monarch

And without doubt will perpetuate his memory

as well in Great Britain as all other

Nations in Europe.

He died, 4th December 1717. Gabriel Boughton, his predecessor in patriotism, dying God knows when, being buried God knows where.

So the epitaph is a trifle over-confident; for Great Britain has a trick of forgetting her most faithful servants.

THE RISE OF THE MAHRATTA POWER

A.D. 1707 TO A.D. 1738

The story of Siva-ji has already been told. His early decease, while it did not materially check the rising flood of Mahratta power, certainly left the invading West a freer hand along the shores of India from Bombay to Calicut.

For Siva-ji seems to have had a genius for sea, as well as for land warfare. It was his unerring eye which, seizing on an island along the coast overlooked hitherto by both Portuguese and English, had it fortified for use as a *point d'appui*, whence he could control the shipping north and south. Indeed, having in view the fact that he was the only person who managed in any way to harass English fleets, it seems not unlikely that, had he lived longer, British commerce would have been longer, also, in finding firm foothold in India.

But he died, and his son Samba-ji died also, meanly, miserably. That, however, only delayed the inevitable for a short time. The Mahratta star was in the ascendant, that of the Moghuls was sinking fast, and the death of Aurungzebe accelerated both ascent and descent.

To begin with, it ended what may be called the Râjput acquiescence in empire; that is to say, their acceptance of "Akbar's Dream" as an ideal, which by good fortune might become real. It was an ideal absolutely foreign to the whole Râjput spirit, the whole Râjput theory of life. In their State-Politic, one chieftain had as independent a position as any other chieftain, and even amongst the followers of those chieftains none was really before or after the other. Every Râjput owed equal fealty to his race, was equally free to defend his own rights as he chose. Yet side by side with this curious individual independence ran what, for want of a better word, we may call a feudal bond betwixt follower and chieftain, between chieftain and suzerain. Akbar's Dream of Empire had been antagonistic to this, yet they had accepted that Dream at his hands, and at his death the mere fact of his heir Jahângir being half a Râjput by birth, had helped them to forget what they had given up to the dead man's genius. Shâhjahân was still more Râjput. In his veins there flowed but one-fourth of the hated Mahomedan blood, so they bore with him. But with Aurungzebe it was different. Born of a Mahomedan mother, the old race intolerance showed in him early, and from the moment he set his foot on the throne, alienation of loyalty began actively, passively, so that by the time the bigot's reign of fifty years was over, every Râjput in India was ripe for revolt; a fact which naturally was in favour of the Mahrattas, since it weakened the power of the Moghuls. It was still more favourable to the advancement of the West, since with India engaged in internecine strife, attention was withdrawn from many a seemingly slight advance which yet was the first step to final conquest. Naturally, after Aurungzebe's anxious efforts to settle the succession by means of a last will and testament, his sons immediately came to blows over the business; in which quarrel the best claimant appears to have gone to the wall, for Azim, the second son, was defeated and killed near Agra by his elder brother, Shâh-Alam, and Kambaksh, the youngest, shortly afterwards drew death down on himself by a desperate defiance near Hyderabâd. Thus Shâh-Alam was left to face the situation for five years under the title of Bahâdur-Shâh. It is worthy of note that he, the first puppet-emperor of Delhi, had thus the same name as the last, the old man Bahâdur-Shâh, who, after dallying with disgrace and deceit in 1857 went to end his miserable life in the Andaman Islands.

Bahâdur-Shâh the First found his hands full. Having pursued Kambaksh to the very confines of the Dekkan, it was necessary ere returning northward to settle the Râjput rebellion (which was becoming daily less restrained), and to temporise in some way with the Mahrattas. And here a piece of diplomacy on the part of the dead brother, Azim, served Bahâdur's turn well. The former, when advancing to dispute the crown, had sought to strengthen his position and protect his rear by giving back to the Mahrattas the rightful heir to Siva-ji's throne in the person of his grandson Sâho, who had been kept in captivity by the Moghuls ever since his father Samba-ji had paid the penalty for blasphemy amongst the Mahomedans, and so been made a martyr by the Mahrattas. It was a wily move, for during the young claimant's long incarceration, another pretender to Siva-ji's crown had arisen. Azim-Shâh, therefore, had deliberately started a successional dispute in the hopes of being thereby freed for a time of troublesome neighbours.

The ruse succeeded, and Bahâdur-Shâh, by ratifying his brother's promise of favourable peace should the young pretender succeed in establishing his claim, managed to keep the Mahrattas quiet for some years.

He was less fortunate with the Râjput confederacy, though he was prepared to give up all things but the mere name of Empire. In the case of Oudipur (Chitore) he went so far as to restore all annexations, to release it from the obligation of furnishing a contingent, to abolish the infidel capitation tax, or *jizyia*, and to re-establish religious toleration as it had existed in the time of Akbar. He could not well have done more; but for once--almost for the only time in Indian history--a faint political feeling is here to be traced. For even the removal of the hated *jizyia* was not enough for the Râjput; he wanted, and he meant to have, independence. This is--or seems to be--the only occasion in all the long centuries of Indian history which gives us a hint of any recognition on the part of the people of political rights, and as such it is peculiarly interesting. Unfortunately, it is so mixed up with the religious motive that it is impossible to say if it really gives ground for supposing that we have here a faint realisation of the rights of the individual.

While Bahâdur-Shâh was engaged in pacifying the Râjputs by the relinquishment of everything, he was suddenly called to the Punjâb by an insurrection amongst the Sikhs.

Nânuk, their original founder, had lived in Akbar's time; a time peculiarly productive of religious enthusiasms all over the world. And Nânuk was a religious enthusiast pure and simple. Of the soldier caste, the son of a grain merchant, he was *devote* from childhood. Much travel and mature manhood turned him into an almost inspired preacher of the Theistic doctrines of Kâbir, who in his turn was a disciple of the great Ramanuja. Concerning this same Kâbir there is a curious legend, the recital of which may serve to impress the memory with the most salient feature of his teaching--his tolerance.

The tale runs that at his death the Mahomedans claimed the right to bury the saint, the Hindus to burn him; in consequence of which there was a free fight over the corpse, in the midst of which the still, white-shrouded form lay, mutely appealing for peace. And lo! when blood had been uselessly spilt, and a compromise effected, it was found that beneath the white sheet was no dead man, only where his holy head had lain grew a sweet basil plant, sacred to the God Vishnu, only where his holy feet had touched, a perfumed *rehan* bush, green as the green of the Prophet's turban!

Nânuk, then, was a preacher, a quietest, and being possessed of this spirit of universal charity, was allowed, naturally, to live in peace during the reign of that past--master in tolerance, Akbar. At his death, however, the rapid increase of the sect attracted the unfavourable notice of Jahângir, and Nânuk was cruelly put to death. The usual result followed. Armed with a sainted martyr, religion became fanaticism. Har-Govind, the murdered man's son, brought revenge and hatred to his holding of the supreme pontiff-ship, and from this time the Sikhs, expelled forcibly from their lands, presented from the mountains north of Lahôre an unbroken front of rebellion to the Government.

It was not, however, till 1675 that, under Govind, the tenth Guru (or spiritual head of the sect) from Nânuk its founder, the Sikhs formed themselves into an aggressive military commonwealth.

Guru Govind was a wise man. Numbers were his first need, so he set to work to establish a creed wide enough to contain all converts, attractive enough to compel them to come in.

Caste was abolished; Mahomedan or Hindu, Brahman or Pariah, were alike when once the oath of fealty was taken, when once the new-made Sikh had vowed to be a religious soldier, to carry cold steel about with him from birth to death, to wear blue clothes always, and never to clip a hair which God had sent to grow upon him. In order still further to emphasise the separation of the Sikh from his fellows, new methods of salutation, new ceremonials for all the principal events of life, were instituted.

Nothing more interesting in the annals of heredity exists than the startling rapidity of the change thus brought about in the Sikhs. They are now--that is, after two hundred years--(as they were, indeed, after a scant one hundred) as distinct a race as any in India, with as well marked a national character as any of the original peoples of India.

So far, therefore, Guru Govind was successful; but his personal mission proved disastrous. Despite his diplomacy, he failed in numbers; his foes were too strong for him, and in the end the pontiff saw all his fortresses taken, his mother and his children murdered, his followers tortured, dispersed, or killed.

This was in Aurungzebe's time, that most bigoted and bloodthirsty of pious kings. The closing years of his reign, however, found him with all his energies centred on the Dekkan, and almost immediately after his death, the Sikhs recovered from their stupor, and having found a new, and this time an unscrupulously cruel leader, broke out into almost incredible excesses of revenge. They ravaged Sirhind, they brutally butchered whole towns, and after penetrating southward as far as Saharunpur, retreated to the Cis and Trans-Sutlej states, which are to this day the stronghold of the Sikh faith.

It was against these stalwart rebels--for one of the quickly acquired national characteristics of the Sikhs is unusual physical height and breadth--that Bahâdur-Shâh had to march in person. He managed with infinite trouble to besiege the chief offenders in a hill-fort, whence, after enduring the utmost extremities of famine, they made a wild sally, headed, apparently, by their leader Banda, who, after making himself conspicuous by desperate resistance, was captured and brought to the Mahomedan camp in triumph. Once there, however, the prisoner threw aside his borrowed *rôle*, openly declared himself nothing but a poor Hindu convert who had dared all to save his Guru, and taunted his captors with having fallen into the trap and allowed the real Banda to escape them!

It is pleasantly noteworthy to find that Bahâdur-Shâh, struck by the man's self-devotion, spared his life.

Before, however, the further endeavours to secure the real leader and crush the Sikhs were successful, the emperor himself fell sick and died, and the usual turmoil of murder and intrigue followed, which ended in the temporary enthronement, at the instigation of Zulfikar Khan (who had been chief instrument in the late king's succession), of the eldest son, Jahândar-Shâh. An inveterate intriguer was this same Zulfikar. He it was who had suggested hampering the hands of the Mahrattas by presenting them with a new claimant for their crown; and now he chose his nominee--despatching the remainder of the royal family *instanter*--because Jahândar, weak, vicious, enslaved by a public dancer, offered himself an easy prey to Zulfikar's desire to be the real ruler.

But Farokhshir, son of one of the murdered princes, who had escaped massacre by being in Bengal, had just sufficient spunk in him to oppose the maker of puppet-kings. Fortune favoured him miraculously, quite irrationally, and--surely to his own surprise--he found himself marching on Delhi, victorious, triumphant. But the whole affair had degenerated--as purely Indian history after the death of Aurungzebe so often does degenerate--into transpontine melodrama and comic opera, and he was met at the gates by an obsequious Zulfikar and his still more obsequious papa, both ready, willing, and eager to deliver up their prisoner, the late Emperor Jahândar, and take the oath of allegiance to the new one, Farokhshir.

But this passed. It was, to use a vulgarism, "too thick" even for a debased Moghul. So the double-dyed traitor was calmly strangled in the imperial tent, Jahândar was quietly put out of the way, and Farokhshir reigned in his stead.

One is irresistibly reminded, as one reads the records of the few following reigns, of the terrible annals of the Slave and Khilji Kings. There is only this to choose between them, that the latter concerned themselves with kings who, however degenerate, were at least real, whereas these occupants of Akbar's throne, Farokhshir, the two infant princes who were in turn raised to power by political factions, and Mahomed-Shâh, were all purely puppets.

The first-named, who owed his kingdom entirely to the ability for intrigue of two Syyeds of Ba'rr'ha, spent his time largely in trying to emancipate himself from their claims on his gratitude. His was a feeble, futile nature, a feeble, futile reign. During it the Mahrattas, becoming tired of their civil war of succession, began to renew their depredations along the Moghul frontiers. But in all ways Farokhshir was a timid creature; so nothing, great was done to hold the marauders in check. He, however, through the aid of a general with an unpronounceable name, was equal to a final tussle and final crushing of the Sikh zealots, seven hundred and forty-nine of whom, defeated and taken prisoners to Delhi, were duly paraded through the streets, exposed to various indignities, and finally beheaded in batches of one hundred and eleven on seven successive days of the week.

Their leader, Banda, was, however, reserved for more refined barbarity. Nothing in the whole annals of history can exceed in devilish malignant cruelty the revolting details of the treatment meted out to this man, who had himself, it is true, led the way in lack of humanity! They are sickening to read, and shall not be repeated here.

Farokhshir only reigned six years. By that time even his masters, the Syyeds, had tired of him, and despite his abject submission, he was finally dragged from the women's apartments, a faint, frightened shadow of a king, and privately made away with.

But these same Syyeds--king-makers as they justly called themselves--were unfortunate in their choice of a successor. They set up one young prince of the blood, who promptly died of consumption in less than three months. They followed him with another, who as promptly followed his example in less time.

The question naturally presents itself--was it tuberculosis or some other toxin? Who can say?

They then, in despair, chose a healthy young man. But the public confidence in them as king-makers was waning, and almost before the new emperor--who was enthroned in the title of Mahomed-Shâh--was firmly settled in his seat, Hussan-Ali--the most powerful of the two Syyeds--was assassinated in his palanquin, and his brother, after vainly trying to hold his own single-handed, was defeated and made prisoner near Delhi, his life being spared out of respect for his sacred lineage--Syyeds being descended directly from the great Prophet.

And all this time, while emperors intrigued against ministers, and ministers intrigued against emperors, while here and there some austere old Mahomedan like Asaf-Jâh (whilom Grand Vizier, and afterwards Governor in the Dekkan), who remembered the bigoted decorum of Aurungzebe's court, lifted up voice of warning and held up holy hands of horror--all this time the Western nibblings continued on the sea-coast, and in the interior the Mahratta power was growing day by day.

For some time the Moghuls kept themselves fairly secure of it by pitting Samba, the one claimant to the crown, against Sâho, the other claimant. But Sâho found a friend in the person of one Bâla-ji, a Brahmin, who began life as a mere village accountant. Ere long, however, he was his master's right hand, and it was by his wits that Sâho found himself no longer a mere vassal of the empire, but an independent ruler, entitled to claim endless minor dues over a large extent of land. A quick wit was this of Bâla-ji's, which recognised the infinite opportunities for encroachments and interference given by widespread, ill-defined rights.

In the confusion worse confounded which ensued, the Mahratta scored invariably against the Moghul, and when Bâla-ji died, his son, still more capable, still more astute, took up the prime minister or Peishwa-ship, and with it his father's life-work.

Now, there is no doubt that this son, by name Bâji-Rao, is, after Siva-ji, by far the ablest Mahratta of history.

He was a warrior, born and bred in camps, a statesman educated ably by his father, a man frank and free, hardy beyond most, content to live on a handful of unhusked grain, vital to the fingertips.

He found himself confronted by a Peace-party, who would fain have paused to consolidate what had already been won, to suppress civil discord, and generally to give a firm administrative grip on the south of India before attempting further conquests on the north.

But Bâji-Rao was clear-sighted; he saw the difficulties of this policy. To attempt the consolidation of what was still absolutely fluid, to bid the bands of predatory horsemen which constituted the Mahratta army suddenly lay down their lances or turn them into ox goads, would be fatal.

The only chance of peace was to form a regular army out of these robber hordes, give that army work to do, and so establish a stern military control as the first and most necessary step towards a fixed Government.

The Moghul empire lay ready to hand, rotten at the core, simply waiting to be overthrown.

He therefore urged his master to "strike the withered trunk, when the branches will fall of themselves," and roused the lazy, somewhat luxurious Sâho to such enthusiasm that he swore he would plant his victorious standard on Holy Himalaya itself.

The career of Sâho-plus-Bâji-Rao was singularly successful. Ere long, after harassing the Dekkan, he forced his rival, Samba, to yield him almost the whole Mahratta country except a portion about Kolapur. Having done this, he turned himself to engage the Moghul force of thirty-five thousand men which had marched on him with the avowed object of delivering Sâho from the terrible tyranny of Bâji. This was defeated, and Sâho-cum-Bâji proceeded to apportion various parts of Southern India amongst the great Mahratta families. The Gaekwars of Baroda date from this time. The Holkar of those days was but a shepherd-soldier, and the Scindias, though of good birth, a mere body-servant of the Peishwas.

Mâlwa was the next emprise, and though its Afghân governor effected his own personal escape by means of a rescue party from Rohilkand summoned by his wife, who sent her veil as a challenge to her brethren's honour, the whole rich province fell into Mahratta hands. The Râjah of Bundulkhund, alarmed, acceded to Bâji-Rao's demands, and Jâi-Singh of Ambêr, hastily summoned by the Moghuls to defend their cause, after a futile and half-hearted resistance, also yielded.

He was more of a scientist than a soldier was Jâi-Singh, and would have been remarkable in any age for his astronomical work. His 'List of the Stars' is still of importance.

Hitherto, all these aggressions had been made by the Mahrattas under cover of claims; those ill-defined, widespread rights of share and taxation which Bâla-ji had started. Now, seeing his opponent's weakness, Sâho-cum-Bâji's demands rose, until even Moghul supineness could not submit to his terms.

Nothing daunted, the former advanced on Delhi itself, but while his light cavalry under Holkar were ravaging the country about Agra, they were attacked and driven back by the Governor of Oudh, a man evidently of some spirit, for he had actually left his own province to defend the adjoining one.

The skirmish was magnified into overwhelming victory by the Moghuls, and this so irritated Bâji-cum-Sâho, that he conceived and put into practice what was more an impish piece of mischief than a serious assault.

Leaving the imperial army which had come out solemnly, solidly, to repel him on the right, he led his swarms of active freebooters by a *detour* to its rear, and then contemptuously disdaining an attack on the pompous martial array, made one almost unbroken march to the very gates of Delhi.

Here was consternation indeed! The Mahrattas at the very steps of the throne, while the court army was seeking them in the wilderness!

His object, however, was mere intimidation; as he phrased it himself: "Just to show the emperor that he could come if he liked."

So, after repelling with heavy loss one sally caused by the Moghul misapprehension of a retrograde movement he made beyond the suburbs (which was due to his desire to prevent damage by his freebooting followers), he retreated as he came, just as the befogged, bewildered Moghul army, duly bedrummed, beflagged, and bedisciplined, was on the eve of arriving at Delhi.

A sheer piece of devilry, no doubt. He had meant to have crossed the Jumna and looted the rich Gangetic plains, but the rainy season was due, and there was more comfortable work to be done in the Dekkan.

Asaf-Jâh, still active though old, followed him so soon as the weather permitted, and he could manage to scrape together sufficient soldiery; but so low had the power of the Moghul fallen by this time, that he had to start with a bare thirty-five thousand men. Then ensued a campaign of some months on the old well-known lines.

The regulars marching with difficulty, the irregulars harassing the line of march. The Moghuls entrenching themselves scientifically, the Mahrattas cutting off supplies, laying waste the country for miles, looting every baggage-train that tried to get in, and finally cutting off all communication with the base. There was nothing for it finally but retreat; a slow retreat of 4 or 5 miles a day, the enemy's light cavalry hanging on the rear, harassing the disheartened army in every possible way. There could be but one end to it--almost unconditioned surrender.

Bâji-cum-Sâho demanded the cession of all Mâlwa, the country between the rivers Nerbudda and the Chumbal, and an indemnity of fifty lacs of rupees, or five millions.

Weighted down with these fateful terms, for which he promised to gain the emperor's sanction, poor Asaf-Jâh continued his way Delhi-wards, Bâji-cum-Sâho marching a few days behind him to take present possession of his conquests. Whether Asaf-Jâh's efforts would have resulted in confirmation of these terms or not cannot be said; for this was in the year of grace 1738, and in the November of that year Nâdir the Persian invaded India.

THE INVASION OF NÂDIR

A.D. 1738 TO A.D. 1742

The old cry once more!

Over the wheat-fields of the Punjâb, just as the seed was bursting into green, that cry--

"The Toorkh! The Toorkh!"

Surely no land on the globe has suffered so much from invasion as Hindustan? The mythical Snake-people first, coming from God knows where.... Then the Aryans, with their flocks and herds, from the Roof of the World.... Next the well-greaved Greeks, leaving their indelible mark on Upper India.... So through Parthian, and Scythian, and Bactrian, to the wild, resistless influx of Mongolian immigrations. Then finally Mahmûd and Mahomed, Tamerlane and Babar ... last of all, Nâdir the Persian.

His was an unprovoked, almost an unpremeditated invasion. It burst upon India like a monsoon storm, swift, lurid, almost terrible in the rapidity with which action follows menace. And like that same storm it came, it passed, and the blue, unclouded sky seemed far away from the desolation and havoc that had been wrought.

In many ways this, the last, was the worst of all the sacks which India had suffered. To begin with, it came so late in time. Towards the middle of the eighteenth century one does not expect a robbing raid on so vast a scale. It seems almost incredible that an army of eighty thousand men should march through a country bent on plunder, and plunder only.

Then its sole object--gold--was such a mean one. No political reason lay at the back of the raid. Nâdir had no ambitions. He did not wish to add to his kingship; it was all wilful, wicked, merciless greed.

Yet Nâdir-Shâh himself was not absolutely a mean man. He was a native of Khorasân, that is to say, an Afghân, born of no particular family, but born a warrior. At the age of seventeen he was taken prisoner by the Usbeks, but after four years of captivity made his escape.

Then he took service with the King of Khorasân, but, believing himself ill-rewarded for a success against the Tartars, gave up his command, and became, frankly, a freebooter.

A few years later, on the shores of the Caspian Sea, he threw in his fortunes with those of a Persian princeling *en retraite*, and in his name fought a variety of battles, in which he was invariably victorious. They ended in the nominal restoration of Tâhmâsp to the throne of his fathers. But behind Tâhmâsp sate Nâdir, who had become the idol of the Persian people; and small wonder, since he had raised the nation from abject slavery to such military glory as Persia has seldom possessed.

It was necessary, however, to continue soldierly exploits; so Nâdir set to work to settle a dispute with the Turks who had taken Tabrîz. He had recovered it, when trouble in Khorasân called him back, and kept him employed for so long, that when he returned to the capital, Isphahân, it was to find that his puppet Tâhmâsp had, during his absence, become a person of much importance, and was exercising all the royal prerogatives.

This did not suit Nâdir, so, on the excuse of lack of statesmanship in concluding a treaty with the Turks, he deliberately deposed Tâhmâsp, and set his infant son in his stead.

This was practically the beginning of Nâdir's reign, but he refrained from assuming the title of King until many victories over the Turks and Russians had strengthened his hold on the Persians.

Then, covered with glory, he assembled all the dignitaries, civil and military, to the number of about one hundred thousand in a sort of mutual admiration conference, when, no doubt by previous arrangement, they offered him the crown, which, after some display of surprise and reluctance, he was pleased to accept.

Now this was all very deep-laid, very diplomatic; but Nâdir's cleverness was at times too clever. In some of his campaigns he had deliberately changed his religion--or rather his denomination--becoming Sunni instead of Shiah, in order to gain over a warlike tribe which was obdurately troublesome; now, hoping to stamp out any sentimental attachment to the dynasty which he had just deposed, and whose claim to kingship rested entirely on its championship of the Shiah tenets, he changed the national denomination, and declared Persia henceforward a Sunni country. It was a mistake; for though the Sunni section was pleased, the Shiahs felt themselves alienated from their new king.

In another way Nâdir showed more sense. It was his greatness as a general which had won him sovereignty, and he recognised that it must be kept by the same means; so he gathered together an army of eighty thousand men and set off to conquer Kandahâr.

L'appetit vient en mangeant. India lay just over the barrier of the Koh-i-Suleiman hills, and the tribes who had hitherto been subsidised by the Moghul Government to keep the peaks and passes, were now sulky over their failure for some years past to squeeze anything out of the bankrupt Government of Delhi.

But even Nâdir required some excuse for bald, brutal invasion. He therefore peremptorily demanded the expulsion of some Afghâns who had fled from punishment to shelter in Indian territory. At all times it would have been difficult to lay hands on a band of wandering Pâthâns amongst the frontier hills, but Delhi was at this time distracted by fear of the Mahrattas, and still all uncertain whether to acknowledge Nâdir-Shâh's claim to kingship.

The hesitation suited the latter; he was over the border, had defeated a feeble resistance at Lahôre, and was within 100 miles of Delhi before he found himself faced by a real army.

There must surely be some malignant attraction about the wide plain of Pâniput! Surely the Angel-of-Death must spread his wings over it at all times, since bitter battle has been fought on it again and again, and its sun-saturated sands have been sodden again and again with the blood of many men.

How many times has the fate of India been decided amongst its semi-barren stretches, where the low *dhâk* bushes glow like sunset clouds on the horizon? First by the mythical, legendary Pândus and Kurus, backed by the gods, protected by showers of celestial arrows. Next, when Shahâb-ud-din-Mahomed Ghori broke down the Râjput resistance, and Prithvi-râj, the flower of Râjput chivalry, was killed flying for his life amongst the sugarcane brakes. Timur passed it by, but his great descendant Babar strewed the plain with dead in his victorious march to Delhi. Here Hemu met with crushing defeat at Akbar's hands, and now Nâdir was to carry on the tradition of death, until that last great fight in 1761, which ended the Mahratta power, and so paved the way for British supremacy.

How many men's dust is mingled with the soil of Pâniput? All we know is that the life-blood of over a million is said to have been spilt upon it.

Nâdir's battle, however, appears to have been a comparatively bloodless rout of an absolutely incapable enemy. Mahomed-Shâh, the so-called emperor of all the Indies, at any rate gave up the struggle incontinently, sent in his submission, and the two kings journeyed peacefully together to Delhi, which they reached in March 1739. Did the populace come out to greet the sovereigns riding in, brother-like, hand in hand, to take up their residence in the palace built by Shâhjahân? It is a quaint picture this, of cringing submission and reckless ascendency.

To Nâdir's credit be it said that, whatever ultimate object of plunder he may have had, he wished to avoid bloodshed. For this purpose he stationed isolated pickets of chosen troops about the city and suburbs to keep order and protect the people. Unavailingly, for a strange thing happened. Whether owing to some deep-laid, well-known plan for poisoning the intruder which failed unexpectedly, or from some other cause, the report was spread abroad within forty-eight hours that Nâdir-the-Conqueror, Nâdir-the-mainspring-of-Conquest, was dead. The rumours blazed like wildfire through the bazaars. In quick impulse the mob fell on the pickets, and seven hundred Persians were weltering in their blood when Nâdir himself rode through the midnight streets, intent, they say, on peace. But the provocation proved too much for his cold, cruel Persian temper.

Struck by stones and mud hurled at him from the houses, the officer next him killed by a bullet aimed at himself, he gave way to Berserk rage. It was just dawn when the massacre he ordered began; it was nigh sunset when it ended, and night fell over one hundred and fifty thousand corpses. Nor did his revenge stop here. The treasure, which he would no doubt have extorted in any case, was now seized on by force, torture and murder being used to make the miserable inhabitants yield up every penny. Every kind of cruelty was employed in this extortion; numbers died from ill-usage, and many others destroyed themselves from fear of a disgraceful death. As an eye-witness writes: "Sleep and rest forsook the city. In every chamber and house was heard the cry of affliction."

The Afghân has always possessed a perfect genius for pillage, and after a short two months Nâdir-Shâh left Delhi, carrying away with him an almost incredible quantity of plunder, which it is very generally estimated at being worth £30,000,000; an enormous sum, but it must be remembered that the famous peacock throne in itself was counted by Tavernier as equal to £6,000,000 sterling.

But Nâdir left Delhi something which, possibly, it might have done better without; for ere leaving, he solemnly reinstated the puppet-king, and swore fearful oaths as to the revenge he would take on the nobles when he returned in a year or two should they fail in allegiance. But he never did return; he really never meant to return. He was a robber *pur et simple*, and he had got all that he had any hopes of getting.

So he disappeared northwards again, to die a violent death ere long. For despite his success, something of remorse had come to him, uninvited, with the spoils of ravaged Delhi. He became cruel, capricious, tyrannical; finally, he grew half-mad, until one night the nobles, whose arrest he had decreed, the captain of his own body-guard, the very chief of his own clan, entered his tent at midnight. Then from the darkness came the challenge in the deep voice which had so often led them to victory.

"Who goes there?"

For an instant they drew back, uncertain; but only for an instant. They went for him with their sabres as they might have gone at a mad dog, and Nâdir, their hero, their pride, their tyrant, their horror, ended his life.

How had he affected India?

First of all it had for the moment checked Mahratta aggrandisement. The appearance of this unknown, hitherto almost unheard-of foe, who traversed with such ease the country he had hoped to annex, and did the things he had meant to do, seemed to paralyse Bâji-Rao. His first impulse was to aid in a general defence of India. "Our domestic quarrels," he wrote, "are now insignificant; there is but one enemy in Hindustan. The whole power of the Dekkan, Hindu and Mahomedan alike, must assemble for resistance."

And even when Nâdir-Shâh had retreated without further progress southward, Bâji-Rao, free-booter, as all the Mahrattas were at heart, must have felt himself frustrated. What use was there in reaching a city desolate utterly, still infected by the stench of unburied bodies; a city whose treasury doors stood wide open, empty, deserted; a city, briefly, which an Afghân had pillaged? So he and his Sâho retired southwards.

As for the effects which Nâdir's sudden swoop on the interior of the plum-cake had on the nibbling mice upon its circumference, there is little to be said. It must have been a surprise to the civilised communities which were so rapidly coming into existence at such centres as Calcutta, Madras, Bombay; centres in which life went elegantly, and people began to talk of the latest news by mail from England. Still, the mere brute-force of the invasion cannot have shocked them much, for Europe itself was a prey at this time to wars and rumours of wars. The 1715 rebellion was over in England; the 1745 had not yet begun. In France affairs were working up towards the Revolution. Spain and Germany were alike, either at the beginning or the end of disastrous struggles.

Yet the mere fact which must have filtered through to the seacoast--*that thirty millions worth of solid plunder had just been filched away from the treasury of India by foreigners*--cannot have been pleasing news. The East India

Company, however, seems to have made no great efforts at aggrandisement during the years between the special granting to it of lands by Farokhshir and 1746, when it formally entered into grips with the French East Indian Company, which about this time began that dispute for supremacy in India which virtually ended with the taking of Trichinoply in 1761.

In truth we have very little information indeed regarding the doings of John Company during this period. All we know is that British imports into India fell from £617,000 in 1724 to £157,000 in 1741, which, taken with a corresponding decrease in dividends, would seem to show some depression, some check to trade.

One thing is certain. The Constitution of the Company was not satisfactory. An attempt had been made to avoid a monopoly of large shareholders by ruling that, no matter what the share held might be, it should only, whether £500 or £50,000, carry one vote for the election of the Court of Directors. But this ruling could be, and was, easily evaded. All that had to be done was to split the £50,000 into a hundred £500 shares, registered in the names of confidential agents, who--in consideration of an honorarium, no doubt--voted according to direction. It was not very straightforward, of course; on the other hand, the original ruling was silly in the extreme, since it prevented those who had a real interest in the Company from exercising their due share of influence.

Unfortunately, this faggot-voting brought with it a corrupt atmosphere. Appointments under the Company were a common bribe, and as the Court of Directors had to be reappointed every year, there was endless opportunity for jobbery.

So, after a time, opposition to the monopoly of the trade began once more to take form. Proposals for yet a new company were floated. Parliament once more took up the matter; which was finally settled by the existing company offering £200,000 to Government, and a reduction of 1 per cent. on the rate of interest payable on the previous loan of some three-and-a-half millions (that is to say, a yearly income of £35,000), as payment for the extension of their monopoly till 1766. This offer was accepted, and in 1744 the term of monopoly was still further extended until 1780, in consideration of a further loan to Government of £1,000,000 sterling at the low rate of 3 per cent. Coming as it did in the middle of a very expensive war, the temptation of this pecuniary assistance must have been potent; but there can be but little doubt that, publicly at any rate, the trade of India suffered considerably from the exclusion of private enterprise.

Certain it is that while the English East India Company found themselves forced to reduce their dividends to 7 per cent, the Dutch Company was dividing 25.

Altogether, then, it is not surprising that, until the French, by assuming the aggressive, forced the East India Company to bestir itself, it did nothing of importance in the way of progress.

THE GAME OF FRENCH AND ENGLISH

A.D. 1742 TO A.D. 1748

The eye of France had been on India for a century and a half, for it was in 1601 that a fleet of French merchant ships set out from St Malo for Hindustan, but failed of their destination.

The first French East India Company was formed in 1604, the second in 1611, a third in 1615; a fourth was founded by Cardinal Richelieu in 1642, yet a fifth in 1664, and finally a sixth, made up by the co-ordination of various older ventures, began in 1719 to trade under the name of "Compagnies des Indes."

There was thus no lack of organisation; of action, there had been, up to 1742, comparatively little. They had secured a factory at Surat, they captured Trincomalee from the Dutch, and they had occupied Pondicherry, which they still hold. Aurungzebe had ceded Chandanagore to them, and they had also obtained Mahé and Karikal, which they bought from the Râjah of Tanjore.

This, then, was the position of France in India when, in the year 1742, the office of Governor was bestowed on one Joseph Dupleix. He had spent his life in India, had amassed a huge private fortune by private trade, but at the same time had done his duty by the company of which his father had been a director.

He was thus saturated, as it were, with the methods and manners of the East, and in addition he had the advantage of a clever wife, who, though European by birth, had been born and bred in India.

Incited, it is believed, by her, he evolved a plan by which he hoped to gain supremacy for France. Competition in fair trade with both the English and the Dutch had failed, but he hoped to gain that by diplomacy which had been denied by commerce. The Moghul dynasty was tottering to its fall. On all sides the petty governors of provinces were aspiring to feeble power, and the balance of parties was often so nearly equal, that a very little support thrown into the scale would determine failure or success. Here Dupleix saw his opportunity, and he set deliberately to work, using Madame Dupleix as his go-between, to make friends for France in this welter of conflicting interests. The work was going on secretly and surely, when in 1744 the war of the Austrian Succession broke out in Europe between England and France.

Dupleix was evidently unwilling that this secret work of his should be interrupted by any outbreak of hostilities in the East, and some little time previous to the open declaration of war, both the French and English Companies had taken steps to provide for peace at any price. But a new factor had arisen on the French side in the person of Admiral Labourdonnais, the Governor of the Isle of France and the Isle of Bourbon.

His had been an adventurous life, and he had often been in and out of favour with those who had employed him. His government of the two contiguous islands was a case in point. He had found a plentiful crop of abuses, he had rooted them out, and in consequence of this, when he returned on private affairs to France, was pursued with unscrupulous enmity and bitter detraction.

In endeavouring to right himself he gave to the Ministers of State and the directors of his Company a full exposition of his views on the Eastern question. It commended itself to the authorities, and he found himself setting sail for the Isle of France in April 1741, backed by a fleet which, with care and training, should be able to secure to his country supremacy in the Eastern seas.

But disappointment awaited him. Long before the declaration of war which he expected, the French Company, who thought it had been made to bear more than its fair share of the cost of fitting out the fleet, sent for their ships, and Labourdonnais was left at a disadvantage. A British squadron was now cruising about the Bay of Bengal, taking the place which he had hoped to fill, and making many French prizes. But he was not a man of discouragements, and the situation having been saved on the Coromandel Coast by the diplomacy of Dupleix, who induced the Nawâb of Arcot to claim Pondicherry as his territory and so save it from occupation by the English, he managed somehow to scrape together sufficient ships and men to try conclusions.

Fortune played a stroke in his favour by the inopportune death of the English captain, by which the command devolved on one who erred on the side of prudence, and who, after the two squadrons had been engaged at long distances until nightfall off the coast, thought it wiser to cut and run under cover of darkness, in consequence of a leak springing in one of his largest vessels.

Labourdonnais, who had suffered far more, and who, in truth, had been anxiously cogitating his best move during the night, thus found himself, as the grey dawn showed an empty sea, a complete victor, and full of relief and pride set sail for Pondicherry. But here a cool reception awaited him, for Dupleix had no notion of having his aims achieved by any one but himself. So the commander by land and the commander by sea were mutually obstructive, and continued to be so; a course which eventually ruined both, destroyed French hopes in India, and for the present saved those of England from almost certain annihilation.

For the British squadron was nowhere. After a month of shelter in the harbour of Trincomalee, it reappeared, only to disappear once more.

Labourdonnais therefore put back to Pondicherry, and prepared seriously to take Madras; which he did, without the least trouble, in September 1746. It was, in truth, incapable of defence.

The French admiral brought eleven ships, two thousand nine hundred European soldiery, eight hundred natives, and adequate artillery against a small fort manned by two hundred men. For the Black Town and the White Town, together with the contiguous five miles of sea-coast, in which were gathered over two hundred and fifty thousand souls, lay absolutely unprotected, at the mercy of all and sundry.

It is said that the English relied for security on the Nawâb of Arcot, who had promised to claim Madras as he had claimed Pondicherry; but, doubtless, Dupleix had been beforehand with them.

This much it is pleasant to record, that the siege, which lasted no less than seven days, was the most bloodless on record. The death-roll was only one Frenchman and five English.

The terms of capitulation were severe. All goods, stores, merchandise, etc., passed to France; all English were prisoners-of-war. A ransom was suggested, but Labourdonnais, while intimating that he was prepared to receive the proposal reasonably, stipulated for previous surrender. Indeed, throughout the whole affair he appears to have behaved honourably and liberally. Not so Dupleix, who, when the subsequent negotiations had commenced, roughly interfered, denied the power of Labourdonnais to dictate terms, claimed Madras as standing in his territory, and generally brought about a dead-lock, during which three more French ships-of-war, with over one thousand three hundred men on board, arrived at Pondicherry.

With this addition to his fleet Labourdonnais could have swept the seas, and Calcutta and Bombay must have shared the fate of Madras; but--alas, for France!--her sons were quarrelling amongst themselves.

And before they could settle their differences the weather intervened. Truly, Great Britain scores something of tenderness from the breezes that blow, by being "set in the steely seas," in the path of the north and the west and the east and the south winds! They saved her once from the Spanish Armada, and now the monsoon rolled up along the coast of Coromandel, and broke in the Madras roads, foundered a French ship of the line, and drove five others dismasted, disabled, out to sea.

It was a crushing blow, one from which France never recovered, and by which poor Labourdonnais, who had consented to be tied by the leg simply from a sense of honour, a determination to stand by his word at all hazards, met with early and disappointed death; for the French Government, filled up with the able lies of Dupleix, sent him to the Bastille, where he lingered for three years, dying soon after his contemptuous and unsympathetic release of poverty and a broken heart.

Dupleix, however, flourished like the proverbial green bay tree. He repudiated ransoms and restorations alike, and seemed likely to remain in possession, when the Nawâb of Arcot intervened, asserting--and no doubt with truth--that the French governor, in order to prevent aid being sent to the English, had promised to make over Madras to him as a reward for quiescence. The intervention was followed by an undisciplined army of ten thousand men. And here, however much the character of Dupleix may arouse dislike, credit must be given to him for showing indubitably the inherent strength of his claim, that European methods should be the weightiest factor in Eastern politics. He met this horde of ten thousand with a body of four hundred half-disciplined native troops--barely half-disciplined--and he literally wiped his enemy out. Henceforward a new element entered into the Eastern problem, for it was abundantly demonstrated that to conquer India it was not necessary to import a whole army. There was that of valour, that of sheer soldiership, amongst the natives themselves, to make them, when properly led, the finest troops in the world. It is hardly too much to say that India practically changed rulers in 1746, when the Nawâb of Arcot was repulsed from Madras.

Out of this repulse (necessary in order to enable Dupleix--despite the promise without which Labourdonnais had refused to budge--to carry through his treacherous intention of repudiating the negotiations, refusing ransom, and holding Madras for the French) arose much. The Nawâb, disgusted, broke with Dupleix and assisted the English at Fort St David, a smaller factory some miles further down the coast. Here the appearance of the undisciplined troops just as the French, imagining themselves secure of victory, were refreshing themselves in a garden, produced such a scare that the victors were across the river again, and on their way back to Pondicherry before they could be rallied.

Dupleix, greatly enraged at his failure, and knowing to a nicety how to deal with natives, now commenced to make the Nawâb of Arcot's life a burden to him by reason of petty raids, until, wearied out, he once more threw the weight of his support into the French scale.

It cannot have been a clean business; it certainly was not an edifying spectacle to see two civilised European communities vieing with one another in their efforts to secure an Oriental potentate, but this much may be said in English extenuation--the French began it.

The case of the English along the Coast of Coromandel now seemed quite desperate. They had lost their only ally, and though an attack by boat on Cuddalore had been repulsed--once more by the aid of Neptune, who always seems favourable to Britain, and who on this occasion swamped half the enemy in the Coromandel Coast, and sent them dripping, half-drowned, with wet powder and soaked magazines, back to sea--they could not hope to avert the renewed assault on Fort St David, which took place in 1747.

But this game of French and English was a series of surprises, a perfect melodrama of dramatic coincidences; for no sooner were the French once more comfortably ensconced in the old garden than--Hey presto!--sails appeared to sea-ward, and in less than no time--hardly long enough for Monsieur's hurried escape--there was a British fleet at anchor in the roads!

It reads like some tale of adventure in which a "God-out-of-a-machine" always appears in the nick of time to save the hero. But so it was, though it must be confessed that beyond a display of *force majeure* the British fleet did nothing. In truth a more incapable fleet never floated. It seems to have spent a whole year in sailing about the Bay of Bengal looking for the French fleet, and when it caught a glimpse of the enemy, promptly changing its *rôle* from hound to hare, and running away itself.

Meanwhile, on land one Major Lawrence--this is the first time that this honoured name appears over the horizon of Indian history--a distinguished King's officer, had come out to take over charge of the Company's forces. At first he certainly distinguished himself, for he began by discovering a deep-laid plot, in which Madame Dupleix was prime mover, to tamper with the fidelity of the few hundred sepoys which the English, following the example of the French, were bringing into discipline. Banishment and death having disposed of this conspiracy, Admiral Griffin and the British fleet were given a chance of more honourable warfare; but, unfortunately, at the time the French vessels showed close in to the coast the admiral and all his officers happened to be ashore enjoying themselves, and so once more honest battle degenerated into the looking for a needle in a bundle of hay; in the midst of which the French vessels achieved their object of landing £200,000 in specie, and four hundred soldiers at Pondicherry.

Major Lawrence, however, almost neutralised this failure by a clever repulse of the French at Cuddalore, which lay but 3 miles north of Fort St David. Hearing that a large force was advancing, he ordered all the guns and stores from Cuddalore to be dismantled and taken in to the former fort. Native spies, naturally, brought the news of this to the enemy, who consequently advanced carelessly, applied their scaling ladders to the walls, and were surprised by perfect platoons of musketry and a shower of grape. The guns removed by day had been restored by night, and the garrison largely reinforced. The result was headlong flight.

Once again it reads like a shilling shocker; one is tempted, almost, to take the whole story as the figment of a super-excited brain.

All this time neither France nor England had--and small wonder--taken this game of French and English on the Coromandel Coast at all seriously; but at long last, in 1748, both the Government and the Company of the latter woke up to the necessity for doing something. The result being such a fleet as no Western nation had hitherto put into Eastern waters. Thirty ships in all, thirteen of them being ships of the line, and none of them less than 500 tons burden.

With these, close on four thousand European troops, three hundred Africans, two thousand half-disciplined sepoys, and the support of the Nawâb of Arcot (who had once more changed sides), Fort St David rightly felt itself strong enough, not only to recover Madras, but also to take Pondicherry.

But here, alas! begins one of the most fateful tales of sheer ineptitude to be found in the whole history of English warfare. Delay, crass ignorance, useless persistence, and exaggerated importance, marked the preliminary siege of Arrian-aupan, a small fort which might with ease have been left alone. For the season was already far advanced, and the object at which it was all-important to strike was, palpably, Pondicherry.

September, however, had well begun ere the attacking force found itself within 1,500 yards of the town, and instantly started, with unheard-of caution, to throw up parallels. Wherefore, save from ignorance, God knows, since in those days 880 yards was the limit for such diggings. On they laboured with praiseworthy persistence until, after a month's work, they reached the point at which they ought to have begun, and found that their toil was useless! Between them and the city lay an impassable morass.

The British fleet, meanwhile, getting as near to their range as strong flanking batteries manned with over a hundred guns would allow, had been pounding away quite uselessly at fair Pondicherry, which lay smiling and peaceful, immaculate as any virgin town behind the white line of surf.

What was now to be done? To begin again was hopeless, to persist useless, so after losing over one-third of its European force from sickness, and expending Heaven only knows how many rounds of ammunition, England retired, having inflicted on France the loss by the fire of her ships of one old Mahomedan woman, who was killed by a spent shot in the street, and by sickness and other casualties some two hundred soldiers.

No wonder Dupleix sang "Te Deums" until he was hoarse! No wonder he wrote bombastic, boastful, letters round to every Nawâb and Râjah, including the Great Moghul, proclaiming that the French were the fighters, and that those who were wise would side with them.

There can be no doubt whatever that this pantomimic siege of Pondicherry lost the English prestige, which it took many years of subsequent victories to regain.

For by the irony of fate, no immediate opportunity of revenge for reparation of their honour was given them.

The Peace of Aix-la-Chapelle terminated the long war between France and England, and one of the provisions of that treaty was the restoration to each power of all possessions taken during the hostilities.

Madras, therefore, was formally receded to England, and the combatants on the Coromandel Coast were left eyeing one another, looking for some new cause of conflict.

But the game of French and English was over.

PLOTS AND COUNTERPLOTS

A.D. 1748 TO A.D. 1751

When the Peace of Aix-la-Chapelle ended open warfare between the French and the English, both naturally turned their eyes more keenly upon India.

What they saw there was stimulating to those who felt within themselves the power of conquest. On all sides were petty wars and rumours of wars. The horrors of Nâdir-Shâh's invasion were being forgotten, but the country was not coming back to its pristine quiet. There was a strange new factor in India now: the factor of a new knowledge of alien races, by whom it was possible to be helped, or who could in their turn give help.

But this, still, was only about and a little beyond the sea-board. Up-country matters went on much as ever. Mahomed-Shâh's majesty crept out of its hiding-place again, and made shift with a pinchbeck peacock throne, a pretence of power.

Bâji-cum-Sâho, the Mahratta, however, almost ere he recovered from his alarm at the Persian hordes, had died, leaving his son, Bâla-ji, as Peishwa in his stead; leaving him also some very pretty quarrels to settle. One with the semi-pirates of Angria, which, involving the Portuguese, ended in the latter being ousted from India in 1739 by the Mahrattas, who, however, admitted to the loss of five thousand men in the siege of Bassein alone.

But Bâla-ji was a strong man, fully equal to the position in which he found himself; and after driving his most formidable private enemy and claimant to the Prime Ministership, Râghu-ji, back to his task of besieging Trichinopoly, he turned his attention to aggression. He began by renewing the long-deferred claim on the court at Delhi, and was granted it, on condition that he aided the Governor Ali-Verdi-Khân to repulse the invasion of Râghu-ji; who, having succeeded in his siege, had made an independent raid into Bengal. This opportunity of killing two birds with one stone was naturally welcome to Bâla-ji, who drove out the intruders without difficulty, and received his reward.

But, so far as Bengal was concerned, it was merely a postponement of an evil day, for Râghu-ji returned to his prey, and finally obtained the cession of a large part of Orissa, and a tribute from Bengal itself.

Thus in 1748 the only ascending power was that of the Mahrattas. On all other sides France and England were spectators of a general scramble for territory, a general assertion of independence on the part of petty chiefs.

And the question naturally came swiftly--"Why should we remain inactive? Why should we not extend our sphere of influence by giving, perhaps even *selling*, our aid?"

The question had already been answered by France. Dupleix had dipped deep into Indian politics, and, by so doing, had undoubtedly strengthened the position of the French. The temptation to follow suit was almost overwhelming, and so in 1749 England drew the sword which was impatiently resting in its scabbard, and became a mercenary in the pay of one Sâhu-ji who claimed the Râjahship of Tanjore. The ostensible bribe offered was an unimportant fort of Devi-kottah, and a slip of country along the coast. The real cause of the coalition being the fact that the large English army, brought eastward during the late war, was eating its head off in idleness.

The whole affair of the Tanjore succession was absolutely trivial, yet almost too complicated for abbreviated detail. It is sufficient to say that one Pratap Singh had reigned for years, that England had recognised him, negotiated with him, and courted his assistance against the French.

Policy, however, changes with the times, and it was now thought advisable, without any further provocation, to assist in dethroning him! No doubt there were excellent reasons for this *volte face*, only at the present they are not in evidence.

This first venture on mercenary lines was not a brilliant passage in the history of British arms. In truth, England in the East did not at that time possess any man fit to carry on similar work to that which Dupleix was doing for France; for Lieutenant Clive, though he had given proof of high courage during the pantomimic siege of Pondicherry, had not yet raised his head above those of his compeers. Indeed, but for a chance he might never have so raised it, since at the taking of Devi-kottah he narrowly escaped death; being one of the four survivors in a rash attempt to cross the river Kolarun on a raft.

So this Tanjore campaign, which began in a tempest[4] that killed all the baggage-animals and severely crippled the whole force, ended ignominiously in another *volte face*. For, finding their *protégé*, Sâhu-ji, had no local support for his claim, the English forces, on condition of his receiving a pension of four thousand rupees, re-transferred their friendship to the original King Pratâp, who, however, was made to ratify the bribes promised by the pretender, and also to pay the cost of the war! The latter being certainly a seething of the kid in its mother's milk.

Meanwhile, France had been busy with more important matters.

To understand what was happening, it is necessary to go back to old Asaf-Jâh, who had begun his career under Aurungzebe, and who only died in 1748 at the extraordinary age of one hundred and four.

A cunning old fox, brave to the death after the manner of foxes when in a tight place, he had, under the title of Nizâm-ul-mulk--a title still held by the rulers of the Dekkan--kept his grip on that country in almost absolute independence of Delhi.

Now, at his death, innumerable points cropped up for settlement. The Carnatic was a fief of the Dekkan, and in the Carnatic were two semi-independent kingdoms, Tanjore and Trichinopoly. The successions of all these were disputed, especially that of the Carnatic, which was held by that very Nawâb of Arcot who had bandied about his allegiance between the French and English. A most immoral proceeding, no doubt, but at a time when civilised and Christian men were palpably only playing for their own hand, it is not to be wondered at if less cultivated, more pagan peoples followed suit. There seems, anyhow, no reason--except the advantage to be gained from having a real *creature*--why Dupleix should have thrown him over and supported the claims of Chanda-Sâhib. But he did; chiefly because Chanda-Sâhib, the only member of a former ruler's family who had sufficient talent for the rise in fortune, had been brought up in the refuge of Pondicherry, and promised important concessions should he succeed. This decision on the part of Dupleix put the English in a quandary. They could not sit still and see France succeed, and yet the chances of success on the other side were small. So they temporised by sending one hundred and twenty Europeans to help Trichinopoly, by which, of course, they committed themselves as much as if they had sent twelve hundred.

They themselves, however, did not seem to think so, for in spite of this absolute challenge to France they refused the English admiral's offer to remain in Eastern waters. So suicidal did this appear to Dupleix that for some time he treated the departure as a mere feint.

So both parties settled down with their "legitimate heir," neither caring one straw for the justice of the claim, since both were equally bad.

Whatever else may be said, this much is certain, that the *protégé* of the French was a better puppet than the *protégé* of the English. Furthermore, he drew into the French net no less a person than Muzaffar-Jung, a grandson of old Asaf-Jâh, who was a claimant for the Dekkan. Truly, therefore, with a Nizam of the Dekkan, and a Nawâb of the Carnatic, both owing their thrones to French interference, Dupleix had a right to expect much for his country.

Their interference, also, was successful. There was a pitched battle close to Arcot, at which the Nawâb was killed (at the most unusual age of one hundred and seven), and only one of his sons escaped with the wreck of his army to Trichinopoly.

Dupleix, it is said, urged the allies to press on after him, but the Oriental mind, as a rule, is satisfied with the present. Chanda-Sâhib and Muzaffar-Jung amused themselves with playing the parts of Nizâm and Nawâb to their hearts' content, and spending themselves and their resources in luxurious pleasures, until the rightful claimant of the former *rôle* appeared on the horizon with an army composed largely of mercenary Mahrattas. A big army, a good army; Dupleix saw victory in it, and he instantly began with his usual unscrupulous diplomacy to attempt negotiations.

In this, however, for once, the English were beforehand with him. They had, as we know, moved by vague fear of the growing French ascendency, sent a few men to support Trichinopoly against possible attacks from Chanda-Sâhib-cum-Muzaffar-Jung, and now, taking heart of grace, Major Lawrence and four hundred troops joined the camp of the rightful Nizâm.

The two armies, that of Nâsir-Jung backed--in truth but feebly--by the English, and that of Chanda-Sâhib-cum-Muzaffar-Jung backed by the cunning of a man versed in all the tortuosities of Indian policy, were now in touch with each other, but they did not come into action.

Thirteen of the French officers resigned their commissions the day before the battle; the disaffection--due to some failure to divide spoils--spread to the men, and their commander, Monsieur d'Auteuil, feeling it unwise in the circumstances to venture anything, took veritable French leave during the night, followed by Chanda-Sâhib. Muzaffar-Jung, thus left in despair, seized the bull by the horns and surrendered himself to the rightful heir, who was in truth his uncle. There is an element of the comic opera in all these incidents which almost preclude their being taken seriously.

But here we have an *impasse*. At Pondicherry all was confusion, and Dupleix driven to despair because his cock would not fight. At Arcot, Major Lawrence trying through an interpreter to warn his cock, the triumphant

Nizâm, against froggy Frenchmen, and seeking to get the reward promised for the loan of the now useless British soldiery.

In both of which attempts he failed. In the first, because the politeness of Oriental manners refused bald translation of the Englishman's home truths. In the second, because wily Oriental astuteness suggested that services having been bought must be given before being paid for, and that Major Lawrence had better serve out his time--if as nothing else--as a boon companion!

This suggestion was refused, and "after speaking his mind freely" (through the polite interpreter!), the English commander and his troops went back in dudgeon to Fort St David.

It took the French less time than it did the English to recover from this fiasco. Dupleix, indeed, was once more deep in diplomacy ere Major Lawrence had made up his mind whether to intrigue or fight.

His decision came too late for success, his indecision too early; for having offered English support for the retaking of the Pagoda of Trivâdi, a strongly fortified place but 15 miles west of Fort St David, he withdrew it when an advance of pay was refused. Whereupon the French stepped in-- the misunderstanding was in all probability the result of their machinations- -and added to their acquisitions by taking the celebrated fort of Jingi, which, situated on a vast isolated mountain of a rock, had been considered impregnable.

It was an exploit of which to be proud, and it is said that after fully realising its natural strength the French force was lost in wonder as to how it had managed to take it!

It was an exploit, also, which roused the Nizâm Nâsir-Jung from his dream of luxurious pleasures. A nation which could take Jingi was evidently the nation with whom to make terms. He therefore offered to negotiate. Dupleix made extravagant demands, and so lured the Nizâm to take the field, for the wily diplomatist was aware that conspiracy was rife amongst the Nizâm's supporters, and hoped by getting in touch with them to rid himself more effectually of a troublesome opponent than by entering into terms with him.

It took fifteen days for the unwieldly army, 300,000 strong--60,000 foot, 45,000 cavalry, 700 elephants, 360 pieces of artillery, the rest being camp followers--to march 30 miles.

Then it was stopped by the bursting of the monsoon. And so, with his enemy blocked hopelessly within 15 miles of him, treachery became possible to the Frenchman. And black treachery it was! To be brief, Dupleix negotiated with the conspirators, and also with the Nizâm; so, finding himself finally in a dilemma as to which side to choose, took the opportunity of a delay in sending back a ratified treaty with the latter, to order the whole French force to attack.

The miserable Nizâm at first refused to believe it possible that those with whom but the day before he had signed a treaty of peace should take arms against him; refused to believe it possible that disloyalty was the cause of half his camp standing sullen spectators of the fray. He mounted his elephant and rode straight to rouse them. It being early dawn, he feared lest he might not be recognised, and rose in his howdah in order to give a clearer view of his person.

Too clear, for he fell in an instant, pierced through the heart by two bullets fired by one of his favourites.

Muzaffar-Jung, thus set free once more, resumed the Nizâmship of the Dekkan, and all went merry as a marriage bell. Both he, the Pathân nobles who had formed the bulk of the conspirators, and Dupleix, had their share of the two and a half millions of treasure said to have been taken from Nâsir-Jung; and much of it was spent in various elaborate festivities, notably in the official installation of Muzaffar; he, in his turn, nominating Dupleix as official Governor for the Great Moghul in all countries south of the Kistna. All the revenues of these countries were to pass through him, and no coins save those minted by the French at Pondicherry were to be current coin of the realm.

It was a tremendous victory for France. The English, who had hitherto been fairly content to exist in India on sufferance, heard their enemy's boast, that ere long the Moghul himself would tremble at the name of Dupleix, with absolute stupefaction. So stunned were they that they did not even object to the commander of their forces choosing this most inopportune moment to return on leave to England.

Fortunately, however, for them, thieves are apt to fall out. The Pathân nobles, discontented with their share of the plunder, once more became conspirators, with the result that Muzaffar-Jung, the creature of the French, was killed.

Fortunately, also, for the honour of England, a man called Robert Clive had been born in Shropshire six-and-twenty years before, and after several years of uncongenial employment as a clerk, had in 1747 received an ensign's commission, from which he had risen in 1751 to the rank of Captain.

And now, when the power of the French was in its zenith, he appeared, young, arrogant, determined to try a sword's conclusions with that past-master of diplomacy, Dupleix.

But before we pass on to the most honourable, the most exciting chapter in the history of British India, a look round must be given to see what had been going on in the far-away north, which lay almost out of touch with Trichinopoly, Arcot, Pondicherry, Madras, the Carnatic, Jingi, Masulipatâm, all those places on which the fingers of France and England had been laid more or less tentatively.

Mahomed-Shâh had died after having successfully resisted the invasion of the Durrâni or Afghân prince, Ahmed-Khân, who, fired by Nâdir-Shâh's example, tried in 1748 to imitate his exploit. He was badly beaten at Sirhind, close to the old battlefield of Pânipat. Before this Ali-Verdi-Khân, Governor of Bengal, had revolted, and become independent; but in his turn had suffered reverse at the hands of the Mahrattas, and had to yield up the province of Orissa.

The latter race had been much exercised over the succession to the throne, for the puppet Sâho, who, combined first with Bâji-rao and afterwards with Bâla-ji, had exercised sovereignty for so long, had no children. The right of adoption, therefore, was his, and, his wife's influence being paramount on personal points, he was inclined to choose the Râjah of Kolapur. This, however, did not suit Bâla-ji. He therefore induced the old queen, Tara-Bhâl, to trump up a tale of a posthumous son of her son, whose birth had been concealed from fear of danger to the child. Sâho, almost imbecile by this time, was deluded into believing the tale of a collateral heir, and ere dying, secretly signed an instrument giving the regency to Bâla-ji, on condition of his supporting the claims of Tara-Bhâi's supposed grandson.

But the ghost of a grandmother thus raised proved a curse to the Peishwa, for Tara-Bhâi, old as she was, did not lack energy or ambition, and at the time of Muzaffar-Jung's death in 1751, she had taken the opportunity of Bâla-ji's absence in the south to meet and crush the combined advance of the French under General Bussy and the puppet they had instantly set up in Muzaffar's place, to proclaim her own story a pure fiction, put the pretended heir into chains, and assert herself Queen of the Mahrattas.

Truly the impossibility at this time of putting reliance on any one's word, the fluctuations of faith, the unforeseen, unexpected complications arising from the general fluidity of morals, makes history read like undigested melodrama.

Such, then, was India when England, all too tardily, found a champion in Robert Clive.

ROBERT CLIVE

A.D. 1751 TO A.D. 1757

Never was the strange susceptibility of India to the influence of personal vitality better exemplified than in the case of Robert Clive.

When, in 1751, he first emerged--a good head and shoulders taller than the general ruck of Anglo-Indians--from the troubled turmoil of conflicting interests, conflicting policies which characterised India in those days, Hindostan was on the point of yielding herself to France; when, in 1767, he finally left the land where he had laboured so long and so well, England was paramount over half the peninsula.

Never in the whole history of Britain was better work done for her prestige, her honour, *by one man*; and yet that one man died miserably from opium, administered wilfully by the sword-hand which had never failed his country; administered as the only escape from disgrace.

It will always be a question whether Clive was or was not guilty of the charges preferred against him. Those who really know the Indian mind, who fully realise the depth of the degeneracy into which that mind had fallen amongst the effete nobility of the eighteenth century, may well hesitate before denying or affirming that guilt, knowing, as they must, how easy a thing is false testimony, understanding how skilfully an act, innocent enough in itself, may be garbled into positive crime.

Either way, this much may be said. The benefits he had conferred on his country were sufficient surely to have ensured him more sympathetic treatment at the hands of that country than he actually received.

But this is to anticipate.

Clive was born--but what does it matter when, where, and how, a man of deeds comes into the world? All that is necessary is to say what he did. Clive, then, was a writer, or clerk, in the East Indian Company's service. It was not, apparently, a congenial employment. Quiet, reserved, somewhat stubborn, he led a very solitary life, knowing, he writes in one of his home letters, scarcely "any one family in the place." A friend tells a tale of him, characteristic, yet hardly sufficiently authenticated for history. He found young Clive sitting dejectedly at a table, on which lay a pistol. "Fire that thing out of the window, will you?" said the lad, and watched. "I suppose I must be good for something," he remarked despondently, when the pistol went off, "for I snapped it twice at my own head, and it missed fire both times."

Whether true or not true, the lad of whom such a story could even have been told must have been something out of the common.

He was rather a tall English lad, silent, with a long nose and a pleasant smile. He was barely one-and-twenty when Dupleix took Madras, and for the first time he found himself a soldier. He returned to his writership, however, for a time, but such a profession was manifestly impossible to his temperament--a temperament admirably illustrated by the following story. He accused an officer of cheating at cards. A duel ensued, in which Clive, with first shot, missed; whereupon his adversary, holding his pistol to Clive's head, bade him beg his life. This he did instantly with perfect coolness, but when asked also to retract his accusation, replied as calmly: "Fire, and be damned to you! I said you cheated, and you did. I'll never pay you."

The adversary, struck dumb by his--no doubt--righteous stubbornness, thereupon lowered his weapon.

Such was the young man who at six-and-twenty, in the absence on leave of Major Lawrence, set off as a captain to the relief of Trichinopoly with six hundred men. He was completely outclassed both in numbers and pecuniary resources, and feeling himself to be so, he returned to Fort St David and boldly proposed a complete *volte face*. The French were thoroughly engaged aiding their ally at Trichinopoly. If he and his small force made a detour to Arcot, the capital, they might find it unprepared. They did; Clive marched in, took possession of the fort before the very eyes of one hundred thousand astonished spectators, and finding over £50,000 worth of goods in the treasury, gave them back to their owners, and issued orders that not a thing in the town was to be touched; the result of such unusual consideration being that, when he finally had to defend his capture, not a soul in the town raised a hand against the strange young *sahib* who seemed to have no fear, and certainly had no greed.

But young Clive had a Herculean task before him. With a mere handful of men--three hundred and twenty in all--he had to defend a ruinous, ill-constructed fort one mile in circumference--ditch choked, parapets too narrow for artillery--from the determined onslaught of ten thousand men. And he did so defend it. Despite failures due to inexperience, rebuffs due to rashness, despite hair's-breadth personal escapes, due to reckless, almost criminal courage, he won through to the end. There is something impish and boyish about the record of these six weeks' siege. How, more out of sheer bravado than anything else, the garrison crowned a ruined tower on the ramparts with earth, hoisted thereto an enormous old seventy-two-pounder cannon which had belonged to Aurungzebe! How they turned it on the palace which rose high above the intervening houses, and letting drive with thirty-two pounds of their best powder, sent the ball right through the palace, greatly to the alarm of the enemy's staff, which was quartered there! How once a day they fired off the old cannon, until on the fourth day it burst and nearly killed the gunners!

All this, and the thrilling story of the mason who--luckily for the garrison--knew of the secret aqueduct constructed so as to drain the fort of water, and stopped it up ere it could be used, would make a fine chapter for a boy's book of adventure. Here it is enough to record that on the 14th November, after a desperate and futile assault, the enemy--French allies and all--withdrew, and Clive found himself free to follow on their heels to Vellore, where he succeeded in giving those of them who were sufficiently brave to stand, a most satisfactory beating; in consequence of which numbers of the beaten sepoys, with the quick Oriental eye for vitality, deserted their colours. Clive enlisted six hundred of the best armed, and returned to Madras, where he was received with acclaim, for victory was then a new sensation to the Anglo-Indian. A month or two afterwards, however, he was out again on the war-path, giving the French-supported army of Chanda-Sâhib a good drubbing at Cauvery-pak. Whilst out, he received an urgent summons to go back to the Presidency town. Major Lawrence was returning from leave, and would resume command.

Despite the urgency, he found time, nevertheless, on his way back to go round by a certain town which Dupleix, in the first pride of victory, had founded under the name of Dupleix-Fattehabad, to commemorate--what surely had been better forgotten--his terrible act of treachery towards Nâsir-Jung in the matter of the ratified but delayed treaty which cost the latter his life. And here, with the same reckless hardihood which had characterised the whole campaign, he paused--though in the midst of an enemy's country--to batter to pieces the pretentious flamboyant column on which Dupleix had recorded his conquest in French, Persian, Mahratti, Hindi.

One can picture the scene, and one's heart warms to the English boy who watched with glee the hacking and hewing, while the natives stood by, their sympathy going forth inevitably to the strong young arm.

Three days afterwards Clive gave up his command, and here his first campaign ends. It was very straightforward, very clear; but what followed was complicated--very!

Trichinopoly was still besieged: the French backing Chanda-Sâhib, who claimed it as Nawâb of the Carnatic; the English backing Mahomed-Ali, who held it as Nawâb of Arcot. To the support of the latter Major Lawrence led his mercenaries, and for a time the siege was raised. By this time, however, the Directors in London were becoming restive over hostilities which interfered with the commerce of the Company. In order to bring the struggle for supremacy to a head, Clive proposed a division of forces, south and north. Whether he was actuated in making this bold proposal by any hope of getting a command over the heads of his seniors or not, certain it is that after agreeing to the proposal, Major Lawrence found it impossible to keep to seniority. The natives flatly refused to go north unless Clive led them.

Here, again, the personal equation--the only thing that has ever counted in India--stepped in. It was a genuine tribute to Clive's possession of that greatest attribute of a good general--*fortunæ*. It heartened him up, and he instantly began a second campaign of success, driving Dupleix to despair, since after every petty victory some of the beaten sepoys, following fortune, invariably deserted to the English side. Clive's army, in fact, was a snowball. It increased in size as it went, and after the big fight at Samiavêram, was joined by no less than two thousand horse and fifteen hundred sepoys. But the young man, for all his gloomy face, his silence, his stubbornness, had a curiously sympathetic personality to the natives. When Seringhâm was taken, and a thousand Râjputs shut themselves up in the celebrated pagoda swearing death ere it should be defiled, Clive "did not think it necessary to disturb them," but at Covelong he drove the frightened recruits back to battle at the point of the sword. After taking Chingleput, the campaign came to an abrupt conclusion. Clive, falling sick, had leave to go to England. This was in 1752.

Major Lawrence, meanwhile, in the south, had been fairly successful. The siege of Trichinopoly raised, the French, who had done all the artillery work, retreated to Pondicherry.

But complications arose. Mahomed-Ali, Nawâb of Arcot, showed indisposition to press his advantage, and to his great chagrin Major Lawrence discovered that Trichinopoly itself had been promised to the Mysore king, one of Mahomed-Ali's native allies. The Nawâb himself was ready to repudiate his promise; the English, it is to be feared, did not favour straightforward fulfilment. The result was a hollow compromise, which in its results showed that honesty would have been the best policy. For the next two years, therefore, Trichinopoly became the scene of constant warfare, and such was the stress of battle that raged round the unfortunate town, that in November 1753 not a tree was left standing near it, and the British detachment and convoy which finally relieved it was forced to go six or seven miles to get a stick of firewood.

The story of the final and futile assault of the French is a thrilling one, especially the incident of the night-attack frustrated by the falling into a disused well of a soldier, whose musket going off, alarmed the garrison, thus rendering of no avail a previous wholesale tampering with the guard. For the French had no hesitation in using underhand means; in this, indeed, lay the strength of Dupleix. On this occasion, anyhow, they suffered for it, since, pinned between the outer ramparts and an inner one, four hundred out of six hundred Frenchmen were either killed, wounded, or taken prisoner.

The year 1740 brought a mutual fatigue of warfare both to the French and the English East India Company. They called a truce to assert that they had never really been at war, the hostile interlude being merely the amusements of mercenaries.

But the whole affair was comic. The Council-of-Negotiation which met at a neutral little Dutch settlement was as unreal as the patents produced on both sides in support of the claims of their puppets. There were seven on the French side for the murdered Muzaffar-Jung's successor, Sâlabut, including one from the Great Moghul. The English, too, had patents for their puppet Mahomed-Ali, also including one from the Great Moghul. Now it is possible that both these contradictory patents were genuine--anything was possible in the India of 1754--but the English one was not produced, and the French one had a wrong seal!

So the affair ended in added exasperation.

But in truth France and England's attention was now awakening to the unceasing hostilities in India. International conferences were held in London, where the Secretary of State, in order to be prepared for refusal of his terms, fitted out a fleet for Eastern waters. The menace proved successful. France, never greatly enamoured of her Eastern Company, gave away the game by sending out one Monsieur Godeheu to take over the Governorship from Dupleix.

It was a bolt out of the blue. Whatever his faults may have been, the latter had spent his life for, and risked his whole fortune in, the Company. He never recovered the blow, but went home, sought bare justice by a lawsuit, and died ruined, broken-hearted, ere his case was decided. So England has no monopoly in ingratitude to her public servants.

Monsieur Godeheu was peaceful, painstaking, praiseworthy. He produced an ill-considered but plausible treaty which rather knocked the wind out of Clive's sails when he returned to Bombay in 1755 with Admiral Watson's fleet, fully prepared to attack the Dekkan from the north. He had to content himself with a campaign against the pirate-king of Anghria, in the course of which a momentous quarrel arose between the English and their Mahratta allies. The latter claimed a share of the plunder, the former refused it, asserting with righteous indignation that deliberate treachery had been proved up to the hilt against their so-called allies, and that consequently they were entitled to nothing. A sordid quarrel at best, which bore bitter fruit in years to come.

From this, Clive sailed to take up command at Madras, where he was met by disastrous news from Calcutta.

Surâj-ud-daula, Nawâb of Bengal, had seized on it, suffocated a hundred and twenty-three of its inhabitants--many of them men in the best positions--in the Black Hole, and had returned to Murshidabad, whence he had issued orders for the destruction and confiscation of all English property in his dominions. Such was the ineptitude of England at that time in India, that two whole months elapsed ere Clive, in a fever of impatience, was allowed to start for retaliation.

While we can imagine him fretting and fuming, we shall have time for a glance back to see who Surâj-ud-daula was, and what was the cause of his action.

Ali-Verdi-Khân, who, it will be remembered, had ceded Orissa to the Mahrattas, had also snatched the Nawâbship from his master's son; a graceless youth, it must be admitted, while Ali-Verdi-Khân himself was, despite many horrid acts, a fairly just ruler. During his lifetime the English had no complaint; but at his death he committed a gross injustice on every soul in his dominions by appointing as his heir his grandson Surâj-ud-daula, a perfectly infamous young man. No one, apparently, had a good word to say for him, except those amongst whom he spent a vicious, depraved life.

His aunt, Ghasîta Begum, at any rate, nourished no illusions concerning him, and being an ambitious woman, anxious to preserve her great fortune for future occasions of conspiracy, took immediate precautions while Ali-Verdi lay dying against any confiscation of her treasures. She employed one Kishen-dâs, a pretended pilgrim to Juggernath, to carry them off in boats down the Ganges. Once on the river, Kishen steered, not for the sea, but for Calcutta. It is difficult to say whether the Governor and Council knew what they were harbouring, but the fact remains that the treasures sought and found British protection, one Omichand, a Hindu merchant, giving Kishen-dâs hospitality.

Surâj-ud-daula took the business very badly. He made a scene at his grandfather's death-bed, and accused the English of siding with the faction that was against his succession. Yet, when that succession was an accomplished fact, and the English agent appeared at his audience to apologise in set terms for a so-called mistake in turning away, as an impostor, from Calcutta, a spy who asserted he bore a letter from Surâj-ud-daula, the latter kept a calm countenance and said negligently that he had forgotten the incident. And yet it was no slight one; for there is little doubt that the Council were not quite satisfied with its own action.

The Nawâb, however, was biding his time, and he soon found it. War was on the point of breaking out once more in Europe between France and England, and orders were, in consequence, sent out by the Directors of the Company to overhaul fortifications. Repairs were at once commenced. This was Surâj-ud-daula's opportunity. He first sent a haughty enquiry as to why, without leave, the English were building a new wall, and, pretending that the reply given was inadequate, followed up his first communication by marching to Kossimbazaar with his army, sending for Mr Watts the Governor, and with threats forcing him to sign an engagement to destroy, within fifteen days, all new works which had been begun at Calcutta, deliver up all the Nawâb's subjects he might call for, and refund any sums the Nawâb might have lost by passports of trade having been illegally granted.

Now, in dealing with these Indian disputes it is notoriously difficult to read through the written lines of the formulated plaint and counter-plaint, and reach the palimpsest below; that palimpsest of fine, complicated motive which invariably underlies the simplest plea, which makes even a petty debt case in India like an English A. B. C. scrawled over a Babylonian brick, covered closely with fly-foot stipplings. But here the stipulation regarding the Nawâb's subjects gives a clear clue. Whether Surâj-ud-daula had any just cause of complaint or not, his real grievance was the loss of his aunt's treasure.

This abject yielding of the English was fatal. Had any one of the type of Clive or John Nicholson been on the spot, events might have been very different; as it was, disaster and destruction followed. Surâj-ud-daula marched on Calcutta, receiving by the way the gift of two hundred barrels of gunpowder from our treaty-bound friends the French at Chandanagore! Reading the record of these few fateful days in June 1756 one knows not whether to laugh or to cry, to let pity or righteous wrath prevail, as the history of silly delay and still sillier activities unfolds itself. The feverish digging of absolutely untenable trenches, the three weeks' delay without any preparation whatever while letters were passing to and fro, the neglect to apply for reinforcements to other presidencies, the imprisonment of Omichand, the miserable fracas in his house, in which a Brahmin peon, mad with rage and professing fear lest high-caste women should be violated, rushed into his master's harem, killed a round dozen of innocent ladies, and then stabbed himself, reminds one of nothing but the fateful days of May a hundred years after, when Englishmen stood by and watched the Mutiny grow from a chance by-blow to a giant unrestrained. Calcutta was taken. Mr Drake, the governor, and Captain Minchin, the commandant, ran away. The ships weighed anchor and sailed out of gunshot, leaving one hundred and ninety deserted men in the fort. But if cowardice showed unabashed, courage was not lacking, and among those who showed it Mr Holwell deserves honourable mention. A civilian himself, he locked the gates of the fort to prevent further desertion, and final resistance being hopeless, did his best by diplomacy to avert absolute destruction. A hard task, for he lost twenty-five of his miserable garrison in one assault, and he lost the aid of more by drunkenness: for the soldiers got at the *arrack* store.

Still, he might have succeeded but for the fact that the Nawâb lost his temper on finding that the treasury only contained £5,000! And he had imagined the English rich beyond dreams. He jumped to the conclusion that there must be treasure concealed, and when none was forthcoming, seems to have cared nothing for the personal safety he had guaranteed to Mr Holwell and his following of a hundred and forty men, women, and children.

The tale of the Black Hole of Calcutta is too well known to need repetition. The unfortunate company were herded at nightfall into a room eighteen feet square, and despite their agonising appeals for deliverance, left to suffocate. By daybreak only three-and-twenty remained alive.

And the ships which could have carried them off ere hostilities began, which even afterwards might have rescued them, were sailing merrily down the river, the full breeze of dawn bellying their sails.

It is an indelible disgrace!

Surâj-ud-daula, disappointed in plunder, retired to Murshidabad fulminating vain thunders against all things British, as he abandoned himself once more to infamous pleasures.

But Clive was on his track. Clive, filled-according to his letters--"with grief, horror, and resentment"; determined that the expedition should not "end with the retaking of Calcutta only, but that the Company's estate in these parts shall be settled in a better and more lasting condition than ever."

The story of his success is a long one, and is, unfortunately, marred by more than one doubtful, almost inexcusable act. But that he should utterly have escaped from the corruption of the whole atmosphere in India at this time is more than any one has any right to expect, even of a hero. He was but mortal, and from the time he was twenty, had had to steer his way through a perfect network of intrigue. Again, his complicity in much that happened is by no means assured, for we know that he was surrounded by enemies amongst his own countrymen, who, jealous of his success, angered with his blunt outspokenness, did not hesitate to injure him. Let us consider for a moment what Clive must have said to Captain Minchin, to Mr Drake, concerning their pleasure-trip down the Hooghly while their friends were suffocating in the Black Hole! We have his opinion of the "Bengal gentlemen" in his letters, which runs thus:--

"The loss of private property and the means of recovering it are the only objects which take up their attention. I would have you guard against everything these gentlemen can say; for, believe me, they are bad subjects and rotten at heart, and will stick at nothing to prejudice you and the gentlemen of the Committee. Indeed, how should they do otherwise when they have not spared one another? Their conduct at Calcutta finds no excuse even amongst themselves; the riches of Peru or Mexico should not induce me to dwell among them."

These are strong words, but they were written under strong emotion. Clive, arriving at Calcutta, after a most fatiguing march of skirmishes along the river, had been mortified by finding that Admiral Watson, who had sailed up it and captured the town after two hours' desultory cannonading, had already appointed a Captain Coote as military governor. This post, naturally, was Clive's by every right, and he objected strenuously. Matters went so far that the admiral threatened to fire on the fort if Clive refused to leave it, and though a compromise was effected, the affair shows the *animus* against the young colonel.

He was hampered on all sides. We find him point-blank refusing to place himself under the orders of the Committee.

"I do not intend," he writes, "to make use of my power for acting separately from you, without you reduce me to the necessity for so doing; but as far as concerns the means of executing these powers, you will excuse me, gentlemen, if I refuse to give it up."

The very existence, therefore, of this friction makes caution necessary in judging of Clive's actions, since, except from his own admissions, we have nothing on which absolute reliance can be placed. He seems to have felt himself overmatched in every way. Certainly he proceeded with more caution than usual, except in regard to his attack on Surâj-ud-daula's camp outside the very walls of Calcutta.

Deputies had been sent overnight to interview the Nawâb with a view to negotiation, and had returned in confusion, lightless, by secret paths, convinced that they were to be assassinated. Huge eunuchs and attendants, made still more terrific by stuffed coats and monstrous turbans, had scowled at them--the Nawâb had been superciliously indifferent. Clive had about two thousand men under his command; the enemy, under Mir-Jâffar, Surâj-ud-daula's general, mustered forty thousand; but instant assault seemed necessary in face of that contemptuous discourtesy.

It began at dawn, and though, owing to fog, it was not so decisive as Clive had hoped, achieved its end, for the very next day the Nawâb proposed peace.

Now in this, again, we must read between the lines. The terms of peace which was duly signed--Clive feeling himself far too weak to continue war, for a time at any rate--were not acceptable to the Committee, for Clive refused to allow the claims of "private individuals to stand in the way of the interest of the Company." The treaty, in fact, was singularly easy on the Nawâb, but it must be remembered that Mr Holwell, who had himself been in the Black Hole, had exculpated Surâj-ud-daula from wilful participation in the ordering of it; indeed, there seems little doubt that it was due to the reckless indifference of subordinates. Thus we see here an honest endeavour on Clive's part to deal with Surâj-ud-daula fairly and squarely. He trusted him, disregarding Admiral Watson's warning that without a good thrashing *first*, treaties with natives were of no avail.

His subsequent disgust at finding this warning had been correct must be admitted in defence of his future actions. After endless intriguing, difficult to follow, and still more difficult when followed to understand--for the friction between Clive and his environment seems to obscure everything--the young colonel (he was but thirty) seems to have reverted to his desire to dislodge the French, with which his services had begun, and, war between the nations being opportunely declared, he attacked and took Chandanagore. This brought about, however, a complete revelation of the perfidy of Surâj-ud-daula, who in letters to the French governor (whom he calls "*Zubat-ul-Tujar*," the "Essence of Merchants"), abuses "*Sabut-Jung*" (the "Daring in War," by which name Clive is still known in India), and promises his heart-whole support. "Be confident," he writes, "look on my forces as your own."

Clive, conscious of having acted against general opinion in trusting the man, resented this personally. Then Suraj-ud-daula was practically a monster in human form. By twenty, his vices were hoary. So it may well have been honest disgust which made Clive first consider the possibility of deposing him in favour of Mîr-Jâffar. Pages have been written inveighing against the enormity of intriguing against a ruler with whom you have a treaty of peace. And it is mean according to Western ideals. Still, Clive did not shrink from it; his verdict is brief: "I am persuaded there can be neither peace nor security while such a monster reigns."

So he did not reign long. Mîr-Jâffar was deliberately nominated; a treaty, consisting of a preamble and thirteen articles, solemnly and secretly drawn up. In this Omichand, merchant, moneylender, spy, informer, a man of infinite influence at Murshidabad, was go-between. As reward for his services and silence--for otherwise he threatened to warn his real master Suraj-ud-daula--he insisted on receiving £200,000. But, in truth, this treaty reads like a huge bill, for in consideration of being made Nawâb, Mîr-Jâffar promised the Company to pay, as damages for the sacking of Calcutta, £1,000,000, to the English inhabitants thereof £500,000, to the natives £200,000, and to the Armenians £70,000.

These were immense sums, but they were the result of absurdly exaggerated estimates of the treasure in Murshidabad, which was currently reported to be at least £24,000,000.

So the farce of friendship went on with the Nawâb. It was a toss-up in the end whether Mîr-Jâffar would be faithful to his master or to the treaty, and on the very eve of the battle of Plassey, that is to say, 23rd June 1757, Clive was still undetermined whether to attempt the final blow or to refrain from it. His reputation would have benefited if he had; for England would have won in the end without subterfuge. Still, for all this excuse is to be found. Even the fact that Clive, in common with half the army and navy, was to receive a stipulated present--in his case a very large one--must not be counted, as it appears to be at the first blush, bribery and corruption. There was no law against the taking of douceurs; the employees of the Company, indeed, were ill paid because of such perquisites, without which they could not live. So, had he chosen to ask for a million of money, he could only have been counted extortionate in his demands. But the trick played upon Omichand with Clive's support and connivance seems--at least--despicable. Briefly, it comes to this. Englishmen were afraid of the scoundrel's blabbing, yet they were determined he should not have the £200,000 for which he stipulated. They therefore drew up two treaties, one with, one without, the stipulation. The one they showed to Omichand was forged; the other was really signed.

It seems almost incredible this should have been done by plain English gentlemen, let alone by one who in many ways was a hero; but so it was.

To avoid paying £200,000 out of revenues which did not belong to us, we resorted to fraud and forgery.

There is but one consolation in the case. Clive himself, the arch-actor, never regretted the act. When arraigned on this charge before the House of Commons he asserted proudly that he thought "it warrantable in such a case, and would do it again a hundred times. I had no interested motive in doing it, but did it with the design of disappointing the expectations of a rapacious man, for I think both art and policy warrantable in defeating the purposes of such a villain."

But was Omichand "the greatest villain upon earth" that Clive held him to be? Even this is doubtful, and our pity is his, no matter what he was, as we read the story, as told by Orme the historian, of the conference which was held the day after the battle.

"Clive and Scrafton went towards Omichand, who was waiting in full assurance of hearing the glad tidings.... Scrafton said to him in the Indostan language: 'Omichand! the red paper is a trick--you are to have nothing.' The words overpowered him like a blast of sulphur; he sank back fainting."

He did not recover the shock, but died a complete imbecile within the year.

No! Whatever way we look at this incident it offends eye and taste. For it was so needless. If Omichand was the double-dyed scoundrel he is said to have been, what more easy than to tell him when all was over: "Yes! the £200,000 is yours, but you shall not have it."

Clive, at any rate, was strong enough for that.

The incident prevents the remembrance of Plassey being a pure pleasure. It was victory complete so far as it went, and by the treaty with Mîr-Jâffar Clive's hope "that the Company's estate in these parts shall be settled in a better and more lasting condition than before" was fully justified; for not only was Calcutta given to it freehold, but also the land to the south of the town, as a *zemindari* subject to the payment of revenue.

England had a real hold on Indian soil at last, and Clive had given it to her.

ROBERT CLIVE

A.D. 1757 TO A.D. 1767

It was in the year 1757, just one hundred years before the Mutiny, that the battle of Plassey was fought, and that by the enthronement of a Nawâb who owed everything to English arms the East India Company became practically lords paramount in Bengal, Behar, and Orissa.

It was in the same year that Upper India was once more disturbed by the inroad of Ahmed-Shâh, the Durrâni king of Kandahâr. Mahomed-Shâh, the Moghul emperor, had once repulsed him, and Ahmed-Shâh, the Afghân's namesake, son and successor of the Great Moghul, had, for the six years of his reign, watched the north-western frontier nervously.

But he died in 1754 without signs of the dread invasion.

It came, however, in Alamgîr the Second's time, through no fault of that distressful puppet, but owing to the arrogance of Ghâzi-ud-din, Grand Vizier, and eldest son of the old fox Asaf-Jâh. Heredity is strong. In his lifetime there was not a political pie in all India into which the latter's wily old finger did not dip, and now his descendants carried on the same game. Sâlabut-Jung, his son, was French nominee for the Nizâmship; Muzaffar-Jung, grandson, for the Nawâbship of the Carnatic. Nâzir-Jung, who perished miserably through the treachery of Dupleix, had been another candidate, and at the effete court of Delhi, Ghâzi-ud-din was virtually king. He chose to insult the widow of an Afghân governor of Lahôre, and Ahmed-Shâh, Durrâni, marched to avenge it.

The vengeance was deep and bitter. Delhi was laid waste; the horrors of Nâdir-Shâh being repeated and excelled, for the Durrâni had not the Persian's hold upon his troops. He also penetrated further down-country than did Nâdir, and harried the Gangetic plain as far as Muttra. The news of his raid, indeed, was one of the many factors in the problem of action or inaction which Clive had had to decide. But the heat drove the hardy northmen back to their hills, and Upper India reverted once more to its old peaceful life, Delhi to dreams. It was a drugged city in those days, winking sleepily in the sunlight, enduring ravishment patiently, returning when the stress was over to watch its pageant king sitting on his pinchbeck peacock throne, pretending to be all-powerful, looking out haughtily, with opium-dimmed eyes, upon a subject world, that in reality cared not one jot for the so-called descendants of the Great Moghul.

In Bengal the English had been king-makers without one reference to the sovereign power. In the very Punjâb itself, the Mahrattas, invited to his aid by Ghâzi-ud-din, came and mastered the length and breadth of the land. In truth, their star was in its zenith. Even in the Dekkan, despite the help of a French force under Monsieur Bussy-by far the ablest commander France ever sent to the East--Sâlabut-Jung could with difficulty keep in the field against them.

And France was beginning to find her hands full. War had been declared in Europe between her and England, and in 1758 the Comte de Lally, a man of great reputation, was sent out avowedly with the intention of breaking the English power in the East.

A bit of a braggadocio was Lally, and all unversed in Oriental likes and dislikes. He began ill by ousting Bussy, in whom the French allies believed utterly, much as the English allies believed in Clive. The secret of this belief may be evolved from the tale of the taking of Bobbili. It was an old fort held by an old family of Râjputs, and Bussy called on it to yield, assaulted it for three days, and finally, on the third night, sounded "cease firing," and waited for the morning to deliver his final blow.

Not a sound disturbed the silence of the night. The primrose dawn showed pale, the old fort rising stern against it. But the gates were open. Bussy entered with caution. The sentries at their posts were dead, the streets were empty, but in the arcades men lay sleeping their last sleep.

The palace doorkeepers were on duty--dead! As he and his staff hurried through the narrow passages, they could see through dark archways women lying huddled up in each other's arms--dead! The Hall of Audience was reached at last; and there, each in his place, the courtiers had drawn their last breath. But the chief was not on the throne; that was occupied by a year-old boy-baby, the beloved heir, playing unconcernedly with the heron's plume of his dead father, who, with his sword through his heart, lay with his head at the feet of his little son. Beside him was the only other living soul in Bobbili, the oldest inhabitant of the town.

Youth and age! The lesson was not unlearnt by Bussy, and Bobbili remains a chieftainship to this day.

Lally, however, was of different mettle. To him, surrounded by well-born, fashionable French officers, all things Eastern were beneath contempt.

What was a Brahmin that he should not do what he was told to do, even though the order involved his being yoked cart-fellow with a sweeper?

It was not conducive to anything but discipline; and discipline in India is limited, like all other things, by caste.

Small wonder, then, that, opposed to such a leader as Captain, afterwards Sir Eyre Coote (for Clive could not leave Bengal), the French fortunes gradually failed, until in 1761 all hold on India was lost by the taking of Pondicherry. Poor Lally! He had pitted himself against Orientalism, and he failed miserably. Yet, once again, he did not deserve to be dragged to execution on a dung-cart for having been "insolent to His Majesty King Louis XVth's other officers" (which was a true count), "and for treason to His Majesty himself" (which was false). Of how many reputations has not India unjustly been the grave? Truly one can echo Lally's last words: "Tell my judges that God has given me grace to pardon them: but if I were to see them again, that grace might go."

It is a wonderfully human speech. One can forgive him much for it, but one cannot forgive his judges as he did; deep down, their meanness, their lack of wide outlook, rankles.

While Eyre Coote, however, was bringing the French power to its end for ever, Clive was consolidating the British hold in Bengal; and still under the stress of utterly uncongenial coadjutors.

"I cannot help feeling," he writes to the Select Committee, "that had the expedition miscarried you would have laid the whole blame upon me." And this was true.

The influx into Calcutta of close on £800,000, paid according to treaty from Surâj-ud-daula's treasure chest--which after all only contained, revenues counted, something under £7,000,000--seems to have roused rapacity on all sides. It is worthy of note, however, that Clive's part in the squabble which ensued is invariably on the side of justice. When Admiral Watson claimed his share of the loot as an actual, though not a formal member of the Select Committee, Clive at once saw the reasonableness of the claim, and set an example--which was not followed--of handing over his share of the additional portion which had to be made up. He also fought strenuously, and overcame, an attempt on the part of the military to exclude the navy from any share in the plunder. Indeed, his reply to the "Remonstrance and Protest" sent him by the soldiers is worthy of quotation.

"How comes it," he asks, "that a promise of money from the Nawâb *entirely negotiated by me* can be deemed by you a matter of right and property?... It is now in my power to return to the Nawâb the money already advanced, and leave it to his option whether he will perform his promise or not. You have stormed no town and found no money there; neither did you find it on the plain of Plassey. In short, gentlemen, it pains me to remind you that what you are to receive is entirely owing to the care I took of your interests."

So, after pointing out that, but for this care, the Company would only have awarded them at the outside six months' pay, he finishes by upbraiding them with their disrespect and ingratitude, and placing the officers who brought him the remonstrance under arrest.

Now this letter, frank and straightforward, enables us to see the position as Clive saw it. The army was purely a mercenary army. From the day on which the English had sided with the Nawâb of Arcot it always had been mercenary. The natives had paid their allies. The question as to the advisability of this did not come in; the fact remained. Therefore, on the supposition that Surâj-ud-daula's wealth was enormous, enormous fees had been asked.

Blame, therefore, could only be given for rapacity, not for the actual taking of any fee. And the advantage to the Company of what had been accomplished was so incalculable that no complaint from *it* was possible.

It had been an easy task to place Mîr-Jâffar on the throne, but it required all Clive's will-power to induce him to do as he was bid. The spoliation of Surâj-ud-daula's treasury had left the former in comparative poverty, and he resented being made by Clive to fulfil his engagements under the treaty. Still, he could not afford to quarrel with one who maintained the peace by crushing rebellion, apparently, by his mere presence.

Just, however, as he was hesitating over an attempt at independence, news came that the Wazîr of Oude was marching upon Bengal, and at the same time an envoy of the Mahrattas appeared, demanding £240,000 arrears of tribute. Fear threw him again into Clive's arms, who, however, had by this time come to see that in choosing Mîr-Jâffar as Nawâb, he had chosen one who would always be a thorn in the side of good government.

"He has no talent," he writes, "for gaining the love and confidence of his officers. His mismanagement of the country ... might have proved fatal ... no less than three rebellions were on foot at one time."

Still, by unceasing efforts, Clive is able to report in 1758 that the Nawâb seems now "so well fixed in his government as to be able, with a small degree of prudence, to maintain himself quietly in it." Under better management, money was flowing in, and the general outlook seemed bright. In the same year Clive was by popular acclaim appointed Governor of Bengal.

The Directors in London had unaccountably overlooked him, possibly because he ought really to have returned to Madras, but the Council in India felt that, without his personal influence with Mîr-Jâffar, their position was critical. The whole English position was, in truth, at this time dubious. The French had been at this period successful on the Coromandel Coast, and the prince-royal of Delhi, having quarrelled with his father, had left the court, and was on his way with a large army to claim the viceroyalty of Bengal. Now, open defiance of the claims of the Great Moghul family was rank sacrilege. Mîr-Jâffar, with a half-eye to ridding himself somehow of British influence, professed horror. Clive's thumb, however, was over him, and escape impossible. The prince-royal was curtly told that, as rebel to his father, he had no authority, and when the Wazîr of Oude arrived in support of the claim, both he and the prince were as curtly and decidedly beaten.

Mîr-Jâffar was now full of gratitude, and determined to give Clive (who, as a recognised official of the Court, ought to have had one) a *jaghir*, or grant of land for services done. No high official of any native ruler is without one. But Mîr-Jâffar was cunning. The *zemindari*, or land subject to revenue, which, under pressure, he had given to the Company was, he saw, really a screw which might be used against him at any time by refusal to pay the just dues.

He therefore hit on the happy idea of killing two birds with one stone. He would give the quit-rent of this to Clive, and leave him and his Company to fight it out between themselves! It really was very ingenious, very acute, as the opposition the plan aroused in the Council clearly proved. It is, in fact, amusing to read the many arguments advanced against it; all of which are in reality founded on the Company's inward determination to use the quit-rent as a set-off against the Nawâb.

He, however, had a perfect right to do as he did, and Clive himself is not to be blamed for sticking to a bargain which gave him some hold of his enemies and detractors. And yet when, after annihilating a Dutch expedition, and forcing on the promoters as conditions of peace that they should never again introduce or enlist troops or raise fortifications in India, Clive announced his intention of going to England on leave, the best part of Calcutta was on its knees to him begging him to reconsider his resolution.

Without him Mîr-Jâffar was a broken reed.

And the Nawâb himself was as urgent in appeal. Without Clive's help, how could he hope to keep the constant encroachments of the Company's servants within bounds?

But Clive was obdurate. He was clear-sighted, and he saw beyond the present. He saw, as he himself writes, that what the future might bring "was too extensive for a mere mercantile company," and he was eager to get home to impress England with his belief, and induce her to stretch out her right hand and take the rich heritage which might be hers. Whether in strict morality she had a right to do this is another matter. Clive thought she had, and in determining the point there can be no doubt whatever that (as he himself writes, "with a thorough knowledge of this country's Government, and of the genius of its people, acquired by two years' experience") one of the chief factors which weighed with him was his conviction that the people themselves "would rejoice in so happy an exchange as that of a mild for a despotic Government."

And that the British Government would be mild was by every evidence part of Clive's faith in himself and in his country. The natives loved him. Nowhere in all his history is there one hint of cruelty in his treatment of them, unless (as in the case of Omichand) hot anger at treachery rose up in him.

"He was the greatest villain upon earth--I would do it again a hundred times over."

Surely if ever Clive gains his deserved memorial, these words of his should find some place upon it in palliation of the offence which tarnished his reputation. An offence which, when all is said and done, has something of the nature of an unreasoning, impish, boyish trick about it which is reminiscent of other incidents in Clive's career, notably the firing of Aurungzebe's old gun at Arcot, and the *détour* to smash up the victory-pillar of Dupleix.

So Clive went home, and, arriving at an opportune moment of national depression after a series of rebuffs abroad, was honoured as something of which England could be proud. He was given an Irish barony. "I could have bought an English one (which is usual), but that I was above," he writes. And yet, apparently, he was not above holding his tongue on many matters of national importance, because he was afraid of irritating the Court of Directors who had the payment of his *jâghir* money. But Clive was ambitious, extraordinarily ambitious, at this time of his career.

"We must be nabobs ourselves," is a phrase which occurs in one of his letters; also this: "My future power, my future grandeur, all depend upon the receipt of the *jâghir* money."

What scheme lay hidden in his brain? One thing is certain. He scrupled at little which would help him to its realisation. He failed, however, in getting a majority in the Council of Directors, though to do so he employed the discreditable tactics of his adversaries by manufacturing votes. In his defence it must be remembered that he was fighting single-handed against a corrupt monopoly, and that throughout the whole quarrel he never flinched from his purpose.

He took the question of his *jâghir*, which the Company refused to pay, into Chancery, but ere the case was investigated, news of so serious a nature was received from India that a sudden and imperious call for Clive to return arose on all sides. He had made our dominion in the East. Only he could save it from destruction.

The story of what had happened during his four years' absence may be briefly epitomised.

Alamgîr II., emperor at Delhi, had been murdered by his minister Ghâzi-ud-din from fear of his intriguing with Ahmed-Shâh, Durrâni, who was once more marching on the Punjâb. Backed by his Mahrattas, the minister thought himself secure; in this he was mistaken. True, the Mahrattas were in the zenith of their power, their artillery surpassed that of the Moghuls, the discipline of their army was better than it had ever been before, but they had in consequence lost something of their lightness, their alertness.

And they were too numerous. When they finally found themselves entrenched on the old historic battle-plain of Pâniput awaiting Ahmed-Shâh's advance, they numbered no less than three hundred thousand. Excellent foragers though they were, supplies soon ran short. On the other hand, Ahmed-Shâh, with the confederacy of Mahomed princes which had joined forces with him, mustered but a third of that number. He saw his advantage, and waited, replying to his Indian allies' importunities to attack: "This is a matter of war; leave it to me." Night after night his small red tent was pitched in front of his entrenchments, whence he watched his enemy. "Do you sleep," he would say contemptuously to the Indian chiefs; "I will see no harm befalls you."

So the day came at last when the Mahrattas were forced by hunger to attack. They fought well; but by eventide two hundred thousand of them lay dead in heaps on the Pâniput plain. Nearly all the great chiefs were slain or wounded, and Bâla-ji, the Peishwa, himself died on the way back to Poona, it is said from a broken heart. Ahmed-Shâh, Durrâni, returned to Kandahâr and did not again enter India.

In consequence of his father's murder the prince-royal, in natural succession, became the Great Moghul. As such it became impossible to further ignore his claims. But he could be, and was, again beaten, together with his ally the Nawâb of Oude. Matters at Murshidabad, however, deprived of Clive's guidance, had gone from bad to worse. Mr Vansittart, Clive's successor in the Governorship, seems to have been weak, and in addition could count on no support in his council save that of Warren Hastings. The end being that Mîr-Jâffar was virtually deposed for misgovernment, and his son-in-law Mîr-Kâssim placed on the throne. It was not a clean business, and Mîr-Jâffar, full of resentment, retired to live in Calcutta on a pension.

Things, however, did not improve under Mîr-Kâssim, though the Prince-Royal-Emperor, who was still hovering on the frontiers, was interviewed by Mr Carnac (doubtless bearing a satisfactory present), and an arrangement entered into by which, in consideration of being confirmed in the Nawâbship, Mîr Kâssim should pay an annual tribute of £240,000. It is easy to be generous with other folks' money!

Thus secured from invasion, Mîr-Kâssim began to try and fill his treasuries, and instantly complained, as Mîr-Jâffar had complained, of the injury done to him and his subjects by the rule which permitted private trade to the servants of the Company, who, not satisfied with using their public position to assist them, claimed the right to be free of all duties, thus ousting the native trader from all markets.

It was manifest, gross injustice; but here again Mr Vansittart and Warren Hastings were alone in condemning it.

Afraid to strike at the root of the evil, while continuing the absolutely indefensible right to private trade, they agreed with the Nawâb that the usual duty should be paid.

This raised a storm in Calcutta, where a full meeting of Council decided by ten to two that the agreement should not stand.

The Nawâb retaliated in kind. Since the Council persisted in their claim, he would extend its bearings to his own subjects. All could now trade free, and let the devil take the hindmost!

It was a fair retort. They tried to intimidate him, but he had the bit between his teeth. Diplomacy had had its day; it was now war to the knife!

Within a month or two the massacre at Patna took place, in which two hundred Englishmen lost their lives in cold blood; but not before the Presidency troops had entered Murshidabad, deposed Mîr-Kâssim, who fled, and reinstated Mîr-Jâffar.

It was a tissue of mistakes from beginning to end, which Major Munro's subsequent victory at Buxar over the combined forces of the Prince-Royal-Emperor (who had not yet managed to recover his capital Delhi), the Wazîr of Oude, and Mîr-Kâssim did little to rectify. For Mîr-Jâffar died shortly after of old age, and the Council was left without a Nawâb to squeeze! After much discussion, however, they decided on putting up Nujâm-ad-daula, an illegitimate son of Mîr-Jâffar's.

Such was the state of affairs when Clive, to whom, in view of the painful state of disorder in Bengal, absolute power had been given, arrived in Calcutta on his second period of Governorship in the beginning of May 1765.

His first act was to decline discussion.

"I was determined," he writes, "to do my duty to the public, though I should incur the odium of the whole settlement. The welfare of the Company required a vigorous exertion, and I took the resolution of cleansing the Augean stable."

He began the work at once, and, undeterred by opposition, did not rest till he had placed the Indian Civil Service on the upward path to its present honoured and honourable position. Perquisites and presents were swept away; unbiassed authority given in exchange.

The only real political work of the next two years was his treatment of, and treaty with, the Prince-Royal-Emperor, Shâh-Âlam, who was more than ever a puppet king after the victory at Buxar, when he had thrown himself on the protection of the English. So anxious, indeed, was he to secure this, that before the answer to his petition was received from Calcutta, he encamped every night as close to the British army as he could for safety!

The treaty into which he then entered contained an important stipulation that the Company should assist him to recover the territories usurped by his late ally Sûjah-daula, Wazîr of Oude.

Hearing of this the Wazîr immediately prepared for resistance by joining forces with Ghâzi-ud-din, the murderous minister at Delhi, and with some bands of Rohillas and Mahrattas.

But they were poor allies, and Clive, coming to the problem with his clear head, proceeded to settle it with a high hand. Sûjah-daula was left with his territories, save for the district around Allahabâd, which was ceded to Shâh-Âlam, the so-called emperor, who was also to receive £260,000 a year as the revenue of Bengal. This was to be payable, not as in the past, by the Nawâb, but by the East India Company itself, who thus became the real masters of the country, and so responsible for its administration, its defences; the Nawâb, Nujâm-ud-daula, reverting to the position of pensioner, a position which he accepted gladly with the remark: "Thank God! I shall now have as many dancing-girls as I please!"

' That the bargains were hard all round none can deny, but it is difficult to see, as has been stated, that Clive derived any pecuniary benefit from them.

On the contrary, it may be observed that special precautions were taken to ensure the legality of the compromise which Clive had entered into with the Directors regarding his *jâghir*, when the public interests, by recalling him to duty, had made some quicker settlement of the question than that of a Chancery suit necessary. Now this compromise, which gave him the revenues for ten years only, or till his death, whichever was the shortest period, was not very favourable to Clive. Its continuance, therefore, should not be urged, as it often is, as proof of his rapacity.

The problem which next employed him was one of extreme difficulty. It was an enquiry into the conduct of officers in regard to their new covenants which prohibited the receiving of presents. As a result of this, ten officials who were dismissed for corruption went naturally to join the ranks of Clive's many enemies.

The question of private trade still remained, and was more difficult of settlement. For the salary of a member of Council was but £350, and he could not keep up the dignity of his position on less than £3,000.

Clive settled this in a somewhat makeshift way, but it is worthy of note that though as governor his pay was largely enhanced by the new scheme, he did not personally take one penny of it, for he had declared his intention of not deriving any pecuniary advantage from his position. The money was spent in augmenting the salaries of his office. All this caused much indignation; many of the Council retired, and to fill their places Clive had the temerity to import outsiders. No sooner was this over than almost every officer of the army mutinied over the withdrawal of double *batta*, or war allowances. No less than two hundred commissions were resigned, and the outlook was black.

Clive set his teeth, and though one of the brigades sent in their resignations *en bloc* in the very face of an enemy, he won through by indomitable firmness, unending patience. The officers of the European regiment at Allahabâd gave most trouble, but a battalion of sepoys, marching 104 miles in fifty-four hours, brought them to reason sharply.

So, when the fight was over, and the ringleaders--only six officers--were tried and punished most leniently (the Mutiny Act of the Company's service proving defective), Clive founded the military fund which still goes by his name, and which has been, and is still, a boon to many a poor widow. Its nucleus was Clive's gift of £63,000.

But his health was failing. His last act ere leaving for England-- never to return--in 1767 was to attend a conference between Shâh-Âlam's representatives, Sûjah-daula, now the Nawâb of Oude, and some Mahratta deputies. The question was a proposal to regain Delhi for the emperor, with the aid of the Company's troops.

Clive at once negatived it. He saw the Mahrattas were now the only possible enemies to peace from whom danger was to be apprehended, and he declined to aid them in any way. On the contrary, he urged the foundation of a confederacy to repel their incursions.

This was his last attempt at diplomacy. He left for England, to find disgrace and disillusionment awaiting him. He had made hundreds, almost thousands of enemies by his just reforms, and with a British public ready, as ever, to be gulled, they had their opportunity. There is no more pitiful and pitiable reading than these records--and in the case of Burke's famous impeachment of Warren Hastings they run to volumes--of these tortuous attempts to twist Western standards of ethics to fit Oriental actions. Putting aside the *animus*, the devilish desire for revenge which inspires most of them, the absolute ignorance of what may be called the atmospheric conditions of India in them remains appalling.

True, Clive had taken £180,000 as his share, when Mîr-Jâffar was enthroned. What then? It was a trifle in comparison with the *sunnuds* gifted to *omrahs* of the court by many a native principality and power to those who served it well. And there was no rule against the reception of honours or presents. Certainly, also, as one follows Clive through all his great services, one can but say that rapacity shows far less in him than in his compeers; one can but echo the words in which the Company, at the time of his departure, summed up those services.

"Your own example has been the principal means of restraining the general rapaciousness and corruption which had brought our affairs to the brink of ruin."

Now, however, by the machinations of those whom he had checked, he was brought to plead for bare honour before the bar of the House of Lords.

"Before I sit down I have one request to make this Assembly, and that is, that when they come to decide upon my honour they will not forget their own."

So he appealed, and the appeal was not fruitless: England was spared the disgrace which France had brought on herself by her treatment of Labourdonnais, Dupleix, and Lally.

But the verdict, that "Robert, Lord Clive, as Commander-in-Chief, had taken a sum of £280,000," but that "at the same time he had rendered great and meritorious services to his country," was not one to satisfy Robert Clive.

He was ill; he suffered from an excruciating disease which opium alleviated, and he ended all his troubles by an overdose of the drug a few months after the day when, with an intolerable sense of injustice at his heart, he quitted the tribunal before which he had been so maliciously arraigned.

For, as he said in his defence, sixteen long years had passed since the offence--if offence there had been--was committed; sixteen long years of silence, of confidence well repaid by faithful service.

HYDER-ALI ET ALIA

A.D. 1767 TO A.D. 1773

While Clive was laying the foundation-stones both of the Indian Empire and the Indian Civil Service in Bengal, Madras had had its share of wars and rumours of wars. It will be impossible, however, to treat of them in detail. All that can be done is to pick out of the seething mass of intrigue, of incident, those things which are necessary to be known, in order that future events shall find their proper pigeon-hole.

The Peace of Paris, signed in 1763, gave back to France her possessions on the Coromandel Coast, and further stipulated that the English nominee, Mahomed-Ali, Nawâb of Arcot, should be recognised by both parties as lawful Nawâb of the Carnatic, and Sâlabut-Jung, the French nominee, as Nizâm of the Dekkan.

Regarding the latter, there is grim humour in the fact, that three years before the Peace was signed poor Sâlabut had been ousted and imprisoned by his brother Nizâm-Ali, and that he was promptly murdered by him the moment news of the treaty reached India! It is not always safe to have the support of the ignorant!

But the Treaty of Paris did more mischief than the murder of the poor prince. It put wind into Mahomed-Ali's head, embroiled him with the Nizâm, led to complications with the Madras Company, which in the year 1765 found itself in the unenviable position of having to pay £900,000 to the Nizâm as tribute for the Northern Circars, instead of holding them rent free from the Great Moghul, as arranged for by Lord Clive. It was a gross piece of mismanagement, and carried with it the perfectly monstrous provision that the Company should furnish troops ready to "settle, in everything right and proper, the affairs of His Highness's government." That is to say, the Nizâm had the right to call the tune without paying the piper!

The very first thing he did was to involve England in a war with Hyder-Ali, an adventurer *pur et simple* who, beginning by being an uncontrolled youth divided between licentious pleasure and life in the woods, free, untamed as any wild creature, forced himself up from one position to another till he held half the territories of the Râjah of Mysore, and had usurped the whole government of that country. Lawless, fierce, without any scruples of any kind, he sided first with one ally then with another, until finally, in 1766, he found himself faced with the fact that Mâhdu Rao the Mahratta, the Nizâm, and the Company, were leagued together for his destruction. The latter had, some time previously, tried to bribe him to proper behaviour, but had failed; for he was, briefly, quite untamable.

Hyder-Ali set to work with his usual fierce energy. He first deliberately bought off the Mahratta mercenaries by parting with certain outlying portions of his stolen territories, and the gift of £350,000 out of his bursting treasures. It was a big bribe, but Hyder-Ali's finances could stand it; for he was a super-excellent robber, with a well-organised army of free-lances for backers.

Meanwhile, the Nizâm's forces and those of the Company under Colonel Smith were approaching Mysore from different sides. It was agreed, however, that the two armies should, when they reached fighting distance, join forces in one camp, so as to show their inviolable unity. But alas! when this happy consummation was reached, the English troops had the mortification of seeing the Nizâm's troops march out as they marched in!

Hyder had been successful with his money-bags once more, and after an absurd and futile farce of palavering on the part of the Company, Colonel Smith prepared to face the enemy's seventy thousand men and one hundred and nine guns with his own meagre seven thousand and sixteen guns. It is astonishing to think how he won his battle and managed to retreat in safety, though he had against his poor thousand of cavalry over forty-two thousand of mounted men, pure freebooters by trade. He seems to have had mettle, this almost unheard-of Colonel Smith, for immediately he received reinforcements he resumed the offensive, and after a time completely defeated Hyder and the Nizâm at Trincomalee. Concerning this battle a nice little story is told. The Nizâm, as is the custom of Eastern potentates, had taken his favourite women with him to the fight mounted on elephants, which stood in line at the rear. The Nizâm, seeing the tide of war going against him, gave orders for the elephants to turn and retire, when from one howdah arose a clear, scornful, feminine voice: "This elephant has not been taught so to turn; he follows the standard of Empire."

And follow it he did, standing alone amid shot and shell, till the royal standards, flying in hot haste, gave him the lead.

But not even this sort of thing could avail. And Hyder's money-bags failed him also in an attempt to suborn an English commandant, who replied to the second flag of truce sent in with a bribe, that if Hyder-Ali wished to spare the lives of his ambassadors, he had better refrain from sending more, as they would be hanged in his sight.

Still, bursting money-bags do much, and ever since the sacking of Bednore, an ancient Hindu city where he had found treasures worth over £12,000,000, Hyder had never been crippled by any lack of gold. Nothing held him. He was here, there, everywhere. Recovering lost territory one day, losing it the next, fighting everybody, even the Mahrattas, like a wild cat, and inwardly raging at his failure to crush the English, who had just entered into a new treaty with his former ally the Nizâm, by which the latter again acknowledged the rights of the Company to the Northern Circars, and further ceded to it, for the annual payment of £700,000, the whole district of Mysore. Thus Madras gained its *diwâni* as well as Bengal.

There is something almost ludicrous in the ease with which territory changed hands in those days, and we are left with the picture in our mind's eye of a be-jewelled potentate and a be-stocked officer hobnobbing over bags of rupees, silk-paper documents, and large seals.

This treaty was a bitter pill to Hyder, who retaliated in every possible way, until one day, by deft stratagem, he took his enemies in the rear, appeared by forced marches before the very walls of Madras, so, with the pleasure-gardens and houses of the councillors at his mercy, almost compelled a treaty of mutual aid and defence.

A *volte face* indeed! Small wonder that the Directors at home, who had been complaining ineffectively of the expenses of the war, became bewildered by the sudden change of *venue*. The general public also, seeing the price of East India stock go down 60 per cent., became uneasy; there is nothing like a drop in Trust-Securities for rousing the national conscience! Dividends were declining, debts were increasing, the glorious hopes of unbounded riches from India had faded; actuaries, nicely balancing debit and credit against the Company, discovered that no less than one and a quarter million of the original stock of four and a quarter of millions had gone, disappeared!

Fateful disclosures these! Public outcry rose loud; voices that had kept discreet silence while profit seemed the certain result of wars, and treaties, and giftings, were now uplifted against rapacity, misconduct, corruption; in the midst of which the alarming discovery was made that the Company required a loan of £1,000,000 from this same public in order to carry on the business. Yet, unless the business was carried on, how could the yearly payments of £400,000 to the royal exchequer, on which the public had insisted, be continued?

Could mismanagement further go?

So three supervisors, vested with full powers, were appointed, and set sail for India in one of His Majesty's frigates. But Fate intervened. They passed the Cape in safety, but were never heard of again.

This was too much. A victim must be found. Therefore Clive was arraigned. That story has already been told, so we can pass on to the mutual recriminations in Parliament, the growing determination on the part of John Bull, honest and dishonest, that something must be done, which found fruit in the first Regulating Act "for the better management of the affairs of the East India Company as well in India as in Europe." By this Act a governor-generalship with a salary of £25,000 was created, together with four councillorships of £8,000. Bombay and Madras were made subordinate to Calcutta, and a Supreme Court of Judicature, appointed by the Crown, was established at the latter place. All the other appointments were to be subject to the confirmation of Parliament, and all the holders of these offices were excluded from commercial pursuits.

The scheme sounded well, but it provided very little aid in reforming the abuses which undoubtedly existed.

It increased the charges upon revenues already overburdened, and the attempt to introduce English ideas of law was calculated to produce more injustice, more oppression, and rouse more alarm and distrust than the previous absence of it had done.

But the dividend for the year 1773 had sunk to 6 per cent.

It was manifestly time to be up and doing--something!

WARREN HASTINGS

A.D. 1773 TO A.D. 1784

It will be remembered that Warren Hastings was the only Member of Council who supported Clive in his decision that all servants of the Company engaging in private trade were bound to pay duty.

Thus, undoubtedly, Clive's enemies must have been his enemies. He had, however, risen with reputation through the various stages of his Indian career; in 1772 he was made President-of-the-Council in Bengal, and immediately set to work to remedy the existing abuses in the collection of the revenue and the whole general administration; a task which was not likely to bring him an addition of friends. While this great revolution in system, which involved the letting of land by public auction, was in full swing, the native potentates beyond Bengal were as usual in a seething state of intrigue. The Prince-Royal-Emperor Shâh-Âlam had at last succeeded in getting the Mahrattas to aid him in recovering Delhi, though he had had to pay a huge price for their help, amongst other things the cession to them of his grant from the English of Allahabad. Consequently, the rich country of the Rohillas (an Afghân race who had settled in India), which reached up from the Delhi plains to the Sivâlik hills, attracted him as a means of again filling his treasury. The Mahrattas were, naturally, nothing loth; so the combined forces marched on Rohilkund, despite the fact that its people were friendly. In the general catch-who-catch-can of India in these days, friendship, honour, truth, counted for nothing it is to be feared, neither with East nor West.

For the tall price of £400,000 the Nawâb of Oude promised to rid the Rohillas of the Mahratta hordes; but being recalled southward by internal dissensions, the Mahrattas, it is said, left of their own accord, and the Rohillas repudiated the bargain. Nothing had been done, they averred, therefore nothing was to be paid.

This gave the Nawâb Sûjah-ud-daula an excellent pretext for war. He had long been anxious to annex Rohilkund, but he needed help to cope with its warlike race. He naturally turned to the English, who had come to aid him (for they were--and small wonder--incensed at the thought of a Mahratta garrison at Allahabad) in repelling a threatened invasion of the

Emperor and his allies. So the Treaty of Benares came to be signed, in which, for a payment of £500,000 yearly, Allahabad was once more ceded by the Company (who had promptly repudiated its cession to the Mahrattas) to its original and rightful owner, the Nawâb of Oude. It was also agreed that for a sum of £21,000 a month the said Nawâb should have the right to the services of a British brigade.

So much is certain. Beyond this, unreliability invades the whole business of the Rohilla war. It has been so distorted, by both sides, in the controversy which arose out of the famous impeachment of Warren Hastings, that the truth is now beyond reach.

Undoubtedly, the British troops were mercenaries; but so they had been from the very beginning, and the exchequer of the Company was at the time very low, whilst behind everything was the great company of British shareholders clamouring for a dividend. Blame may be poured as vitriol on the reputations of many men, but the great offender was the general greed of gold *in England*.

Hastings, however, was already on his defence for this apparently unnecessary war (which yet brought in grist to the mill) when he was appointed the first Governor-General of India under the New Act.

This same Act, however, brought out from England his and Clive's bitterest enemy, Philip, afterwards Sir Philip Francis, as one of the four councillors.

So, from the very beginning, Hastings' hands were tied, for General Clavering and Mr Monson had come out in the same ship with Mr Francis, and were led by the nose by him, leaving only Mr Barwell to form an ineffectual minority with the Governor-General.

It was as if the desire at home had been to stultify reform, since quarrel began at once. Warren Hastings declined even to consider the recall of the Resident in Oude, who had been appointed by him under the old rules. The Triumvirate not only recalled him--a man of whom they knew nothing good, bad, or indifferent--by their majority of one, but appointed in his stead a Colonel Champion of whom they knew less, save that he was the author of various highly-coloured, sensational, almost hysterical letters on the iniquities of the Rohilla war; the appointment, therefore, tells its own tale of bias. The instructions given to the Colonel were incredibly foolish. He was to call for instant payment (within fourteen days) of the £400,000 the Nawâb had promised to pay on the conclusion of the war, failing which he was to withdraw the brigade at all costs. Anything more unscrupulous than this demand for what the Triumvirate was pleased to call "blood money," while appearances were to be saved by, possibly, withdrawing aid at a critical moment, could not be imagined. But despite Warren Hastings' vehement opposition, the instructions were issued, though Fate intervened in the cause of common-sense ere they could be carried out, by the news that the war was over!

The dissensions in the Council soon became notorious; the natives--time-servers by nature, and quick to seize on any opportunity of ingratiating themselves with those who have the whiphand--lost no time in trumping up charges against Warren Hastings. These, even one which alleged that out of a bribe of £90,000, only £1,500 fell to the Governor-General's share--a charge which refutes itself by sheer absurdity--were enquired into with reckless, indecent animosity.

Finally, the complaint of one Râjah Nuncomâr brought matters to a crisis. In this matter it is almost impossible to blame sufficiently the conduct of the Triumvirate, who used their wretched majority of one, not for any public purpose, but simply to gratify private spite. Small wonder was it that, confronted with such absolutely unscrupulous animosity, Warren Hastings took up the glove and fought fairly enough, but with every weapon he could lay his hands upon.

There was a Supreme Court in Calcutta, and Nuncomâr had, amongst other and many villainies (for he was known to be a desperate and unprincipled intriguer), a bad habit of forgery.

He had been on trial for this once before, and Hastings had interfered for his release. Now he let the law take its course, and Râjah Nuncomâr, duly tried and sentenced, suffered the extreme penalty, for forgery was then in England a hanging matter.

The execution had immediate effect. The crowd of native informers ready to pour their lies into the ears of the Triumvirate disappeared as if by magic, but the animosity remained; and in the years to come the death of Nuncomâr was used with immense effect in the great impeachment.

Meanwhile, the Nawâb of Oude had died, and his son reigned in his stead. Out of this arose fresh disputes on the Council. The Triumvirate being all for imposing exceedingly harsh terms on the new Nawâb, Asaf-daula; Mr Hastings refusing to sanction what was "no equitable construction of the treaty with the late Nawâb," and was indeed an extortion which the new ruler had "no power to fulfil."

The Directors at home, however, continuing their career of persistent greed, after first refusing to agree with the Triumvirate on the ground that "their treaties with Oude did not expire with the death of Sûjah-daula," suddenly changed their opinion when they realised the immense pecuniary advantage to be derived from the new arrangement. The extortion, therefore, was carried out, Mr Hastings protesting. And now two new problems arose: one in Madras, one in Bombay, both presidencies being subordinate to that of Calcutta. The first concerned the re-installing of the Râjah of Tanjore, which country had been made over to the Nawâb of the Carnatic. This was a quarrel which, like a snowball, grew as it went along, and ended in most extraordinary fashion, by the arrest and imprisonment of Lord Pigot, the Governor of Madras, at the hands of a vice-admiral of the Fleet! The bewildering complexity of complication in the whole case would take pages to unravel, and the result--the death of one poor old man (for Lord Pigot succumbed to the ignominious treatment meted out to him)--would no doubt, in the opinion of the Directors, scarcely justify the expenditure of so much pen and paper.

The trouble in Bombay arose out of the taking of Salsette, and involved conflict with the Mahrattas, who had persisted in refusing possession of it to the English.

The state of affairs amongst the Mahrattas was at this time confusion itself. Râgonâth-Rao had been made regent by Bâji-Rao, who, it will be remembered, had died during his son's minority of grief, after the fatal day of Pânipat. The boy Peishwa had since been murdered; conspirators had declared that his wife had borne a son; claims and counterclaims, intrigue and counter-intrigue, had reduced the Mahratta Government to an invertebrate condition, which the Bombay Council considered favourable to their earnest desire to keep the Portuguese from again acquiring the peninsula (or island) of Salsette, which virtually commands the harbour at Bombay. They therefore temporarily annexed Salsette, and made its cession foundation of an offer to aid Râgonâth-Rao (commonly called Râgoba), who was then in very low water, against the opposite faction. The temptation was great; a treaty was signed, by which the East India Company, in addition to gaining Salsette and Bassein, were to be paid £225,000.

But here the Supreme Council at Calcutta intervened--why, it is impossible to say--declared in one breath that the treaty with Râgoba was "unpolitic, unreasonable, unjust, and unauthorised," and advised one with the opposite faction.

The quarrel, as usual, becomes complicated in the extreme, and is rendered more confused than it need have been, even in those days of bewilderment, by the double interference from Calcutta and from England. Considering that about six months was necessary to secure a reply from the former place, and about two years from the latter, it is marvellous how any action at all could be decided upon. In the end, however, a treaty was signed with Râgoba's enemies, which raised great indignation in Bombay, not because it involved any breach of honour, but because it brought in less to the Treasury.

Warren Hastings, however, was now busy over financial reforms, and despite the quibbling and captious criticism of the Triumvirate, evolved a scheme which showed real grip of the problem at issue, as indeed might have been expected from a man of his intelligence and vast Indian experience. It was, however, rejected by the Three, who at the same time excused themselves from suggesting any other scheme, because they were not "sufficiently qualified by local observation and experience to undertake so difficult a task."

Surely fatuousness could no farther go? We have here men who consider themselves qualified to criticise, while they admit total ignorance of the subject criticised!

Stung, no doubt, by this obvious retort, Mr Francis finally produced a scheme--a scheme which, containing as it does the very first inception of the "Great Mistake" which has dogged the footsteps of England in her dealings with India, had better have been hanged like a millstone round its promulgator's neck, and he drowned in the sea, than that it should ever have seen the light.

For amid quotations, no doubt, from Adam Smith and Mirabeau--the latter in French, after his usual wont--Philip Francis, mastertype of the self-satisfied Western mind--the mind which degenerates so easily into that of the crank, the faddist--started the cardinal error of all errors in India; that is, the statement that the property of the land is not vested in the Sovereign power, but belonged to the people.

Looking down the years, seeing the manifold evils which this pernicious engrafting of Western ideals on Eastern actions has produced; the alienation of the land, the hopeless slavery of the cultivator to the money-lender, the harsh evictions rendered necessary by the loss of the tenant's credit (which had ever been due to his *unalterable* hold on the land, combined with his *inability to sell it*), one can but wish that the millstone had done its work!

The evil, however, was scotched for the moment. Colonel Monson died, and Warren Hastings, by his casting vote as Governor, now ceased to be in the minority.

He immediately used his newly-acquired ascendency to appoint what was practically the first Settlement Commission in India. That is to say, a body of tried and experienced officers, who should "furnish accurate statements of the values of lands, uniform in design, and of authority in the execution," which should serve as a basis for revenue, and would also "assure the ryots (peasants) against arbitrary exactions," and "give them perpetual and undisturbed possessions of their lands."

"This," he goes on to say in his Minute, "is not to be done by proclamations and edicts, nor by indulgences to *zemindars* (large proprietors) or farmers. The former will not be obeyed unless enforced by regulations so framed as to produce their own effect without requiring the hand of Government to interpose its support; and the latter, though they may feed the luxury of the *zemindars* or the rapacity of the farmers, will prove no relief to the cultivator, *whose welfare ought to be the immediate and primary care of Government.*"

Bravo, Warren Hastings! If there was anything to forgive, one would forgive much for the sake of such a creed.

His success spread consternation amongst his enemies. Something must be done, and done quickly.

One Colonel Macleane had gone home, arriving in February 1776. In a moment of great depression in the previous year, Warren Hastings had entrusted him with a letter of instruction to be conveyed to the Directors, in which he declared that he "would not continue in the Government of Bengal unless certain conditions" were accepted.

No use was made of this letter till the 10th October, when, after a stormy attempt on the part of the Company to oust Warren Hastings, Colonel Macleane wrote announcing that he held the Governor-General's resignation!

These are the bald facts. Eager to catch at any excuse for the removal of an opponent, the resignation, absolutely unauthorised, wholly tentative, was accepted without any discussion of the conditions, and a Mr Wheler appointed as successor.

The English mail of the 19th of June 1777 which conveyed this astounding piece of news to Calcutta took almost every one by surprise; except, apparently, General Clavering and Mr Francis. At any rate, on the very next day the former boldly issued orders signed "Clavering, Governor-General," and requested delivery from Mr Hastings of the keys.

A free fight indeed! That day *two* councils were held: one by General Clavering, with Mr Francis as sole supporter; one by Warren Hastings and the ever faithful Mr Barwell.

Could animosity, pitiful squabbling, disreputable intrigue, further go?

Luckily, there was another power in Calcutta capable of deciding the rival claims, and to it Mr Hastings, ever inclined to toleration, appealed.

The Supreme Court decided unanimously in favour of Warren Hastings, and so the matter ended for a time; Mr Wheler, who had come out to be Governor-General, taking Colonel Monson's place, and, naturally, restoring the Triumvirate, which, however, after a brief interval, dwindled again by the death of General Clavering.

All this is very petty, very uninteresting, in the face of the vast questions which were surging up for settlement all over India, but it is instructive as showing the absolute futility of the India House in its attempts at control, in its inept shilly-shallying between greed of gold and its desire to implant Western ethics on the East. So the quarrel went on, involving amongst other things a duel between Warren Hastings and Mr Francis, in which the latter was badly wounded and had to go home!

Meanwhile, the Mahrattas were more than ever at loggerheads amongst themselves. Râgoba's claims were readmitted by a large number of the faction who had formerly been against him, and with whom a treaty had been made. They applied for help under that treaty (to reinstate Râgoba this time!) and received it; no doubt all the more readily because that gentleman had been the Bombay Council's original nominee. Also because, about this time, the arrival of a French ship at Bombay with a mission purporting to be from Louis XVI. to the Mahratta Court at Poona caused some alarm. For hostilities seemed not far off in Europe between France and England, and the chief member of the so-called embassy was one Chevalier St Lubin, who was known to have previously been with the Mahratta forces.

And here followeth a welter of confused incidents, claims, and counterclaims, which pages would not suffice to unravel.

The Triumvirate, reduced to two, opposed help. Warren Hastings with his casting vote carried it, but ere the brigade sent from Calcutta arrived at the seat of war, Râgoba's half of the Poona court had whacked the other half, and having gained ascendency, proposed to do without their candidate!

Here was an *impasse* for people whose Western minds could not follow such mental somersaults. To add to their confusion, war had been again declared between France and England, and before the Council had had time to recover from their surprise, the victorious Poona party had been again overthrown, and the now ascendant one of Nuna Furnavese was known to harbour Chevalier St Lubin, and to have French proclivities!

There seemed to be nothing for it now save once more to make Râgoba a figurehead.

In truth, as one follows in the maelstrom of Indian intrigue, even as briefly as is possible here, the efforts of these harassed, distracted Western diplomatists to keep their honour above water, one is filled with pity for them. It would have been better not to fight at all, if their code of ethics forbade them the full use of the weapons used against them.

So the weary Mahratta war dragged on and on, backed at first by the hearty approval of the Court of Directors, who pointed out "the necessity of counteracting the views of the French at Poona."

This same war was full of incident. Scindiah and Holkar flash over its horizon, now in alliance, now in defiance; territories and towns were taken, and lost, and retaken; the whole wide, central plain of India and all the western coast-line was perambulated by soldiery; and in the end, in 1782, a treaty was entered into at Sâlbai which was utterly disadvantageous to the English, and which wrung from the Bombay presidency the despairing cry that it must "henceforward require from the Bengal treasury a large and annual supply of money" to carry on the concern.

Meanwhile, in Madras, affairs had not been much more happy. During the war with France, Pondicherry had been assaulted and had capitulated with the honours of war, but in all other ways success was absent. Friction arose between the presidency and the Nizâm over the question of a French garrison, and though the matter was outwardly smoothed over and friendly alliance continued, it formed the basis of a confederation between the Mahrattas, Hyder-Ali, and the Nizâm, having for object the *total expulsion of the English from India.*

Hyder-Ali, whose sword had been rusting in its scabbard since the Peace of 1763, had his own private grievance of help promised by treaty and withheld, because the object for which it was asked was deemed unworthy. This was a constant cause of the endless dissensions between the British and the native princes, and shows clearly the absolute folly of attempting, as the Company did, to run with the hare and hunt with the hounds; that is to say, to compound a treaty on one ethical basis, and carry it out on another.

He instantly commenced operations in the Carnatic, and, though the Nizâm was bought off by the conciliatory measures of the Bengal Council, continued his attack with unhesitating ferocity. He was, frankly, a murderous madman, who, as the phrase runs, "saw red" on the slightest provocation. But even *his* excesses were no warrant for Edmund Burke's blatant rhetoric in his celebrated impeachment, where "menacing meteors blacken horizons," and "burst to pour down contents (?) on peaceful plains" (?). Where "storms of universal fire blast every field," and "fleeing from their flaming villages, miserable inhabitants are swept by whirlwinds of cavalry into captivity in unknown and hostile lands."

What dictionary did Burke use, one wonders, and how comes it that his cheap rhodomontade passes for eloquence?

Hyder-Ali, however, made himself very disagreeable, and in the short space of twenty-nine days brought one disaster after another to the British arms. They began to look on defeat as their portion.

Madras being, apparently, unable to grapple with its enemy, Sir Eyre Coote was sent from Bengal to take command. But he found every military equipment faulty. The commissariat was beneath contempt, and for months the British force was kept stationary, unable to close with Hyder, who, aided by French officers, flashed here and there at his pleasure. But the day of reckoning came on the 1st July 1781, when Hyder-Ali lost ten thousand men, and the English but three hundred and sixty.

Though fortune continued to waver between the combatants, this was practically the turning-point in the war. France, it is true, sent a fleet to interfere on the native side; England sent one to checkmate it; but it was death which finally intervened--death who conquered wild, untamable, almost irresponsible Hyder. He died suddenly, at the age of eighty, from a carbuncle on the neck.

He left a worthy tiger cub behind him, and Tippoo-Sultân continued his father's fierce fighting with unvarying ferocity and varying success, helped in all ways by the French, so long as that nation continued at war with England. When that ended, he fought still, off his own bat, and the war, which completely crippled Madras, dragged on with markedly increasing arrogance on the one side, and increasing submission on the other, until in 1784, in spite of Tippoo-Sultân's many vile crimes, his shameless murderings of English officers, his still more terrible offences towards women and children, peace was concluded with him; a peace, certainly, without honour. To the minds of some it may seem the most indelible stain on the reputation of the British in India.

Warren Hastings, at the time the treaty was signed by the other members of the Supreme Council, was in Lucknow, whither he had gone by way of Benares.

The Râjah of this place had in 1775, it will be remembered, found British protection by the treaty with Asaf-daula, Nawâb of Oude, which Warren

Hastings had condemned as unfair, and of which one of the articles was the cession of Benares. As usual, an immediate dispute arose as to what revenue and charges were to be paid; a dispute which waxed and waned until 1781. There can be no doubt but that on the English side increasing impecuniosity prompted growing demands, while on the Râjah's side was as constant a desire for the evasion even of just claims.

That Warren Hastings considered his position unassailable is evidenced by the fact that, when, in 1781, on his way to Oude he paused at Benares, he placed the Râjah (who, it may be said, was a man of no family whatever) under arrest in his palace to await further explanations, in the charge of some companies of sepoys who did not even *carry* ball-cartridge. Palpably, therefore, no violence was intended. It could not have been, since Hastings had but a small escort. Rescue, however, was immediately resolved on by the populace; a general rush was made for the palace, the sepoys were cut to pieces, and the Râjah made good his escape. Almost immediately afterwards, in consequence of the annihilation of a small British re'ief force from Mirzapore, the whole countryside rose in the Râjah's interest, and some time elapsed ere a force sufficient to cope with the insurrection could be gathered together. Finally, the Râjah (who had throughout protested his desire for peace, even while preparing at all points for war) fled to a fort, whither he had previously conveyed most of his treasures. Warren Hastings, therefore, at once began to form a new Government. A grandson was selected as successor, the tribute payable was increased, and the whole criminal jurisdiction of the province (which had been wretchedly administered) vested in Bengal. After this the late Râjah was pursued to his fort, whence he fled, leaving his women behind. His mother attempted defence, but finally capitulated on the promise of personal safety and freedom from search; the latter stipulation was, however, undoubtedly violated, as the payment of "10 rupees each to the four female searchers" occurs in the accounts of the incident. But this in no way implicates Warren Hastings, who asserts his great regret that the breach of faith should have occurred. It may be mentioned that some £300,000 was found in the fort, which, with the amount that the Râjah had, doubtless, carried away with him, effectually disposes of a poverty which prevented a payment of £50,000. (These details are necessary because of the great stress laid by Mr Burke in the impeachment on this Benares incident.)

The Governor-General had intended passing on to Lucknow, but the Nawâb Asaf-daula, put out by the delay at Benares, was in a hurry, and met Warren Hastings at Chunar.

Here a new treaty was signed. It will be remembered that when the last one was entered into on the occasion of Asaf-daula's accession, Warren Hastings had protested against it as unfair. He now, therefore, exempted the Nawâb from all expenses of the English army quartered on him, with the exception of the single brigade arranged for by his father, Sûjah-daula, and from all other expenses to English gentlemen excepting the charges of the Resident and his office.

As a set-off to this nothing was exacted; but leave was given to the Nawâb to resume certain *jâgkirs*, on condition that in all cases where such grants were guaranteed by the Company, equivalent value to the annual revenue should be given yearly. Not an unfair arrangement, since a fixed revenue, though uncertain through the mutability of the person who has to pay it, is less uncertain than one dependent on fluctuating crops.

But there were two *jâghirs* which, so to speak, filled the Nawâb's eye: they were those held, and illegally held, by his mother and his grandmother. In addition to the vast stretches of land, the revenues of which made these two princesses not only independent, but as possessors of small armies, dangerous factors for strife in internal politics, they were known to possess, and wrongfully possess, the treasure, estimated at £3,000,000, of the late Nawâb. To all this they had no possible claim. Under Mahomedan law the widow takes one-eighth only of her husband's personal possessions, the mother nothing. There is no possibility of will, no possible over-riding of the law. They were, therefore, robbers, and that the Nawâb should have refrained from violence for so long is to his credit. This, however, was due to an unwarrantable interference on the part of the British. Mr Bristow, the Resident appointed by the Triumvirate, had, with their consent, and despite Hastings' dissent, guaranteed immunity to Asaf-daula's mother. As a matter of fact, no foreign power was admissible in a family dispute; in addition, the Begum was in the wrong.

There can be no doubt that Warren Hastings knew the justice of Asaf-daula's claim to the treasure, or that English troops accompanied the Nawâb to Fyzabad, where the Begum resided.

Beyond this, we have "diabolical expedients," "torturing processes," "works of spoliation," besides a variety of rhetorical and eloquent abuse, on the one side; on the other, unconvincing affidavits of the Begum's complicity in the Benares insurrection and a matter-of-fact and apparently credible denial *in toto* of diabolical expedients *et hoc genus omne*.

And behind all we have a very virtuous, very greedy British public, which insisted on being paid £400,000 a year by a bankrupt and overburdened concern.

For that was now the condition of the Honourable East India Company. It had attempted too much, or rather its servants had done these things which ought to have been done, without regard to dividends. At the close of Warren Hastings' administration--he resigned his office on the 8th February 1785, practically compelled thereto by the action of the Board of Directors-- the revenues of India were not equal to the ordinary expense of Government.

A terrible indictment, truly! For which, however, some excuse may be found in the following short chapter on administrations and impeachments.

ADMINISTRATIONS AND IMPEACHMENTS

A.D. 1761 TO A.D. 1785

Clive and Warren Hastings need to be bracketed together in the history of India. They were the men who made our Empire, and they were both impeached for their methods by their countrymen.

And both were acquitted. How came this about?

There is a little sentence in the History of India by James Mill the historian (father to John Stuart Mill), a man presumably above sordid considerations, a man whom one would never suspect of commercialism, which answers the question:--

"In India the true test of the Government as affecting the interest of the English nation is found in its financial results."

This is not intended as blame. On the contrary, Mill goes on to make the deliberate but not quite accurate statement that Warren Hastings' administration *must* have been bad, because, though in 1772, when that administration began, the revenue was but £2,373,750, as against £5,315,197 in 1785, the additional income did not provide for 5 per cent. interest on the additional debt incurred.

That and that only was the *fons et origo mali*. England wanted gold.

Doubtless the expenses of the ruinous wars which devastated India during the latter half of the eighteenth century were a terrible charge upon the revenues; but the revenues increased during the same time, and were more than equal to current expenses, only they did not provide for £400,000 a year tax, and the payment of more than 5 per cent. interest.

In truth, England had not yet grasped the significance of the White Man's burden; she wanted to be paid for carrying it. That is the bitter truth.

But during the administrations of both Clive and Warren Hastings an effort, at least, was made to make that administration worthy of Englishmen. Clive spent his whole force against corruption; Warren Hastings spent his in an attempt to govern the people peacefully and righteously. So much attention is absorbed, as a rule, by the question of his guilt or innocence in regard to certain specific charges, that none is given to the masterly way in which he turned his brief ascendency in the Council, caused by Colonel Monson's death, not to any scheme for personal aggrandisement or even to public money-getting, but to the passing of a revenue settlement which should protect the peasant. In the course of the argument against Mr Francis' views (which necessarily formed part of the scheme) Mr Hastings made a remark which deserves quotation, if only because it seems to have roused no denial, not even from the irrepressible Francis.

"It is a fact which will with difficulty obtain credit in England, though the notoriety of it here justifies me in asserting it, that much the greatest part of the *zemindars*" (big proprietors, petty Râjahs, and Nawâbs, etc.) "are incapable of judging or acting for themselves, being either minors, or men of weak understanding, or absolute idiots."

This is a sweeping indictment which, had it not been incapable of denial or mitigation, must certainly have met with censure. But even Mr Francis acquiesces. He admits that "many of the *zemindars* will at first be incapable of managing their lands themselves."

Now we have here a most ominous admission which gives us the clue by which we can unravel much more in this tangled web of eighteenth-century India.

It was the upper class which was corrupt, which was degenerate utterly. Long centuries of unpunished crime, of depravity without one check, had done their work. The scions of the small nobility were born decrepid; they died early, outworn by vice, leaving heirs as degenerate as themselves. In lesser--ever, thank Heaven!--in lessening degree this has remained the great problem in India: how to give freedom to its hereditary rulers, and yet to ensure that the race shall not suffer, yet to give it freedom from hereditary evils.

In the eighteenth century the men of courts and cities were, as a rule, vicious to the core. If evidence be needed on this point, go to Delhi, go to Lucknow, and there, in the dregs, and lees, and off-scourings of what was once a dynasty, you will still find some of the meanest specimens of humanity on God's earth.

It was with the far-away ancestors of these off-scourings of dead courts, full, then, of pride and power, that men like Clive and Hastings often had to deal. Small wonder, then, if they often dealt with them unwisely, harshly, angered by their hopeless treachery.

But the great factor in all the many oppressions which, undoubtedly, formed part of English annexation in India was not private rapacity, it was public greed.

What, for instance, was even Clive's asserted £300,000 of plunder beside the £400,000 of yearly tribute to the English Exchequer? As for Warren Hastings' fortune, he left India an impoverished man, with scarce enough wherewithal to pay the expenses of defending himself from the charge brought against him by his country for unbridled peculation.

Both Clive and Hastings had hard parts to play, and, considering the difficulties against which they had to contend, they played them well. Though, perhaps, neither of them realised (and certainly no one else did) that the times in which they lived were transitional, that the very existence of the East India Company as a purely mercantile concern was fast drawing to a close, and that a new life of responsibility--the life of true empire--was opening before it, they acted as if they had so realised it. They flung rupees behind them to stay the gold-grubbing multitude, careless, over-careless of how they gained them; but--but they took their own way! Hastings especially identified himself with the people of India; he learnt their language, knew their hoarded wisdom, and often appealed to the lessons of their past history.

This in itself was an offence to the self-sufficient West, which failed, and often still fails, to find excuse for a breach of its own laws in the different ethical standards of the East.

Take Clive's rapacity. There was no law forbidding the reception of presents. He did great things, very great things for Mîr Jâffar, and under the same misconception of enormous wealth which made the country itself claim one million of money as compensation for a loss of £5,000, he accepted a fee of £180,000.

Regarding the Omichand incident--the only other accusation formulated against him which is of any importance--it is, at least, arguable that when bare existence for your countrymen depends on outwitting a traitor, an informer, a villain, any weapon is legal.

In like manner, if it is possible to disentangle the actual charges made against Warren Hastings from the network of words in which Sheridan and Burke caught the unwary minds of many ignorant people, it will be found that in every charge which went up to trial a simple excuse bars the way of blame.

The charge concerning his responsibility for the extermination of the Rohillas, of which he was acquitted even by the House of Commons, finds answer in his vehement dissent from the treaty forced on him by the Triumvirate, and by which he was bound to provide the Nawâb of Oude with troops.

That concerning his cruelty to the Râjah of Benares is met by the undoubted fact that no article in the treaty with the latter gives colour to the contention that the tribute payable was a fixed and unalterable sum, while the fact that £300,000 worth of treasure was discovered in the possession of the Râjah's women, disposes effectually of the plea that poverty prevented payment.

Against the accusation of his having aided and abetted the Nawâb of Oude in seizing and confiscating the personal property of the Begums, stands the undoubted fact that these ladies could not, by the laws of India, possess such property; while the charge of undue cruelty in the treatment of these same ladies is absolutely unprovable, by reason of the conflicting evidence on both sides.

Then the charge of having, during his administration, raised the cost of the civil establishment some £5,000,000, is more than met by his undenied efforts to place the Government of India on a basis worthy of England, and by the necessity for either accepting and carrying through new responsibilities, or allowing the Company to sink back into its former state, when a paltry £20 a year was all the salary it could afford to pay men whom it yet vested with almost unlimited power of extortion.

The eighth and last count--for it is as well to confine refutation to what actually went up for trial--his personal rapacity and corruption is answered conclusively by the undoubted fact that when he retired, the sum of some £72,000 represented his entire fortune.

Truly, there was some justification for the bitter cry with which he ended his defence--a defence which lies practically in denouncing English greed for gold:--

"I gave you all, and you have rewarded me with confiscation, disgrace, and a life of impeachment."

He was on his trial for no less than nine years.

These two great men left India a very different place from what they had found it. The East India Company was trying now to govern, as well as to make money. There was scarcely a district throughout the length and breadth of the land into which the thought of England had not entered; few in which the lives of Englishmen did not form a not always wholesome example. In Lucknow, however, Claude Martin, soldier of both France and England, quaint admixture of honour and dishonour, while he aided and abetted the Nawâb in cock-fighting, drew the line at debaucheries, though he kept a considerable number of wives. This, however, was forced on him by his own merits, since the courtly, good-looking, middle-aged Frenchman's favourite charity was the educating of orphans, and the girls for whom he performed this kindly office had a trick of refusing the eligible *partis* offered them, and electing to remain with their guardian!

Walter Reinhardt, nicknamed the "Sombre," was not so estimable a creature. He was, undoubtedly, the murderer, while in the Nawâb of Bengal's service, of the English at Patna in 1763, and the arch-factor in many other crimes. But he met his dues by marrying one of the most remarkable women of India. It was no light task to be the husband of the Begum Sumroo, who buried a laughing girl at whom the blue-eyed German from Luxembourg had cast an approving glance, under her chair of state; buried her alive, and sat on her for three days. Four was not necessary; Walter the Sombre had learnt his lesson in three!

After his death she ruled her state of Sirdhâna, not very far from Delhi, until she died in 1838, a very old woman, who possibly, despite her conversion to Roman Catholicism, looked back on her youth as a dancing-girl in Delhi with a vague regret.

Then there was George Thomas, an Irishman, whilom favourite of the aforesaid Begum, who cherished the hope--so he says--"of attempting the conquest of the Punjaub, and aspired to the honour of placing the British Standard on the Attock." He only succeeded in establishing for himself an independent principality near Hânsi, which he yielded to Lord Lake in 1803.

But all over India, in almost every town of import, Englishmen were to be found in positions of trust under native rulers. Briefly, they had come to stay; and no amount of legislation by Parliament, no prohibition of diplomacy, no exhortation to refrain from treaties or from meddling in native politics, could now avail to prevent England from becoming first factor in India.

It may be worth while to glance round that India and gain, as it were, a pictorial view of it at the time when England and the English Parliament first assumed political responsibility in regard to it by the establishment of a Board-of-Control appointed by the Crown.

In the far north, Kandahâr and Kâbul were, as ever, engaged in petty warfare, the sons and grandsons of Ahmed-Shâh Durrâni each striving for the mastery. The Punjâb was held by the Sikhs so far as the Sutlej. What are now called the Cis Sutlej States including the great battlefield of Pânipat, being under Mahratta influence. This influence had also made itself felt at Delhi, where the Great Moghul, Star-of-the-Universe and Defender-of-the-Faith, Shâh-Âlam by name, led the life of a pensioner, a prisoner, his authority gone save as a watchword to rouse strife. Oude was in the hands of the British debauchee Asaf-daula. Thence passing through Benares lay the English-held Bengal, Behar, Orissa. Westward was Poona, Guzerât, almost all Râjputana, Agra, and a great part of Central India; these were strongholds of the Mahrattas. Mysore, headquarters of the man-monster Tippoo-Sultân, murderer-in-chief after his father Hyder-Ali's death, marched with Central India the Dekkan fief of that half-hearted ally the Nizâm. Below that, again, came the Carnatic, held by that most troublesome and expensive of potentates the Nawâb of Arcot, tame bear (and bore) to the Madras Presidency, which must have wished its *protégé* at the bottom of the sea many and many a time.

And under all these broad classifications, such a welter of proud, poor principalities and grasping, vicious courts as surely this world's history shows nowhere else. The horrid outcome of unlimited, unbridled power in the past.

And below this again?

Below this, again, the dreaming heart of India, unchanged, unchangeable.

THE BOARD OF CONTROL

A.D. 1786 TO A.D. 1811

The heroic age of the history of British India is now past. Forced by Fate and by the strong right hand of two strong men, England, with one eye still fixed on gold, had had to turn the other on the duties of empire. So the Company was, as it were, split in twain. The old commercial interests were dealt with, as heretofore, by the Board of Directors, but the control "of all acts, operations, or concerns, which in any wise relate to the civil or military government or revenues of the British possessions of the East Indies," was vested in a Board of six members, all appointed by the Crown.

The word "British" is noteworthy in conjunction with possessions, and shows the ease with which the English nation, while still loudly condemning the action of the East India Company, availed itself of the result of such actions. The chief point of interest in the New Act was the power given to Parliament to pay the salaries, charges, and expenses of the Board of Control out of the revenues of India, provided this charge did not exceed £16,000. This was the nucleus of the present payment of £144,000 in the India Office alone.

As regards the Constitution in India few changes were made, and, after a brief tenure of office on the part of Mr Macpherson, Lord Cornwallis went out to India as Governor-General. He had served successfully in Ireland, but with disaster in America. Considering his entire ignorance of even the first conditions of Eastern life, his Governor-Generalship was much less disastrous than it might have been, though it was marred by the crystallisation of the Great Mistake which Mr Francis had first presented in nebulous form; that is to say, the engrafting on India of the Western idea that the land cannot possibly belong to the State, but that some proprietor most be found for it.

But ere this was embodied in the Permanent Settlement of Bengal, Lord Cornwallis found his hands full of minor diplomacies. Tippoo-Sultân was at war with the Mahrattas, and the latter had foolishly been given promise of assistance by the British.

"An awkward, foolish scrape," writes the Governor-General. "How we shall get out of it with honour, God knows; but out of it we must get somehow, and give no troops."

That, practically, was the first charge on his administration. How to get out of minor squabbles, and leave the prime movers to fight it out amongst themselves. Hitherto the British troops had been mercenaries. As such they had made their influence felt in every corner of India. Now all was changed. England was a power in the East, hostile or friendly as she chose, not to be bribed to the support of any one. His next task was to interview the Nawâb of Oude on the subject of the protection of *his* state, and in so doing rather to sidewalk round this firm non-mercenary position adopted by the Board of Control. For £500,000 was taken yearly as payment for two brigades which were to bring "the blessings of peace" under the ægis "of the most formidable power in Hindustan." Asaf-daula, however, was hardly worth protecting. He extorted every penny he could get from everybody in order to spend it on debauchery, and allowed his ministers to cheat and plunder both him and his country.

Another and a more worthy visitor pleaded for an interview, and was refused the favour. This was Jîwan Bakht, the heir-apparent to the Emperor Shâh-Âlam. He had been received by Warren Hastings, who, possibly because he saw in him a promise not often to be found in the Indian potentates of those days, allowed him £40,000 a year as maintenance. "Gentle, lively, possessed of a high sense of honour, of a sound judgment, an uncommon quick penetration, a well-cultivated understanding, with a spirit of resignation and an equanimity almost exceeding any within reach of knowledge or recollection."

Such was the character given by the great Proconsul after six months of daily intercourse; but caution was now the order of the day.

"The whole political use that may be derived" (from an interview) "is at present uncertain, but there may arise *some future advantage* if we can gain his affection and attachment ... but I have already prepared his mind not to expect many of the outward ceremonials usually paid in this country to the princes of the House of Timur, as they would not only be extremely irksome to me personally, but also, in my opinion, improper to be submitted to by the Governor-General at the seat of your Government."

So wrote Lord Cornwallis, and Jiwan Bakht, with spirit *and* resignation, contented himself finally with a request that he might be allowed at least asylum under British protection. He died of fever shortly after at Benares. Poor, proud prince of the blood royal! Was he really next-of-kin, as it were, to the Great Moghuls? If we had given him a chance, as we gave it to the monster Tippoo, to half-a-hundred scoundrels all over India, would he have regained the empire of Akbar? Who knows? He vanishes into the "might-have-been" with his high sense of honour, his spirit, and his resignation.

After this, Lord Cornwallis with a light heart took in hand the abuses of both the civil and the military services, and managed, by "making it a complete opposition question" which "brought forth all the secret foes and lukewarm friends of Government," to obtain higher salaries and better positions for both soldiers and civilians.

So far well. Then once more Tippoo-Sultân intervened, and in a trice India was back in the old days of intrigue, secret treaties, allies, and war. Even Lord Cornwallis, the Liberal pillar of upright, straightforward policy, fell before the peculiar temptations of Oriental diplomacy. There is much to be said for him. Tippoo was an unwarrantable survival. He ought long before to have been hanged, drawn, and quartered. As it was, he burst in upon the coming civilisation and culture, as Mr Burke's 'meteor' burst upon the 'peaceful fields.'

It would take too long to tell the tale of the four years' war during which the Mahrattas, the Dekkanites, and the English, hunted Tippoo ineffectively from pillar to post, and he retaliated in kind. Finally, in 1792, he was cornered at Seringapatam, and once more peace was concluded with a man who deserved nothing but the death of a mad dog.

Then ensued a partition of spoil after the old style; each ally receiving so many lakhs of money, so much territory. After which Lord Cornwallis, covered with glory, found leisure to address himself towards crystallising into our rule for ever--unless some Government arises strong enough to put the wheel back and start afresh--the Fundamental Error, the Great Mistake of the British Empire in India.

In 1793 Mr Dundas and Mr Pitt, neither of them possessing a scrap of first-hand knowledge of their subject, "shut themselves up for ten days at Wimbledon" (Heaven save the mark!) and evolved out of their inner consciousness the Permanent Settlement; thus once and for ever--unless for the forlorn hope of a strong Government--alienating from the Sovereign power of India a possession which had been the Crown's by right beyond the memory of man--in all probability for over five thousand years.

As usual with all overwhelming errors, it was done from the purest motives of truth and honour, mercy and judgment; that is to say, from the Western definitions of these virtues. As Lord Cornwallis writes, he was restoring the rightful landowners "to such circumstances as to enable them to support their families with decency and give a liberal education to their children according to the customs of their respective castes and religions," thus securing "a regular gradation of ranks ... nowhere more necessary than in this country for preserving order in civil society."

It sounds quite unassailable to Western ears; but the results opened Western eyes. The measure was passed in 1794; in 1796 one-tenth of the land in Bengal, Behar, and Orissa was on sale. The ancient order of *zemindars*, so far from giving a liberal education to its children, was fast disappearing, glad to accept the small amount of hard cash, if any, which remained over after settling up ancestral debts. A new race of proprietors was as rapidly taking the place of the old, to the disadvantage of the peasant. For as Sir Henry Strachey writes:--

"The *zemindar* used formerly, like his ancestors, to reside on his estate. He was regarded as the chief and father of his tenants. At present the estates are often possessed by Calcutta purchasers who never see them."

Nor were the judicial reforms of Lord Cornwallis much more happy. "Since the year 1793," says Sir Henry Strachey, "crimes of all kinds have increased, and I think most crimes are still increasing."

This was a natural result, first of the attempt to graft English law with all its legalities on Eastern equity, but mostly of the crass ignorance of native life everywhere displayed. Mr Shore, afterwards Lord Teignmouth, expresses this well when he says:--

"What judge can distinguish the exact truth among the numerous inconsistencies of the natives he examines? How often do those inconsistencies proceed from causes very different from those suspected by us? How often from simplicity, fear, embarrassment in the witness? How often from our own ignorance and impatience? We cannot study the genius of the people in its own sphere of action. We know little of their domestic life; their knowledge, conversations, amusements; their trades and castes, or any of those national and individual characteristics which are essential to a complete knowledge. Every day affords us examples of something new and surprising, and we have no principle to guide us in the investigation of facts except an extreme diffidence of our opinion, a consciousness of inability to judge of what is probable or improbable.... The evil I complain of is extensive, and, I fear, irreparable. The difficulty we experience in discerning truth and falsehood among the natives may be ascribed, I think ... to their excessive ignorance of our characters and our almost equal ignorance of theirs."

The last sentence is perhaps scarcely strong enough, for Lord Cornwallis failed to find one civil servant of the Company in Madras who was "tolerably acquainted with the language and manners of the people."

Meanwhile, war had once more broken out between France and England, and though it had not yet disturbed India, Tippoo-Sultân, with his usual hardihood, bragged of the marvels of the French Revolution to the English officer charged, now that the ransom had been paid, with the duty of restoring the Sultân's sons, who had been kept as hostages. A trifle, which yet showed the way the wind was blowing. The Nizâm of the Dekkan, also, irritated by the tepid neutrality of Lord Cornwallis, had fled for help to French arms. Nor was Scindiah better pleased. Though of low caste, being sprung from the slipper-bearer of Bâla-ji, the first Peishwa, no Mahratta house claimed higher honours. Practically, it was master of half Hindustan, and it had been greatly offended by the refusal of Lord Cornwallis to accept its offer of help against Tippoo in consideration of a like number of troops to those promised to the Nizâm. So on all sides there was hostility--a hostility increased by Sir John Shore's policy (he succeeded Lord Cornwallis as Governor-General) "to adhere as literally as possible to the strictest possible interpretation of the restrictive clause in the Act of Parliament against entering into war."

Naturally, the fat was soon in the fire. The Mahrattas, always eager for a fray, fell upon the wretched Nizâm, who, fortunately for him, failing British aid, had that of France; but so had Scindiah. Therefore Monsieur Raymond and Monsieur de Boigne crossed swords; until the death of Ragoba the Peishwa turned all Mahratta thought to the choice of a new ruler.

English thought, also, was at this time (1798) engaged in a question of succession. Asaf-daula, the Nawâb of Oude, had died, acknowledging a certain Wazeer-Ali as his son and successor. So the dissolute, disreputable lad of seventeen was promptly placed by the British Government on the throne with all honour: it did not do to divert the weather eye, which was always open for "future advantage," to such trivialities as kingly qualities. But alas and alack for the British Government, its choice was instantly challenged by Sa'adut-Ali, the late Nawâb's brother, who brought proof that not only Wazeer-Ali, but all Asaf-daula's reputed children, were spurious.

At first England hesitated at deposing her Nawâb. Then? Then it is extremely difficult to know what the real motive underlying the action was, but in 1798 we find Sa'adut-Ali on the throne of Oude, no longer an independent ruler, but a mere vassal of the British Crown. The plea of adoption raised by Wazeer-Ali had been dismissed, and in honest truth, not absolutely without cause. For the Mahomedan law does not specifically recognise it, especially when near blood-relations exist.

These events, together with the death of old Mahomed Ali, Nawâb of Arcot, aspirant to the Nawâbship of the Carnatic--whose debts had been a veritable millstone round the neck of his consistent backer, the East India Company--saw Lord Cornwallis and Sir John Shore through their term of office, and Earl Mornington, afterwards Marquis Wellesley, reigned in their stead. He landed in April 1798 and found himself instantly confronted with the results of the non-interference policy; that is to say, with renewed war with Tippoo-Sultân, who--the remark has been made before--ought long ago to have been hanged.

It is somewhat refreshing to find that immediate negotiations were carried on both with the Nizâm and the Mahrattas in absolute defiance of Mr Pitt's famous minute against diplomacy! But nothing restrained Tippoo, not even considerations of personal safety. He was well backed by the French, with whom the English were still at war. So he tried conclusions with splendid audacity. And failed. Seringapatam was once more taken, and this time Tippoo was found dead under a heaped mass of suffocated, trodden-down corpses in the north gate. But he, apparently, had died a soldier's death, for the flickering light of the torches by which the search was made showed that a musket ball had crashed into his skull above the right ear.

It was a better death than he deserved, for though his territories were well administered, and though Seringapatam was found to be fortified, garrisoned, provisioned, better than many a modern fort, and though in every way his vitality was superhuman, it was the vitality of a devil, and not of a man. Hyder-Ali, his father, had been wild, untamable, given to long solitudes in the jungles, remote from all save savage beasts. Let the only excuse, therefore, which can be made from Tippoo-Sultân be given him--he was born with insanity in his blood.

Relieved from the Tiger-cub--the golden Tiger-head footstool of the throne found in the royal audience chamber at Seringapatam is now at Windsor--who had kept Madras in a constant state of alarm for close on half a century, the Board of Control settled down to various pieces of policy, for it must not be forgotten that all political work had been taken out of the hands of the East India Company. This is a point frequently overlooked, so it must be borne in mind that for all actions after 1784, the Board of Control, that is, a body of unbiassed English politicians appointed by the Crown, are entirely responsible. They settled a disputed succession in Tanjore, they ousted the Nawâb of Arcot, and by putting a nominee of their own on the throne with a pension of one-fifth of the revenue only, became vested with the whole of the rest of the Carnatic. They then turned their attention to Oude, where the Government of Sa'adut-Ali was in a shocking state of disorder. Reformation being urged upon him, he wilily announced his intention of abdicating, and thus gained some delay. Rather to his disadvantage than otherwise, since Lord Mornington was not long in producing a cut-and-dried scheme by which the Company should "acquire the exclusive authority, civil and military, over the dominions of Oude"; and also that by "secret treaty, not by formal abdication," the Nawâb, in consideration of receiving a liberal pension, the family treasure and jewels, should agree to his sons' names being "no further mentioned than may be necessary for the purpose of securing to them a suitable provision."

It was a big order, and to it the Nawâb naturally objected. But the screw was too tight. He had yielded himself vassal in order to gain the throne. His government was atrocious. It was practically impossible for the New Code of Western Ethics, which was everywhere raising its head in menace to the iniquities of the East, to look on such things and live. So in the end the treaty was signed; and whatever else the result might be, one thing is certain, the inhabitants of Oude were none the worse for the change of rulers.

A trivial detail in the confused complication of this transaction deserves unstinted blame, and that was Lord Mornington's acceptance of the offer made by one of the Begums of Oude to constitute the Company her heir. This was openly avowed to be a means of escaping from the extortions of her grandson the Nawâb, but though it seems equitable enough to Western ears, it must not be forgotten that the India law of inheritance of those days allowed no right of will, neither did it sanction the possession by any widow of wealth beyond a certain small proportion of her husband's real and personal property, which in this case could not have included anything but personal effects, the rest belonging to the Crown.

Volumes might be written on this question of the English action in regard to Oude, but practically there are but one or two facts, one or two admissions, to be made on both sides.

First, it is at best doubtful if we had any right to depose Wazeer-Ali in favour of his uncle. True, the right of adoption does not hold good in Mahomedan Common Law, but Indian history gives countless examples of Mahomedan sovereigns nominating their own successor, though it must be admitted that this nearly always only held good where there was no collateral heir. Second, this deposition was undoubtedly in our favour. By elevating Sa'adut-Ali, a small pensioner to the throne, we gained a hold on him which enabled us to dictate our own terms at the time, and, by the mere fact of the vassalage to which we reduced him, to enhance these terms at our convenience.

On the other hand, none can deny that the state of affairs in Oude strained patience to the uttermost; nor that in essence, the throne of Oude was of our own creation. It had only a history of a hundred years, and owned its very existence to the protection of England.

The year 1800 showed the outlook all over India more than usually threatening; so lowering indeed, that Lord Mornington, now the Marquis Wellesley, consented to prolong his service in India in order to tide affairs over the crisis which seemed about to come.

The chief factor in the unrest was Mahratta jealousy. The Nizâm of the Dekkan, their hereditary enemy, had just been granted a new treaty. Under it he had been promised a definite protection of troops in consideration of his ceding territory to the revenue amount of the subsidy which he would otherwise have had to pay--and, no doubt, would have paid irregularly.

It may here be remarked that this desire to secure regular payment for the mercenary troops necessary to maintain prestige and power, was nearly always the cause of English aggression and annexation in India.

This treaty affronted the Mahrattas, but ere they could formulate their grievances, internecine war broke out amongst them, consequent on the death of Nâna Furnavese, the Peishwa who had for so long opposed Ragoba. Over this Holkar and Scindiah, who for some time past had been at each other's throats, fought furiously, and the new Peishwa, Bâji-Rao, feeling himself in danger of falling between the two stools of his unruly vassals, applied to England for the protection of six battalions of British-trained sepoys, and promised in return to cede territory of the annual value of £225,000.

It was granted to him, but the treaty contained other stipulations regarding future relations which practically reduced the Peishwa to a state of dependence.

Holkar and Scindiah, on the part of *their* sections of the Mahrattas, resented this fiercely. As usual, they refused to be bound by the Peishwa's pusillanimity. So war was declared; a war which for the time taxed even Sir Arthur Wellesley's military genius to the uttermost, for the Mahrattas were born fighters. But the battle of Assaye, fought on the 23rd of September 1803, broke their power in Central India. They had over ten thousand disciplined troops commanded by Europeans, chiefly French officers, and a train of one hundred guns, in addition to nearly forty thousand irregular infantry and cavalry. Against these Arthur Wellesley had but a total of four thousand five hundred men, but they included the 78th Highlanders, the 74th Regiment, and the 19th Dragoons.

It was a fine fight; a double fight, for when, overwhelmed by a real bayonet charge--the first, possibly, they had ever seen--the Mahrattas fell back on, and passed, their guns, the artillery men, feigning death, flung themselves in heaps on the ground. So, ridden over by the pursuing cavalry, treated as dead, spurned as things of no account, they remained until, the tyranny overpast, they were up and at their guns again, bringing *volte face* destruction to their enemy's rear. It needed a desperate charge of the Highlanders, with Arthur Wellesley himself at its head, to retrieve the day.

The number of British killed was one thousand five hundred and sixty-six, more than one-third of their total force.

England, however, was now finally on the war-path; hesitation was over, the Mahratta power all over India had to be crushed. No less than fifty-five thousand British troops of all arms were gathered together in India, and these were divided out between the Dekkan, Guzerât, Orissa, and Hindustan proper. Of the foremost of these divisions the record has just been given; the two next, though successful, were in all ways of minor importance. The last, under General Lake, was the largest, and consisted of nearly fourteen thousand men all told. He advanced up the Gangetic plain, and the battle of Alighur was fought before that of Assaye. It was practically fought against Scindiah's forces under General Perron, the celebrated French commander, who, with De Boigne and Raymond, had been for many years the backbone of resistance against England. But it was fought in the name of the blind Shâh-Âlam, puppet-emperor of India; for the Mahrattas, always good fighters, had sent round the fiery cross on every possible pretext of personal and national loyalty, of tribal faith and racial adherence.

But on the 16th of September, after a pitched battle before Delhi in the low-lying land across the river Jumna--the country sacred now to pig-sticking!--General Lake rode with his staff to the palace which Shâhjahân in all his glory had built, there to have the first interview which a conquering Englishman had ever had with the Great Moghul himself.

It was a fateful interview. In the palace, glorious still in its lines of beauty, an old man, blind, decrepid, seated under a tattered canopy, poverty-stricken, miserable. By his side, soon to be Akbar II., was his son, and his grandson, the man who afterwards, as Bahâdur-Shâh, served out the measure of his crimes in the Andaman Islands.

It reads like some bad nightmare, does that circumstantial description given by Lake of his ride through the thronged city at sunset-time, when the people, wide-eyed, curious, expectant, crowded so close that the little cavalcade could scarce make a way for itself.

Of what were they thinking, those poor Delhi folk who had suffered so often at the hands of so many men? Were they still faithful to the memory of the Moghuls, or did their eyes seek wistfully in the faces of the newcomers for a new master?

Certainly on that 16th of September at sunset-time, after the interview had fizzled out with the exchange of empty titles, and as "Sword of the State," "Hero of the Land," "Lord of the Age," and "Victorious in War," Lake and his staff left the old palace to nightfall, and the old king to dreams, a pale ghost may well have walked through the halls of audience beneath the reiterated pride of that legend: "If there be a Paradise upon Earth, it is this, it is this, it is this," and asked itself what might have been it instead of a fever-stricken grave at Benares, it had found help to recover kingship?

Poor Jiwan Bukht! Had you, indeed, as your name implies, the Gift of Life?

Perhaps you had--and we squashed it!

But there was more to be done by Lake's force ere on the 27th February 1804 Scindiah, who was in reality the man behind the gun, gave in, and a treaty was signed which enabled the Governor-General to give vent to his feelings in the following bombast:--

"The foundations of our empire in Asia are now laid in the tranquillity of surrounding nations, and in the happiness and welfare of the people of India. In addition to the augmentation of our territories and resources, the peace manifested exemplary faith and equity towards our allies, moderation and unity towards our enemies, and a sincere desire to promote the general prosperity of this quarter of the globe. The position in which we are now placed is such as suits the character of the British nation, the principles of our laws, the spirit of our constitutions, and that liberal policy which becomes the dignity of a great and powerful empire. My public duty is discharged to the satisfaction of my conscience by the prosperous establishment of a system of policy which promises to improve the general condition of the people in India, and to unite the principal native states in the bond of peace under the protection of the British power."

After which there was naturally nothing to be done save to whack Holkar also; for he had kept out of the scrimmage discreetly. This campaign was not so successful. The fort of Bhurtpore withstood four assaults, and might have withstood four more, had not peace with honour and a donation of £200,000 intervened.

This--for the Râjah of Bhurtpore was an independent ally of the Mahrattas--rather upset Scindiah's calculations, for he was on the point of rejoining Holkar in defiance of all treaties. So the ultimate issue stood deferred when the Marquis of Wellesley ceased to be Governor-General.

He had deviated horribly from the "restrictive policy," and had consistently acted in the way which Parliament had pronounced to be "repugnant to the wish, the honour, and the policy of our nation."

But that policy had been a broken reed. It was virtually the policy of folding the arms, and awaiting the blow in the face that was bound to come sooner or later.

Nevertheless, the expense of Marquis Wellesley's wars told against his reputation; he went home obscured by a cloud of deferred dividends, and Lord Cornwallis returned for a second attempt at Indian administration. Age had undoubtedly cooled the ardour of his blood, for he immediately made most pusillanimous concessions to Scindiah for the sake of peace, passing over flagrant breaches of treaty with an easy diplomacy, and might have done infinite harm had he lived longer. But he died at Buxar within two months of his arrival in India.

Sir George Barlow took his place, but thereon arose a fine dispute between the Directors of the India House and the Ministers of the Crown concerning the patronage of this appointment.

Perhaps this was the reason why England failed to learn a lesson which would have been of use to her fifty years afterwards; for the little mutiny at Vellore occurred in 1806, and the Great Mutiny in 1857.

Yet the causes were identical. In 1857 it was a greased cartridge, in 1807 it was a cap; but beneath both lay unreasoning fear of forcible conversion to Christianity. A fear which grew to bloodshed, and which found the Europeans, as ever, totally unprepared. Nearly one hundred of them lost their lives, and but for Colonel Gillespie's swift ride from Arcot, and the wisdom of the officers in command at Hyderabad, the mutiny might have spread, as did the one at Meerut in May 1857. And it must be admitted that those sepoys of Vellore had greater cause of offence than they of later years; for they were asked to shave to European pattern, to wear a hat-shaped turban, and appear on parade minus their caste marks.

All this, including Sir William Bentinck's recall (he was Governor of Madras at the time), went on while the India House and the Crown were at daggers drawn over the Appointments question.

The latter meant to nominate the Earl of Lauderdale, who, as a pronounced free-trader, threatened to break up the Indian monopoly. The fight ended by the Earl of Minto, President of the Board of Control, taking up the appointment in 1807, which he held till 1811. It was an uneventful administration, the extinction of the Company's monopoly, which marked its close, being the only feature in it which claims a place in this modest outline of history; this, and perhaps the fact that owing to greater facilities of borrowing the Company was enabled to pay off its old debts which it had contracted when the rate of interest was 12 per cent., and renew them at 6 per cent.; thus effecting a reduction of half a million in expenditure.

As an instance of how little the Board of Control and the policy of inaction had benefited the finances of the Company, it may be mentioned that whereas its debt was in 1793 but £7,000,000, in 1811 it was £27,000,000.

But the world was beginning now to count it as a gift--as the cost of Empire.

THE EXTINCTION OF MONOPOLY

A.D. 1812 TO A.D. 1833

The Act of Parliament which inaugurates this period did not entirely extinguish the monopoly of the East India Company; that was reserved for the Act which marked its close. Yet the one promulgated in 1813 was sufficiently wide in its scope to partake of the nature of a revolution; for although the trade with China--chiefly tea--remained on its old close footing, that with India was thrown open to any one who possessed a licence, such licences not to be solely obtainable through the Council of Directors, but also through the Board of Control. But there were two additional clauses in the bill which, though grafted in upon it during its lengthy passage through Parliament, were of more gravity than some of original import. One was the forming of a regular Church Establishment in India--a formal declaration, as it were, of the creed of the new master; the other the inclusion of missionaries as persons to whom a licence to pursue their trade might be given. Taken together, these two clauses went far towards an admission that it was the duty of England to uphold her own faith. The speeches that were delivered for and against these clauses in Parliament are excellent reading; perhaps the most informing of them being one by Sir J. Sutton, who, attempting to hedge, as it were, objected to the open avowal in the clause that persons were to be sent to India for "the introduction of religious and moral improvement," as calculated to alarm and annoy, and suggested that the words "various lawful purposes" should be used instead. The suggestion was treated seriously; Mr Wilberforce, the great speaker on the missionary side, assuring his hearers that it was extremely unlikely that the natives of India would *ever read the clause*, and ending with an impassioned assertion that unless actual mention of religion was made in the Act it would stand tantamount to a decision that though Christianity was the faith of England, the creeds of Brahma and Vishnu were to be upheld by England in India. There was a strong religious party in the House, representing a stronger one in England. And feeling had been roused by Lord Minto's refusal to allow certain Baptist missionaries to print, publish, and disseminate pamphlets calculated to arouse indignation amongst the people of other faiths. So, despite a very able protest from Mr Marsh, who asserted that it must be remembered that the people "we wished to convert were in the main a moral and a virtuous people, not uninfluenced by such ideas as give security to life, and impart consolation in death," the clause was passed.

There is also an excellent speech made by Mr Tierney on the Commerce question, in which he pertinently remarks that amongst all the benefits which he was told were to accrue to the people of India from free trade, he had never *heard* even of a proposal to allow one manufacture of India to be freely imported into Great Britain! But such remarks were of no more avail then than they are nowadays, when the manufactures of India are stinted by the duty on cotton twists, and her markets glutted by free Manchester muslins.

The whole history of the cotton trade, in truth, is grievous. At this time, when Parliament was piously purposing to preach to so-called heathen the religion which claims first place as teaching the duty of doing to others as you would be done by, the woven goods of India could have been sold in England at rates 50 and 60 per cent. cheaper than similar goods manufactured in England. What then? Were they so sold? or sold at a price which would have brought wealth to the miserably poor Indian craftsman? No! The mills of Paisley and Manchester were protected by a duty of 70 and 80 per cent. on these Indian goods, thus sacrificing those to whom we wished to teach Christianity to those who, at any rate, said they had that faith.

Ere going on to the events of the next few years it must be mentioned that the East India Company, while vehemently protesting, had some sops thrown to it by this Act. One was that the "commercial profits of the Company were not in future to be liable for any territorial payments until the dividend claims had been satisfied." This was extremely comforting. Furthermore, £1,000,000 sterling was to be set aside from the surplus revenue (when it existed, but up to the present it had not) to meet any failure.

With this, and a few more scraps of comfort, H.M.E.I.C.S. had to be satisfied and start fair with a new Governor-General, Earl Moira. One is irresistibly reminded, when following this history of English dealings with India, of the fable concerning King Log and King Stork; for after a calm, there comes invariably a storm. How many governor-generals have not sailed out to India, loudly protesting peace, prepared at all points to uphold the non-interference clause? How many have sailed back again with reputations either marred, in English eyes, by change of policy, or kept intact by leaving behind to their successors a state of affairs out of which war was the only escape?

Earl Moira, therefore, suffered from Lord Minto's efforts after economy by his undue reduction of the army, by his refusal to see what was going on around him. So the first thing to be faced was the necessity for war in Nepaul if the boundaries of Oude were to be preserved intact. Hitherto Great Britain had been pacific over invasion to the point of pusillanimity, dreading, and not without just cause, a campaign amid the ascending peaks and passes of the Himalayas, backed by the unknown regions of its eternal snows.

But at last these dangers had to be faced. It took a whole year of hill-fighting in the finest scenery in the world, and in a climate which must have been some compensation for other hardships, ere a treaty of peace was signed at Segowlie, by which England gained in perpetuity the magnificent provinces of Kumaon and Gharwal.

Meanwhile, India was not happy. The well-meaning Western attempt to raise money by a house-tax in large cities had nearly brought about an insurrection in Benares, where the *pandits* had, not without cause, claimed the whole city as a place for worship, and as such exempt; while an assessment for municipal police led to hard fighting at Bareilly.

But by this time Earl Moira's eyes had been opened. On every side he saw dangers to the State-politic which could not be averted save by action. The predatory system, so often the curse of divided India, was in full swing. In truth, no power wielded sufficient authority to keep the others in order. What was happening in 1815 was what would happen in 1915 if the alien rulers of India were to adopt a policy of non-interference. The Pindârees were the chief offenders; since time immemorial their hordes of free-booting horsemen had been a terror, and of late years they had aided and abetted the Mahrattas. But, despite growing atrocities, it was not until 1816 that Parliament would permit them to be coerced.

Meanwhile, Râjputana was smouldering. After the murder of the Emperor Farokhsîr the various states fell into the hands--as did almost all India--of the Mahrattas; not without hard fighting, not without bitter beatings, and still more bitter upbraiding, as when after one defeat the Rana of Oudipore made a common courtesan carry the Great Sword-of-State, avowing that in "such degenerate times it was no better than a woman's weapon."

So matters had gone on from bad to worse, while Scindiah, dissociating himself from the Peishwa, became paramount, until in 1778 Râjah Bhîm came to the throne of Mêwar (Oudipore, Chitore). During his reign Scindiah and Holkar fought almost continuously over the hills and dales of Râjputana, and the former threw the weight of his savage influence into the pitiful tragedy of Kishna Kumari, the Virgin Princess. Her story is well known, but if only for the strangeness of such an incident being possible in the nineteenth century, and in a court where Englishmen came and went, it may be given here.

Kishen Kumari, the Virgin Kishen, was beautiful exceedingly. She was promised in marriage to the chief of Jeypore. Scindiah, incensed at non-payment of a claim by the latter, opposed this in favour of the chief of Marwar; and in the ensuing struggle to the death, Bhîm Singh, seeing ruin before him, determined to sacrifice his daughter's life as the only way of ending the strife.

They tried to poniard her, she standing calm; but the dagger fell from the hand of the brother appointed, as one of sufficient rank, to the deed. Then they tried poison. She drank it three times calmly, bidding her grief-distracted mother remember that Râjput women were marked out for sacrifice from birth, and that she owed her father gratitude for letting her live so long. But the poison refused its work; so, as calmly, she asked for a *kasumba* draught to make her sleep. It was prepared. Sweet essence of flowers, sweet syrup of fruits, concealed the deadly dose of opium; she laid herself down and slept, never to wake.

A terrible tale, which merits the comment made on it by old Sagwant Singh, chief of Karrâdur, who, riding hard for Oudipore, flung himself breathless from his horse with the quick query: "Does the princess live?" And hearing the negative, went on without a pause up the stone steps of the palace, through the wide courtyard, adown the passage, till he found Mâhârâjah Bhîm upon his throne. Then he unbuckled his sword.

"My ancestors," rang out the passionate, protesting old voice, "have served yours for thirty generations. To you, my king, I dare say nothing, but never more will sword of mine be drawn in your service."

So, laying it with his shield at the feet of the weakling, he left.

A fine old Râjput was Sagwant Singh; one feels glad he said his say.

This, however, is by the way. Nine years after it happened--that is to say, in 1819--after the war with the Pindârees (which, of course--since war is ever bred of war in India--involved hostilities with the Peishwa, with Holkar, with Scindiah, with all the native states, briefly, who tried to bar the progress of the new master), Râjputana found itself eager to claim alliance with a power which, instead as of old protesting against protection, was now not only willing to grant it, but prepared to make its promise good against all comers.

For once, then, in the sweeping changes which the year ending in 1819 brought about, the English gave as good as they got. No great battle had been fought, but Scindiah was humbled, Holkar's aggressions had been stopped, the Peishwa's very name had disappeared, and on all sides alliances had been formed--durable alliances, which would no longer require the sword to enforce them.

And all this arose out of Parliament's hesitating admission that certain predatory robbers must be restrained, and Earl Moira's wise interpretation of that scant assent into action which, after two weary years, settled the great territorial question of India as only it could be settled; that is to say, as the Earl (afterwards Lord Hastings) phrases it: "by the establishment of universal tranquillity under the guarantee and supremacy of England."

But the Gurkha or Nepaulese war, and the third and final Mahratta war, unfortunately, only form part of Lord Hastings' work. He was not so happy in dealing with the question of Oude. It had simmered for long: the Nawâb, who had been encouraged by Lord Minto, complaining of the interference of the Resident; the Resident complaining of obstinate obstruction on the part of the Nawâb. In the middle of the quarrel Sa'adut-Ali died, leaving treasure, despite his plea of poverty, to the amount of £13,000,000. He was succeeded easily, quietly, with the help of British influence, by his eldest son, who, to show his gratitude, offered one of his father's millions to the Company as a gift. It was accepted as a loan at the usual rate of interest, 6 per cent.

But the young Nawâb was even more turbulent than his father, and when a second million was asked for on the same terms as the first, took the opportunity of practically demanding the withdrawal of the Resident. Now it is impossible to be harsh with a potentate who has just loaned you two millions of money out of his private purse. Without for a moment doubting the decision that Major Baillie the Resident had been wanting in respect, the fact remains that he went to the wall, and that the Nawâb was set free of all control in his administration. Furthermore, after a treaty signed in 1816, by which the loan of the second million was written off against the cession of a piece of territory scarcely worth the sum, the Nawâb was further encouraged and advised to assume the title of King; thus once for all asserting his equality with, and not his dependence on, the shadow of the Great Moghul at Delhi.

So, to the extreme indignation of the latter's sham Court and the scandal of all true Mahomedans, he proclaimed himself "Ghâzi-uddin-Hyder, King of Oude, the Victorious, the Upholder of Faith, the Monarch of the Age."

Not such a very poor specimen at that, whether taken at native or English estimate; for he was at least amiable--a kind, not overclever princeling, who cultivated the Arts in a dilettante fashion.

For the rest, though the long service--over nine years--of the Marquis of Hastings was eminently successful, it was not likely that one who rode rough-shod over the faddists' cry for noninterference at home could escape without censure. But regular impeachment was impossible towards one who had actually augmented the public revenues by £6,000,000 a year! So he escaped the fate of Clive and Warren Hastings.

He was succeeded by William Pitt (Lord Amherst) after an interregnum during which a Mr John Adams, armed with supreme, if brief authority, carried on a crusade against the press which, in view of recent occurrences, is singularly informing. The censorship had been abolished by Lord Hastings in rather bombastical language, which scarcely matched the severe inhibitions that followed against anything like criticism; the actual result being, that while the name of an invidious office was abolished, the press was left to face prosecution. In the case of the *Calcutta Journal*, against which Mr Adams tilted, the end was deportation of the editor to England!

The Burmese war, however, occupied Lord Amherst until 1826, when various minor campaigns became necessary; one against a Sikh mendicant, who announced himself as the last of the Avatârs of Krishna, incarnated for the express purpose of ousting all foreigners from India. Bhurtpore, also, had to be finally taken, a usurper expelled, and a six-year-old râjah established on the throne, under the guidance, naturally, of a British resident. Such things had to be if the standard of Western ethics was to be enforced in Government.

There remained also Oude, that perennial thorn in the side of those who had created it. Ghâzi-ud-din-Hyder had lent a million and a half more money to the Company--had lent it at 5 per cent.!--but yet, he complained, there was no pleasing the English master! There is something pitiful about the good-natured king's plea that misgovernment *could* not exist, because Oude from one end to the other was cultivated like a garden; there was not even a waste place in it whereon an army might encamp! And as for the disturbances on the British borders, was he responsible for the landholders being Râjputs by tribe, soldiers by profession, and so refusing to pay except by force? And for what did he pay English soldiers, except to use force?

There was force, anyhow, in his arguments, but his grievances remained unredressed at his death in 1827, when he was succeeded by his son, Nâsir-ud-din-Hyder.

So, without any great excitement save the Burmese war, Lord Amherst's Governor-Generalship came abruptly to an end, owing to sudden illness in his family, which prevented his awaiting any arrangement for his successor. This is somewhat typical of one who never seems to have taken any personal interest in Indian questions, who, in fact, seems to have wearied of the East. He was the first Governor-General who found a Capua at Simla.

Then, after much striving, Lord William Bentinck, who had been deprived of the Government of Madras in 1807 in consequence of the mutiny at Vellore, was appointed in Lord Amherst's place. It was a great triumph for him, being, as it were, an admission that he had been unjustly dismissed in the first instance. His administration, however, did much to justify his early treatment, for there can be no question that he showed an almost phenomenal want of tact. Indeed, but for the fact that the final extinction of the monopoly of trade did not take place until 1835, this chapter would end on the assumption of office by Lord William Bentinck in 1828, since there can be no doubt that many of his well-meaning efforts should be included amongst the causes which led up to the mutiny of 1857. The best plan, therefore, will be to catalogue them briefly here, and discuss them in connection with others of a like nature after 1835. The first, which brought him great disfavour with the military, was not, strictly speaking, his action, but that of England. His only responsibility for what is called the half-*batta* (extra allowance) order is that he did not, as Lord Hastings and Lord Amherst had done, refuse to obey his superiors. It was a silly retrenchment, since for the sake of a paltry £20,000 a year it gave umbrage to a very deserving body of men, who could ill afford to lose the money. The scheme was condemned by all competent judges in India as "unwise and inexpedient, fraught with mischief, and unproductive of good."

But Lord William Bentinck had come out bound hand and foot to economy, social reform, and missionary effort, so he spent his years in adding up and subtracting, in framing laws, such as that against *suttee*, and the forfeiture which, under Hindu law, followed on conversion to a different faith.

For political work he had but one catchword; the catchword of his employers--non-interference. The puppet-emperor at Delhi complained bitterly; his complaint being unheard, he actually sent an agent--no less a person than Râm-Mohun-Rao, the founder of the Brahma-Somâjh, the modern Theistical sect of India--to plead his cause in England. But he also was unheard. His mission had been kept secret, and so his credentials were "out of order."

In Oude, Nâsir-ud-din, realising this policy of non-interference, began a series of petty aggressions against Âga-Mîr, the finance minister, whom the British Government supported. These ended unsatisfactorily for all parties by the minister being conveyed out of the reach of Nâsir-ud-din's vindictive hatred. The Nawâb then refused to appoint any one in Âga-Mîr's place, and, being totally unfit, by reason of his dissolute habits, to manage the state himself, everything fell into confusion. Finally, driven, for once, out of non-interference by the effect of it, Lord William Bentinck not only refused friendly intercourse if a responsible minister were not appointed, but told the drunken, disreputable occupier of the throne himself in so many words, that if he did not mend his ways he would be deposed.

So far well; but when, appalled by this prospect, Nâsir-ud-din besought advice how to govern, this was refused. The policy of which the Governor-General was the mouthpiece would not allow him to interfere!

Humanity is at times hard to understand; in this instance peculiarly so, unless, as was stated at the time by the respectable courtiers--and even in that sink of iniquity, Lucknow, there were some just men--the real object of the English was not to improve government, but to find an excuse for usurping it.

But in Jeypore, in Jodhpore, in Bundi, in Kotah, and many another minor state, to say nothing of larger ones, the almost slavish adherence of Lord William Bentinck to the order he had received brought strained relation$. And yet all the while he was attempting purely diplomatic *râpprochements* with outlying states. The Russian scarecrow had begun to trouble the slumbers of Indian statesmen, and this curious creature, destined to remain a nightmare for generations, led to interest in the affairs of Kâbul. In Lord Minto's time Mr Mountstuart Elphinstone had, with great difficulty, met the then Ameer Shâh-Sujah at Peshâwar, and arranged the terms of a treaty with him, but ere this could be ratified Shâh-Sujah himself had been turned out of his throne. He had pleaded for help to recover it; but Lord Minto being one of the non-interference faction, aid had been refused. The Ameer had, however, been allowed a pension, on which he had lived in Ludhiâna, a Sikh town on the Sutlej river.

Here Lord William Bentinck found him in 1832, when he had an interview with Runjeet-Singh, the Sikh king of the Punjâb.

There can be little doubt that the question of aiding Shâh-Sujah to recover his throne was mooted by Runjeet-Singh, and was negatived by the Governor-General; there is also little doubt, however, that *too much cold water* was not thrown over the scheme, since Dost-Mahomed, the Kâbul usurper, was suspicioned with Russian proclivities and was being watched.

But these are minor points compared to the changes which were coming over the East India Company at home. Its charter expired in 1834, and the question as to whether that charter should be renewed had to be answered. It was answered in the negative, and on the 22nd April 1834 India ceased to be a land of restrictions. It was thrown open to the wide world. During the course of the twenty years which had passed since the semi-extinction of the Company's power, but 1,324 licences to go to India had been issued. What proportion of these had been issued to those whose object was "the introduction of religious and moral improvements" is unknown, but in 1833 mission work had begun almost all over India; indeed, the concluding years of the period between 1813 and 1833 were marked by greatly increased efforts and results in proselytising the natives. One cause of this being the shortening of the ocean passage to India by the adoption of the Red Sea route. On the 20th March 1830 the *Hugh Lindsay*, a small steamer, left Bombay harbour, arriving in Suez in thirty-two days, and on her next voyage reduced the time to twenty-two. Thus, before the year 1836, despatches from London arrived in Bombay in two instead of six months; the time taken now is twelve days.

It may seem extravagant to say that the lessening of sea-sickness brought about the Indian Mutiny, but taken seriously, it is true. That is to say, the sudden letting loose on a country which had hitherto been reserved to especially licensed persons, of all and sundry, the dregs as well as the cream of the West, together with the removal of the great personal discomfort and expense of a six months' journey round the Cape, which had hitherto militated against travel in India, combined to produce such a change in that country as was bound to create alarm, distrust, and resentment, amongst the most Conservative people in the world.

FREEDOM AND FRONTIERS

A.D. 1834 TO A.D. 1850

What was the cause which led England to refuse a continuance of its charter to the East India Company?

It was the price of tea. Before this, all considerations as to whether the Company had done its duty to India or not vanish into thin air. As Mr Mill the historian says succinctly: "The administration of the Government of India by the East India Company was too exclusively a matter of interest to India to excite much attention in England." But with tea it was different. That was a question for every Englishman's breakfast table. Hitherto China had been debarred from free trade, and the price of tea was high; therefore monopoly was a bad thing for the consumer of tea. Q.E.D.

So on the 22nd April 1834, India was thrown open to the world, and though "John-Company" still ruled its destiny, it did so on a different footing. For the rest, the story of the dispute concerning territorial and commercial assets, the haggling over bargains between the Court of Directors and Parliament, is not edifying, as may be judged by the fact that the latter suggested the abolition of the salt-monopoly, not from the slightest consideration for the taxed native of India, but from a desire to secure a new market for Cheshire!

One of the first results of the new arrangement was an unseemly struggle over the filling up of the Governor-Generalship made vacant by Lord William Bentinck's retirement from ill-health. That the appointment should have been bestowed on Sir Charles Metcalfe is certain; he had served India well in many capacities. But parties objected. Then Mr Mountstuart Elphinstone came into the running, also Sir Henry Fane, Lord Heylesbury, Lord Glenelg, until at last a perfectly colourless appointment was made in the person of Lord Auckland, a most amiable and estimable nobleman, with no experience of India. He arrived in Calcutta in 1836, the interregnum, during which Sir Charles Metcalfe had carried on the work, having lasted for over a year. He immediately started on judicial reform with the aid of a law commission, of which Mr, afterwards Lord Macaulay, was president. It was he who drafted the Indian Penal-Code, which, founded on common-sense and the old Roman Law, remains to this day practically unaltered, a standing challenge of concise clearness to the confused medley of old precedent and new practice which so often does duty for equity in England. While this work was in progress unexpected trouble in Oude occurred. Nawâb Nâsir-ud-din-Hyder died suddenly, leaving no children. It may be remarked that the constant occurrence of heirlessness amongst the reigning families of India at this time tells its tale all too clearly. There were two boys favoured by the Queen-mother, whom the Nawâb had once acknowledged, but had since formally disavowed. He himself had no brothers, and the succession therefore reverted to the heirs-male of Sa'adut-Ali, his grandfather. Under British law the next-of-kin would have been the children of an elder son; under Mahomedan law it was the younger but still living son. Of this there can be no possible doubt. Looking back on Indian history, though, as a rule, the failure of direct heirs-male brought about a general free fight over the succession, a younger uncle has always claimed above a cousin. Thus in Oude there were instantly three claimants in the field. The Queen-mother's boy Mura-Jân, the younger uncle Nâsir-ud-daula, and Yamîn-ud-daula, who claimed to be son of an elder uncle, and was therefore a first cousin.

Naturally, the British supported Nâsir-ud-daula. Legally, he was the heir, though after a time another first-cousin-pretender, asserting that he and he only was the rightful Nawâb, actually travelled to England in order to urge his title. Meanwhile, on the Nawâb's sudden death, old Nâsir-ud-daula, the English nominee, had been dragged out of bed, promptly conveyed to the palace, and left to take an hour or two's sleep before the fatiguing ceremony of being installed on the cushion of State.

This was the Queen-mother's opportunity. She nipped in from her palace at Dilkusha with half the loose riffraff of the town (which in Lucknow floats about aimlessly awaiting such an opportunity), seized on the person of old Nâsir-ud-daula-it is a wonder they did not murder him--and promptly put Mura-Jân on the throne; he occupied it for about one hour and forty-five minutes. Then the British troops having returned and cleared a way with a few charges of grape, the coronation of the poor, miserable, by this time nerve-collapsed old uncle went on in due course!

Small wonder that he signed every obligation which he was asked to sign. This does not, however, in any way exonerate those who, taking undoubted advantage of the position, made him sign an unconditional engagement of submissiveness.

Still, signed it was; and for a very distinct and palpable "good consideration." Therefore its legality is beyond question.

The year 1836, however, brought up another political question for decision. The Râjah of Sattârah, quite a small princeling, had given trouble ever since the English had most unwisely rescued him from poverty and imprisonment and placed him in power. His proceedings, eventually, became so outrageous, that the Government deposed him, and elevated his brother to the vacant throne.

This is mentioned because the incident is made use of as evidence for the "annexation at any price policy" of the English. In this case, at any rate, they did not err.

But now, over the horizon of a fairly peaceful India, its statesmen saw, looming in the distance, the shadow of Russia, and all thought, all energies, turned to the north-west frontier. Between it and the territory already swayed by Calcutta lay the Sikh nation and the five fruitful Doabas of the Punjâb. Of these England knew little, save what she had learnt from Megasthenes the Greek, and Arrian's Anabasis.

One or two courteous interviews had passed with Runjeet-Singh, the Sikh king, but that was all. It was sufficient, however, to show him able, a man not to be easily swayed. His life-history confirms this. Left king at the age of twelve, with a profligate mother who for years had carried on an intrigue with the chief Minister-of-State, and an exceedingly ambitious mother-in-law, he managed to rid himself speedily of their influence, and ere long take his position as monarch of a far larger kingdom than he had inherited. His conquests eastwards were, indeed, only checked by meeting with British-protected states, and he kept an eye steadily on both Kâbul and Kashmîr. The former he hoped to gain by using Shâh-Sujah, the deposed Ameer, as a stalking-horse; and as a bribe for help promised, but never given, he succeeded in extorting from the latter the celebrated Koh-i-nur diamond. The latter, and Peshawar, he wrested from the Afghâns, with the aid of two French officers who opportunely arrived on the scene. So much for the Punjâb. Below it, still on the western border, lay Scinde, an independent state. Beyond it, Persia, with which England already had relations. But what of Afghanistan? There Mr Elphinstone's attempt to establish connection had ended with Shâh-Sujah's flight.

It was determined, therefore, to attempt an embassy to Dost-Mahomed, his usurping successor, and Sir Alexander Burnes was chosen as the delegate.

He was a man who had travelled all over Central Asia, who was in every way qualified for his task. Unfortunately, or fortunately, he was too well qualified for carrying out the simple commercial instructions with which the English Government had tentatively, perhaps timidly, entrusted him. But the discovery of Russian intrigues in full swing at the Kâbul court sent commerce to the right-about. Burnes was in the thick of diplomacy without delay, and ere long formal questioning and reply was going on between Russian and English ambassadors regarding the former's influence on the Indian borderland, which elicited a categorical denial of any ulterior object on the part of Russia.

But Dost-Mahomed for all that refused to accede to England's somewhat impertinent request, that he should dismiss the Russian agent from his court. And so began a quarrel which is barely settled to-day.

Sir Alexander Burnes left Kâbul in dudgeon, and almost immediately after his departure matters came to a crisis by the Persians--avowed allies of Russia--besieging Herât. Now, Herât was considered by diplomatists and the military alike the key of India, and in 1838, after many *pour parlers*, manifestoes, and embroglios, the combined armies of the tripartite alliance, that is to say, the British, the Sikhs, and Shâh-Sujah, marched on the Punjâb to reinstate the latter on his long-vacated throne in Kâbul. In all the long history of India no more unwarrantable invasion was ever undertaken, though half a hundred good reasons were given for it at the time, and could be found for its defence even now by those who fail to see that Dost-Mahomed was, as Eastern potentates go, quite a decent ruler. There is but one possible excuse. England chose her career deliberately, thinking not at all of Afghânistân, but of Russia.

After a halt at Ferôzepore, where the allies assembled and where festivities were held, Runjeet-Singh, an old man now, blind of one eye, desperately marked with smallpox, and inconceivably ugly, tripped over a carpet, to the horror of his court (who considered it an evil omen), and fell flat on his nose at the feet of a big English gun he was examining; and where, also, Henry Havelock, one of the new school of the Church-Militant, exclaimed in horror at "the ladies of a British Governor-General 'watching' choral and dancing prostitutes" (surely a somewhat over high-toned description of that deadliest of dull and decorous entertainments, an Indian *nautch*). After all this a fairly-triumphant march was made through Scinde (where the Ameer of that country, after a distinct promise that no riverside forts should be touched, was fairly diddled out of the one at Bukkhur, on the shameless plea that it stood on an island), through Quetta to Kandahâr and Ghuzni (which made a good resistance); so to Kâbul, which was entered on the 7th August 1839, when Shâh-Sujah ran about the passages of the Bâla-Hissâr palace like a child, clapping his hands with delight at finding himself back again after thirty years' absence.

So far good. But, meanwhile, Runjeet-Singh had died, and our rear was endangered by the almost open enmity of his successor. Thus a limited garrison, only, had to be left in Kâbul; and in addition, Dost-Mahomed's first flight had proved to be but a prelude to desperate resistance. Still, armed occupation was held of the town of Kâbul, cantonments were built for the British regiments and sepoys which formed the garrison, in which the troops passed the winter and summer of 1841 in comfort. Then came disaster.

What caused the outbreak is a mystery. So far as one can judge, it began in private revenge upon Sir Alexander Burnes. His house was the first attacked on the 2nd November 1841 by a mob thirsting for blood and plunder. He attempted to calm them by harangue. He offered large sums for his own and his brother's escape, but they were both cut down, every sepoy murdered, every man, woman, or child on the premises brutally killed.

And here follows *in petto* an anticipation of what occurred some fifteen years later, when a like massacre broke out at Meerut in 1857. A general paralysis seems to have attacked those in authority. Here, there, everywhere, in isolated posts, Englishman and sepoy fought together and fell together bravely; but at headquarters decision disappeared, and Brigadier Shelton finally settled, weakly, to hold the cantonments, instead of retiring on the fortified and almost impregnable Bâla-Hissâr, where there was a plentiful store of provision. The mistake was fatal. Within a month a treaty had to be signed which was practically unconditional surrender. Dost-Mahomed was to be reinstated; Shâh-Sujah allowed to follow his friends back to India. "The terms secured," writes Sir William McNaghten, "were the best obtainable." At any rate, at the time, it was hoped that they would save the lives of some fifteen thousand human beings. But fate was against it. Sir William McNaghten, failing in a side-intrigue which, even had it succeeded, would have been barely possible with honour, was foully murdered, and on the 6th of January about four thousand five hundred fighting-men and twelve thousand camp followers, men, women, and children, were driven out into the inclement winter cold to find their way, as best they could, over peak and pass back to Hindustan.

The horrors of that terrible march will scarcely bear telling. Over three thousand found freedom at once by being massacred, wantonly massacred by mountain tribes in the first pass; the rest, without food, without fuel, without tents, pressed on, fighting fiercely as they forced their way eastwards.

It was on the 13th of January that the English garrison at Jellalabad, looking out up the passes, saw one man swaying in his saddle, scarce able to keep his seat, urging his jaded, outworn pony eastward, still eastward!

It was Dr Bryden, the only man who came through. But he brought the welcome news that some women and children, and a few men, were prisoners, and so far safe.

Naturally, there was no more question now as to the rights or wrongs of war. These captives had to be rescued, and punishment meted out to many murderers. Both objects were accomplished within the year, but not by Lord Auckland; for Lord Ellenborough succeeded him at the time of the Kâbul disaster, when matters were at their worst. There was some difficulty in finding a candidate for the throne. Shâh-Sujah himself had in the interval been shot through the head, and his son, whom the mob of Kâbul had first set up as a puppet-king and then imprisoned, had no stomach for further sovereignty. A younger member of the family was, however, eventually found willing to face assassination for the sake of a doubtful crown.

His kingship, which only lasted till the British forces were withdrawn, at least secured the preservation of the Bâla-Hissâr, which otherwise, as a punishment to Kâbul, would have been razed to the ground; as it was, the Great Bazaar, a building entirely devoted to commerce, was destroyed instead, possibly because Sir William McNaghten's body had been exposed upon it.

Thus, in 1843, the first Afghân war came to an end with the absurd incident of the Gates of Somnâth. These were supposed to be still hung at the entrance of Mahomed-the-Despoiler's tomb at Ghuzni. So, with an odd mixture of sham Orientalism and latter-day romanticism, they were taken down, carried back to India to form the subject of a most marvellous effusion addressed to the chiefs and peoples of India, which goes by the name of "Ellenborough's Song of Triumph," in which these gates, "so long the memorial of your national humiliation," are said to have "become the proudest record of your national glory!"

And after all, they were *not* the Gates of Somnâth!

Almost immediately after this the relations with Scinde became strained. The Ameer had, in truth, just cause of complaint in a breach of treaty regarding the passage of troops across the Indus, and after much discussion the sword became the only possible arbiter. So Sir Charles Napier commenced the war which, conducted by consummate skill throughout, ended virtually with the victory of Miani and the annexation of Scinde.

It was towards the end of the next little war, this time with Scindiah, that Lord Ellenborough was recalled, and Sir Henry Hardinge, being sent to govern in his stead, found himself instantly plunged in a war of far greater magnitude with the Sikhs, with whom, after the death of old Runjeet-Singh, friendly relations had ceased. In truth, the kingdom was in a state of tumult.

The army, which consisted of almost the whole nation (since every Sikh is by birth and faith a fighter), realising that the whole power was virtually in its hands, clamoured for new conquests. Dhuleep-Singh, the heir, was a minor; his mother, nominally guardian, had no influence, and finally, forced by circumstances, gave her consent to an invasion of British territory. It was an unprovoked, and yet not altogether unwelcome assault, and it met with instant and overpowering reply. On the 13th December 1845 the Sikh army crossed the Sutlej in force, and on the very same day a British proclamation was issued, formally declaring that all possessions of Mâhârâjah Dhuleep-Singh, on the British bank of the river, were annexed. Swift battle followed. At Moodki on the 18th December, on the 22nd at Ferozeshâh, on the 20th January at Aliwâl; finally, the 10th February saw the last stand made at Sobrâon, a village which stood then on the eastern bank of the sliding river. It stands now on the western, for the Sutlej has shifted.

Swift, and short, and sure, was the campaign, curiously enough leaving little of rancour behind it amongst the tall, upstanding Sikhs. "You were so much better than we were," said an old Sikh worthy, who had gone through the four defeats, as he showed an infinitesimal slice of his little finger tip; "just so much--no more! but you were better led." And the keen old eyes ranged cheerfully over the wide wheat plain, intersected by silver-shining streaks of sliding river, that had once been the battle-field of Sobrâon, and the old voice went on exultingly over the tale of how he had knelt to receive the British cavalry at Aliwâl, and knelt on, through three consecutive charges, until he had fallen unconscious amongst his dead comrades.

A treaty of peace was signed at Lahôre twelve days after Sobrâon, which stipulated for the formal cession of the whole Cis-Sutlej country and an indemnity of £1,500,000, £500,000 of which was to be paid immediately, and the remaining £1,000,000 to be discharged by the cession of Kashmîr and Hazâra.

This practically ended Lord Hardinge's Governor-Generalship, and late in 1847 Lord Dalhousie took up the office.

The whole of the next year was taken up with a war in Scinde which spread to the northern half of the Punjâb beyond Lahôre, which--despite the cession of Hazâra--still remained practically unsubdued. After the taking of Multân and the defeat of Mulrâj's troops, Lord Gough marched northwards against Shere-Singh, defeated him at Râmnuggar, fought an indecisive battle against him at Chillianwâla, and finally, on the 21st February 1849, at Gujerât, completely annihilated the Sikh army, taking all their guns.

Resistance was thus at an end, and the Punjâb as far as Peshawar was coloured red in the map of India.

The proclamation of the Governor-General in announcing the fact is worthy of quotation as a finish to the long history of English dealings with Hindustan.

"The Government of India formerly declared that it decreed no further conquest, and it proved by its acts the sincerity of its profession. The Government of India has no desire for conquest now; but it is bound in its duty to provide fully for its own security and to guard the interests of those committed to its charge. To that end, and as the only sure mode of protecting the state from the perpetual recurrence of unprovoked and wasting wars, the Governor-General is compelled to resolve upon the entire subjection of a people whom their own Government has long been unable to control, and whom (as events have now shown) no punishment can deter from violence, no act of friendship can conciliate to peace."

The question arises, how much of this admirable effusion is strictly true? In the case of the Punjâb there can be no doubt that the Sikhs began the struggle by wanton and unprovoked assault. But was this always so? Certainly not always. Yet once begun, there was no possibility of turning back in England's career of annexation. She had put her hand to the plough, she was driving a Western furrow over the uncultivated wilds of the East, and as she sowed and scattered seed, the necessity for protecting the crop-scanty though it was at first--arose immediate and insistent.

People say England has brought poverty to India. Perhaps she has. Poverty is the handmaid of so-called civilisation. But she has also brought peace--and population!

MANNERS, MORALS, AND MISSIONARIES

A.D. 1850 TO A.D. 1857

Beyond the second Burmese war and the annexation of Oude there is little to be recorded in this short period of seven years. The former passed on, as did every war, to annexation; yet once again there seems little doubt that this was brought about by obstinate refusal to keep the treaty which ensured "the utmost protection and security" to British ships trading to Burmese ports.

The question of the annexation of Oude, however, falls into another category, and is so often cited as one of the chief causes of the Great Mutiny of 1857, that it is best discussed among the many other reasons for resentment and rebellion which undoubtedly existed in India at this time. One of these was the change of manners in the ruling white-faced race.

In the old days of a good year's voyaging and sea-sickness round the Cape few women had been found to face it; and so the Englishmen in India had formed irregular connections with native women, often of very good birth. These connections, though, of course, contrary to our marriage laws, were not exactly immoral; they were, indeed, often as regular as the differing codes of Christianity, Hinduism, and Mahomedanism would allow. And, naturally, they greatly bridged over the gulf between the rulers and the ruled.

The short sea-passage changed all this. English ladies came out in crowds, and seeing themselves surrounded by native sister-subjects who thought differently to what they did on almost every conceivable social subject, held up holy hands of horror at everything they saw, oblivious, apparently, of the obvious fact, that if the native sister appeared a bogey to them, they also must have been a bogey to the native sister.

She, however, by her very seclusion, was prevented from airing her opinion. Not so the Englishwomen and young girls who began to come to live amongst those who were generally called the heathen. There is no more charitable and kindly soul than the average British matron, and in the days before '57 she was beyond measure romantic. This was the time when, escaping from the stern rule of papa and mama, who had been ready with bread and water for "miss" if she refused an eligible *parti*, the English girl looked on Love with a big L, as something only a trifle less divine than the God whom she worshipped. She was not, therefore, likely to find anything but militant pity and charity for a social system which began by ignoring love as synonymous with passion. Thus the Englishwoman was no factor for peace in the new order of things. Then the changes inaugurated by the inclusion of the "introduction of religious and moral improvement" as a licensable trade had borne much fruit. One has only to read missionary reports to find out how enormously organised effort to convert the people of India had increased since 1813, and still more from 1833. In the year 1840 Dr Duff's Christian college at Calcutta numbered over six hundred pupils, and in 1845 came the added interest to the cause of Missions brought by the great Evangelical movement, not only in the Church of England, but throughout all Europe. This wave of religiosity left no Christian sect untouched, and part of its result was the introduction into India of a race of Church-Militant officials, admirable in character, in work, who, despite their faithful performance of duties to Cæsar which demanded absolute impartiality, could not divest themselves absolutely of their other duty (as they held it) to God; that is to say, to influence the natives for good--in other words, to Christianity. Without attempting praise or blame, it is impossible to deny that the example of such strong and militant Christians as the Lawrences, as Havelock, as half a hundred other well-known names, to say nothing of the hundreds of lesser-known ones who in civil stations and cartonments were encouraging mission work with all their might and main, must inevitably have attracted the attention of *pandits* and *moulvies*, whose profession, whose bare living, was bound up in so-called heathendom.

Then, ever since the days of Lord William Bentinck, legislation had favoured the new faith. It will be remembered that he was mixed up with the mutiny at Vellore--a mutiny, if ever there was one, caused by abject fear of enforced conversion. His abolition of *suttee*, his tinkering with Indian law so as to free Hindu converts to Christianity from disabilities in succession (or as it has been put, "to free them from the trammels of their former superstitions and secure them in the full possession of Christian freedom"), had passed muster at the time, but as their effects became palpable, their interference in matters of custom and religion was resented. The very inauguration of female education was an offence, and as the years went on, bringing ever more and more missionary effort, and, above all, more support to that effort on the part of the ruling race, fear of wholesale conversion sprang up amongst the ignorant people, and was carefully fostered by the priests and preachers who had all to gain and nothing to lose by revolt.

And behind all this lay slumbering a great resentment. Say what folk would, be the excuse what it might, the fact remained that the last hundred years had seen every Indian prince reduced to the position of a pensioner, his land annexed. And the years between 1850 and 1857 produced a large crop of such annexations and usurpations. To begin with the petty state of Sattârah. When Pertâp-Singh the ruler (given his chiefship by the British who hunted him up, prisoned, poverty-stricken) had to be deposed childless, England forebore to annex, and placed a brother on the cushion of State; but when that brother, also childless, adopted a son but a few hours before his death, she refused to recognise his right to do so in regard to the succession. Such a son was legal heir to personal property, but Sattârah, being a dependency, could not by Indian law pass by adoption without the permission of the lord-paramount, which in this case had not been asked. Legally, she was right; but the sting of annexation rankled.

Then the case of Kerowli occurred, in which adoption was made without permission; but here the Governor-General's order was over-ruled by the Directors, who held that though "Sattârah had been originally a gift and creation of the British Government, Kerowli was one of the oldest Râjput states, and merited different treatment." Annexation was not, therefore, carried out; but the very considerateness of the decision intensified feeling in the other case.

Following this came the Jhânsi case, involving an area of about 2,000 square miles. Here, again, no issue--almost no collateral relationships--was the cause of an unauthorised adoption which, because the chiefship was, again, a creation of the English, was held inadmissible.

Then, as if these three almost forced annexations, occurring in 1849,1852, and 1853 respectively, were not enough to damn British policy in the eyes of disaffection, yet another case came up for settlement in 1853; for on the 11th of December died Râgoji-Bônsla, the Râjah of Berâr. He left neither issue nor collateral heir, neither had he attempted to supply their place by adoption; thus the question of the state lapsing to the Crown arose in its simplest and clearest form. The decision was, naturally, that by the Râjah's "death *without any heir whatever*, the possession of his territories has reverted to the British Government which gave them"; a decision without any doubt legal.

Now, ere passing on to the annexation of Oude, which stands on a totally different footing, it is as well to notice the drift of what may be read between the lines of this long record of principalities passing by lack of heirs of the body to the lord-paramount. What does it mean? Doubtless, it points first to degeneracy, to the fading away of families which is due to dissolute life. But this life in high places was no new thing; the English had found it rampant when they came. Therefore some other reason for the necessity of State interference must be found. What was this?

Plainly, on the very face of things, the answer is to be found. It was the order, the law, the freedom from conspiracy, assassination, self-aggrandisement, which English protection had ensured. In the old times an heirless râjah of past fifty would have been the centre of a snatching crowd of nobles, and the strongest would have asserted his right, and possibly hurried on the death of the dying king, or ever the lord-paramount had time to interfere; and then a payment in gold would have satisfied authority! So degeneracy did not matter; a new family always took the place of the dead one.

Now there was a hard and fast law which had to be obeyed by king and subject alike; a bitter lesson for any Oriental to learn, whose very idea of kingship is its superiority to order.

The trouble in Oude began--when did it not begin!

In 1760 Sûjah-ud-daula, its hereditary wazîr, well beaten by the Company for aggression on Bengal, ceded Allahabad and Korah, but was left undisputed master of the rest of his territories. In 1768, again in consequence of defeat, he was bound over to reduce his army. In 1773 he once more bound himself to further dependence in return for troops. In 1775 Sûjah-ud-daula died, and his son Asâf-ud-daula, in return for "good consideration," ceded territory as perpetual payment of the said troops, and afterwards, by various treaties, promised, in return for the guarantee of the possession, protection, and administration of Oude, to govern "in such a manner as would be conducive to the prosperity of his subjects"; also, to act on the advice of the British Government. Sa'adut-Ali, his successor, ratified these treaties, and showed, by the mere fact of his amassing treasure to the amount of £14,000,000 during his reign of fifteen years, that they were not, at least, pecuniarily hard. Ghâzi-ud-din, the next Nawâb or wazîr, regained a certain independence, not by treaty, but by loaning out his father's millions to the Company. The sop of being allowed to assert his independence of Delhi and call himself King was thrown to him; but he was no ruler, and the aid of British troops being refused him, "except in support of just and legitimate demands," he defied the treaty which limited his own army, and kept sixty thousand native troops, two-thirds of whom were entirely without discipline, living naturally by rapine and robbery. His son Nâsir-ud-din, hopeless debauchee, continued and increased these evils, drawing down on himself the solemn warning of Lord William Bentinck in 1829, that deposition must surely follow on such misrule. Unfortunately, however, advice how to rule was refused, and on Nâsir-ud-din's death--

of course without issue--advantage was taken of the accession of the old man--almost in his dotage--Nâsir-ud-daula, to obtain a fresh and still more stringent treaty, by which, if misrule continued, the British Government reserved the *right to administer, rendering account to the Nawâb,* and so far as possible maintaining existing forms so as to *facilitate the future restoration of power to its rightful owner.* In other words the Nawâb was, if contumacious, to be put under trustees for the time. This was in 1837. At Nâsir-ud-daula's death in 1842 his son succeeded, and in 1847 another son rose to the throne by his brother's death--of course without issue. Now Wajîd-Ali-Shâh, the last Nawâb or King of Oude, was utterly worthless. One has but to read the journal of the Resident, General Sleeman, to recognise how hopeless was the problem of peace, prosperity, or progress, under his rule. Surrounded by fiddlers, prostitutes, poetasters, eunuchs, he wasted half the revenues on these creatures, by whom he was led about, a silly imbecile, with drugged brain and diseased body.

"There is not, I believe," writes General Sleeman--a man of infinite knowledge of the native, infinite sympathy with them--"another Government in India so entirely opposed to the best interests and most earnest wishes of the people as that of Oude now is. People of all classes have become utterly weary of it."

No better case for deposition, for the removing of a whole people from the grip of fatuous immorality and crass misrule, could be found than this; but the means chosen to effect the desirable consummation were mean in the extreme. There were two definite treaties regarding the government of Oude. The one signed in 1837, gave as the punishment for misrule, the placing of the administration *under trustees only.* That signed in 1801 gave a guarantee of British protection in return for the cession of certain territories, *provided the administration of Oude coincided with the advice of the Company.* In this case, therefore, the only penalty was palpably the *withdrawal of protection.*

Neither of these penalties satisfied the desire for a total change of policy. Instead of saying this openly, instead of boldly running up the flag of England, and saying: "This passes! It can no longer be permitted, that, under the protection of England such vice, such fraud, such extortion, such downright devilry, should exist. This crazy, imbecile, lecherous, drunken scoundrel shall take his pension and cease to be a tyrant." Instead of all this, with at least some backbone of righteous indignation to carry it through, Lord Dalhousie the Governor-General and his advisers informed the Nawâb that the treaty of 1837 had never been ratified in England, but that by some mistake the fact had never been notified to him! And this after Lord Hardinge in 1847 had threatened the Nawâb with the penalty laid down in that treaty, and no other!

It is almost incredible! But there is more to tell. By thus setting the treaty of 1837 aside, that of 1801 remained, under which the English had no power to do more than withdraw their protection from Oude. Thus annexation stood less justified than ever, except on the plain ground of the greatest good of the greatest number.

Oude was annexed in 1856. It was the recruiting-ground of a large portion of our native armies, and there is no doubt whatever that we have here the great political cause of disloyalty. In the previous two or three years, also, many measures had been passed to rouse religious resentment and suspicion, such as the Hindu widows re-marriage Act, and the Act to remove all forfeiture of property due to a change of religion. Nor were these things, as of old, too remote to touch on the common lives of the people. In Lord Dalhousie's term of office alone 4,000 miles of electric telegraph wires had spread a network over India, railways were every day eating into the heart of the land, a road, metalled, duly laid out for posting, stretched 2,000 miles from Culcutta to Peshâwar, schools were starting up in the rural districts, and letters--stamped letters--carrying God knows what of lies born of fear or fraud, were being delivered for a trifle to almost every town and hamlet in India.

A mighty change this, bringing with it at every point the defiling touch of the Feringhi.

Nor was this all. Government was changing. It might be for the better--at any rate, it could not be for the worse--but still it was strange. The man to whom the revenue would in future be paid would have a white face, and that in itself was disturbing.

Yes! without doubt, the West was encroaching fast

Oude, it has been said, was the great recruiting-ground of our native cavalry, but also for our table attendants. The first went home to hear tales of annexation, of order which gave the brotherhood-of-arms that had remained at home no chance of plunder as in the past. The latter took home with them on their holidays long tales of the mem-sahibas, and the sahibs' command that all servants should attend family prayers; and of the *bakshish* of kindness to be gained by professing interest in the new faith.

So, fostered by professional agitators, by disappointed claimants--even as the present unrest is fostered in India nowadays--the indefinite fear of something grew in the years between 'fifty and 'fifty-seven.

THE GREAT MUTINY

A.D. 1857 TO A.D. 1859

Heaven knows there were not wanting signs and portents in India before "'fifty-seven" which might have put statesmen on their guard--had they known of them.

But the terrible fact is that they did not know of them. Why? Because those whose duty it was to keep their fingers on the pulse of the body corporate, whose duty it was to note every passing symptom of the new organism of whose life so much remained to be learnt, did not, as a rule, know enough of the language of India; the language by which alone they could gather information at first hand.

Reading the records of these fateful two years, plodding through question and answer in many a weary enquiry or trial in which long pages of evidence are given by officers who required an interpreter in dealing with the men under them, the connection comes home startlingly, that the greatest cause of the Indian Mutiny was the ignorance of Englishmen. And this much is certain; that in every case where incipient rebellion was quelled, where officers seemed to have had some hold over their subordinates, the influence came through "knowledge of the vernaculars."

Yet so great was the ignorance of England, that even General Hearsay, a man noted for his tolerant friendliness with his sepoys, could write on the 11th February 1857: "We have at Barrackpore been dwelling on a mine ready for explosion."

Still some there were who saw, who feared and even gave expression to their fears, like Sir Charles Metcalfe.

"I expect to wake some fine day and find India lost to the English Crown."

Fateful words, which might have come true but for the national characteristic of Englishmen: their readiness to die in order to retrieve the mistakes they have lived to make.

What, then, were those signs. There were many. Chief amongst them the steady distribution northwards and westwards of the hearth-baked cake which passed from the hands of one village watchman to the other, with the mysterious message? "For the elders; from the south to the north, from the east to the west." What did it mean? Heaven knows. Most likely it was merely an attempt to arouse in the calm, steadfast lives of the peasants in their fields, something of the unrest which was being felt wherever native life impinged upon the life of the new master. It failed, of course. Throughout the whole Mutiny, the India of the wide wheat-fields, the flooded rice-patches, the sugarcane brakes, the tall millet-stretches, and the snow-tufted cotton bushes, dreamt on peacefully.

Then there was the general grievance, started craftily in Calcutta and carried throughout every native regiment in India, of the grease-defiled cartridges. Was the tale true or untrue? In the beginning, at Dum-Dum, there may have been a possibility of suet smearing. Afterwards there was none. But that mattered little. Agitators, professional agitators, were abroad, and in India no lie is too gross to be believed.

Then the commissariat flour was defiled purposely by bone dust--(it may have been of malice prepense, for agitation in India *sticks at nothing*); no righteous man could eat of it and live. This was a dish prepared for the high-caste Brahmins, and Kshatriyas of Oude; and for the Mussulmans a like poisoned *plât* was made ready by the English shiftings and shufflings over the annexation of that country and the deposition of its king.

Taking this, and a like anger from every decadent court in India, the absolute brutality of the Mutiny ceases to be inexplicable. Every scoundrel in India was against us. Doubtless, honest dread of wholesale conversion, even a sense of duty, drove many fairly honest men to murder; but the whole Mutiny was, so to speak, engineered by lust of power which had passed.

The 34th Native Infantry began the ball at Barrackpore, about 100 miles north of Calcutta, and so within reach of the priestly power that gathers always round Mai-Kâli's famous and bloody shrine. Thanks to General Hearsay's prompt action, it was quelled. The story of the old man's gallop across the parade-ground, revolver in hand, accompanied by his protesting son as aide-de-camp, is well worth telling, but there is no time for it here. Then fires began to break out in cantonments all over India, showing a state of unrest, which made old General Hearsay give the warning so early as the 18th of April, that "the Hindoos, generally, are not at present trustworthy servants of the State."

By the 2nd of May his words were found true in Lucknow, where a regiment of irregular cavalry--part of the late Nawâb's marauding army-

-mutinied openly over the greased cartridge question--which had now so openly become a pretence--and was disarmed by Sir Henry Lawrence's prompt action. But India had not an indefinite supply of heroes and hard-headed old campaigners ready and able to cope with danger, and the 10th May at Meerut found hopeless, helpless weakness.

In order to abate the growing grievance of the cartridge, orders had been issued that they were no longer to be bitten as of old, but torn, thus obviating, it was thought, all possible danger of caste-defilement. It was a mistaken order, since it gave credence to the lie of their being greased at all. Consequently, the 3rd regiment of Light Cavalry (Oude-recruited almost to a man) refused even to handle them. On the 9th of May, eighty-five men, condemned to ten years' penal servitude for mutiny, were, by General Hewitt's senseless severity, degraded publicly before the whole garrison, and marched off to prison; he the while watching the proceedings complacently from his buggy, for he had already been removed from the Peshâwar command on account of physical unfitness for duty.

Ere twenty-four hours had passed, he proved himself also mentally unfit to grapple with a great emergency. Meerut was in flames, women and children lying murdered, yet His Majesty's 60th Rifles, the 6th Dragoon Guards, the European Artillery, and no small loyal contingent from the native regiments, were cooped up, inactive; not even one man sent to warn Delhi, but 30 miles away!

How the heart aches as one reads of brave men on their knees begging for a squadron! Only a troop! For a gun! for anything! wherewith to dash down the broad, white road, and guard the way to Delhi--begging, and being refused!

All one can say is that, inadvertently, General Hewitt did good service to his country, in that his folly precipitated, and made premature, an outbreak which, had it gone on to full growth, would surely have lost us India for a time.

"To Delhi! To Delhi!" That was the one cry of the half-dazed mutineers, feeling freedom full in their faces; unexpected, unhoped-for freedom. Yet, even so, the old habit was strong on them. They must have a master; if the new one hid like a coward, they must find another. And at Delhi was the representative of the House of Timur, of Akbar, whose memory still lingered in the hearts alike of Hindu and Mahomedan. He, the man without a State-religion, the man who had held the balance true, to whom all religions equal, was master indeed! Whether old Bahâdur-Shâh, his degenerate descendant, who since Akbar II.'s death had dozed and dreamed away a drugged life full of causeful and causeless complaints, was in the plot beforehand, or whether it took him by surprise to find himself acclaimed King instead of Puppet, is a moot point. All that is to be known of this is, that a nine months' trial--a trial, be it remembered, by a victorious, autocratic accuser which thus, in a country like India, where strength ever goes to the strong, could have its pick of witnesses--failed to find evidence of complicity.

Not that it mattered, save to one poor, dottled old man saved thus from the hangman's noose, whether he knew or did not know. Events marched with terrible rapidity, murderous certainty, whether the palace gave orders for them or whether it watched, stupefied, expectant. The Ridge was swept clear of Englishmen, women, children, save for the few who sought refuge in the Flagstaff Tower, thus deferring for a time their inevitable fate. Dawn had brought the first troopers to shoot down the captain of the palace guards and savagely to cut to pieces Simon Fraser, the Commissioner, who attempted to harangue them, and all day long massacre had gone on unabashed; but even the blood-drunken assassins paused and held their breaths when at sunset, with a great roar, a shaking of solid earth which by force made the bodies of the mutineers shiver, the "Glorious Nine" in the Arsenal sent their message of defiance to the skies. Truly, that blowing-up of the magazine by the "Nine"-by Willoughby, Forrest, Scully, Buckley, and five others--may be likened to the roar of the British Lion, as yet half-asleep.

It was the only note of defiance that was heard at Delhi for five long weeks.

Women and children were murdered; the Palace, roused from its dreamings, took the goods the Gods gave--and small blame to it, seeing how coincident had been the dwining of the Moghuls' power with the widening of English influence; the mutineers looked in each others faces, almost appalled at their own success; yet still the master made no sign. Truly had it been said that their rule was but to be one hundred years, and was not this the centenary of Plassey, when Sâbat-Jung, the "Daring in War," had first laid finger on Hindustan?

If the "Daring in War" had been here now! That was a thought which surely must have been in the minds of many of these hereditary soldiers whose fathers may have fought against Clive. But there were no such sahibs nowadays; Surâj-ud-daula--on whom be peace!--had said sooth when he held the English but a small nation--scarce ten thousand warriors all told!

In good sooth, however, there was some excuse for inaction. Of personal courage--take a stronger word and say heroism--there was no lack, but of national preparedness, nothing. Mutiny spread like mushroom spawn in the dark, and everywhere took authority by surprise, so holding back the power which otherwise would have been free for giving help where help was needed. Fortunately, some places found a man able and willing to take the lead. At Benares, two hundred Europeans faced and overpowered two thousand sepoys, chiefly owing to the personal vitality of Colonel Neill, and at Lucknow Sir Henry Lawrence, after crushing one rebellion, was calmly making his preparations for the next, which he knew must come ere long. Whether in his sagacious head lay the thought that by holding Lucknow at all costs he might lessen the pressure of Delhi, and so divert the attention of some mutineers from that central point, who can say? But his action undoubtedly saved the whole situation. Had Lucknow--the defenders-- gone, thus setting free the hordes of rebels investing it, the forlorn hope of attackers who clung to the Red Ridge of Delhi in almost helpless defiance all the long hot summer could not have held their own.

So when the question is raised as to which heads the list of importance in this history of the Mutiny--the Defence of Lucknow or the Forlorn Hope of Delhi--the only possible answer is, that they both form part and parcel of the one desperate effort to retain hold of Empire in India.

The fact that a whole month elapsed ere the blow given at Meerut was returned, made the task of the Red Ridge a harder one. But for the loyalty of the Punjâb the counterblow might have been even longer in coming. Sir John Lawrence, however, was at Lahôre, and none of the Lawrences ever failed their country. Still, Fate was unkind, and Englishmen--brave, patriotic Englishmen--still more unkind in their lack of comprehension. When the blow was finally struck at Budli-keserâi, and the mutineers ran pell-mell for Delhi, 6 miles off, they were not followed, though the Kashmîr and the Mori gates were open wide, though the populace were waiting, waiting, watching for the master's return. But we condemned Delhi unheard. We held every man in it a rebel, and so, as night fell, the open gates were closed once more. How many men's life-blood was spilt thereinafter in trying to open them as wide again? God knows. So the army clung to the Red Ridge instead, and as the heat grew and the rocks seemed to blister and the sunshine to scorch, half of it gave up the struggle for a quiet sleep in the shadow of Earth's breast. Even the generals died; but the change of command brought no change in action, until, on the 5th of August, a tall, lank, black-bearded man rode into camp ahead of the relief column with which he had marched from Peshâwar. It was John Nicholson.

By a curious coincidence, a faint echo of the challenging roar which Willoughby and Forrest, Buckley and Scully, had sent to the skies just three months before, greeted his entry as the powder factory in the rebel camp blew up. But this was no challenge; it was a salute. Within ten days of the arrival of the four thousand who had come to relieve the six thousand on the Ridge, the battle of Nujufghur had been won. On this occasion the troops under Nicholson marched 36 miles through a morass, and fought a desperately hard fight in six-and-thirty hours. But Nicholson did not spare others, because he did not spare himself. Then ensued a wait of nine days, ere the siege-train arrived; a wait that was full of work. The man saw what had to be done, and made up his mind to do it, despite all difficulties placed in his way; for he was but six-and-thirty, and the older officers had not his fire, his dash.

It was on the 14th of September 1857, at three o'clock in the grey dawn, that the assault of Delhi commenced: by noon it was taken, but the man who had taken it lay shot through the breast. He had attempted the impossible. He had seen his own regiment--Jacob's rifles, the 1st Bengal Fusileers--hesitate, and hesitate perhaps rightly, seeing that the storming of that lane by the Burne bastion had been attempted many times and failed. So he had given the old call, "Forward, Fusileers! Officers to the front!" and had led the way.

The rush did not fail that time. The Burne bastion was taken, but the heart and soul of the man who had arisen for this purpose had orders for recall. John Nicholson lay dying.

He lived to see the whole city taken, the English flag floating over the Palace. Concerning the charge that drunkenness amongst the English army was the cause of the five days' delay in achieving this end, much has been written. Field-Marshal Earl Roberts, who was on the staff, has given an authoritative denial to this charge, by stating that he did not see a single drunken man throughout the day of the assault, although in the "discharge of his duty, he visited every position held within the walls."

This sounds satisfactory, were it not for the fact that this inspection was immediately followed by a general order for fatigue parties to destroy all liquor found in the shops (though some of it was urgently needed by the hospital); and also for the subsequent despatch which says, three days later, that an attempt to take the Lahôre gate had failed, "because of the refusal of the European soldiers to follow their officers."

But Delhi was taken, and, practically, the Mutiny was at an end. For the sepoys could not live without a master, and the master, a trembling, distracted old man, had given himself up from his hiding-place in his great ancestor Humayon's tomb, to Major Hodson, of Hodson's Horse. Concerning the yielding up of, and the subsequent shooting down of, the Delhi princes, much again has been written. Whether honourably or treacherously given, they richly deserved their fate; but the validity of the excuse that the shooting down was a sudden necessity which arose out of the fact that rescue was attempted while Major Hodson was conveying them under escort to Delhi, is fatally injured by a tiny scrap of evidence, irrefutable absolutely.

Hodson's favourite orderly, in telling the story in after years, invariably gives this detail: "Prince Abûl-bakr wore a talisman on his arm; so I said to Hodseyn-Sahib: 'Wait a bit, Huzoor! to kill him with that on will bring ill-luck. I'll take it off ere we shoot him.'"

No hurry there, no stress of circumstances surely, to make the immediate use of a revolver necessary?

But, once again, Delhi was taken. "If ever India needs a deed of daring done, John Nicholson is the man to do it." So had said a comrade-in-arms years before, and now the deed was done. Delhi, which had focussed rebellion for four long months, was taken by assault.

And how of defence?

Lucknow still held out, despite the death of the man who had made defence possible, for Henry Lawrence died from a shell-wound on the 4th July; but he left stout hearts behind him. And then, with all justice be it said, the besiegers were but half-hearted. They must have been so, else how could a scant garrison of fifteen hundred, in a weak position, with scarce a palisade in some places between them and the foe, have held their own against close on twelve thousand soldiers, backed by the wildest, wickedest, most wanton town-rabble in all India? And the population of Lucknow runs into hundreds of thousands.

Meanwhile, English troops on their way to China had been stopped and diverted to India by telegraph; England, grasping the magnitude of the disaster, was sending out regiment after regiment, and divisions were being formed up and sent hither and thither to quell and to punish. Amongst the commanders of these, Henry Havelock stands first, and at the head of a movable column, started for Cawnpore in July. Too late to save the beleaguered garrison, pent up foolishly in untenable entrenchments; too late even to save the horrible tragedy of the well at Cawnpore, into which, by the wanton wickedness of a courtesan, two hundred English women and children were thrown, after being foully murdered.

They did not, however, die in vain; for from the moment the news of the awful massacre reached the English camps there was no more hesitation. Not by God, but by the slaughter-house at Cawnpore, every man swore that retribution should be bitter and deep. How deep, how bitter it was, it is not well to say. Let the dead past bury its dead. It was hard for the British soldier to believe that the peasants whose villages he entered in his forced marches scarcely knew that war was abroad. But so it was. Within 20 miles of Delhi itself there are villages which passed through the Great Mutiny time knowing no more of it than that "the Toorkh"--the bugbear of Indian rustic life--had appeared again. That sometimes with a dark face, sometimes with a white one, he appeared, plundered the grain-stores, perhaps cut down a man or two, mayhap ravished a woman, and then disappeared. That was all. To the vast, the overwhelming majority of the people of India, that was all!

But to those who had sworn by the festering, blood-stained well at Cawnpore, all life seemed bound up in those two thoughts: "Will Delhi fall ere we reach it to help?" "Will Lucknow hold out ere we can relieve it?"

There was so much to be done. All over the country isolated resistances were staring death in the face bravely. At Arrah, half a dozen civilians held a miserable thatched bungalow for days, almost amusing themselves in its defence, strengthening its possibilities with mud from the garden, and using their sporting rifles with deadly effect on their foes. In another place a magistrate used his bulky files to fortify the public office roof, writing afterwards to report coolly that for impenetrability he could recommend a good criminal case, full of hard swearing.

All this, and hundreds of other heroisms, filled up the long hot summer of '57. The rains fell copiously, the crop was a bumper one, the peasants, mercifully, had no time to think, even, of aught save its harvesting and husbanding; there was so much to be done.

On the 25th of September, just five days after the final fall of Delhi, Havelock and Outram, with a small force, had pushed their way through to Lucknow, but, though the garrison was relieved, the generals did not feel themselves strong enough to march out and face the rebels. So once more, but now heartened up by the certainty of success which came to every Englishman in India with John Nicholson's daring deed, Lucknow waited for more help.

It came with Sir Colin Campbell's force on the 16th of November, when, leaving Outram to hold the Alumbagh with three thousand five hundred men, the general marched back as he had come, triumphantly carrying with him the women, the children, and the sick.

Thus the Defence had ended, the Attack had succeeded, and only Retribution remained.

By this time the Delhi column, set free from its task, had marched southwards for further assault. Agra, Jhânsi, Central India generally, had to be settled, and settled they were satisfactorily.

By the 11th of May 1858 the Mutiny had disappeared, as the mutineers themselves had disappeared on that fateful day in late September 1857, when, having retreated--some fifty or sixty thousand strong--from Delhi to the plains about Agra, the dusk found them encamped, still coherent, still resolved on struggle, and the night glittered with the watch-fires of a vast army. But the dawn, coming cloudily, reluctantly, found only the dead ashes of a resolve that had passed in the night; the men who had made it had vanished into thin air. They were hurrying back to their homes, eager to be found peacefully at work when the master should once more come on his tour of inspection.

The 2nd of August in that same year a bill for the "Better Government of India" passed into law.

It had eighty-five sections, but its general object was to transfer the whole administration of India from the Company to the Crown.

Whether better government has resulted, or not, is a question which it is to be hoped the English reader of this mere sketch of Indian history may be more qualified to judge than he (or she) was before the perusal of these slight pages.

INDEX

----laws,

Asaf-daula,

Asaf-Jâh,

Asôka,

Assaye,

Astronomy,

Asva-medha,

Attock,

Auckland, Lord,

Aurungzebe,

Babar,

Bactrians,

Bâhmani dynasty,

Baji-rao,

Battlefield,

Beâs,

Begums,

Begum Sumroo,

Benares,

Bentinck,

Bernier's views,

Bhattinda,

Bhim-si,

Bhishma,

Bimbi-sâra,

Bindu-sâra,

Birbal,

Black Hole,

Nâsir-ud-din,

----,

Nawa-ratani,

Nawâb of Bengal,

New Rajagrîha,

Nine gem necklace,

----Nandas,

Nizâm,

Nuncomâr,

Nurjahân,

Nyaya,

Omichand,

Oude,

Oudipur,

Outlying provinces,

Padmani,

Palibothra,

Pandu,

Pâniput,

Parthians,

Pataliputra,

Patna,

Peace of Aix la Chapelle,

Permanent settlement,

Persistency of creed,

Personality,

Pertap,

Pillars of Asôka,

Pirates,

Plassey,

Pondicherry,

Portuguese,

Porus,

Prithvi-Râj,

Private trade,

Punjâb,

Puranas,

----creed,

Queen Elizabeth,

Rajagrîha,

Râjputni heroism,

Râjputs,

----confederacy,

----resistance,

Râmâyana,

Râzia Begum,

Reinhardt,

Religion,

Rig-Veda,

Rock edicts,

Sa'adut-Ali,

Sabaktagîn,

Sai-nair,

Sâkas,

Salîm,

Samûdra-gupta,

Sanchi,

Sandracottus,

Sankhya,

Sanwat era,

Sarâswati,

Scythians,

Seleukos Nikator,

Self-choice,

Serpent kings,

Ses-nâga kings,

Shahâb-ud-din,

Shâhjahân,

Sidi Dervish,

Sikhs,

Siva-ji,

Sivalak,

Slave kings,

Smith,

Soma,

Somnâth,

Sonpût,

St Thomas,

Successions,

Sunjogata,

Surâj-ud-daula,

Susceptibility to personal equation,

Sûtra,

Syyeds,

FOOTNOTES

Footnote 1 : Comparable in modern mythology to Minerva.

Footnote 2 : This assemblage, or fair, still exists, under the name of the Mâgh-mela.

Footnote 3 : A Ghazi is the title of honour given to one who has killed the infidel.

Footnote 4 : It was in this storm that the admiral's ship, *Namur*, went down, with seven hundred and fifty men.